Boydell & Brewer Ltd

27 SOUTH MAIN STREET, WOLFEBORO, NEW HAMPSHIRE 03894

FOR REVIEW

WILLIAM OF MALMESBURY

by R.M. Thomson

#0-85115-451-4; Cloth; 196pp.; $39.50
Publication Date: April 1987

For further information, please contact
Ruth Corrigan at (603) 569-4576

**We would appreciate receiving two
copies of your review when it appears.**

WILLIAM OF MALMESBURY

WILLIAM OF MALMESBURY

Rodney Thomson

THE BOYDELL PRESS

© Rodney Thomson 1987

First published 1987 by The Boydell Press
an imprint of Boydell & Brewer Ltd
PO Box 9, Woodbridge, Suffolk IP12 3DF and
Wolfeboro, New Hampshire 03894-2069, USA.

ISBN 0 85115 451 4

British Library Cataloguing in Publication Data
Thomson, Rodney M.
  William of Malmesbury.
  1. William, *of Malmesbury*   2. Historians
  – England
  I. Title
  942'.0072024   DA3.W4/
  ISBN 0-85115-451-4

Library of Congress Cataloging-in-Publication Data
Thomson, Rodney M.
  William of Malmesbury
  Includes index.
  1. William, of Malmesbury, ca.1090–1143.
  2. Historians – Great Britain.   I. Title
  DA3.W48T47   1986   942.01'092'4 [B]   86-2632
  ISBN 0-85115-451-4

Printed in Great Britain by
St Edmundsbury Press Ltd, Bury St Edmunds, Suffolk

CONTENTS

LIST OF PLATES

Between pages 116 and 117

PREFACE AND ACKNOWLEDGEMENTS

IN 1974, HAVING for some years studied a monastic scriptorium and library (that of Bury St Edmunds abbey in the twelfth century), I found myself in search of a *person*, an English man of letters from the same period, whose intellectual life might repay investigation. I found William of Malmesbury, via M. R. James's lecture 'Two Ancient English Scholars'. To my astonishment and delight, no-one seemed to have followed up the evidence of William's extensive and unusual reading presented by James and by Stubbs before him. My immediate reaction was to begin a card-index of works known to William at first hand, as a means of gaining access to his mental and intellectual world. In due course I was led to study the methods by which he acquired and copied his texts, the use which he made of them (notably as historical sources), his contacts with other libraries and monastic scholars, and his achievement and influence as a writer. The result was a number of articles scattered through nine different journals. The notion of a complete monograph did occur to me as a daunting task, and I owe to Richard Barber the idea that the articles themselves might be usefully made into such a book. Acting upon his suggestion, I found that the articles, put into a rational sequence, formed a reasonably complete and coherent structure. This is not to say that the 'structure' amounts to a well-rounded or final portrait of William. For one thing, much remains to be done. It would be possible, for instance, to continue the list of studies of William's sources which form part II of this book, and certainly this would reveal more of his scholarly techniques and attitude. Much more, undoubtedly, could and will be said about William as a historian. But it is also the case that a complete portrait of William will never be realizable; he was too reticent to reveal much of himself to his readers, and there is little evidence outside of his writings to compensate for his own silence. The emphasis of this book is on William's scholarship not merely because that is my own principal interest, but because it is in this, and in very little else, that William reveals himself to us. And it is this, in any case, which constitutes his claim to historical importance.

Each chapter below, then, is based upon work that has already appeared elsewhere, but the relationship between the present and the earlier version differs from chapter to chapter and must be explained here. Chapter 1 is substantially new, but includes part of 'John of Salisbury and William of Malmesbury; Currents in Twelfth-Century Humanism' in *The World of John of Salisbury*, ed. M. Wilks (Studies in Church History, Subsidia 3, 1984), pp. 117–125. Chapter 2 is a heavily-revised version of 'William of Malmesbury as Historian and Man of Letters', *Journal of Ecclesiastical History*, 29 (1978), 387–413. Chapter 3 is based upon three articles: 'The Reading of William of Malmesbury', *Revue Bénédictine*, 85 (1975), 362–402, 'The Reading of William of Malmesbury; Addenda et Corrigenda', ibid., 86

(1976), 327–335, and 'The Reading of William of Malmesbury; further Additions and Reflections', ibid., 89 (1979), 313–324. Appendix I is a corrected conflation of the Handlists provided in those articles. Chapter 4 is based upon 'The "Scriptorium" of William of Malmesbury', in *Medieval Scribes, Manuscripts and Libraries; Essays presented to N. R. Ker*, ed. M. B. Parkes and A. G. Watson (London, 1978), pp. 117–142, and 'More Manuscripts from the "Scriptorium" of William of Malmesbury', *Scriptorium*, 35 (1981), 48–54. Five of the eighteen plates which accompany this chapter are new. Chs. 5–8 are slightly revised and corrected versions of 'Identifiable Books from the pre-Conquest Library of Malmesbury Abbey', *Anglo-Saxon England*, 10 (1981), 1–19, 'William of Malmesbury's Edition of the *Liber Pontificalis*', *Archivum Historiae Pontificiae*, 17 (1978), 93–112, 'William of Malmesbury's Carolingian Sources', *Journal of Medieval History*, 7 (1981), 321–337, and 'William of Malmesbury and the Letters of Alcuin', *Mediaevalia et Humanistica*, new ser. 8 (1977), 147–161. Chapter 9 is a more extensively revised version of 'William of Malmesbury and some other Western Writers on Islam', ibid., 6 (1975), 179–187. Finally, ch. 10 is based upon 'William of Malmesbury and the Noctes Atticae', *Hommages à André Boutemy*, ed. G. Cambier (Collection Latomus, 145, Bruxelles, 1976), pp. 367–389. Appendix II to this chapter is new.

For permission to republish earlier material I am indebted to the editors of the journals concerned, to Cambridge University Press (chs. 2, 8, 9), the Scolar Press (ch. 4), and the Ecclesiastical History Society (ch. 1). The plates are published with the permission of the The Bodleian Library, Oxford, The Master and Fellows of Merton College, Oxford, The Warden and Fellows of Lincoln College, Oxford, The Master and Fellows of Trinity College, Cambridge, and Lambeth Palace Library, London.

Help provided for the original articles by scholarly friends has been acknowledged there. Since their appearance many of the same and other colleagues have offered helpful criticism and information; in particular I would like to thank Professors Michael Reeve, Janet Martin, Donald Bullough, Christopher Cheney, Drs Martin Brett and Michael Lapidge, and Ms Carlotta Dionisotti. In a more general way this book reflects – I hope – the influence of a group of Oxford scholars whom I have been fortunate to know, and whose generosity and friendship I should like to acknowledge here: Richard Hunt (+), Neil Ker (+), Beryl Smalley (+), Sir Richard Southern and Sir Roger Mynors. And last – but by no means least – I wish to thank Marion Gibbs, who first awakened my interest in the cultural history of early Europe, and who showed many young Australians at the University of Melbourne what it was like to have studied under Sir Maurice Powicke and Sir Frank Stenton.

Rodney M. Thomson
1986

ABBREVIATIONS

AbAm	William of Malmesbury, *Abbreviatio Amalarii*, ed. R. Pfaff in *Récherches de Théologie ancienne et médiévale*, 48 (1981), 128–171
AG	William of Malmesbury, *De Antiquitate Glastonie Ecclesie*, ed. and trans. J. Scott, *The Early History of Glastonbury* (Woodbridge, 1981)
ASC	*The Anglo-Saxon Chronicle*, trans. D. Whitelock, D. C. Douglas and S. Tucker (London and New Jersey, 1961)
ASE	*Anglo-Saxon England*
BHL	*Bibliotheca Hagiographica Latina*, ed. Bollandists (Brussels, 2 vols, 1898–1901)
BL	British Library
BN	Bibliothèque Nationale
Carter, 'Thesis'	P. N. Carter, 'An Edition of William of Malmesbury's Treatise on the Miracles of the Virgin', D.Phil. diss., Oxford University, 2 vols, 1959
CCSL	*Corpus Christianorum, Series Latina*
CLA	E. A. Lowe, *Codices Latini Antiquiores* (12 vols, Oxford, 1934–71)
Clavis	E. Dekkers and A. Gaar, *Clavis Patrum Latinorum* (Steenbrugge, 2nd edn, 1961)
Comm. Lam.	William of Malmesbury, *Commentary on Lamentations*, as in Oxford, Bodl. Libr. MS Bodl. 868
CSEL	*Corpus Scriptorum Ecclesiasticorum Latinorum*
CUL	Cambridge, University Library
De Miraculis B.V.M.	J. M. Canal, *El Libro De Laudibus et Miraculis Sanctae Mariae de Guillermo de Malmesbury* (Edizioni 'Ephem. Mariol.', Rome, 1968)
EHR	*English Historical Review*
Farmer, 'Life and Works'	D. H. Farmer, 'William of Malmesbury's Life and Works', *Journal of Ecclesiastical History*, 13 (1962), 39–54
Farmer, 'William of Malmesbury's Commentary on Lamentations'	D. H. Farmer, 'William of Malmesbury's Commentary on Lamentations', *Studia Monastica*, 4 (1962), 283–311
GP	William of Malmesbury, *Gesta Pontificum Anglorum*, ed. N. E. S. A. Hamilton (RS, London, 1870)

GR	William of Malmesbury, *Gesta Regum Anglorum*, ed. W. Stubbs (RS, London, 2 vols, 1887–9)
HN	William of Malmesbury, *Historia Novella*, ed. and trans. K. Potter (London, 1955)
James, *Two Ancient English Scholars*	M. R. James, *Two Ancient English Scholars* (Glasgow, 1931)
Ker, 'Handwriting'	N. R. Ker, 'William of Malmesbury's Handwriting', EHR, 59 (1944), 371–6
Leland, *Collectanea*	J. Leland, *De Rebus Britannicis Collectanea*, ed. T. Hearne (London, 2nd edn, 6 vols, 1770–4)
Leland, *De Scriptoribus*	J. Leland, *Commentarii de Scriptoribus Britannicis*, ed. A. Hall (Oxford, 2 vols in 1, 1709)
MGH	*Monumenta Germaniae Historica*
MLGB	N. R. Ker, *Medieval Libraries of Great Britain* (London, 2nd ed, 1964)
Ogilvy, *Books known to the English*	J. D. A. Ogilvy, *Books known to the English, 597–1066* (Cambridge, Mass., 2nd edn, 1967)
PH	William of Malmesbury, *Polyhistor Deflorationum*, ed. H. Testroet Ouellette (Binghamton, 1982)
PL	*Patrologia Latina*
RS	*Rolls Series*
Stevenson, 'A Contemporary Description of the Domesday Survey'	W. H. Stevenson, 'A Contemporary Description of the Domesday Survey', EHR, 22 (1907), 72–84
Stubbs, *Memorials*	W. Stubbs, (ed.), *Memorials of St Dunstan* (RS, London, 1874)
TCBS	*Transactions of the Cambridge Bibliographical Society*
Texts and Transmission	L. D. Reynolds et al., *Texts and Transmission; A Survey of the Latin Classics* (Oxford, 1983)
The Writing of History in the Middle Ages	R. H. C. Davis, J. M. Wallace-Hadrill et al., *The Writing of History in the Middle Ages; Essays presented to Richard William Southern* (Oxford, 1981)
TKI	L. Thorndike and P. Kibre, *Incipits of Mediaeval Scientific Writings in Latin* (rev. ed, Cambridge, Mass., 1963)
TRHS	*Transactions of the Royal Historical Society*
VD	William of Malmesbury, *Vita Dunstani*, in Stubbs, *Memorials*
VW	William of Malmesbury, *Vita Wulfstani*, ed. R. Darlington, *Camden Third Series*, 11 (1928)

PART I

CHARACTER AND ACHIEVEMENT

WILLIAM OF MALMESBURY AND HIS ENVIRONMENT

AT THE TIME of William of Malmesbury's birth, not long before the year 1100, England was well along the path of recovery from the chaos which followed the Norman Conquest. In addition it was beginning to benefit from the substantial, if sometimes painful innovations made by its new masters. As in the realm of government, law and order, so in the world of learning and religion: the new ecclesiastical hierarchy was determined to sweep away the purely insular elements in English cultural and religious life, which they regarded as unauthoritative and barbarous, and to bring the country back into the mainstream of Latin Christendom as they understood it. The reforms which had come to Normandy from Italy were now to be transmitted to England; and the process, entailing the imposition of a style of Christian life and organization modelled on the Benedictine institutions and ethos, was to be carried out briskly and rigorously.

Not that the English were prepared to acquiesce in the loss of their valued traditions without a struggle. Initially it seemed as if the invaders would triumph by brute force; but as the years passed it became obvious that native traditions had not been entirely obliterated, and that it might even prove beneficial if some were allowed to re-emerge. Local saints and festivals, Latin writings such as Bede's, vernacular records such as the Anglo-Saxon Chronicle and royal Law-Codes began to return to legitimacy and even prominence by the late eleventh century. The confrontation and eventual osmosis of imported and revived native culture took place (or is at least most visible to us) within the greater religious institutions of England, in particular in the monasteries of the south.[1] It was in such a place, and as part of this process, that William of Malmesbury was to make his notable

---

[1] For this process see R. M. Thomson, 'The Norman Conquest and English Libraries', in P. F. Ganz (ed.), *The Role of the Book in Medieval Culture* (Turnhout, 2 vols., 1986), II, pp. 27–40.

contribution to both English and European literature and learning.[2]

William was born apparently c.1095 and not far from Malmesbury in Wiltshire.[3] He tells us that he was of mixed parentage, and that his father, who is likely to have been the Norman partner, ensured that he had some education (presumably via a private tutor or local grammar school) before his entry into the cloister of Malmesbury at an early age.[4] The region of south-west England, roughly corresponding to ancient Wessex, was to produce a distinctive culture within the Anglo-Norman world of the twelfth century, and signs of this were already apparent before c.1100. That culture was ecclesiastical and Latin, focussed on a group of ancient cathedral and monastic foundations, and emphasizing biblical studies, history and hagiography, classical reading and scientific research, primarily in the area of astronomy. The reasons for this peculiar fecundity can only be guessed, but surely one explanation must be the long-term survival of Anglo-Saxon intellectual activity initiated by Alfred, developed by the monastic reformers of the late tenth century, represented by vernacular and Latin texts still held in the libraries of ancient foundations, supplemented and fertilized after 1066 by new books and new blood from the continent.[5]

Malmesbury abbey, of which William was a monk from adolescence until the end of his life, was typical of the region. Founded by Aldhelm himself, it had existed almost continuously, if without particular distinction, ever since, and had managed to preserve a legacy of literature, learning and religious ideals from his time.[6] Not that that legacy was so very strong in the early twelfth century. William has little to say in detail of the history or internal life of the abbey before 1118, and Stubbs suggested plausibly that he may have been absent from the cloister during these years, in pursuit of further education.[7] In his *Gesta Regum* William describes the broad outlines of his education – 'Logic, which gives arms to eloquence, I contented myself with merely hearing; medicine, which ministers to the body's health, I studied

---

[2] On William's career see W. Stubbs in GR I, pp. xi–xliii; Farmer, 'Life and Works'; A. Gransden, *Historical Writing in England c.550–c.1307* (London, 1974), ch. 9.

[3] There are some difficulties about this date, discussed and resolved (as far as they can be resolved) by Stubbs in GR I, pp. xiii–xvii.

[4] GR II, p. 283; I, p. 103; GP, pp. 433, 436–9. Cf. the similar background of William's contemporary, the historian Orderic Vitalis; M. Chibnall, *The World of Orderic Vitalis* (Oxford, 1984), pp. 7–11.

[5] For some studies of this regional culture see R. W. Hunt, 'English Learning in the late Twelfth Century', in *Essays in Medieval History*, ed. R. W. Southern (London, 1968), pp. 110–124; R. W. Southern, 'England's Place in the Twelfth-Century Renaissance', in his *Medieval Humanism and other Studies* (Oxford, 1970), pp. 166–174; R. M. Thomson, 'England and the Twelfth-Century Renaissance', *Past and Present*, 101 (1983), 11–15.

[6] On the history of Malmesbury abbey see below, p. 98 n. 1.

[7] GR I, pp. xxii–xxiv.

somewhat more closely; but now, having intimately explored the various branches of ethics, I bow down to its majesty, because it spontaneously unveils itself to those who study it and directs their minds to moral behaviour; and especially history which, by the felicitous recording of great deeds, inspires its readers, by example, to the pursuit of good or the avoidance of evil.'[8] This seems to suggest something more than an elementary, grammar-school education and something other than a monastic one, but there is no information as to where William got it. William does provide one piece of information about his first abbot, Godfrey of Jumièges (1087 × 1091–1106): that he found the library disappointing and set about augmenting it. This leads William to refer to his own activity in strengthening the legacy by the acquisition and writing of books.[9] Eventually he was to extend his endeavours to other houses such as Glastonbury, and then to England as a whole in his ecclesiastical history, the *Gesta Pontificum Anglorum.*

William was, like Bede before him, a man without career-ambition or achievement. By c.1137 he held the office of precentor at his abbey, and in that capacity doubtless acted as its librarian.[10] He was at the Council of Winchester, perhaps representing his leaderless abbey, in 1139. In the following year he was offered and refused its abbacy, and that is all.[11] He is very coy about referring to himself or his friends, and no-one else had any reason to write about him. Even the date of his death is uncertain, inferred to be 1143 because he broke off his *Historia Novella* in the previous year and there is no record of his existence thereafter. His importance and contemporary and modern reputation rest entirely on his writings, some of which we can date reasonably precisely, and from which we can at least infer something of the author's character and beliefs. Even so, he was a detached scholar who does not often give himself away by offering opinions other than those conventional within a Benedictine community of the time.

The first precisely fixed point in William's biography is the completion of the first edition of his *Gesta Regum Anglorum,* in 1125.[12] This enormous work, on which much of his modern reputation rests, was designed to cover the secular history of England from Bede's time until his own; in the *Gesta Pontificum* he would do the same for English religious history. Such a grand project obviously entailed a prolonged and rigorous education, wide reading, considerable research both within and outside his abbey, and some previous experience in the construction of more modest historical works.

---

[8] ibid., pp. 103–4.
[9] GP, pp. 431–2.
[10] He is given that title in the letter of Robert of Cricklade written at about that time; see below, p. 74.
[11] GR I, pp. xxxviii–ix, xli; HN, pp. 29–34.
[12] GR I, p. xix.

Yet the chronology and details of all these things are thoroughly obscure. William himself indicates how his studies led him towards historical writing. Following the passage quoted earlier, he continues: 'When, therefore, at my own expense, I had procured some historians of foreign nations, I proceeded, during my domestic leisure, to inquire if anything concerning our own country could be found worthy of handing down to posterity. Hence it arose that, not content with ancient writings, I began myself to compose; not indeed to display my learning, which is trifling, but to bring to light events lying concealed in the confused mass of antiquity'.[13] We know that some at least of the *Gesta Regum* was completed before 1118, the work having been commissioned by Queen Matilda, who died in that year.[14] Whether William was selected at that date as its sole author, or whether it was a task laid upon the community and begun as a team effort cannot be said. We do not know what claim, if any, William had by then to be regarded as the ideal person to entrust with a task of such magnitude. That he might have had such a claim is at least suggested by his production of a unique, if derivative version of the *Liber Pontificalis*, completed between 1119 and 1125, probably nearer the earlier date.[15] This was already a work of considerable scope which must have been some years in the making. Its constituents show that William had travelled widely in order to ransack other monastic libraries. Possibly this task originated as a continuation of Abbot Godfrey's programme of library-acquisition, and perhaps it was this activity which shaped William's literary proclivities in the direction of history.

For a period of a little more than a decade, 1125–c.1137, William's literary activity was extraordinary, and he must have been released from a good deal of regular discipline in order to make it possible. The first edition of the *Gesta Pontificum* was completed later in 1125, and the second edition of the *Gesta Regum* a decade later.[16] In the meantime, shortly after 1129, he visited Glastonbury and wrote first the Lives of its local saints, Patrick, Dunstan, Indract and Benignus, and then his famous historical monograph, the *Antiquity of Glastonbury*.[17] As well as writing original works, he was evidently still collecting writings and books for the abbey library, and making digests and collections of material relevant to his historical labours. In 1129 he produced, partly in his own hand, a digest of Roman imperial history which still survives as Oxford, Bodl. Libr. Arch. Seld. B. 16, of which much more will be said below.[18]

---

13 ibid., pp. 103–4.
14 See below, pp. 15, 34–5.
15 See below, ch. 9.
16 GR I, pp. xix, xxxi.
17 GR, pp. 1–5.
18 See below, pp. 25–6, 57, 62–4, 66–7, 92–3, 112.

From c.1137 we have the only surviving contemporary reference to William, in a letter of Robert of Cricklade, then canon of Cirencester.[19] In it Robert praises William as a writer, naming his *Defloratio Gregorii, De Miraculis Beatae Virginis Mariae* and Commentary on Lamentations. In his introduction to the latter William implies that King Henry I is dead, indicating that he was writing after 1135, and incidentally describes himself as 'quadrigenarius'.[20] He also professes to regret his long and exclusive immersion in historical studies, to be remedied by the composition of the biblical commentary. Presumably much the same fit of conscience lies behind the composition of the *De Miraculis* at about the same time. Hagiography probably did not come under the same ban. William visited Worcester cathedral priory in 1113–24 and again between c.1124 and 1142, between which dates he wrote the Life of St Wulfstan.[21]

But he did not finish with history. After 1135 he revised the *Gesta Regum* again, and by 1140 was engaged upon its continuation, the *Historia Novella*, in which he refers to his 'three books of chronicles', now lost.[22] In this year he produced a second recension of the *Gesta Pontificum*, and wrote another work now lost, the *Itinerarium Iohannis Abbatis*, a description of the journey of Malmesbury's new abbot to Rome.[23]

William's original works, then, represent only one extremity of a wide spectrum of literary, historical and bibliographical activity. They shade off into compilations and 'collected editions', in some of which the texts have been manipulated in various ways. At the far end are the manuscripts of varied contents copied by him or under his direction. The compilations include his florilegium, the *Polyhistor*, the edition of the *Liber Pontificalis* mentioned above, and collections of materials for Imperial and Frankish history.[24] Digests rather than compilations are the *Abbreviatio Amalarii, Defloratio Gregorii*, and collection of texts on grammar and orthography (BL Harl. 3969).[25] The 'collected editions' are those of Cicero's works (CUL Dd. 13. 2), of ancient military strategy (Oxford, Lincoln Coll. lat. 100), and computistica (Oxford, Bodl. Libr. Auct. F. 3. 14).[26]

In his scholarly and literary achievement William is representative of the concerns, traditions, virtues and limitations of Benedictine monasticism. He was living near the end of the great age of Benedictine scholarship, and though he apparently sensed that new forces were at work, associated with the continental Schools, he had little contact with them. Some idea of what

19 Noticed by Hunt, art. cit., pp. 117–8; for the date see below, p. 74 and n. 205.
20 GR I, pp. xiii–xiv, cxxii.
21 VW, pp. viii–ix.
22 HN, p. 1.
23 GR I, pp. xxxviii–xl.
24 See below, pp. 13–14, 25–7, 32–4, 37, 57, 62–3, 66–7, 92–3, 112, chs 6, 7.
25 ibid., pp. 29, 32–4, 37, 95–6.
26 ibid., pp. 32, 50–55, 83–5, 87.

this meant can be gained by comparing William's scholarly and literary outlook with that of his younger contemporary and fellow-countryman, John of Salisbury. The two almost certainly never met, though they read some of the same books, probably because of their mutual plundering of the Canterbury libraries.[27] Let us take as a subject for comparison their interest in and treatment of Greco-Latin antiquity. This is a good example because it is central to their scholarship, a major preoccupation in their works, and provides a key (and if we were to add biblical and patristic antiquity as well, *the* key) to their thinking about their contemporary world.

For John antiquity was above all a storehouse of authoritative models and *exempla*. The sources for these things possessed the same minimal authority because of their common membership of the storehouse; indeed, it sometimes appears as though John was prepared to invest them with a roughly equivalent absolute value. The models and *exempla* themselves were of many types and were put by John to many uses, ranging from mere *bons mots*, examples of literary wit and elegance, to the more characteristic extended models of rational thought and moral action. John applied these *exempla* to the large contemporary problems which confronted and vexed him, producing some distinctive and original syntheses and solutions.[28] Secondly, John had recourse to antiquity as an excuse and justification for his more controversial and potentially divisive statements.[29] He sought to direct his readers' attention from his own responsibility for them, by mobilizing the wisdom of antiquity. The outstanding instance of this is his employment of 'Plutarch' in Book 5 of the *Policraticus*.[30] Another is his habitual use of apposite classical pseudonyms for the objects of his disapproval and ridicule.[31] This application of antiquity involved, and helps explain, the elements of prominent display, of name-dropping, and the tracts of near-verbatim (though often subtly altered) quotation. Thirdly, it has become increasingly clear that John's real acquaintance with Greco-Latin pagan authors was more restricted than would appear at first sight.[32] He very

[27] ibid., p. 58.
[28] H. Liebeschütz, *Mediaeval Humanism in the Life and Writings of John of Salisbury* (Warburg Institute Surveys 17, London, 1950), pp. 66–73; P. von Moos, 'The Use of *exempla* in the *Policraticus* of John of Salisbury', in *The World of John of Salisbury*, ed. M. Wilks (Studies in Church History, Subsidia 3, Oxford, 1984), pp. 207–261.
[29] J. Martin, 'The Uses of Tradition: Gellius, Petronius and John of Salisbury', *Viator*, 10 (1979), 57–76.
[30] John of Salisbury, *Policraticus*, ed. C. C. J. Webb (Oxford, 2 vols, 1909), I, p. 281ff.
[31] Of these 'Cornificius' in the *Metalogicon* is the most notorious; many more examples may be found there, and in the *Policraticus* and *Entheticus*.
[32] For instance, P. Lehmann, 'Nachrichten und Gerüchte von der Überlieferung der *Libri Sex Ciceronis De Republica*', in his *Erforschung des Mittelalters* (Stuttgart, 5 vols, 1959–62) IV, pp. 98–102; H. Liebeschütz, 'John of Salisbury and pseudo-

frequently quoted at second hand, made heavy use of epitomes, and often misattributed quotations, or misquoted. As we know, he could invent both authors and their statements. In the *Policraticus* he condemns those who read anthologies in order 'to seem to know that which they do not know'.[33] Ironically, this is a reasonable description of what he did himself.

For William antiquity was similarly, but to a much more limited extent, a source of models and *exempla* applicable to contemporary situations.[34] He saw it, rather, as a total civilization, differentiated from his own and superior to it in learning and culture, and he sought to recapture at least its compatible values, as far as possible, by preserving and disseminating its literary *Nachlass*. But he was evidently captivated by it irrespective of its applicability, or of the possibility of its contemporary resuscitation. These attitudes are held in tension in his *Polyhistor*. In its introduction, addressing a monk called Guthlac, he promises a collection of *flores* relevant to the pursuit of the religious life.[35] He warns against reading certain pagan writings, including some of Cicero's. This is all very conventional and cautious. Yet much of the collection's content is amoral, and none of it is closely geared to the Christian moral system. In fact it is principally characterized by a self-delighting fascination with 'ancient peoples and places'.

Then again, William really was extraordinarily well-read. He knew, at first hand, at least some four hundred works of two hundred authors, his reading of classical and late antique secular authors being almost exactly a quarter of this total.[36] Like John he knew some uncommon works. He appears to be unlike John in having internalized some of this reading to a considerable degree. Most of his borrowings from Virgil are unacknowledged and absorbed into the fabric of his own prose; for William Virgilian style had become instinctual.[37]

The figures just quoted are restricted to first-hand quotation. William

Plutarch', in *England and the Mediterranean Tradition* (Oxford, 1945), pp. 33–9; *M. Tullii Ciceronis De Divinatione*, ed. A. S. Pease (Urbana, 1920–3 and Darmstadt, 1963), pp. 34–5 and n. 217; J. Martin, report of her dissertation 'John of Salisbury and the Classics' in *Harvard Studies in Classical Philology*, 73 (1969), 319–21, and 'John of Salisbury's Manuscripts of Frontinus and Gellius', *Journal of the Warburg and Courtauld Institutes*, 40 (1977), 1–26; R. H. and M. A. Rouse, 'The Medieval Circulation of Cicero's *Posterior Academics* and the *De Finibus Bonorum et Malorum*', in *Medieval Scribes, Manuscripts and Libraries; Essays presented to N. R. Ker*, ed. M. B. Parkes and A. G. Watson (London, 1978), pp. 351–2.

[33] *Policr.*, II, pp. 179–80.
[34] See below, pp. 25–31, 47–61.
[35] PH, p. 37.
[36] These figures are compiled from the list given below, Appendix I.
[37] See below, pp. 29, 47–8.

rarely used his authors in any other way, and the only exceptions known to me – four in all – are for authors whom he could not possibly have found without an extended tour of ancient religious foundations on the continent.[38] But he did conduct just such a search virtually the length and breadth of England, and also borrowed books from across the Channel.[39]

William approached his classical reading as a 'professional' historian. He liked to date his authors, in relation to each other and to major rulers and events.[40] He quite explicitly preferred the earliest source of a story, unless there were reason to do otherwise, in which case he explained why.[41] He liked to know who copied from whom, and had little time for mere plagiarizers.[42] But his interest was also philological. I have already mentioned his 'collected editions' of works by the same author (Cicero) or on the same topic (military strategy, grammar and rhetoric). He sometimes embellished these books with biographical introductions and commentary, and often edited the texts in them.[43] His editorial work needs further study, but enough has already been done to indicate that he could collate, that he preferred early manuscripts, and that he could emend by conjecture, on the basis of his own exceptional latinity.[44]

It is particularly illuminating to compare John's and William's use of the Latin author whom they both most revered – Cicero. In his *Entheticus* John said 'Orbis nil habuit majus Cicerone latinus', and William habitually calls him 'that great (or "most eloquent") orator'.[45] There is a considerable disparity between each scholar's knowledge and use of Cicero, and in both respects the two men differ from each other. John makes heavy use of Cicero's writings in absolute terms, and in proportion to his first-hand acquaintance with them. The reductionist tendencies of recent studies of John's reading have had particular impact here. That he did not know the *Republic* (any more than William) or the *De Divinatione* has long been known; now we must also subtract the *De Finibus* and *Posterior Academics*.[46] Apparently he did know a collection of the letters, uncommon even on the

---

[38] The exceptions are Plautus, *Pseudolus* (see below, p. 49), Livy (below, p. 16; not in England until Becket's time), Petronius (below, p. 61; brought to England in John's time), and Cicero, *Orator* (below, p. 55).

[39] See below, pp. 72–5.

[40] ibid., pp. 17–19.

[41] ibid., pp. 40–1.

[42] ibid., pp. 13–14, 59–61, 66–7.

[43] ibid., pp. 51–3.

[44] ibid., pp. 64–6, Martin, 'John of Salisbury as Classical Scholar', in *The World of John of Salisbury*, pp. 182–3, and A. C. Dionisotti, 'On Bede, Grammars and Greek', *Revue Bénédictine*, 92 (1982), p. 133 and n. 1.

[45] John of Salisbury, *Entheticus de Dogmate Philosophorum*, ed. R. Pepin (New York, 1975), line 1215; see below, pp. 21, 55.

[46] See the works by Lehmann, Pease and Rouse cited in n. 32 above.

continent, unknown in England and to William.[47] William's case is the reverse. He knew between nineteen and twenty-eight of Cicero's works at least.[48] Two of these were at second hand, but I count them because he not only acknowledged his failure to find them, but attempted, *moderno more*, to reconstruct them from quotations in works of Augustine.[49] On the other hand he quotes Cicero rarely, though judiciously (I do not count the *Polyhistor* extracts), drawing on six works, of which five were rare at the time.[50] To some extent the differences between John's and William's use of Cicero may simply reflect the different kinds of work that they wrote. William had little call or opportunity to quote Cicero in his historical writings, and composed nothing remotely resembling John's major treatises.

The differences between William's and John's treatment of antiquity generally are due to more than one factor. One of them is their very different careers. John was a hard-pressed administrator, probably working consciously towards the bishopric that he belatedly obtained. He was particularly heavily engaged during the years prior to the writing of his two major works, and complained of lack of leisure for reading and study.[51] In relating his learning to his administrative work, John saw himself in terms of a definite antique model: the Senecan or Ciceronian model of the virtuous, articulate public man who speaks and writes to instil moral sense into his country's rulers.[52] The monk William, by contrast, was by choice a careerless man. About his self-ideal there is likewise no doubt: his hero was Bede, a model of detached and selfless devotion to Christian learning, to the recovery and promotion of the legacy of the past.[53] In other words, in comparing John and William we are comparing a scholastically-trained *curialis* with a monastic autodidact, and we are comparing two styles of reading: rapid skimming as against meditative absorption.

It is also instructive to compare their audiences. John wrote primarily for a small, élite circle of highly-educated ecclesiastics. Their expectations constitute another reason for the ostentatious parade of *auctores* in John's works, including his correspondence.[54] William's readers, the monks of Malmesbury and nearby houses, were of humbler rank and attainments, and

---

[47] On MSS and knowledge of Cicero's *Epistulae ad familiares* see *Texts and Transmission*, pp. 138–142.

[48] See below, p. 201.

[49] ibid., pp. 51–2.

[50] ibid., pp. 55–6.

[51] *Policr.*, I, p. 14.

[52] Liebeschütz, *Mediaeval Humanism*, pp. 79–84.

[53] See below, pp. 18–20, and GR I, pp. 58–67, 69; II, pp. 389, 518, 567.

[54] John's audience can be gauged from his correspondence, and from the circulation of the earliest manuscripts of his major works, on which see A. Linder, 'The Knowledge of John of Salisbury in the Late Middle Ages', *Studi Medievali*, ser. 3, 18 (1977), 319–22.

but Robert of Gloucester?

even the noble patrons of some of his works were not necessarily learned.[55] In any case self-expression seems to have been at least as important as considerations of readership in influencing William's literary output.

Finally, we need to remember not only the different milieux in which John and William operated, but also that John was a generation younger, witness to, and participant in an ineluctable process by which scholastic education became streamlined, vocationally-oriented, and thus in his view barbarized. Despite his call for a more thorough grounding in the *auctores*, John was himself a prisoner, as well as critic, of Cornificianism. He calls its products 'philosophers baked overnight', who say 'There is no point in studying the rules of eloquence'.[56] But John himself argues for the severely practical advantages of eloquence in fine Cornifician style: 'Who are the most prosperous and wealthy among our fellow citizens? Who the most powerful and successful in all their enterprises? Is it not the eloquent?'[57] William, the detached monk, could afford the luxury of reading the *auctores* for their own sake; John, the overburdened administrator and responsible adviser, could not.

And yet the two men have sufficient in common to be regarded as products of, and notable contributors to the 'twelfth-century renaissance' in England, and as making a distinctively English contribution to European intellectual life. This distinctiveness consisted in the mobilization of the literature of antiquity and its application to the study of contemporary society, its nature and problems. For John, the application was by means of satirical and philosophical comment on political life and structures; for William it was done by writing the history of his country.[58]

---

[55] For William's *Kulturkreis* see below, pp. 34–7, 72–5. Many of William's works fall under the heading of 'teaching-material'.

[56] John of Salisbury, *Metalogicon*, ed. C. C. J. Webb (Oxford, 1929), pp. 11–12.

[57] ibid., p. 23.

[58] On the English contribution to the twelfth-century Renaissance, including comment on the role played by William and John, see the articles by Southern and Thomson cited in n. 5 above.

2

WILLIAM AS HISTORIAN
AND MAN OF LETTERS

AS A HISTORIAN and man of learning, William has over the last century drawn very diverse reactions from those scholars whose work has brought them into contact with him. At one end of the spectrum, praise has been lavished on his wide reading, critical acumen and historical judgement; at the other, his credulity, carelessness, wilful mishandling of evidence and meandering irrelevance have been stigmatized. He has sometimes been seen as head and shoulders above, and in advance of his time, a 'modern' writer;[1] while others have seen him as the creature of his epoch and immediate environment in a pejorative sense.[2] The fact is that hardly any modern scholar apart from William Stubbs has given attention to William for himself alone, or attained such a command of his output as to be able to offer an overall assessment of it. Even Stubbs did not claim to be attempting this and, in any case, was unacquainted with several of William's works, and misattributed others.[3] Of course William is best known now, and perhaps always was, for his major historical writings. His other literary and intellectual activities have been passed by, although it is scarcely possible to offer a comprehensive judgement upon his achievement as historian without considering it in the context of his other literary and intellectual interests. It is also debatable whether he saw himself as a historian first and foremost,

[1] R. Darlington, *Anglo-Norman Historians* (London, 1947); R. W. Southern, 'Aspects of the European Tradition of Historical Writing IV: the Sense of the Past', TRHS, 5th ser., 23 (1973), 255; B. Smalley, *Historians in the Middle Ages* (London, 1974), pp. 90, 92–3.
[2] Carter, 'Thesis', I, ch. vi; W. Stubbs in GR II, pp. xv–cxlii, esp. pp. cxli–cxlii; R. B. Patterson, 'William of Malmesbury's Robert of Gloucester', *American Historical Review*, 70 (1965), 983–997.
[3] Stubbs did not know, for instance, of William's canon law collection (Oxford, Oriel College MS 42), his collection of Cicero's works (CUL MS Dd. 13. 2), his copy of John the Scot (Cambridge, Trinity College O. 5. 20) or of Martianus Capella (Cambridge, Corpus Christi College MS 330); he wrongly attributed to William the version of the *Passio S. Indracti* in Oxford, Bodleian Library MS Digby 112, and the *Miracula S. Andrei* really by Gregory of Tours.

rather than a Christian man of letters for whom the rescuing, collecting and editing of Latin literature, the writing of history and hagiography, the compilation of biblical commentaries and works of moral edification were all legitimate and important tasks which suited his talents, and which would benefit his and other monastic communities.

In attempting an overall assessment of William as Benedictine scholar, let us begin with his reading. The first impression conveyed by the list of his reading which is Appendix I is surely that he read everything on which he could lay hands.[4] I believe that this is correct so far as it goes; that is, that William was a voracious and omnivorous reader who attempted in all seriousness to read for himself, or to obtain for his local library the totality of what was available to the western world of his time. Of course he was not successful. Some fields are under-represented, although this might reflect only the paucity of our information. For example, William certainly knew many more patristic works than I have been able to identify. But I do not think that any general area in which reading was available or of interest to a religious of the early twelfth century is unrepresented in my list. The implied qualification is important, for there is so far no evidence that William read any early scholastic writings. Otherwise there were certainly some individual works that he did not find. In some cases these were writings, particularly classical, which circulated mainly or solely on the continent; others were everywhere rare and little read. William did the best he could with texts that he badly wanted but could not obtain, by collecting together quotations and fragments.

But, although omnivorous, William was not undiscriminating. He had his preferences, the most notorious of which, a cause of guilty concern to him and of periodic self-justification, was his love for the pagan classics. The other main focus of his attention, this time a legitimate one, was the writings of the Fathers. These are the two major emphases of William's wide reading and, except for the extent of his interest in the first, they are typically Benedictine.[5] Not that they were his only interests, but he habitually preferred what was antique to what was more recent, and when he praised the work of his contemporaries, it was generally because they were once again respecting the great models of classical and Christian Rome.[6] He was always on the lookout for works of history, as he says in the *Gesta Regum*,[7] but largely for a utilitarian purpose, unless they were about ancient Rome; he needed them to compile his own. Thus he read and used Ethelweard,

---

[4] See below, pp. 197–207.
[5] As outlined by J. Leclercq, *The Love of Learning and the Desire for God* (New English edn, London, 1978), chs 6 and 7.
[6] GR II, pp. 338–340, 402–3, 513, 516. GP, p. 173.
[7] GR I, p. 103.

although he found his style disgusting.[8] He acknowledged the fundamental contribution of the Anglo-Saxon Chronicle to his reconstruction of the history of England after Bede, while affecting to despise it as a primitive and lowly form of literature.[9] On the other hand he enthused over the verse of Hildebert of Le Mans and Godfrey of Winchester because they represented a revival of correct Latinity and of antique literary and ethical values.

Although William sometimes quotes an author without providing any indication that he had read him, this is rare, and what is perhaps more impressive than the mere list of authors and works known to him is the evidence of his thorough knowledge and absorption of so many texts. By what means he learned so much of the *Aeneid* one cannot say, but the fact remains that he appropriated its text to the point where it became a major, unconscious, instinctual influence on his style, with verbatim and easily identifiable quotations shading off into echoes, reminiscences and tricks of style. A better test is an obscurer author, Palladius. William's brief note on the contents of the *De Agricultura* is sufficient to demonstrate his careful reading of it, with special attention to its sources, lost to him but which he probably made some effort to locate.[10]

William is especially remarkable among twelfth-century literati for his awareness of the relationship between texts. His copy of Paul the Deacon's *Historia Romana*, for instance, is accompanied by marginal notes indicating what was copied from Eutropius, Orosius and Jordanes, and what was peculiar to Paul himself.[11] He was well aware of the debt which Ambrose's *De Officiis* owed to Cicero's work of the same name.[12] Even more interestingly, his comments on the Pliny extracts in his florilegium, the *Polyhistor*, show how he had made himself aware of the interrelationship of a whole series of texts on geography and natural history. Thus:

> I shall give some excerpts from Pliny's Natural History, from which Solinus and Isidore took whatever they wrote about geography and ethnography, the nature of animals, and wonders to be found on land and sea.[13]

And again:

> But there are many idle things in Pliny; and also Pliny took much from Valerius, while Valerius took almost all of his material from Cicero.

---

[8] Ibid., pp. 1, 3, 121. On the style of Ethelweard and other Anglo-Latin writers criticised by William, see M. Lapidge, 'The Hermeneutic Style in Tenth-Century Anglo-Latin Literature', ASE, 4 (1975), 67–111.
[9] GR I, p. 11ff.
[10] See below, p. 59.
[11] Oxford, Bodl. Libr. MS Arch. Seld. B. 16, ff. 73–134v; below, pp. 66–8.
[12] See below, p. 40.
[13] PH, p. 45.

But I do not think it inappropriate to include these things here, in order that you may know what each borrowed from the other.[14]

He took a similar course with the Gellius excerpts in the same collection,[15] and a particularly revealing example of this kind of research is found in the prologue to his *Abbreviatio Amalarii*:

> Now the first two books [of Rabanus's *De Officiis Ecclesiasticis*] are transcribed verbatim from Augustine's *De Doctrina Christiana*, the third from Gregory's *Pastoral Rule*. And what is there in his *De Natura Rerum* that is not already in Isidore's *Etymologiae*? What in his *De Compoto* that is not in Bede's *De Temporibus*, apart from some discussions of allegories?[16]

I shall return to the important criticisms embodied in this last excerpt later; here it is enough to note that William had managed to discover Rabanus's principal sources, presumably by the only way open to him, painstaking textual comparison. It would be possible to multiply examples to illustrate this point, and others are given in the next chapter.[17] They show that William worked hard at his reading, comparing different versions of the same story, operating within a firm chronological framework, so that he was able to give an accurate account of their relationship. Where did he learn this technique? Perhaps it was from Bede, who in his New Testament commentaries provided marginal indications of his main sources.[18]

I have already mentioned William's wide-ranging search for literary materials. Most of the specific evidence that he had visited a particular place

[14] Ibid., p. 61.
[15] See below, pp. 60–1, 186–7.
[16] GR I, p. cxxix; AbAm, pp. 128–9.
[17] See below, pp. 40–1, 60–1, 66–7. To these examples can be added PH, p. 44: 'Possem plura de libris Ciceronis quos habemus excerpere, nisi quod et quedam iudico inania, et quedam scio a Valerio et Plinio excerpta quamuis et aliqua eorum que illi excerpserunt ego hic scienter apposuerim. Sane laudem Lucii Luculli qua eum in libro de Achademicis extulit propter claritatem dictorum non preteribo', and p. 118: (after a series of excerpts from Cicero, *De Senectute*) 'Hic animaduertat lector me pretermisisse de Atheniensibus, qui hoc quod Temistocles dixerat utile quoniam honestum non erat dimiserunt, de falso testamento Minutii Basuli, de profuga Pyrri qui uenit ad Fabricium, de octo milibus Romanorum quos uiuos cepit Hannibal; hec enim omnia in Valerio Maximo leguntur. Dimisi etiam quod Marius criminacione Metelli acquisierit consulatum, quoniam in Salustio copiose legitur; preterii nichilominus quod Titus Manlius tribunum plebis pro criminacione prioris sui uoluerit necare, quoniam copiosius in Seneca de Beneficiis inuenitur; quedam tamen que alii dixerunt apposui, quoniam eos illa ex Tullio excerpsisse qui eos tempore precessit sciui'.
[18] M. L. W. Laistner, 'Bede as a Classical and a Patristic Scholar', in *The Intellectual Heritage of the Early Middle Ages*, ed. C. Starr (Cornell, 1957), pp. 103–4.

and used its literary resources is found in the *Gesta Pontificum*. There is enough of it to show that he had travelled virtually the length and breadth of the land, visiting most of its major cathedrals and abbeys by 1125, the date of the first edition of the *Gesta*.[19] The evidence is such that we have to envisage at least one grand tour, entailing a long absence, perhaps a year or more, from his house, and prolonged stays at certain other monasteries, exploring, noting, summarizing and copying. Once the dimensions of William's bibliographical travels are realised, a number of questions have to be answered: what precisely was its object? How did he obtain his abbot's permission for such a long absence from Malmesbury? Who supported him financially? – for his travels and stays at other houses must have been costly. As to the first question, his trips were obviously related to his work in stocking the inadequate abbey library, a project in which he might have assisted Abbot Godfrey when a young man (before 1106),[20] and to the planning of his major historical writings. Although most of the evidence is found in the *Gesta Pontificum*, this is a coincidental consequence of its topographical organisation, and I believe that the *Gesta Regum* was the main object and beneficiary of William's travels. This means that William's long journey, which certainly took place before 1125, was probably undertaken even before 1118. The evidence for this will be discussed shortly.

Bringing the *Gesta Regum* into the picture solves the problems of how William obtained permission and money for his travels. The recently printed dedicatory letters prefacing the *Gesta* in Troyes, Bibliothèque Municipale MS 294 (*bis*) clearly shows that the production of this work was a task originally laid upon the whole Malmesbury community by Queen Matilda of England (d.1118).[21] In the letter to her daughter and namesake, at least part of which seems certainly by William himself, it is explained that some of the *Gesta* was written while the queen was alive; on her death he hesitated to proceed, but finally went ahead, because of the project's intrinsic importance, and because of his friends' urging.[22] I should consequently suggest that William's 'grand tour', sponsored by his abbey and perhaps by Queen Matilda directly, had been undertaken by this date, presumably c.1115.

But this was not the only time that William went searching for materials outside his own library. Between 1125 and 1135 he stayed at Glastonbury, writing the lives of its local saints and the *Antiquity*, digging into its archives and hagiography. Within the same period he was at Worcester, a visit connected with the writing of the *Vita Wulfstani*.[23]

---

[19] See below, pp. 72–5.
[20] GP, pp. 431–2.
[21] Ed. E. Könsgen, 'Zwei unbekannte Briefe zu den Gesta Regum Anglorum des Wilhelm von Malmesbury', *Deutsches Archiv*, 31 (1975), 204–214.
[22] Ibid., pp. 213–4.
[23] VW, p. viii.

William's literary travels were both extensive and purposeful. To write the individual histories of England's monasteries and cathedrals meant, for William, a visit to each of them, using their charters, domestic chronicles and hagiography, talking with senior and responsible inmates. But he also carried, in his head if not written down, a list of his 'wants', of which Cicero's *De Re Publica* was clearly one.[24] In the *Polyhistor* he mourns that, although Cassiodorus had stated that Jerome's commentary on Jeremiah contained 20 books, 'nusquam inuenitur nisi vi'.[25] These and other examples show William attempting to move from text to text, using the evidence of one writer to help him find the work of another. His ability to do this puts one on one's guard. When, in his *Historia Novella*, he proudly quotes Livy, it is at second hand, via Orosius.[26] In the *Gesta Pontificum* he refers, correctly, to a passage in a rare play of Plautus, but the form in which he gives it shows that his real source was Jerome.[27] And yet he seems only to have done this when the original work was not available to him; when it was, he quoted at first hand. For example, in the *Gesta Regum*, describing the last days of the Venerable Bede, William says:

> Plerumque spe metuque libratis, cum neutrum praeponderaret, inferebat, 'Horrendum est incidere in manus Dei uiuentis. Non ita inter uos uixi ut pudeat me uiuere, sed nec mori timeo, quia bonum Dominum habemus'; sanctissimi Ambrosii morientis dictum mutuatus.[28]

What work concerning Ambrose is William quoting here? If we turn to his source for the circumstances of Bede's death, the famous Letter of Cuthbert to Cuthwine, we find the same words, also ascribed to St Ambrose.[29] They are taken from the Life by Paulinus of Milan.[30] One would be entitled to assume that William simply lifted the quotation and reference from Cuthbert's Letter, but that is not so, for some small variations in the quotation, and the tell-tale addition of 'morientis' after 'Ambrosii' show that William also consulted the text of Paulinus.

It is worth considering, for a moment, William's use of literary material as historical evidence. Sir Richard Southern has recently emphasised the variety

---

[24] See below, pp. 51–2.

[25] PH, p. 136. Cf. Cassiodorus, *Institutes* i. 3. 3: 'Hieremiam ... etiam sanctus Hieronymus uiginti libris commentatus esse monstratur; ex quibus sex tantum nos potuimus inuenire ...'. In fact Jerome never completed more than these books.

[26] HN, p. 34, where the reference to Livy is not commented upon by the editor. It was M. R. James (*Two Ancient English Scholars*, p. 26) who recognised that this quotation was at second hand.

[27] See below, p. 49.

[28] GR I, p. 65.

[29] *Baedae Opera Historica*, ed. C. Plummer (Oxford, 2 vols, 1896), I, p. clxii.

[30] Paulinus, *Vita Ambrosii*, 45 (PL 14. 43).

of the material out of which William pieced together domestic, biographical and national history.[31] He himself considered chronicles and annals of greatest weight, although he regarded the second as the inferior form of the two. But among the sources of the *Gesta Regum*, the work which best illustrates this point, can be found both prose and verse, hagiography and biography, letters and charters. One of William's most impressive characteristics is his ability to squeeze some historical insight from a piece of writing in itself of only marginal relevance to his theme. Sometimes the same material could be used for more than one purpose. A case in point is Hildebert's great poem 'Par tibi Roma nihil'.[32] William cited it to justify his admiration for Hildebert, to illustrate his general point that antique culture was experiencing a rebirth in his own time, and to amplify his account of the city of Rome, its topography, antiquities, traditions and current political situation.

A different kind of material, William's use of which has been much admired, was the early charters of Glastonbury, the ungrateful soil from which he tried to disinter the dates and sequence of the pre-Conquest abbots of the house.[33] He could not, of course, distinguish the false from the genuine documents, and this led him into error; but even modern researchers have found the same task difficult, and William is nearly unique at this time in realising how these documents might be used, even if his *modus operandi* was not sufficiently refined to ensure the most accurate of conclusions.[34]

In parenthesis, it should also be noted that William, sometimes censured for mere 'book-learning',[35] did not exclusively rely on literary sources for his historical information: oral testimony, the traditions of the 'seniores', first-hand or reliable second-hand observation, monuments such as the famous Glastonbury 'pyramids', its ornaments, inscriptions, tombs and buildings were all grist to his mill, in his desperate endeavour to construct a connected account of the ancient history of this house, as of his own and others.[36]

Naturally William's sources sometimes gave him conflicting information

---

[31] Southern, art. cit., pp. 254–5.
[32] GR II, p. 403; A. B. Scott (ed.), *Hildeberti Carmina Minora* (Leipzig, 1969), no. 36.
[33] Southern, art. cit., p. 254; J. A. Robinson, *Somerset Historical Essays* (London, 1921), ch. 2; AG, pp. 18–20.
[34] Southern, ut supra; AG, pp. 197–209.
[35] R. W. Southern, *St Anselm and his Biographer* (Cambridge, 1963), pp. 274, 326 and n. 1.
[36] Southern, 'Aspects of the European Tradition of Historical Writing IV', p. 255. This, of course, does not invalidate his opinion that William's judgements were more usually based on his reading than on his first-hand encounters with people and events.

about the same events. In general he faced up to such cruces consciously and honestly. Early in the *Gesta Regum* he explicitly notes different regnal dates assigned to an Anglo-Saxon king by Bede and the *Chronicle*.[37] When he wrote his detailed treatment of the career of Wilfrid in the *Gesta Pontificum* he had both Bede and Eddi at hand, and was well aware of the differences between their accounts. In an interlinear note to his copy of Eutropius he mentions that Suetonius gave a different date for Domitian's death.[38] This awareness in itself makes William one of a small elite among early European historians. Did he go further and pronounce a definite opinion on which of the conflicting sources was the more reliable, or develop criteria for judging his sources?

Although I believe that the answer to both questions is affirmative, it must be said that William was not consistent. Perhaps if the chronology of his works were better established, we might be able to perceive a development in his attitude to problematic source–material and in his expertise in handling it. Thus, the difference between the dates in Bede and the *Chronicle* which he records is left to the reader to resolve. William evidently felt that he had done what was required of him by faithfully recording what two authoritative sources said, and bringing the discrepancy to his readers' attention. This was, of course, a common conception of the historian's role, and Bede himself might have been William's model for it.[39] On the controversial aspects of Wilfrid's career he simply followed the more discreet, Canterbury-oriented Bede. This is understandable, since William was committed by his close connections with Canterbury to the acceptance of its own, official, propagandist view of its past.[40] His interlinear note on the date of Domitian's death gives no indication of preference.

Nonetheless, William developed some criteria of reliability, and we can observe him applying them to difficult source–problems. First of all, the 'veritas' of a record might be guaranteed by the 'auctoritas' of its writer. This 'auctoritas' was a complex of several elements: antiquity, tradition, learning, orthodoxy, intellectual importance. No doubt this consideration played a part in his preference for Bede's account over Eddi's, and the terms in which William habitually refers to Bede illustrate that William did indeed regard his writing as 'authoritative'.[41] And yet he would not on that account prefer his dating to that given in the *Chronicle*, and on other occasions felt free to

---

[37] GR I, p. 13.
[38] See below, pp. 57–8.
[39] *Baedae Opera*, I, p. 8.
[40] For William's connections with Canterbury writers see below, pp. 46–7, 73–5; for his quotation of the 'Canterbury Forgeries' see GP, pp. 46–62, GR II, pp. 342–8, R. W. Southern, 'The Canterbury Forgeries', EHR, 73 (1958), 193–226, and below, pp. 134, 137.
[41] GR I, pp. 1, 2, 46, 53, 57, 60–67 etc.

criticise him, as for his scanty treatment of Aldhelm's career.[42]

Another criterion was style, for which William had an uncanny feel. In his collection of Leo's sermons he correctly identifies the two *spuria* by noting that they are not in the pope's style.[43] As the prologue to his *Gesta Regum* clearly indicates, William thought that the historian had a particular responsibility to present his material in worthy dress: in other words the good historian should be a good rhetorician.[44] William was putting himself in line with those writers of Roman antiquity familiar to him, for 'worthy dress' and 'rhetoric' meant for him, apart from other things not strictly related to style, the writing of a neoclassical Latin – 'exarata barbarice Romano sale condire', as he himself expressed it.[45] From this viewpoint he compared his task with Bede's, and commented adversely on such a writer as Frithegod.[46] Sarcastic judgements on the literary abilities of the writers of later Anglo-Saxon England are common in William's works.[47] In his belief in elegant presentation as an important duty for the historian, although not in this consistent and scathing criticism, he is of a piece with many other major chroniclers of the period from the ninth to the thirteenth century.[48] But he rises above the ruck (such as Richer and Dudo of St Quentin) in two respects: firstly, he did not see this as the historian's *sole* task. He explicitly distinguished, for example, between Ethelweard's careful recording of events and his ungainly style, between the reliability of the *Chronicle* and its dry, spare form. Conversely, he liked Osbern of Canterbury and Faricius of Abingdon as latinists but thought their accounts of Dunstan and Aldhelm unsatisfactory because insufficiently based upon the early sources.[49] The historian, William implies, must wed accuracy and completeness to elegant presentation. This viewpoint is clearly and forcefully expressed in the prologue to Bede's *History* and it is interesting to note that, like Bede in that place, William in the prologue to the *Gesta Regum* cites his principal authorities.[50] Secondly, although William was passionately fond of good Latin, he praised writers in or translators into the vernacular. King Alfred is the most famous recipient of praise at his hand for his translations,[51] but he also complimented the humble Colman who wrote an Old English Life of St

---

[42] GP, p. 330 and cf. pp. 293, 296.
[43] See below, p. 71.
[44] GR I, pp. 1–3.
[45] Ibid., p. 2.
[46] Ibid., and GP, p. 22.
[47] GR I, pp. 1, 3, 31, 144; GP, p. 344; VD, p. 250.
[48] R. W. Southern, 'Aspects of the European Tradition of Historical Writing I: The Classical Tradition from Einhard to Geoffrey of Monmouth', TRHS, 5th ser., 20 (1970), 177–188.
[49] VD, pp. 250–252 (these, however, are not his only criticisms of Osbern); GP, p. 331. Faricius's Life is in *Acta Sanctorum*, Maii VI, pp. 84–93.
[50] GR I, pp. 1–2; *Baedae Opera*, I, pp. 6–7.
[51] GR I, pp. 132–3.

Wulfstan, by translating him without 'change in the order of events, altering nothing in the true relation of fact'.[52] William's admiration for such men can be attributed, I think, to pride in his English ancestry, and to his interest, as humanist and teacher, in the dissemination of learning. Was he yet again influenced in this direction by his profound admiration for Bede? In his account of Bede's last days, mentioned earlier, William includes the information that he was engaged in translating the Gospel of St John into Old English up until the day of his death.[53] I shall document this interest of William's later.

Age was another criterion by which evidence might be tested. Implicit in William's account of the relationship between two or more sources is the assumption that the earliest version is the most reliable and authoritative, and in at least one place this is made explicit. In William's copy of the *Collectio Canonum Quesnelliana* he claims to be using a very ancient manuscript which, by means of marginal signs and comments, he compares with the modern exemplars.[54] I have given reasons below for believing that the ancient copy might have dated from the late eighth or early ninth century.[55] At one point William notes a major variation between this version and the modern texts but, he says, this version is to be believed because of its venerable age.[56] This, of course, is a step towards the modern science of source-criticism. Conversely, he despised plagiarism, unless there was a particular reason for it. As noted earlier, he roundly abused Rabanus Maurus for mere scissors-and-paste work in the *De Universo* and *De Computo*.[57] He himself, in the prologue to his *Miracula Beatae Virginis*, asks the reader's pardon for repeating in his own words stories already recounted by others, on the ground that where the earlier sources are not to be had, the stories might at least be available in his version.[58] In this case repetition is justified on the grounds of increased availability; once again William is concerned about dissemination.

Finally, William was capable of criticising a source on the basis of its content and relation to its historical context. Thus, he noted that Caedwalla's confirmation of a Glastonbury grant was signed with a cross, even though the king was a pagan at the time.[59] This charter, the text of

---

[52] VW, p. 2 (citing from the translation by J. H. F. Peile [Oxford, 1934], p. 2); Gransden, *Historical Writing in England c.550–1307*, pp. 87–9.

[53] GR I, p. 65.

[54] See below, pp. 64–5.

[55] Ibid., pp. 65–6.

[56] Ibid., p. 65.

[57] GR I, p. cxxix; AbAm, p. 129.

[58] *De Miraculis B.V.M.*, p. 63.

[59] Southern, 'Aspects of the European Tradition of Historical Writing IV', p. 254.

which is extant, certainly has suspicious features.[60] Whether William actually thought it suspect but made nothing of this in deference to his patrons, the Glastonbury monks, one can only conjecture. But it is possible to provide a more certain illustration of such criticism. In his *Polyhistor* William has this to say about Jerome's letters:

> Nunc quia ad epistolas ad Demetriadem uirginem scriptas uenimus, moneo te amice ne putes illam que ita incipit 'Si summo ingenio' Iheronimi esse licet in omnibus exemplaribus hunc titulum habeat et Sanctus Aldelmus in libro De Virginitate idem astruat. Quod uero Iuliani Pelagiani sit, Beda in primo libro super Cantica Canticorum ostendit, insanos sensus eius arguens. Sed et beatus Augustinus in epistola ad Iulianam eiusdem Demetriadis matrem [Ep. 188] uerba Iuliani in hac epistola multum detestatur. Ea sunt huiusmodi: 'In hiis es laudanda bonis, que nisi in te et ex te esse non possunt'. 'Quod ait', inquit Augustinus, "non sunt nisi in te", cibus est. Quod uero ait "non nisi ex te" uirus est' [Ep. 1. ii. 4–5]. Hac ergo reiecta, altera secure legatur, que ita incipit 'Inter omnes materias' [Ep. 130]. Ex hac uocis mee pro uirili parte non deerit testimonium in eius uirtutibus explicandis, cuius (ut incliti oratoris utar sentencia) magis spes laudanda quam res est.[61]

Notes on the authorship of this letter are found in other English sources. At least two twelfth-century manuscripts of Jerome's letters, and the fourteenth-century *Catalogus Scriptorum Ecclesie* by Henry de Kirkestede contain notes similar to each other and to William's, although briefer.[62] Another twelfth-century copy of Jerome's letters has a much longer critical note added in the fourteenth-century.[63] The relationship of William's note to these others is unclear, but he probably adapted and developed his from one already attached to manuscripts of Jerome's correspondence. Whatever the case, his note illustrates his ability to deploy his wonderful knowledge of his texts to critical advantage, arguing from internal evidence against that of all the exemplars which he had examined and against his admired patron Aldhelm, although, as he says, Bede has already made the same observation. Nevertheless, William is not content to rest on Bede's *auctoritas* alone, but reproduces his reasoning, supporting it with further evidence, Augustine's

---

[60] AG, pp. 93, 198.
[61] PH, p. 87.
[62] The twelfth-century examples are in Oxford, New College 129, f. 158v, and London, BL Roy. 6 A. iii, f. 41; Kirkestede's *Catalogus* is in CUL Add. 3470, the note being on p. 86.
[63] Oxford, Bodl. Libr. MS Bodl. 365, f. 340.

letter to Juliana. Modern scholarship agrees that both Bede and (by implication) William were essentially correct.[64]

I said that William was not consistent in his application of the principles of textual and source-criticism. In his canonistic collection, a few folios after his boast of the excellence of his 'most ancient exemplar', he inserted a lengthy note pointing out that his source did not include the 'filioque' clause in the Nicene Creed, in contrast to the 'modern exemplars', thus agreeing with the Greek Church against the Roman of William's day.[65] Significant is the absence of any value-judgement or comment upon this fact, although William's copy is faithful to his 'most ancient exemplar'. His sense of orthodoxy and of discretion, both strong, were two agents which compelled him to draw back when his historical sense seemed to urge him towards a particular conclusion. These same concerns, of course, led him to a correct decision in the attribution of the Pelagian letter to Demetrias.

The other major limitation upon William's criticism of his texts is his 'credulity'. A sensitive examination is required of this trait, seen most clearly in his hagiographical works, and in the marvel-stories in the later books of the *Gesta Regum*. Somehow it coexisted with a Bedan rationality, humanity and common sense. Not the 'credulity', part of the *Weltanschauung* shared by the society in which William lived, but the juxtaposition, is what is curious. The delimitation of these (to us) radically different attitudes, the conditions under which now one characteristic now the other came to the fore and temporarily dominated in William's work and personality, are matters which require elucidation. It must be said, of course, that in the light of modern research into medieval historiography, the contrast probably seems greater to us than it would have to William and his generation.[66] It is probable, indeed, that they perceived no disjunction at all. What we are seeking to reconstruct, therefore, is William's vision of history, the window through which he viewed reality. It would certainly be useless and misleading to award him praise or blame for being sometimes rational and 'modern', sometimes credulous and 'of his own time'.

This much can be said, by way of simple, introductory generalisation: that William is at his coolest and most intellectual when dealing with the remote past, and vice versa. It is the present, or more often the immediate past, not antiquity, which he mythologises. This is most clearly seen in the *Antiquity of Glastonbury*, once it is stripped of the later interpolations.[67] William's account of the earliest, possibly apostolic origins of the abbey are restrained,

---

[64] Ogilvy, *Books known to the English*, pp. 187, 218. The letter is probably not by Julian but by Pelagius himself: *Clavis*, no. 737.

[65] See below, p. 65.

[66] Cf. R. D. Ray, 'Medieval Historiography through the Twelfth Century: Problems and Progress of Research', *Viator*, 5 (1974), 33–59.

[67] AG, pp. 6–33.

rational and cautious, with elaborate citation of his sources.[68] It is when he comes to the decade or two previous to his writing that he tells stories such as that of the bleeding crucifix.[69] So also with the *Gesta Regum*: the early books are a judicious selection and combination of Bede, the *Chronicle* and other incidental information. Much later we have the famous legends of Gerbert the magician, the witch of Berkeley and the two clerks of Nantes.[70] When he comes to write contemporary history in the *Historia Novella* rationality reigns again. This strange shifting of attitude sets William apart from the majority of ancient and early European historians for whom mythology generally increased with remoteness in time and thinness of factual information. William introduces marvels when his source-material is most abundant, and gratuitously, to the extent that they contribute little or nothing to his main theme.

This, of course, only carries our enquiry a stage further back, for it raises the question: why was William like this? One's first impulse is perhaps to look for possible models from which he could have derived this tendency to mythologise the recent past, and indeed a not dissimilar process is discernible in Bede.[71] Bede's concise account of Roman, Celtic and pagan Anglo-Saxon Britain is relatively free from myth or miracle. It is with the coming of the Augustinian mission that an era of signs and wonders begins. For Bede these supernatural happenings are pregnant with theological meaning: they are signs of God's favour, they are intimately related to the spirituality and moral virtue of the performer or recipient, and they are told in order to edify. They are expressions of the Gospel's ascendancy, of the victory of Christ and His followers over the forces of darkness, and of their power over the laws of nature. Little of this applies to William's miracles. They are not linked to any particular movement of spiritual revival (though he was aware of such movements in his time),[72] they are not necessarily manifestations of the sanctity of any individual, and they have little or no theological or moral content. The workers of William's marvels are more often demonic than saintly. These differences, profound though they are, do not prove that Bede was not William's model in this particular area: rather they show that William's spirituality and the spirituality of his age were very different from Bede's. In function and content William's *miracula* have more

<hr>

[68] William's original account, minus the interpolations, is in AG, pp. 168–172.
[69] Ibid., pp. 157–9.
[70] GR I, pp. 194–203, 253–4, II, pp. 294–5.
[71] See J. Rosenthal, 'Bede's Use of Miracles in "The Ecclesiastical History"', *Traditio*, 31 (1975), 328–335. A rediscovery of Bede seems to have been a crucial component of Anglo-Norman historiography; cf. C. N. L. Brooke, 'Geoffrey of Monmouth as a Historian', in idem, D. E. Luscombe et al. (eds), *Church and Government in the Middle Ages; Essays presented to C. R. Cheney* (Cambridge, 1976), pp. 77–91.
[72] GR II, pp. 380–385.

in common with those told by Guibert of Nogent than with Bede's.[73]

But perhaps we should look to something other than a model to help explain William's ambivalent attitude to the past. Is it too much to suggest that William's wide reading and studies had led him into a position where he was in danger of breaking out of the ideological framework within which his monastic training had taught him to view the world? He was not bold enough to make the break radically, but he found himself, whether entirely consciously or not, most able to break free from it when discussing remote periods. When he came to deal with his own time he could hardly dismiss miracles, signs and wonders without provoking questions from others and discomfort in his own psyche. Even so, those that he introduces into his historical works are of a comparatively trivial nature, and do not function as the causal agents for important actions, developments or changes. This is, of course, to suggest that William did feel to some degree the disjunction mentioned earlier, that his 'window on reality' did not at all points perfectly correspond with that which was utilised by most writers of his time, or, to put it another way, that he was attempting to use the 'window' accepted by most of his contemporaries, but found that it did not permit a consistent interpretation of all the material which he came to scrutinize. This implies a degree of inner conflict and, indeed, there is evidence for this in William's *Miracles of the Virgin*. In its lengthy introduction William scrapes together, with great difficulty, the opinions of the Ancients about the Virgin's powers and qualities. Towards the end of this almost fruitless exercise, he expresses his surprise that the Fathers had had so little to say about her:

> There is yet another point to be made about the sublimity of this Virgin not as unquestionable fact but as a matter still open to argument and without prejudicing the caution of the ancients who had nothing to say of her Assumption or Ascension nor the verdict of those of our own day who are inclined to think that such a thing is possible. For certain of those among whom I count myself one are not a little disturbed by the problem of why our authorities have either omitted it after due consideration or have kept silent because they could not make up their minds and of why they have not categorically asserted that the Lady Mother of the Lord has now risen and ascended into heaven with her virginal body.[74]

William maintains that these matters are capable of dialectical proof and proceeds to argue accordingly. Even so, his worry remains:

---

[73] J. F. Benton (ed. and transl.), *Self and Society in Medieval France; the Memoirs of Abbot Guibert of Nogent* (New York, 1970), passim, but espec. iii. 18–20.
[74] *De Miraculis B.V.M.*, pp. 57–8 (following the translation of Carter, 'Thesis', II, pp. 291–2).

These are almost all the things mentioned by our ancestors in praise of the blessed Mary in so far as they can be discovered ... However, if, with the permission of the saints, one may say it, there is still much that needs to be said in literary compositions concerning this quite exceptional woman. For they have been completely silent – perhaps accidentally or perhaps deliberately – about these matters which are particularly useful, I think, for the souls of simple men in kindling their love for Our Lady; examples, I mean, of her piety and miracles whose abundance is made manifest to the world in accounts which deserve serious consideration.[75]

Nearly all of William's writings, whether his original compositions or 'collected editions', are concerned with the past and its great figures. His attitude to the past and its relationship to the present is a subject of considerable importance.

William was conscious of major changes in the course of English history, of the impact and contribution of new peoples and cultures. He could also appreciate some of the distinctive features of a quite different civilisation, such as that of Islam.[76] But could he envisage the civilisation of the past as an entity quite separate from his own? To put it another way: did he, like most of his contemporaries, see his own world as an extension of the world of antiquity, and vice versa?[77] I think it might be claimed that he was capable of differentiating the two, but did not wish to and shied away from doing so. The evidence for this comes in part from the Selden Collection on Roman history.[78] This collection is quite unique of its kind: it is a series of chronicles, arranged in chronological order, beginning with Dares and concluding with Hugh of Fleury, brought up to date with some genealogical material. The chronicles are followed by a copy of the *Breviarium Alaricum*. William does not directly explain his purpose in stringing together these histories, but he provides passages of commentary at intervals, from which his aim emerges quite clearly. This is a 'potted history' of the Roman Empire, and once this much is realised, certain of William's assumptions are easily grasped.[79] He begins with the sack of Troy and the foundation of Rome, then, with Orosius, Jordanes, Eutropius and Paul the Deacon, we

[75] *De Miraculis B.V.M.*, p. 63 (Carter, 'Thesis', II, p. 296).
[76] See below, ch. 9.
[77] C. Morris, *The Discovery of the Individual 1050–1200* (London, 1972), pp. 51–7.
[78] Oxford, Bodl. Libr. MS Arch. Seld. B. 16. For its contents see below, pp. 66–8.
[79] Some of these commentaries are printed in GR I, pp. cxxiv–v, cxxvii–cxl, and below, pp. 63, 66–7. The only other of any length is on f. 140: 'Quos successores Carolus Caluus habuerit in illa parte Galliae quae nunc Francia dicitur, quamuis in gestis Francorum inueniatur, tamen hic occasione Caroli Magni non omittam. Eorum ergo hic sunt nomina ...'.

proceed through the *fasti* and deeds of kings, consuls and emperors; thence to the east for the rise of the Byzantine Empire, then back to the west with Charlemagne's coronation, continuing on to the conclusion of Hugh of Fleury's account, the reign of Louis the Pious. William's genealogical additions are lists of the Eastern and German emperors and – somewhat irrelevantly as he himself confesses[80] – the kings of France. All this, with the *Breviarium* as its keystone, shows that William saw the history of early Europe as a direct continuation of the history of Rome. Despite the transition from paganism to Christianity, the change of language in the East and the religious differences between East and West, the shift of the centre of civilisation in the West from the Mediterranean basin to the north-west, the collapse of Roman administrative and political institutions and the formation of new ones from crude beginnings, William still saw, or wished to see the history of the previous millennium as a continuum. The elements of continuity, in particular the imperial title, were more important for him than the cataclysmic changes. The rise of Rome had a greater effect upon the subsequent history of western Europe than did the beginnings of Christianity, which do not rate a mention in the Selden Collection. I say that William *wished* to see it this way, and yet I believe that there were forces urging him to think differently. My evidence for this is his attitude to ancient Rome and all she stood for, which brings us to William's view of the past as humanist and man of letters.

In his treatment of the past, William concentrated on two main areas: as a historian (and patriot?) he was interested in early England; as both historian and humanist he was passionately interested in ancient Rome. William's attitude to the works of pagan antiquity is complex, and his attempts to justify it indicate that he did not fully understand it himself. The justifications occur in two places: the prologue to his *Polyhistor*, and the famous note in his collected edition of Cicero's works.[81] In the *Polyhistor*'s introduction, addressed to a monk named Guthlac, William distinguishes between those pagan works which can be read by a religious with profit for his morals and way of life, those which are about rhetoric, and those which, although their matter is repugnant for one reason or another, are still useful as models of style. As examples of the first type William mentions Cicero's works which treat of the vices and virtues, and the writing of a polytheist (Hermes) which exhorts the worship of one God, although countenancing the existence of lesser gods made by Him. Here again one sees William seeking common ground between Christianity and other religions, and pleased to find some in a work which he knew only at second hand, through St Augustine. It ought to be said, however, that he did not merely or primarily include in the *Polyhistor* moral or ethical reflections, but

---

80 See the quotation in the previous note.
81 PH, p. 37; below, pp. 51–2.

miscellaneous information on the natural world, on famous Greek and Roman men and women, on ancient peoples and places. In the note in his Cicero-manuscript, William explicitly addresses himself to those who might criticise him for reading 'as many pagan authors as I do'. Citing Jerome's letter to Eustochium he admits that those who love pagan writers to the neglect of the Scriptures sin greatly; on the other hand their study in order to aid the understanding of the Bible and to write eloquently is a virtue; in support he cites Augustine, whose reading of Cicero's *Hortensius* set him on the road to monotheism and ultimately to Christianity, and Jerome's letter to Magnus. The letter to Eustochium evidently touched William's conscience, for he quotes from it Jerome's description of his spiritual crisis no less than four times in his own works.[82]

How much do these *pièces justificatives* tell us? Certainly they are evidence that William was conscience-stricken about his exceptional love of the classics, and that he was probably the recipient of some criticism on this account. But they are less illuminating than they appear as to the real reasons why he persisted in his reading. The reasons given: to instruct in moral virtue, to improve one's style and eloquence and to increase one's understanding of Holy Scripture, are all conventional, their basis lying in passages from Jerome and Augustine which by William's time were traditionally cited for this purpose.[83] One is worried, for instance, when in the *Polyhistor*'s introduction he cites Seneca as good for moral instruction, while his quotations from Seneca's letters in the body of the same work are exceptional among such medieval selections in being chosen not for their ethical content but for their wit.[84] Plainly we need to get beyond William's justifications to the actual use he made of the pagan classics in his own works.

William did on occasion use pagan authors to make a moral point, but not often. A notable instance is in his *Commentary on Lamentations*, where he says: 'We should await the end, not the beginning of our pleasures – as Aristotle says so beautifully, and I think not in an inferior manner to any Christian'.[85] Most of William's citations of this kind are general, platitudinous moralisations, often in the *Sprichwort* category. More typical is his 'magis spes laudanda quam res est' from Cicero via Jerome, in the *Polyhistor*.[86] It goes without saying that none of this moral advice has any

---

[82] In the passage in the Cicero-collection printed below, p. 52; in *De Miraculis B.V.M.*, p. 132, in PH, p. 87, and VW, p. 15.
[83] R. R. Bolgar, *The Classical Heritage and its Beneficiaries* (Cambridge, 1954), pp. 51–4, 204–5. Cf. Ogilvy, *Books known to the English*, p. 174, for the use of Jerome, *Ad Eustochium*, by Bede, Aldhelm and Alcuin.
[84] L. D. Reynolds, *The Medieval Tradition of Seneca's Letters* (Oxford, 1965), pp. 115–122.
[85] See below, p. 62.
[86] PH, p. 101.

specific Christian content and, indeed, as a body it has only tangential contact with the Christian system of values. Thus the *Polyhistor* has many anecdotes illustrative of the virtues of ancient men and women of note: the characteristic excellences which they display are courage, probity, justice, sagacity, seeking after wisdom, loyalty and patriotism. Piety, of course, is absent, and so are love (in the Christian sense) and humility. It is not that the values implicit in William's examples are anti-Christian, but that they are not necessarily those which are given high priority within the Christian scheme of things. If a particular value-system is represented by William's selections and quotations from the pagan classics, it is Stoicism. William was not alone at this time in being influenced by Stoicism, especially through Seneca.[87] In this connection a very telling passage is found in his *Miracles of the Virgin*:[88]

> Philosophers have always taught this: that it is important for right living to have continually in mind some person or other of utterly blameless life so that you are ashamed to sin in the sight of that person, if the sight of God is in itself not sufficient to deter you. Anyone who does this either never or hardly ever sins. And gradually proceeding from that point, he will fall into the habit of loving God alone and of taking pleasure in good for its own sake, when once he has begun to act morally for the sake of respectability.

The same idea is expressed in very similar language in William's *Vita Wulfstani*.[89] Such a citation of a pagan ethical proposition and its harmonisation with Christian principles is an example of a tendency noted recently by D. E. Luscombe who, however, finds it more characteristic of the Schools and of the second half of the twelfth century.[90] Monastic writers tended to be censorious of such relativism.

There is less difficulty about William's use of the classics for stylistic purposes. He was steeped in the Arts of grammar and rhetoric, and if the historical works are omitted, the classical texts which he is known to have read most thoroughly nearly all come within these classifications. But of course works of history ought not necessarily to be excluded. In the margins of his Orosius William often notes 'Declamatio' opposite a speech – a sure

---

[87] P. von Moos, *Hildebert von Lavardin* (Stuttgart, 1965), passim (see Index under 'Stoa' and 'Seneca') and G. Verbeke, *The Presence of Stoicism in Medieval Thought* (Washington, 1983), pp. 8–14.

[88] *De Miraculis B.V.M.*, p. 116 (Carter's translation). The source seems to be Seneca, *Ep.* 11. 8–10.

[89] VW, p. 5.

[90] D. Luscombe, 'The *Ethics* of Abelard', in *Peter Abelard (Medievalia Lovanensia, Ser.I/Studia II*, Louvain and The Hague, 1974), pp. 66–73.

but he to expose to use 'declam.' in history

sign of rhetorical interest.[91] The fact that he compiled a collection of grammatical manuals comprising pseudo-Caper, Agroecius, Bede and Alcuin indicates the seriousness of his interest in this area;[92] so do his citations of Cicero's *De Inventione* and the (pseudonymous) *Ad Herennium*.[93] Neither of these works is included in William's great Cicero-collection;[94] this is so odd that I can only assume that he had a separate collection of treatises on rhetoric comprising these two works and perhaps others. Although William knew Cicero's philosophical and rhetorical treatises best, he habitually refers to him as 'that great (or "most eloquent") orator'.[95] I have already remarked on the heavy debt to Virgil which William shows as a stylist. This shows most markedly in vocabulary, in particular expressions (such as 'pede retro sublapsa' or 'terque quaterque beati'), and in echoes and citations. When we look at the structure of William's sentences, however, the influence of Suetonius and Sallust is apparent, at something like cross purposes to other, more 'modern' techniques such as rhyming *clausulae*, popular in William's time, and which he used freely, although not as much as some other contemporary monastic writers. Thus, quite apart from the citations which so liberally sprinkle all of William's works, and especially those at which he worked most assiduously, it can be claimed that the classics deeply influenced his prose style. We also recall that when he criticised earlier English writers for their over-elaborate Latin, it was because they did not conform to the canons of classical writing.[96] The writing of history was most appropriately done 'more Romano'.[97]

There is little evidence that William took seriously his expressed view that the pagan classics could be an aid to understanding the Scriptures. True, in his *Commentary on Lamentations* references to Cicero, Seneca and others abound, but the fact remains that William was not first and foremost a biblical scholar.[98] Significantly, he wrote his commentary in a fit of conscience at having to such an extent expended his powers on 'frivolous'

---

[91] Oxford, Bodl. Libr. MS Arch. Seld. B. 16, ff. 11–72v passim; cf. the instance of a twelfth-century Sallust similarly annotated in Smalley, pp. 19–20 and pl. 9.
[92] Contained in London, BL MS Harl. 3969.
[93] See below, p. 55.
[94] Ibid., pp. 50–3.
[95] See above, p. 21, and 'rex facundiae Romanae' cited below, p. 55.
[96] See above, notes 46 and 47.
[97] GR I, p. 2.
[98] For a good (and rare) example of William's deployment of his knowledge of classical rhetoric in the service of biblical scholarship, see Comm. Lam., f. 113: 'Isti more strutionum negligunt oua sua. Dicuntur hec hyperbolice; hyperbole porro est dictio fidem excedens, usitatissima tam gentilibus quam nostris. Verbi causa: Dixit Virgilius de cuiusdam equis 'Qui candore niues anteirent, cursibus auras'; candidiores Nazarei eius niue, nitidiores lacte, rubicundiores ebore antiquo, safero pulchriores'.

works of history.[99] The broad education and literary fluency which his wide reading gave him were undoubtedly aids to scriptural study, but it could hardly be claimed that William primarily employed them for that purpose.

When all is said and done, William's justifications for his classical reading are too negative to reveal much of his real motivation. They explain why *it is not bad* or why it is permissible to read the pagans; they do not explain why it might be a positive virtue, or why one should be as enthusiastic about it as William was. Why did he choose to be so exceptional in his time – a position of which he was uncomfortably conscious?

I think that the answer lies in William's psychology, that it is complex and for lack of evidence hard to articulate, but I would locate a key to it in William's full citation in the *Gesta Regum* of Hildebert's great poem on ancient Rome 'Par tibi Roma nihil'.[100] This poem is a noble lament on Rome's fall and present ruinous and anarchic state contrasted with its former grandeur. For Hildebert (and I would suggest that William well understood and agreed with him) Rome was the symbol of a total civilization for which he felt a profound admiration, from which he felt regretfully alienated, and to which he felt inferior: 'Quam magni fueris integra, fracta doces'; even the ruins are a lesson in Rome's past greatness, and under present conditions there is no possibility of restoration. The skill, creativity and organisation have vanished. Of course, Hildebert wrote a sequel to this poem, 'Dum simulachra mihi', on Christian Rome,[101] which William almost certainly knew,[102] but did not see fit to copy into the *Gesta*. He shared the critical attitude of many of his contemporaries towards the venality of the Rome of his day;[103] it influenced his interpretation of Pope Urban's motives in preaching the first Crusade.[104] For William, then, ancient Rome represented an integrated civilisation superior to his own, particularly in the realms of learning, eloquence and good government. But was this the Rome of Cicero or of Jerome? – 'classical' or 'late antique', to use the modern terms? It is a commonplace that this distinction was not generally made by scholars before the fifteenth century; but William did make it. He explicitly distinguished, for instance, between Roman authors who were 'pagani' or 'gentiles' and 'Christiani'.[105] In the *Polyhistor* Seneca and Cicero come under the first head, Tertullian, Jerome and Augustine under the second. It might

---

[99] See the introduction printed in GR I, pp. cxxii–cxxiii.
[100] See above, n. 32.
[101] Scott, *Hildeberti Carmina Minora*, no. 37.
[102] See the arguments advanced below, pp. 71–2.
[103] J. Benzinger, *Invectiva in Romam* (Lübeck and Hamburg, 1968), p. 75 and n. 10. Cf. *De Miraculis B.V.M.*, p. 129: 'Domestico et naturali Romanis malo ut sint auarissimi, sicut in ueteribus historiis est legere et his temporibus approbare'.
[104] GR II, p. 390.
[105] PH, p. 37, and below, pp. 51–3.

be argued that this division reflects a particular religious viewpoint, not a historical periodisation. But William also distinguished periods implicitly by his stated estimates of ancient Roman writers, and by the way in which he uses them. All Roman writers are 'authorities' to some degree; but only 'classical' writers are authorities or models for style; both groups, especially the Christians, might be useful for matter. William, therefore, never praises or uses Macrobius for his style; but he quotes some of his stories and uses his information.[106] In other words, while the pagans are obviously less useful for doctrine, William recognises that theirs was the great age of Latin literature. 'Par tibi Roma' and the tales in the *Polyhistor*, which concern only people and events of the 'classical' period, suggest that William saw it as the great age of Roman thought and government as well. Perhaps the only way in which William saw the Europe of his own day as superior to the classical world was in its possession of Christianity. Indeed it upset him that the ancient Romans were not Christian, and it was probably this which led him to emphasise the points of contact between the Stoic and Christian ethics. From this angle, harking back to our earlier point, the Selden Collection can be seen as an attempt to maximise the elements of continuity between Roman and European civilisation by one impressed by the superiority and 'otherness' of the earlier culture in relation to his own. Also to be seen in this light are William's praise for those of his contemporaries who were reviving the art of writing according to the ancient canons, and his comparisons of the English kings of his day with rulers of pagan antiquity.[107]

William would have heartily endorsed the advice of Hugh of St Victor: 'Learn everything; it will all come in useful somewhere',[108] for he seems to have operated according to that very principle. I cannot think of an explicit statement by William on the value of learning as an end in itself; the nearest indication that he held some such belief is the passage in the *Gesta Regum* in which he describes his own educational background.[109] But there is plenty of indirect but clear testimony to the value which he placed upon it. One thinks, for instance, of those passages in which he connects standards of religious life with standards of learning.[110] For William these things tended to stand or fall together. He puts into Urban II's mouth the opinion that the

---

[106] This has to be inferred (a) from his almost exclusive use of 'classical' writers for his *Schmuckmittel* and (b) from his occasional laudatory comments: e.g. Cicero 'rex facundiae Romanae' (below, p. 55) and GR II, p. 465.

[107] See above, p. 13; for the latter, see especially M. Schütt, 'The Literary Form of William of Malmesbury's *Gesta Regum*', EHR, 46 (1931), 255–260, and G. Townend, 'Suetonius and his Influence', in T. Dorey (ed.), *Latin Biography* (London, 1967), p. 107.

[108] Useful, that is, in a Christian context: J. Taylor (ed. and transl.), *The Didascalicon of Hugh of St Victor* (New York, 1961), pp. 18, 137.

[109] GR I, p. 103. See above, pp. 2–3.

[110] Ibid., II, pp. 132–3, 166–174, 304–5.

northern 'barbarians' do not even deserve the name of Christians precisely because of their barbarity.[111] If asked, William, of course, would have justified his immense learning in terms of its relevance to the pursuit of biblical studies, the ability to expound and preach, and to live a more godly and properly directed life. We have already discussed the evidence for this.[112] But the conformation of his studies, and its chief areas of emphasis correspond imperfectly to this professed aim, at least if it is interpreted strictly, just as the *Gesta Regum* can hardly be seen, in its totality, as an exercise in the inculcation of Christian principles of right conduct, although it purports to be, and although it contains moral lessons passim.[113] William loved the study of the past, and good reading both past and contemporary, for its own sake, although he had no doubt that it all contributed, in the broadest sense, to the building up of the Christian character and to a better understanding of the Faith.

William also believed in the dissemination of learning; he was not content selfishly to absorb without passing on. His role as teacher has been grossly underestimated, indeed ignored. To be sure there is little enough information on this aspect of his character. He does not speak of it, nor does anyone else. The evidence, however, is solid enough, and consists of certain of his original works, but particularly his *collectanea*: the *Polyhistor, Defloratio Gregorii, Commentary on Lamentations, Abbreviatio Amalarii,* his copy of John the Scot's *Periphyseon* and of Anselm's works, and the collections of texts on grammar, canon law, Roman history, and military strategy.[114] The first five of these have dedicatory letters setting out the reason for their manufacture, and the principles on which they have been organised. The seventh and eighth have prefatory verses in William's own hand, addressed to the reader.[115] At least four appear to have been genuinely prompted by the requests of various persons, in three cases individuals, in the case of the *Defloratio* the whole community of Malmesbury, for whose use it was expressly intended.[116] It is not clear whether the individuals

---

111 Ibid., p. 395.

112 See above, pp. 27–30.

113 Cf. what William says he is about in his dedication to Earl Robert of Gloucester: GR I, p. 355.

114 For the manuscripts of these collections, other than those already mentioned in this chapter, see below, pp. 87–93, 95–7.

115 Oxford, Lincoln College MS lat. 100 (Collection on Military Strategy), f. 3: 'His sua Willelmus detriuit tempora libris/ Coniungens studiis haec quoque parua suis./ Quos animi causa poteris percurrere lector;/ Nam cum summa grauant, inferiora iuuant'; London, Lambeth Palace Library MS 224 (Collection of Anselm's works), f. ii: 'Disputat Anselmus presul Cantorberiensis./ Scribit Willelmus monachus Malmesburiensis./ Ambos gratifice complectere lector amice'. These are reproduced in facsimile in Ker, 'Handwriting', pls 2 and 3.

116 The prologue, where this is stated, is printed by Farmer, 'William of Malmesbury's Commentary on Lamentations', pp. 8–10.

concerned were members of the same house, although they were all monks. As we know that William travelled to many other houses and executed commissions there, to guess would be hazardous. Considered together, these collections and summaries were designed to fulfil four main functions. Firstly, they were to facilitate easy reference by gathering together between two covers texts by the same author or on the same subject – the collection on grammar is a good instance. William was also concerned to provide good texts. A detailed study of this endeavour would prove rewarding. The Oriel College collection of conciliar canons is the outstanding example of this, and it has been frequently noted that William was wont to correct his exemplar, usually unauthoritatively but always intelligently.[117] He did this to Jordanes and the *Breviarium* in the Selden Collection, to Leo's sermons in Oriel College MS 42, and to Tertullian's *Apology* in his copy of Lactantius and Tertullian. William compared manuscripts of Bede's *Historia* belonging to different classes,[118] and in the *Gesta Regum* comments upon a major variant distinguishing two of them. The implication is that he took special pains to secure the best possible text of Bede before using it as the basis for his own account of early Anglo-Saxon England. Then there was the aim of selection and summarisation; here he had in mind 'light reading' or the needs of novices. The *Polyhistor* was for casual browsing, the *Defloratio* and *Abbreviatio* more for the serious beginner. In the case of the *Defloratio* he went a step further, by classifying his selected passages under a very systematic and useful set of headings, the method of which is explained in his preface.[119] His aim here was the improvement of monastic life; thus, he explicitly states that he has omitted all passages dealing with questions of dogma. Finally, William could rarely resist adding some comment of his own to elucidate, correct or supplement his texts. In a collection of several very disparate texts, such as the Selden Collection, his accounts supply linkages between them; in the *Abbreviatio* he supplements the information in his main text with more recent material; in the Oriel manuscript he compares different versions of the same texts. The *Commentary on Lamentations* is, perhaps, the best example of all, for whereas it purports to be no more than a summary of Paschasius, there is much additional comment by William himself, some original, some from classical or patristic sources. For instance: 'Quod autem Paschasius dicit fuisse sinagogas super

---

[117] For the Collection on canon law see below, pp. 64–6, 97–8; on the corrections to William's text of Tertullian see H. Hoppe, *Tertulliani Apologeticum* (CSEL 69), p. xxvi and nn. For Jordanes see T. Mommsen, *Jordanis Romana et Getica*, MGH Auct. Antiqu., 5. i, p. liv; on the *Breviarium* see below, pp. 62–3, and on William's text of Leo's works ibid., pp. 42, 97, 124, 132–3.

[118] GR I, p. 260; *Baedae Opera*, I, p. cxiv n. 1.

[119] Farmer, 'William of Malmesbury's Commentary on Lamentations', pp. 209–210.

montem Oliuei non constat. Ipse uiderit si uerum sit; ego nusquam alias legi'.[120]

One kind of annotation, of particular interest and common to most of William's *collectanea*, is the short, bio-bibliographical preface giving information about the author and the historical context of each work. The edition of Tertullian and Lactantius has prefatory passages from three different works of Jerome,[121] the grammar collection from Cassiodorus's *Institutes*, the *Defloratio* from the *De Viris Illustribus* of Gennadius and John the Deacon's *Vita*,[122] and the Oriel College collection of Pope Leo's works from Gennadius and the *Liber Pontificalis*.[123] Sometimes, too, William provided tables of contents.[124] These annotated collections convey an impression of orderliness, consistency, scholarship and intellectual magnanimity. They were William's contribution towards the building up of a community of Christian scholarhip at Malmesbury and elsewhere. William's hand appears in most of them. We shall see below how he organized their copying.[125] Starting, so it seems, from scratch, he succeeded in putting together a team of at least two or three competent scribes, and in mobilising the rest of the convent to offer occasional supplementary assistance. These men sometimes did more of the actual copying – at least of the final version – than did William himself, but they always worked under his overall supervision. On the other hand, there is no evidence that he succeeded in establishing an exceptional intellectual tradition at his rather provincial abbey. He was not to know that he lived at the far end of the great age of Benedictine learning.

Be that as it may, there are enough scattered clues to enable some account to be given of William's *Kulturkreis*. His earliest known patron was also his most illustrious: Queen Matilda of England, as revealed by the prefatory letters in the Troyes manuscript of the *Gesta Regum*.[126] The second of these, addressed to her daughter, has a postscript divided from the rest of the letter by a paragraph-mark.[127] The speaker in this section, although still referring to himself in the plural, is probably William, since the conversation recorded in it could hardly be conceived other than as between two people, one of them a historian. According to this postscript, on a certain occasion the queen inquired 'of us' about her family tie with St Aldhelm. William (as I

---

[120] Comm. Lam., f. 122v.

[121] Namely, from two letters, the *Chronicle* and *De Viris Illustribus*.

[122] The extracts in the *Defloratio* are omitted from Farmer's printed list of contents (art. cit., pp. 310–311); they follow the prologue.

[123] Oxford, Oriel College MS 42, ff. 90–90v.

[124] In Oriel College MS 42, Lambeth Library MS 224, and the *Defloratio*.

[125] See below, ch. 4.

[126] Könsgen, pp. 211–214.

[127] The division, not noted by Könsgen, occurs at p. 213 of his edition, with the paragraph beginning 'Solebant sane ...'.

identify the speaker) replied that it was through the genealogy of the West Saxon kings, upon which she requested a written account.[128] This was supplied – it is referred to as an 'exigua scedula' – and the queen declared that the subject called for more ample and dignified treatment, thus encouraging the undertaking of the *Gesta Regum*. While Matilda's patronage helps explain some puzzling features of that work, it also raises further questions: how was it that William, a young man with no known writings to his credit, was already esteemed highly enough to be engaged in historical discussion by the queen (or by his community on her behalf), and to be treated by her as something of an authority? Who was his teacher, and where was he trained? Perhaps he had already written the lost works he mentions later in his career: the 'three little books called Chronicles', and a metrical Life of St Aelfgifu.[129] All this is tantalisingly conjectural, and all that is certain is that before 1118 William and his fellow-monks were on intimate terms with Matilda, who inspired him to begin his greatest work and who, as I have earlier suggested, may have actively supported its prosecution.

The letters to David of Scotland and the Empress Matilda do not entitle us to regard them as patrons of William or his monastery in the same way. They and the accompanying copies of the *Gesta* were sent with a very particular object in mind: to encourage the recipients to end the abbey's long vacancy and give them an abbot. The gesture was not successful, for Roger of Salisbury held Malmesbury in his own hands for another thirteen years, until his death in 1139.

The friendship with the elder Matilda explains why the second edition of the *Gesta*, as well as the *Historia Novella*, was dedicated to her son, Earl Robert of Gloucester. It cannot be ascertained, however, whether William's relations with him were as close as they apparently were with Matilda, or whether he actively supported William's literary projects. With the English kings, strangely only in the case of Henry, William seems to have had little contact. Naturally he has been accused of favouring the cause of Robert and the empress,[130] and he himself recognised the difficulties of writing

---

[128] However in GP, p. 332, William explicitly denies Aldhelm's alleged relationship with the West Saxon royal house, referring to the evidence of the *Anglo-Saxon Chronicle*. This does not necessarily contradict our argument, for William could have altered his opinion in the course of his researches.

[129] For the 'Chronicles' see HN, p. 1; for the lost poem on St Aelfgifu, GP, p. 187.

[130] See particularly the articles by R. B. Patterson, 'William of Malmesbury's Robert of Gloucester', pp. 893–7, and (less conclusively) 'Stephen's Shaftesbury Charter; another Case against William of Malmesbury', *Speculum*, 43 (1968), 487–492. William has been effectively defended by J. Leedom, 'William of Malmesbury and Robert of Gloucester Reconsidered', *Albion*, 6 (1974), 251–265. And cf. D. Crouch, 'Robert, Earl of Gloucester, and the Daughter of Zelophehad', *Journal of Medieval History*, 11 (1985), 227–243.

contemporary history from an unbiased viewpoint.[131] And yet he remained remarkably independent. It is possible that the copy of the *Gesta* sent to King David and Empress Matilda stopped short at about 1118, prior to the deaths of Alexander of Scotland and Queen Matilda of England.[132] If so, the reason may have been William's desire to save his honesty while avoiding the danger of causing offence.

All of William's other known patrons were monastic, and merge with the category of friends. We have already mentioned them: Henry of Blois and the Glastonbury monks for his *Antiquity* and hagiographies, Worcester priory for the *Vita Wulfstani* and his local community as a whole, and individual monks there and perhaps elsewhere for others of his works. In the next chapter I shall advance arguments for meetings between William and other scholars in the course of his travels: with Eadmer and Alexander at Canterbury, with Faricius at Abingdon, and with his fellow-historian John at Worcester.[133] Dr Martin Brett has shown that John and William worked closely together, exchanging information while their works were in progress.[134] I would like to think that the manuscript of Hildebert's poems which William had before 1125, and which was put together after 1114, was obtained directly from the author himself, whom William so much admired.[135] But there is no evidence for William having had personal contact with any continental scholar, let alone for his having travelled outside England.

The audience for whom he wrote most of his works was also monastic: some of his writings he doubtless never intended to have any real circulation at all. There was no reason why the *Antiquity* should have been known outside Glastonbury, or the *Vita Aldhelmi* outside Malmesbury.[136] But even with this proviso, some of William's minor works were never popular. The sobriety of his historical judgements did not appeal to a wide audience. Not long after its composition, the Glastonbury monks altered William's *Antiquity* out of all recognition. By the thirteenth century it seems to have survived only in this interpolated form. On the other hand, the *Abbreviatio*

---

131 GR I, pp. 357–8, 465–6.

132 At least this is true of the text in the Troyes manuscript, which I assume derives from one or other of the copies sent to the king and empress. The most likely alternative explanation of its incompleteness, loss of leaves in its exemplar, accounts ill for the fact that it ends with a complete sentence.

133 See below, pp. 46–7, 73–5.

134 M. Brett, 'John of Worcester and his Contemporaries', in *The Writing of History in the Middle Ages*, pp. 113–7.

135 See below, pp. 71–2.

136 Manuscripts of the *Antiquity* all seem to come from Glastonbury; it was, however, also known to Gerald of Wales; see AG, pp. 36–9, 182–4. For manuscripts containing the *Vita Aldhelmi* see GP, pp. xi–xxvi.

Amalarii had a reasonable English audience.[137] The *Polyhistor* was known to Ralph of Diss by the 1180s, and was at St Augustine's Canterbury by c.1300; the *Commentary on Lamentations* was at Worcester by the mid twelfth century.[138] Robert of Cricklade, writing from Cirencester c.1137, knew several of William's works.[139] The *Miracles of the Virgin* were paid the doubtful compliment of being subsumed into several later compilations; even so, a good many manuscripts of the original work remain, and by the thirteenth century it was known on the continent.[140]

Quite different were the *fortunas* of his major historical works. He himself was conscious that he was writing them for a different and larger readership. Within his own lifetime they were known throughout southern England at least. By 1200 they were read all over England and on the continent, and rivalled Geoffrey of Monmouth in forming the bases of later chronicles of national and European history.

The above is offered as an introductory sketch of William as scholar, reader, writer and teacher. Much more could and will yet be said: in particular of his aims as a historian and of his historical method, his treatment of character, motive and causation, his philological expertise, vision of history and so forth. It is plain that William was a man at conflict with himself, and this is what makes him so difficult to categorise. I should have liked to present him as a humane, reasonable, scholarly Benedictine in the best Bedan tradition. That is, I suppose, how he would have wished to be remembered. Surely he would have echoed Bede's description of his long life: '... while I have observed the regular discipline and sung the choir offices daily in church, my chief delight has always been in study, teaching and writing'.[141] But this attractive picture, although in large part accurate, is marred by William's snobbery, anti-Semitism,[142] love of inconsequential marvels and subservience to the contemporary establishment, political and

---

[137] Five manuscripts, all but one English, are used by R. Pfaff for his edition (AbAm). Only two have known provenances: Lanthony and Cambridge University: R. Pfaff, 'The Abbreviatio Amalarii' of William of Malmesbury', *Récherches de Théologie Ancienne et Médiévale*, 47 (1980), 77–9.

[138] For Ralph of Diss's use of the *Polyhistor* see P. K. Marshall, J. Martin and R. H. Rouse, 'Clare College MS 26 and the Circulation of Aulus Gellius 1–7 in Medieval England and France', *Mediaeval Studies*, 42 (1980), 374. John Leland saw a copy of the *Polyhistor* at St Paul's: *Collectanea*, IV, p. 48. Cambridge, St John's College MS 97 (*Polyhistor*) is a St Augustine's book; the main manuscript of the Commentary (Oxford, Bodl. Libr. MS Bodl. 868) is mid-twelfth century, from Worcester Cathedral Priory.

[139] See below, p. 74.

[140] The *fortuna* of this work is studied in detail by Carter, 'Thesis', I, pp. 17–36, 58–78; cf. *De Miraculis B.V.M.*, pp. 29–31.

[141] Bede, *Hist. Eccl.*, V. 24.

[142] See P. N. Carter, 'The Historical Content of William of Malmesbury's Miracles of the Virgin Mary', in *The Writing of History in the Middle Ages*, pp. 146–154.

religious. When he rose above or advanced beyond the common opinion of his time, as he did so often and so remarkably, it was not as a rebel or protester, but as a 'professional' scholar with a slightly priggish concern for intellectual precision. William's mental exertions and considerable learning were subject to the constraints and pressures imposed by his ideological environment, and they can only be viewed intelligently in that context.

3

WILLIAM'S READING

ONE OF THE most fundamental prerequisites of the 'Twelfth-Century Renaissance' was a dramatic increase in the range and availability of reading matter, both old and new. One need only compare the writings accessible to Bede, Rabanus or Alcuin with the library-catalogue of a sizeable twelfth-century abbey to see the force of this. The rediscovery of ancient texts, both pagan and Christian, was arguably the most important facet of this new enthusiasm for reading, for the assimilation of the literature of antiquity supplied a common and assured basis for further advances in knowledge and creativity. In this process an important role was played by the monastic Order, in particular by the larger and longer-established Benedictine communities. This particular monastic contribution to Europe's intellectual development has probably been underestimated, since the twelfth century also saw the end of monasticism as the dominant spiritual force within Christian society, and since the Schools were so clearly becoming the principal environment within which were made the most considerable advances in knowledge in the most central disciplines. This underestimation has applied also to England, where traditional Benedictine culture remained important until the end of the century, and to William, who has some claim to be regarded as the best-read European of the century.

In this chapter I propose to study, quite simply, *what* William read, my pattern being Max Laistner's famous article on the library of the Venerable Bede.[1] It is entirely appropriate that I take a work on Bede as a model, for William himself looked to Bede for instruction in reading and writing. Everyone is familiar with his reference to Bede's *Historia* in the prologue to his own *Gesta Regum*,[2] and it is easy to demonstrate that he was interested in Bede's non-historical writings as well. It is even possible that Bede's

---

[1] M. L. W. Laistner, 'The Library of the Venerable Bede', in A. Thompson (ed.), *Bede; His Life, Times and Writings* (Oxford, 1935), pp. 237–266, reprinted in Starr, *The Intellectual Heritage of the Early Middle Ages*, pp. 117–149.
[2] GR I, pp. 1–2.

reading was to some extent the pattern, or at least starting-point for his own. Towards the conclusion of his study, Laistner warned that by Bede's 'library' he did not necessarily mean what was on the shelves (or rather, in the cupboards) at Wearmouth and Jarrow.[3] That warning is doubly necessary in an essay on William of Malmesbury's reading. Although he spent all his adult life within his abbey, and although he was concerned to build up its library, we know, and will abundantly demonstrate, that he travelled the length and breadth of England in search of books and documents, transcribing, extracting and summarizing. I am therefore not concerned here to establish anything about the library of Malmesbury, merely what William himself read.[4]

I. THEOLOGY AND BIBLICAL STUDIES

The foundation of all monastic reading, apart from the Bible and Benedictine Rule, was the Church Fathers. We should be surprised if there were not ample evidence for William's reading of at least the four great Latin doctors, Jerome, Ambrose, Augustine and Gregory. Ambrose's *De Obitu Theodosii* seems to be the source for a passage in the *Gesta Regum*, and William extracts from the *De Officiis, Hexaemeron, De Virginitate, De Paenitentia* and some of the letters in his *Polyhistor*.[5] His *De Officiis* extracts are prefaced by a note which demonstrates his familiarity with both it and Cicero's work of the same name:[6]

> Liber beatissimi Ambrosii De Officiis plenus est exemplis memorabilibus, que quoniam uel in diuina Scriptura repperiuntur uel in Tullio De Officiis hic non posui. Duo tamen non pretereunda putaui ...

From Augustine, 'omnis sciencie fons', as William calls him,[7] I have found traces of twenty-two works, of which fourteen are extracted in the *Polyhistor*. Among them are letters and sermons, and the great treatises such as the *De Civitate Dei, Confessions, De Trinitate* and *De Doctrina Christiana*.[8] Jerome was at least as popular; besides some quotations which I

[3] Laistner in Starr, *Intellectual Heritage*, p. 145 n. 79.
[4] For information about the library in and before William's time see below, chs 4 and 5.
[5] GR I, p. 6; II, p. xviii; PH, pp. 78–81, 138.
[6] PH, p. 78. A quotation from Ambrose which I cannot place is Comm. Lam., f. 93 'Magna nobis est benefaciendi necessitas, qui habemus indicem quam et occulta non fallant et honesta delectent et turpia offendant'.
[7] PH, p. 89.
[8] A quotation which I cannot place occurs in GP, p. 425: 'mens mali conscia ipsa sibi tormentum est, anticipatque uiuens mortuorum suplitia'.

cannot place,[9] I note twenty-three works which William certainly knew, twenty-two of them extracted in the *Polyhistor*. We are not surprised to find letters and the major apologetic works among them, and there is also a series of Old Testament commentaries. Prefacing the extracts in the *Polyhistor* is his note:[10]

> Quia ordine ad beatissimum Iheronimum uenimus, nemo a nobis expectet eius sentencias, quibus libri eius et maxime epistole iocunde et incomparabiliter splendent; pauca tamen alibi non lecta de libro Contra Iouinianum et de eius epistolis posui, que alios fecisse uel dixisse narrat; omisique multa gratissima ab ipso quidem commemorata, sed ab aliis antedicta.

Finally, there is St Gregory, and here there is enough evidence to suggest that William knew virtually all of his works, including his correspondence: quotations can be found in the *Gesta Regum, Gesta Pontificum, Abbreviatio Amalarii* and *Commentary on Lamentations*,[11] but the most striking evidence of William's interest (reflecting that of his abbey) is his own *Defloratio Gregorii*, made before c.1137, a classified set of extracts from five of the pope's works, made for the 'instructionem communem' of the Malmesbury monks, as the preface states.[12]

These cases, considered together, occasion less surprise at the breadth of William's reading than at its profundity. But with the exception of Gregory, there can be little doubt that our evidence for the extent of William's acquaintance with the works of the great Latin Fathers is very imperfect. We should certainly expect him to have known Jerome's commentary on the Psalter, and his quotations from two of Jerome's commentaries on the Pauline epistles suggest that he had access to the complete set. There is a high probability that further study of William's works will reveal his acquaintance with more writings of these men, but it is certain that much evidence for this acquaintance has not survived at all.

It is possible to list another twenty-seven patristic writers with whose works William was familiar. Among the commoner ones should be mentioned Cassiodorus and Isidore, in both of whom William had a multiple interest: theological, historical and bibliographical. Less common

---

Comm. Lam., f. 75 'Ea sunt ... apud Hebreos saphico metro composita, ita ut singuli uersus per singula litterarum incipiant elementa'; f. 107v 'ut die Ierosolimitani excidii, Iudei annuatim aduentantes, a milicie custode locorum, magno emerent, quatinus eo loci licenter plorare possent'; GR II, p. 358 'Si placet, legant; si non placet, abiiciant'.

[10] PH, p. 81.

[11] *Dial.*, GP, p. 357, GR II, p. 204; *Reg. Past.*, Comm. Lam., f. 108v; *Hom. in Evang.*, AbAm, p. 135; Comm. Lam., f. 27.

[12] Farmer, 'William of Malmesbury's Commentary on Lamentations', p. 309.

are Cyprian, Julian of Toledo, Fulgentius and Leo, of whose letters and sermons William owned a remarkable collection, put together by himself from a number of sources.[13] But the really striking representatives of this class, as commented long ago by M.R. James, are Tertullian and Lactantius.[14] Both of these writers were rare, particularly in England.[15] William's own collection, containing Tertullian's *Apology* and three of Lactantius's works, survives in late copies.[16] For the Lactantius treatises William's copy, belonging to the 'mixed recension', is derived, together with Casinensis 595 (c.1100) from a lost archetype;[17] the text of the *Apology* is close to that in the 'Codex Luganensis', now Oxford, Bodleian Library MS Lat. theol. d. 34, an English manuscript of the early twelfth century.[18] These were apparently the only works of these two authors known to William; the *Apology*, for instance, enjoyed a manuscript-tradition quite separate from the rest of Tertullian's works.[19] Presumably William made his original copy from two separate exemplars, and it demonstrates his solid historical sense that he decided to combine works of the two early Latin Fathers in the same book. In Tertullian, 'eloquentissimus', as he calls him,[20] William had a special interest, extracting from the *Apology* in the *Polyhistor*.[21]

William shows a surprising degree of interest in Carolingian and early English writers on theology and biblical studies. He had copies of Alcuin's Commentary on Ecclesiastes and letters, many of which are quoted in the

---

[13] Cyprian, *Quod idola dii non sint*: PH, p. 78; *De Mortalitate*: ibid.; Comm. Lam., f. 44; Letters (Ep. 63. 13): AbAm, p. 159; *De Orat. Domini*: AbAm, p. 161. Julian: PH, pp. 101–2; Fulgentius, *De Fide*: VD, p. 323; *Serm. III*, 83–4: Comm. Lam., f. 27v 'iugis non desit in ore correptio, nec simplex in corde dormitet oratio'.

[14] James, *Two Ancient English Scholars*, p. 20.

[15] Apart from William's, three Tertullian MSS of English provenance are recorded; for a now lost fourth, containing works other than the *Apologeticum*, see below, pp. 108–111. There are no other known English MSS of Lactantius, and I know of no references to either author in English medieval library catalogues.

[16] Oxford, Balliol College 79; Gotha, Forschungsbibliothek Membr. I. 55.

[17] *Lactantii Opera* I, ed. S. Brandt (CSEL 19), pp. li–lii. The editor notes that William's collection has been emended unauthoritatively but intelligently by a learned scholar (ibid., p. liii and n. 1, referring to the Gotha MS and a 'MS from Emmanuel College', which is Cambridge, Emmanuel College 238, written in Bruges in 1424). This was doubtless William himself.

[18] *Tertulliani Apologeticum*, ed. Hoppe, pp. xi n. 7, xxi and n. 67, xxvi. I have examined Bodl. Lat. theol. d. 34, but can find no marks to connect it directly with William or Malmesbury. Another English copy of the *Apologeticum*, BL Roy. 5 F. xviii (c.1100), has recently been identified as made at and for Salisbury Cathedral. Its text too is apparently related to that in Bodl. Libr. Lat. theol. d. 34 (Hoppe, pp. xxi–ii).

[19] CCSL 1, pp. 78–84.

[20] PH, p. 75.

[21] ibid., pp. 75–8. Printed by Lehmann, 'Tertullian im Mittelalter', in his *Erforschung des Mittelalters*, V, pp. 194–7.

Gesta Regum and *Gesta Pontificum*.[22] The same writer's *De Orthographia* is found in William's collection of early grammatical manuals.[23] Some time before c.1137 William summarized the *De Ecclesiasticis Officiis* of Amalarius for the use of the local monks.[24] This was his *Abbreviatio Amalarii*. Dr Pfaff has shown that William's copy of Amalarius was of the first edition in three books, known from sixteen manuscripts, none of them English.[25] The presumption is that William had the use of a continental manuscript. The *Abbreviatio* survives in five manuscripts, in four of which it is preceded by Isidore, *De Ecclesiasticis Officiis*, and followed by a conflation of Drogo of Laon, *De Divinis Officiis* and the *Micrologus*, under the name of 'Ivo of Chartres'.[26] This perhaps suggests that William, as was his wont, made a collection of liturgical manuals consisting of these three texts, and we may therefore tentatively include the Isidore and pseudo-Ivo items among his reading. His prologue to the *Abbreviatio* and *Letter to Peter* indicate that he knew Ivo's sermons and probably *Decretum* as well.[27] In the *Gesta Regum* is a passage from the *Panormia*.[28]

But to return to the Carolingians: William shows that he knew Rabanus's *De Officiis Ecclesiasticis*, *De Universo* and *De Computo* by noting their main sources in the prologue to the *Abbreviatio*; later in that work he uses the same writer's *Enarrationes in Epistolas Pauli*.[29] Paschasius's *De Corpore et Sanguine Domini* is cited in the *Gesta Regum*, and his commentary on Lamentations was used by William as a basis for his own.[30] In the *Gesta Pontificum* he cites Florus's *Contra Ioannis Scoti Erroneas Definitiones Liber* in a way which suggests that he had read it,[31] and this brings us to William's most unusual Carolingian author, John the Scot himself.

In the *Gesta Regum* and *Gesta Pontificum* William mentions his translation of pseudo-Dionysius, *De Hierarchia Celestia* and the *Periphyseon*.[32] Of this last work, which experienced a revival in the twelfth century, we have William's personal copy.[33] The precise relationship of all

---

[22] The Commentary on Ecclesiastes is in Oxford, Merton Coll. MS 181, for which see below, pp. 93–5. On William's use of Alcuin's letters see below, ch. 8.
[23] London, BL Harl. 3969.
[24] Pfaff, 'Abbreviatio', pp. 79–80.
[25] ibid., pp. 80–82.
[26] ibid., pp. 77–8.
[27] AbAm, p. 171.
[28] *Panorm.* 8. 135: GR I, pp. 250–1, summarized. It is reproduced verbatim in a marginal note in Oxford, Bodl. Libr. MS Lat. class. d. 39, f. 144 ('Ex decretis'), for which see below, pp. 142, 144.
[29] AbAm, pp. 128–9, 137, 165.
[30] GR II, p. 341; I, p. cxxiii.
[31] GP, p. 393.
[32] GR I, pp. cxliv, 131; GP, p. 393.
[33] Cambridge, Trinity College MS O. 5. 20 (1301), for which see below, pp. 90–2.

extant *Periphyseon* manuscripts is not yet established, but we know that William used two exemplars for his copy, acquired separately and probably at a distance in time from each other.[34] Both were copied again later in the century: that for the first part of William's text in north-east Ireland, the other at Mont St Michel.[35] Both were presumably continental, although the abbey already had an interest in John the Scot, having developed a tradition that he spent his last days there.[36] William, so far as we know, was the first Englishman to know both John's *Periphyseon* and his translations of pseudo-Dionysius. The latter William knew in a standard version which included glosses and a prefatory letter from Anastasius the Librarian to Charles the Bald.[37]

Except in the case of Bede, whose works were always popular in European monasteries, William's interest in early English writers is remarkable. I find evidence for his knowledge of sixteen Bedan works, seven of which he copied in full. They represent a cross-section of Bede's historical, computistic and biblical works, plus his elementary teaching-manuals. As with the patristic works, there seems little doubt that William actually knew more of Bede's writings than the surviving evidence suggests. Scarcely any of Boniface's letters were preserved or circulated in England, and William seems to have known only two of them, with which he flanks his resumé of the Acts of the Council of Cloveshoe.[38] In British Library Cott. Otho A. I, an Anglo-Saxon manuscript of the eighth century, mainly burnt in the 1731 fire, the Acta were followed by the same two letters, and this was presumably William's exemplar for all three items. Unfortunately its provenance is unknown.[39]

He did a little better with Aldhelm's correspondence. As the founder of his monastery, Aldhelm had a special attraction for William, who cites nine of his letters in his two major historical works, some found nowhere else or in one other manuscript.[40] In the *Gesta Pontificum* he mentions the loss of others by 'incuria nostrorum antecessorum'.[41] Hamilton seems to have doubted whether William knew Letter 4 (to Geruntius) 'de Pascha', since William refers to it as destroyed.[42] But William only says that it is the

---

[34] ibid., pp. 90–1.
[35] ibid., p. 91.
[36] I. Sheldon-Williams and L. Bieler (eds), *Iohannis Scotti Eriugenae Periphyseon* I (Dublin, 1968), pp. 4–5, 21–3.
[37] See below, p. 104.
[38] GR I, p. 80; GP, pp. 9, 11; W. Levison, *England and the Continent in the Eighth Century* (Oxford, 1956), pp. 280–1.
[39] CLA, I, no. 188.
[40] GP, pp. 333, 335, 337–9, 341, 343, 358; *Aldhelmi Opera*, ed. R. Ehwald (MGH Auct. Antiq. 15), pp. 475–516.
[41] GP, p. 344.
[42] GP, p. 361 and n. 3.

'Britons' who have lost it, and his resumé of its contents suggests that he had read it. The *De Laudibus Virginitatis*, *Carmen de Virginitate* and *Enigmata* are also cited, and reference made to alleged sermons.[43] Among more recent English ecclesiastical writers William knew Aelfric, whom he confuses with the abbot of Malmesbury of the same name, citing the *Vita Ethelwoldi*, the *Abbreviatio Passionis S. Edmundi*, and mentioning 'libros multos ex Latino uersos'.[44] He wrote a Life of Bishop Wulfstan, but it is not certain that he knew the writings which he attributes to him.[45]

William certainly read Old English, for his *Vita Wulfstani* just mentioned is a translation of the vernacular Life by Colman. He used a version of the *Anglo-Saxon Chronicle*, and shows an interest in those, such as Aelfric and King Alfred, who did translation into the vernacular.[46] In his *Vita Dunstani* he indicates his knowledge of Ethelwold's English translation of the Benedictine Rule, in a version with a prologue also recently identified as Ethelwold's.[47] William however does not mention him by name as translator or author.

This intense interest in English writers reflects William's pride in his half-English descent, his curiosity about the history of his own house, the chance results of searching its ancient library, and his special admiration for Bede. But William was also part-Norman. In his treatment of the Conquest, following Bede's interpretation of the Saxon invasion, he considered that the English had lost their morale and were ripe for reinvigoration by God's chosen instrument of reformation, the powerful and energetic Normans.[48] Some of William's reading, then, reflects his intellectual contacts with learned men in France and Normandy, and with the centres of the new, imported monasticism in England, notably Canterbury. He quotes a letter of Fulbert of Chartres, mentioning a 'uolumen epistolarum inter alia opuscula', which the bishop wrote.[49] Some idea of the contents of this volume can be gained from the eleven surviving copies, of which no less than four are English, and date from just before 1100 to the second half of the

---

[43] GP, pp. 343, 143; GR II, p. 410; GP, pp. 335, 344.
[44] GP, pp. 406–7.
[45] Cf. VW, p. 3. But as William was translating from Colman's lost Old English version, he may just be repeating the words of his source.
[46] For his use of the *Chronicle* see below, pp. 70, 151; for his comments on Aelfric and Alfred see GP, pp. 406–7, GR I, pp. 132–3, GP, pp. 333, 336, 405–6.
[47] VD, p. 290. In his note Bishop Stubbs refers to the prologue of the *Regularis Concordia*, noting an O.E. version. But the information given by William is not found there, and he refers distinctly to a bilingual version of the Rule, which the *Regularis Concordia* is not. His source is now conclusively identified by D. Whitelock, 'The Authorship of the Account of King Edgar's Establishment of Monasteries', in *Philological Essays ... in Honour of H. D. Meritt*, ed. J. L. Rosier (*Janua Linguarum, Ser. Maj.* 37, Paris, 1970), pp. 125–136.
[48] GR II, pp. 304–6.
[49] GR I, p. 226.

century.[50] Fulbert's Easter Hymn is quoted in the *Gesta Pontificum*, and his Marian writings were used by William in his *De Miraculis B.V.M.*[51] Honorius Augustodunensis, Guitmund of Aversa and Ivo of Chartres are other continental contemporaries known to William. In the case of Honorius this was almost unavoidable, since he is now known to have stayed and written at Canterbury before c.1125.[52] William knew his *Speculum Ecclesiae* and copied his *Sigillum Beatae Mariae*.[53] In the *Abbreviatio Amalarii* he notes 'de situ et structura et dedicacione ecclesie abunde plures doctores et nuperrimo tempore Iuo Carnotensis episcopus significacione dixere',[54] probably referring to the *Decretum*. In a marginal note to his copy of Anselm's works William mentions Robert of Tombelaine as the author of a commentary on the Song of Songs,[55] and this may mean that he had read it; William, so far as I can judge, was no mere name-dropper. Another continental contemporary whose works he greatly admired was Hildebert of Le Mans; but I propose to enlarge on William's knowledge of Hildebert's verse in a different connection.

William's Canterbury contacts are particularly fascinating. We know that he visited both Christ Church and St Augustine's more than once,[56] and these visits are directly reflected in his reading. He cites some of Lanfranc's letters, his *De Corpore et Sanguine Domini*, and he knew the *Collectio Lanfranci*, the archbishop's abbreviated version of the pseudo-Isidorean Decretals.[57] Lambeth Palace Library MS 224 is William's own collection of St Anselm's works. It contains fifteen treatises and a unique collection of letters derived from early drafts which William doubtless found at Canterbury.[58] Only one Meditation is in Lambeth 224, and none of the *Orationes*, but the *Orationes* and *Meditationes* are mentioned in the *Gesta Pontificum*, and William cites *Oratio* VII in his *De Miraculis*, so he probably

[50] F. Behrends (ed. and transl.), *The Letters and Poems of Fulbert of Chartres* (Oxford, 1976), pp. xlii–l.

[51] GP, p. 440; *De Miraculis B.V.M.*, pp. 48, 82–3, 112n.

[52] Southern, *St Anselm and his Biographer*, pp. 211–217.

[53] *De Miraculis B.V.M.*, pp. 137–8: Honorius Augustodunensis, *Speculum Ecclesiae*, PL 172. 852; Oxford, Merton College MS 181: *Sigillum Beatae Mariae*.

[54] AbAm, p. 151.

[55] Ker, 'Handwriting', p. 373.

[56] See below, pp. 70, 73–5.

[57] Letters: GP, p. 39ff, 63ff; *Scriptum de Primatu*: GP, pp. 39–46, M. T. Gibson, *Lanfranc of Bec* (Oxford, 1978), p. 222. The work is contained in London, BL Cott. Cleo. E. i and Nero A. vii, but William knew a separate version. *De Corpore et Sanguine Domini*: GP, p. 73, GR II, p. 338; on the *Collectio Lanfranci* see below, pp. 66, 131–3.

[58] On the MS see below, pp. 87–9; on its contents, F. S. Schmitt, *Sancti Anselmi Opera Omnia* (new edn, 6 vols in 2, Stuttgart-Bad Cannstadt, 1968), I, pp. 165*–171*.

knew the complete set.[59] Some stories related about Anselm in the *Gesta Regum* are found in Recension B (written c.1115) of Alexander of Canterbury's *Dicta Anselmi.* A comparison of the versions, however, suggests that William may have had these stories orally from Alexander while at Canterbury, rather than from the text of the revised *Dicta*.[60] By c.1137, however, William certainly knew the *Dicta*, referring to them by name and quoting them in his *De Miraculis B.V.M.*[61]

This brings us up-to-date with William's biblical and theological reading. Although we have no evidence that he read anything in this field written later than c.1115, or that his contacts on the continent extended much beyond a handful of Norman religious houses, he was certainly aware of different and completely new currents in learning, as appears from the prologue to his *De Miraculis*:[62]

> Vtile autem quod hic et superius nominaui, eo sensu uolo accipi secundum beatum Ambrosium De Officiis, ut idem sit utile quod honestum, et honestum quod utile, *quamuis in secularibus scholis aliter difiniatur.*

II. CLASSICAL AND LATE ANTIQUE WRITINGS

We must now retrace our steps in time to examine William's most remarkable and characteristic area of reading, for which his enthusiasm made him, according to his own words, notorious in his own day: the Latin classics.[63] The relevant evidence is rather better than for his theological reading, and we can deduce what must be a reasonably complete list of classical and late antique works which he had read. His *Polyhistor*, full of extracts of this type, is particularly helpful, and so are several of William's *collectanea*, plus the quotations and echoes embedded in his original works.

William's two favourite classical authors show his good taste, for they are Virgil and Cicero. William's knowledge of Virgil has to be reconstructed piecemeal from the many quotations, echoes and reminiscences in his own works. These are especially frequent, although rarely noted by the editors, in the *Gesta Regum* and *Gesta Pontificum*. My own list, which is certainly not

---

[59] GP, p. 76; *De Miraculis B.V.M.*, p. 56.
[60] R. W. Southern and F. S. Schmitt, *Memorials of St Anselm* (Oxford, 1969), p. 211 n. 20.
[61] *De Miraculis B.V.M.*, p. 131.
[62] ibid., p. 50.
[63] James, *Two Ancient English Scholars*, p. 22; see above, pp. 26–31.

complete, totals sixty, of which fifty-one are from the *Aeneid* (all books), seven from the *Georgics* and the remaining two from the *Eclogues*.[64] William appears to have memorized a prodigious quantity of Virgil's text, especially the *Aeneid*. Very few items in my list are verbatim quotations of any length, or introduced by an authorial comment. Most are embedded unobtrusively in William's own prose. While some of this was doubtless the product of deliberate artifice, much seems to be natural and unconscious. A passage in the *Historia Novella* shows that he also knew Servius's commentary.[65]

M.R.James noted that Virgil was William's favourite classical poet, adding 'but Juvenal, Persius, Lucan and Terence are quoted often enough to show familiarity with them. Plautus and Horace seem to have but one reference apiece. Ovid is rare, Statius, so popular in the medieval period, he apparently did not know. He, and the tragedies of Seneca, which were known to Aldhelm, are the most remarkable absentees'.[66] These judgements, based mainly on the *loci citati* identified by Stubbs and Hamilton, need modification. Like most twelfth-century literati, William was familiar with the satirists; I find six quotations from Juvenal and five from Persius in his major historical works.[67] He knew at least three plays of Terence, *Andria*, *Eunuch* and *Heauton Timorumenos*, but since all six invariably travelled

[64] *Aen.* 1. 3: GP, p. 426; 1. 33: HN, p. 68; 1. 87: GP, p. 377; 1. 94: Comm. Lam., f. 2; 1. 126: GP, p. 98; 1. 150: ibid., p. 416; 1. 172: ibid., p. 378; 1. 174; ibid., p. 429; 1. 286: GR II, p. 402; 1. 305: GP, p. 399; 1. 372: AG, p. 40; 1. 590: *De Miraculis B.V.M.*, p. 68; 1. 742–3: GP, p. 281; 2. 1: GP, p. 440; 2. 120: ibid., p. 302; 2. 132: ibid., p. 419; 2. 169: GR I, p. 181, Comm. Lam., f. 45v, HN, p. 39; 2. 204: GP, pp. 104, 230; 2. 389: GR I, p. 22; 2. 426: Comm. Lam., f. 96; 2. 435–7: ibid.; 3. 48: GR I, p. 255; 3. 357: GR II, p. 300; 3. 592: GP, p. 377; 4. 262: GR I, p. 52; 4. 522: GP, p. 427; 5. 206: GR II, p. 497; 5. 344: GP, p. 313; 5. 415: ibid., p. 81; 6. 304: GP, p. 96; 6. 644: ibid., p. 373; 6. 743: GR I, p. 184; 6. 748: *De Miraculis B.V.M.*, p. 112; 6. 853: GR II, p. 487; 6. 854: GR I, p. 266, GP, p. 154, but this is probably from Abbo of Fleury; 7. 84: GP, p. 412; 7. 279: GR I, p. 150; 7. 586: HN, p. 70; 7. 781: GP, p. 178; 8. 406: *De Miraculis B.V.M.*, p. 106; 8. 483: GR II, p. 330; 9. 641: GP, 275; 10. 474–487: GR I, pp. 258–9; 10. 641: GR I, p. 135; 11. 72: GR I, p. 52; 12. 84: Comm. Lam., f. 113; 12. 668: GR II, p. 374; 12. 764–5: HN, p. 34. *Georg.* 1. 30: Comm. Lam., f. 13; 1. 103: GR II, p. 411; 1. 467: HN, p. 12; 2. 484 (Cassiodorus, *Inst.* 1. 28. 5): Comm. Lam., f. 98; 3. 10–11 (from Aldhelm): GP, p. 336; 4. 198–9: AbAm, p. 149; 4. 425–8: GP, p. 8. *Ecl.* 6. 9: GR I, p. 3; 9. 4: GP, p. 434. But William's prose is full of Virgilian echoes.
[65] HN, p. 43.
[66] James, *Two Ancient English Scholars*, p. 25.
[67] Juvenal: 1. 43: GR II, p. 446; 2. 40: ibid., p. 326; 4. 89: HN, p. 45; 4. 149: GR I, p. 57; 6. 223: GP, p. 220; 7. 202: GR I, p. 53; 10. 114–132: CUL Dd. 13. 2, f. 192; 14. 99: Comm. Lam., f. 41. Persius: 1. 35 (Jerome, *Ep.* 54. 5. 3): GP, p. 258; 1. 85: GR II, p. 361; 2. 69: ibid., p. 384; 3. 87: *De Miraculis B.V.M.*, p. 142; 5. 184: Comm. Lam., f. 41.

together, he probably read the remaining three as well.[68] Lucan, who appealed both to William's historical and literary interests, is quoted at least seventeen times.[69] On the other hand, William's single quotation from Plautus is via Jerome.[70] This would be no cause for wonder, were it not that instances of William quoting indirectly are so rare. In this case there was a good reason. The play from which he quoted, the *Pseudolus*, was one of the group of twelve which circulated separately from the remaining eight. It survives only in three German manuscripts dating from the tenth and eleventh centuries and was not revived in the twelfth century.[71] It is perhaps more surprising that William did not quote any of the first eight plays, of which a copy was made at and for Salisbury Cathedral in the late eleventh century.[72]

Neither was James correct in crediting William with only a single quotation from Horace, and it would be surprising if William had not known him better. I find ten quotations, drawn from the *Odes, Ars Poetica, Epistles* and *Satires*.[73] While the number of passages identified is still small, the distribution is significant; it is often noted, for instance, that use of the *Odes* in early Europe was rare compared with the *Satires*.[74] It is typical of William that he should diverge in this way from average contemporary taste.

[68] *Andr.* 1. 61 (Jerome, *Ep.* 108. 21. 4, or 130. 11. 1): GP, p. 293; 1. 68 (Jerome, *Comm. in Gal.* 4. 15–16): VD, p. 324; 2. 1. 5–6: HN, p. 68, AG, p. 160 (H. Walther, *Lateinische Sprichwörter und Sentenzen des Mittelalters* [5 vols, Göttingen, 1963–7], no. 26156); 4. 1: GR II, p. 295; *Heaut.* 77: Comm. Lam., f. 75; *Eun.* 2. 2. 44: GR II, p. 481.
[69] 1. 70–1: GP, p. 409; 1. 144–5: GR I, p. 220; 1. 320–3: CUL Dd. 13. 2, f. 118; 2. 515: GR II, p. 374; 2. 592–3: Comm. Lam., ff. 8, 41; 3. 58: GP, p. 197; 4. 97: GR II, p. 418; Comm. Lam., f. 26v; 4. 93: GR II, p. 419; 4. 579: ibid., p. 417; 4. 819: GP, p. 152; 5. 290: ibid., p. 432; 5. 580: GR II, p. 374; 8. 384: ibid., p. 395; 9. 725: AG, p. 42; 10. 132: VD, p. 263.
[70] GP, p. 22; Jerome, *Adv. Jov.* (PL 23. 211).
[71] *Texts and Transmission*, pp. 302–307.
[72] London, BL Roy. 15 C. xi, ff. 113–194; see R. M. Thomson, 'British Library Royal 15 C. xi: a Manuscript of Plautus' Plays from Salisbury Cathedral', *Scriptorium*, 40 (1986), 82–7.
[73] *Carm.* 1. 4. 13: GR I, p. 253; 1. 12. 11: II, p. 428; 1. 18. 84: *De Miraculis B. V. M.*, p. 76; 2. 10. 12: ibid., p. 165; *Ars* 96: Comm. Lam., f. 38; 97: GP, p. 112; *Sat.* 1. 2. 31: GP, p. 275; *Ep.* 1. 1. 100 (Jerome, *Comm. in Eccles.*): HN, p. 38; 1. 1. 90: GR I, p. 84; 1. 2. 69 (Jerome, in several works: H. Hagendahl, *Latin Fathers and the Classics* [Göteborg, 1958], pp. 102 n. 1, 105, 125, 181, 282, 326): GP, p. 403.
[74] C. H. Haskins, *The Renaissance of the Twelfth Century* (Cambridge, Mass., 1927), pp. 109–110; L. D. Reynolds and N. G. Wilson, *Scribes and Scholars* (Oxford, 2nd edn, 1974), pp. 85–6.

Similarly he knew Ovid quite well, quoting the *Tristia, Amores, Fasti* and, at least three times, the less favoured *Metamorphoses*.[75] Two quotations from Statius's *Thebais* are in the *Gesta Regum*, and an adaptation in the *Gesta Pontificum*;[76] I have found none from the *Achilleis*. It would, *pace* James, be remarkable if William knew Seneca's *Tragedies*, as they went unread during the eleventh and twelfth centuries, to emerge only after c.1200 at Paris.[77] Finally, William occasionally adapts and quotes from Martial.[78]

William's intimate acquaintance with Virgil has to be demonstrated by laborious unearthing of quotations from his original writings; his interest in Cicero is much easier to document. M .R .James first drew attention to the massive corpus of Ciceroniana in Cambridge University Library which is a fifteenth-century copy of a collection first put together, so he thought, by William.[79] It contains not less than twenty-two works by Cicero, including twelve speeches, plus the pseudonymous *Invectiva in Sallustium*. Of course James, in pulling this rabbit out of his hat, was loud in William's praise, comparing this with the other famous Cicero-corpus made up by Abbot Wibald of Corvey in the same century.[80] No-one else of the period invites comparison in the knowledge of so many Cicero's works. Recently, however, warning notes have been sounded, for the textual affinities of some of the contents of the Cambridge manuscript are continental, and it has been suggested that while the philosophical works in it stem from William's original collection, the speeches were added in Germany, where the manuscript was copied for William Gray, bishop of Ely.[81] The manuscript must clearly be examined more closely.

First of all, those items can be assigned to William's original corpus which have his prefaces, and which are used in his works. On the basis of the introductory matter we can say that William read the *De Natura Deorum, De Fato, De Divinatione, Academica Priora*, the fragments of *Hortensius* and *De Re Publica* which he put together from Augustine, Cicero's *Timaeus* translation, the *De Paradoxis, De Milone, Phillippics* and *Tusculans*. Of these

---

[75] *Trist.* 9. 5–6: GR I, p. 47, Comm. Lam., f. 5; *Amor.* 3. 4. 17: GR I, p. 194; 1. 15. 1: ibid., p. 57; *Fast.* 1. 547: HN, p. 6; *Met.* 2. 846: GR II, p. 293; 7. 115: I, p. 255; 15. 160: ibid., p. 374.

[76] 2. 495: GR I, p. 237?; 9. 559: ibid., p. 58. A possible echo of 2. 16 is in GP, p. 137.

[77] *Texts and Transmission*, pp. 378–381.

[78] *Ep.* 1. praef. 9: *Letter to Peter* (GR I, p. cxliv); 2. 11: GR II, p. 355; 14. 154: II, p. 36n.

[79] CUL Dd. 13. 2. James, *Two Ancient English Scholars*, pp. 21–3.

[80] Berlin, Staatsbibliothek der Stiftung Preussischer Kulturbesitz lat. 2° 252, on which see *Texts and Transmission*, pp. 58–142, passim.

[81] R. A. B. Mynors, 'A fifteenth-century Scribe; T. Werken', TCBS, 1 (1949–53), 98; idem, *Catalogue of the MSS of Balliol College Oxford* (Oxford, 1963), p. 377; *Texts and Transmission*, pp. 80–1.

the first three and the *De Paradoxis* were among the commonest of Cicero's works in the twelfth century, the *Phillippics* reasonably so. The little introductions themselves are fascinating, and as few have been printed, and none in full, I give them here.[82]

The first follows the text of the *De Fato*, on f.87:

> Vt autem intentio auctoris Tullii in libris De Deorum Natura, De Diuinatione et Fato melius intelligatur, liber beati Augustini De Ciuitate Dei quintus diligenter respiciatur, in quo libro capitulis viii. et x. et xi. intencionem, errores et raciones Tullii in predictis libris apertissime reprobat et confutat. (Then follow extracts from *De Civ. Dei* V. 9 and VI. 2.)

The *Academics* are preceded by a passage from *De Civitate Dei* VI. 2, and followed by the famous passage headed 'Ex libris eiusdem De Re Publica aliisque fragmenta quedam ex Augustino' (f.106v), and, in the margin, 'Verba Willelmi de Malmesbury collecta ex libris Augustini et Tullii Ciceronis; istis dicta etiam exprimuntur'. It begins:

> Cicero in inicio secundi libri De Diuinacione dicit se fecisse quattuor libris Achademicos, quorum primus est in quo sicut supra posui ex dictis beati Augustini libro sexto De Ciuitate Dei laudat idem [et] citat dicens se disputacionem de Achademicis habuisse cum M. Varrone: 'homine', inquit, 'omnium acutissimo facile et sine ulla dubitacione doctissimo'. 'Non ait', inquit Augustinus, 'eloquentissimo' (*De Civ. Dei* VI. 2; William repeats this story in the *Polyhistor*.[83])

Then William:

> Hic liber primus Achademicorum in Anglia non inuenitur, sed nec secundus in quo Catulus pro Achademicis disputans introducitur, sicut ex multis que in hiis libris proxime scriptis animaduerti potest. Tertius uero et quartus liber Achademicorum hi duo sunt qui proprie Lucullus appellantur, quia in uno introducitur Lucullus contra Achademicos disputans, in altero Tullius ei pro Achademicis respondet. Dicit item Cicero in principio secundi libri De Diuinatione se composuisse librum in quo introduxit Hortensium hortantem ad studium philosophie. Dicit eciam ibidem se sex libros De Re Publica composuisse. Qui libri quia in Anglia non reperiuntur, ego Willelmus Malmesburgensis more meo hic apposui quicquid de materia et intentione eorum in beato Augustino inuenire potui. Simul et hic

---

[82] Extracts may be found in James, *Two Ancient English Scholars*, p. 22 (in translation), J. S. Reid, (ed.), *The Academica of Cicero* (London, 1885), pp. 67–8, and F. E. Harrison, *Millennium: A Latin Reader* (Oxford, 1968), pp. 100–1.

[83] PH, p. 97.

inuenta occasione notandum puto, ne quis me reprehendat quot libros gentilium lego et scribo. Qui enim hac intentione illos legit quia fastidit uel uilipendit diuinas Scripturas grauiter et penaliter peccat; unde et beatus Hieronimus se castigatum et cesum profitetur in libro ad Eustochium De Virginitate Seruanda (Ep. 22). Qui uero eos ideo legit ut si quid ornate et eloquenter dicunt ipse in scriptis suis ad Dei et sanctorum eius gloriam opportune transferat, tenens apostoli regulam ut omnia probet, quod bonum est teneat, ab omni specie mala se abstineat (I Thess. 5. 21), nullo modo eum delectione gentilium librorum peccare crediderim. Quod si michi non creditur, epistola eiusdem Ieronimi ad oratorem Magnum urbis Rome legatur (Ep. 70; extracted in the *Polyhistor*[84]).

William then gives passages from Augustine, *Confessiones, De Trinitate* and *De Civitate Dei* containing references to, and quotations from the *Hortensius* and *De Re Publica*.

The preface to the *Timaeus* (f.108v) reads thus:

In sequenti libello transfert Cicero sensum Timei Platonis de genitura mundi pretermissis omnibus que Calcidius transtulit in principio de Socrate et Hermocrate et Critia. Ista uero translacione utitur beatus Augustinus in libro De Ciuitate Dei terciodecimo ubi Plato in[tro]ducit Deum concionantem ad minores déos (XIII. 16). Cuius concionis secundum hanc translacionem hoc est principium ...

William then gives Augustine's extract and Calcidius's version. Thus this passage indicates, what we should have anyhow guessed, that William knew Calcidius's translation of the *Timaeus* as well as Cicero's less complete version.

The *De Paradoxis* is prefaced by a long series of extracts from Macrobius, *Saturnalia* 2. 1 and 2. 3 (f.114).

On f.118, before the *Pro Milone*:

Milo quidam miles Pompei magni occidit P. Clodium Rome, unde uocatum ad iudicium cum Cicero defendisset et parum promouisset Pompeius inducta armatorum manu in ciui eripuit. Inde Cesar loquitur in Lucano: (Here is quoted *Phars*. 1. 320–3).

A long passage is prefixed to the *Phillippics* (f.192):

Demosthenes fuit Athenensis orator CCCis annis ante Tullium, sicut idem Tullius in fine secundi libri De Diuinacione dicit. De quo Demosthene eleganter ad Tullium dictum est: 'Demosthenes, Marce

---

[84] ibid., p. 86.

Tulli, preripuit tibi ne esses solus orator ne primus' (Jerome, Ep. 52. 8. 3). Is ergo Demosthenes oraciones illas appelauit Phillippicas quas contra Philippum regem Machedonum patrem Alexandri magni edidit qui tirannice Athenas inuaserat. Ad cuius imitacionem Marcus Tullius Cicero oraciones illas appellauit Phillippicas quas contra Anthonium edidit qui tirannidem affectabat super Romanos post interitum Gaii Cesaris sicut commemorat beatus Augustinus in libro tercio De Ciuitate Dei (III. 30) sed enim uterque pro Phillippicis suis occisus est, Demosthenes a Phillippo, Tullius ab Anthonio, unde Iuuenalis: (Here is quoted *Sat.* 10. 114–132).

William repeated the quotation from Jerome in his *Polyhistor*.[85] Finally, remarks from Jerome, *Super Ep. ad Galat.*, and Augustine, *De Origine Animae*, are prefixed to the *Tusculans* (ff.274–5).

There may have been more of these notes, but the opening leaves of several of the individual works have been excised for the sake of their initials. Those that remain indicate not only which texts in this collection William certainly knew, but his acquaintance with other writings about them, and his desire to provide a little background information about them for his own benefit and that of other readers, no doubt in particular his fellow-monks at Malmesbury. The note on the *De Re Publica* suggests, in addition, how keen he was to obtain works which he knew existed, without having seen copies. We shall show conclusively that when he stated that no copy was to be found in England, it was on the basis of a thorough search up and down the country. This intensive quest for particular ancient works known to William from their mention in other texts makes him almost unique among twelfth-century men of letters.

But we can establish that he knew other texts in the corpus besides those with introductions. The *De Senectute* is extracted in the *Polyhistor* and quoted in the *Gesta Pontificum*.[86] The *Catilines* are mentioned and briefly characterized in the introduction to the *Polyhistor*;[87] William's exclamation 'O tempora, O mores' in the *Gesta Pontificum* presumably comes from that source.[88] The *Philippics* are mentioned in the *Polyhistor*, and the *De Officiis* is extracted there, quoted in the *Gesta Regum* and *Commentary on Lamentations*, and in Oxford, Bodleian Library MS Rawl. G. 139 we have a copy of it made under William's direction.[89] Also in the *Gesta Regum* is a

---

[85] ibid., p. 84.
[86] ibid., pp. 112–4; GP, p. 19.
[87] PH, p. 37.
[88] GP, p. 421: *Cat.* 1. 2. But it might also have come, with less likelihood, from *Verr.* 2. 4. 55, *Pro Dom.* 137 or *Pro Deiot.* 31.
[89] PH, pp. 37, 114–8; 2. 15: GR II, p. 368; 3. 21: ibid., p. 462; 31. 1: GR I, p. 65, Comm. Lam., f. 93.

passage from the *Pro Milone*.[90] Finally, in a marginal note to his collection of Carolingian chronicles William refers to and quotes from the *Pro Marcello*,[91] one of the three Caesarian Orations. Since these seem always to have been copied together, William presumably also knew the *Pro Ligario* and *Pro Rege Deiotaro*.[92] All this assures us that he knew at least fifteen of the Ciceronian works in the Cambridge manuscript, including some of the speeches.

The main argument which has been advanced for these speeches having been taken from a continental exemplar unconnected with William is that earlier copies of them are more or less rare, in nearly all cases continental, and in very many confined to Germany.[93] The group from the *Pro Caelio* on is found, with similar lacunae and textual displacements, in a manuscript of about the same date from the Belgian abbey of Parc, while the texts of the *Pro Milone* and *Tusculans* are closely related to another contemporary manuscript written near Bonn, in which the *Pro Milone* even has the introduction found in the Cambridge manuscript.[94] But both of these continental manuscripts, which used to be dated earlier than the Cambridge one, are now known to be its twin textually, and therefore do not in themselves prove that the relevant speeches were copied from continental exemplars. It has not yet been proved that any of the texts in the Cambridge manuscripts derive from earlier continental copies.

The Cambridge manuscript was written in 1444 by Theodore Werken, a professional scribe from southern Holland, for Bishop Gray, then in Cologne.[95] At least two other manuscripts were written there at about the same time for Gray, both copied ultimately from collections made by William. One is a copy of his 'Selden Collection' of historical writings, the other is the manuscript of Tertullian and Lactantius mentioned earlier.[96] The exemplar of the latter was copied again on the continent to produce Gotha, Forschungsbibliothek Membr. I. 55.[97] All three of Gray's manuscripts have

---

[90] GR I, p. 129 '... ut quidam ait, leges inter arma sileant'; cf. *Pro Mil.* 10 'Silent enim leges inter arma' and Jerome, *Ep.* 126. 2. 2 'Quodsi iuxta inclitum oratorem silent inter arma leges'. Both Jerome and William were probably quoting from memory.

[91] See below, pp. 142–3.

[92] *Texts and Transmission*, pp. 65–7.

[93] ibid., pp. 80–2; Mynors, *Catalogue*, p. 377.

[94] Brussels, Bibliothèque Royale 14492; Bonn, Universitätsbibliothek S 140. Moreover the Bonn MS also contains (ff. 233–57) book 6 of Lactantius's *Institutes*, closely connected by its readings with William's text as in Oxford, Balliol Coll. 79 (another of Gray's books) and Gotha, Forschungsbibliothek Membr. I. 55 (*Lactantii Opera*, ed. Brandt, pp. liv–lv); see above, p. 42.

[95] Mynors, op. cit.

[96] Oxford, Balliol College 125, copied from Bodl. Libr. Arch. Seld. B. 16; Balliol Coll. 79. See Mynors, *Catalogue*, pp. 64–5, 103–5.

[97] ibid., p. 65.

marginal annotations in the hands of his scribes, thus copied from the exemplars. These annotations appear in all parts of the Cambridge manuscript, not just the part considered to derive definitely from William's collection. The texts quoted by the annotator indicate that he wrote no earlier than the fourteenth century; the existence of the Selden manuscript, which has no such annotations, shows that they were not made to William's original *collectanea*, but to later copies of them. If the annotation was done in England, as seems most likely, then it means that Gray brought all the exemplars with him to Cologne. On this basis, though tentatively, I am inclined to accept the whole of the Cicero-collection in Cambridge University Library Dd. 13. 2 as William's.

But, as James pointed out, this manuscript does not represent the full extent of William's knowledge of Cicero's writings. The *De Amicitia* is mentioned and extracted in the *Polyhistor*, and the *De Legibus* quoted in the *Gesta Regum*.[98] James thought that William did not know many of Cicero's works on rhetoric,[99] but that is not true. The *De Inventione* is mentioned in the introduction to the *Polyhistor*, extracted in the same work, and drawn on in the prologue to the *De Miraculis B.V.M.*[100] We have William's own copy of the rare *Partitiones Oratoriae*.[101] His single reference to the pseudonymous *Ad Herennium* is worth detailed consideration, as it illustrates yet again William's close attention to his texts and staggering memory. In the *Gesta Regum* he refers to a piece of turgid writing as 'eo dicendi genere quod suffultum rex facundiae Romanae Tullius in rhetoricis appellat'. This is adapted from Osbern's *Vita Dunstani*, but Osbern did not say which work of Cicero's was involved.[102] In fact 'suffultus' is used in such a connection only once in all Latin literature, and that is in the *Ad Herennium*.[103] In his own *Vita Dunstani* William has a quotation from the *Orator*, but he probably lifted this from Augustine's *Tractatus in Iohannem*.[104]

We can safely say, then, that William knew at least nineteen, and perhaps as many as twenty-eight works of Cicero, if we count the fragments from the *De Re Publica* and *Hortensius*. James remarked that William did not quote Cicero as often as one might expect, and even after further research that judgement remains sound, for apart from transcriptions and extracts, I find only nine quotations in William's writings.[105] But he knew nearly all of Cicero's philosophical treatises, some of the rhetorical works, and at least

---

98 *De Amic.*: PH, p. 114; *De Leg.* 1. 2. 6: GR II, p. 434.
99 James, *Two Ancient English Scholars*, p. 23.
100 PH, pp. 37–8, *De Miraculis B.V.M.*, pp. 47–52.
101 Oxford, Bodl. Libr. Rawl. G. 139. See below, pp. 86–7.
102 GR I, p. 144; Osbern, *Vita Dunstani* in Stubbs, *Memorials*, p. 70.
103 *Ad Her.* 4. 5. 8.
104 VD, p. 288; *Orator* 132; Aug., *Tract. in Ioann.* 58. 3.
105 See above, notes 86, 88–91, 98, 100, 102.

four speeches. Some of these were not by themselves uncommon in large twelfth-century libraries, but William is extraordinary in knowing so many of them.

Addressing his friend Guthlac in the prologue to the *Polyhistor*, William says: 'All Seneca's books except that on the death of Claudius and the *De Causis* are almost as full of profit as they are of words'.[106] This shows that he did not distinguish between the writings of the two Senecas, a normal medieval confusion somewhat surprising, however, for William. By the 'De Causis' he apparently meant the elder Seneca's *Controversiae*, from which he quotes in the *Gesta Regum*.[107] The twelfth century saw a marked revival of interest in the works of the younger Seneca, and William occupies an important place in this development.[108] The uncommon *Apocolocyntosis* interested him; it is mentioned in the *Polyhistor*, quoted twice in the *Gesta Pontificum*, and once in the *Gesta Regum*.[109] We should expect William to be acquainted with the moral treatises, but there is evidence only for his reading of *De Beneficiis*, which is extracted in the *Polyhistor*.[110] As it invariably travelled with the *De Clementia* William presumably knew that too.[111]

William's knowledge of Seneca's letters, studied in detail by Reynolds, is particularly fascinating. Letters 71, 7 and 72, 3 are quoted in the *Commentary on Lamentations*, and 11–120 are extracted in the *Polyhistor*.[112] Since late antiquity Seneca's letters had circulated in two separate collections, one containing letters 1–88, the other the remainder. Both collections were little known before c.1100, and then it was the first 88 letters which gained popularity. Hildebert of Le Mans, for instance, one of the earliest writers to seize eagerly on Seneca's works, only knew letters 1–88. William is the earliest of four known twelfth-century writers who knew letters 89–124, and Reynolds was able to show that the next earliest, Robert of Cricklade, knew *only* these later letters. This makes William the first person after late antiquity to know both parts of the collection. Textual evidence suggests that William found separate manuscripts of the two parts and put them together himself, and this would be consistent with his known habits as a bibliographer and editor.

---

[106] PH, p. 37.
[107] 1. 9: GR I, p. 64.
[108] On twelfth-century interest in Seneca see K.-D. Nothdurft, *Studien zum Einfluss Senecas an die Philosophie und Theologie des zwölften Jahrhunderts* (Leiden-Köln, 1963); von Moos, *Hildebert von Lavardin*; Reynolds, *The Medieval Tradition of Seneca's Letters*.
[109] GP, pp. 24, 291; GR II, p. 329; *Texts and Transmission*, pp. 361–2.
[110] PH, pp. 139–143.
[111] *Texts and Transmission*, pp. 363–5.
[112] Reynolds, op. cit., pp. 117 and n. 2, 120–3. Ep. 71. 7: Comm. Lam., f. 13v; 72. 3: ibid., f. 18; PH, pp. 104–111.

There is evidence for William's knowledge of some thirty other prose writers of the classical and late antique periods. I will comment only on some of the more interesting.

First, a ghost must be laid. Cato's *De Originibus* survives today in fragments only, collected together in the last century.[113] In his own collection of works on Roman history, William included a short passage which he entitles 'Excerptum ex libro Catonis de originibus'.[114] This passage, describing the mythical origin of the Trojan people, is not included in the modern editions of Cato. Is it then a hitherto and otherwise unknown fragment of genuine Cato? Alas, no. The passage is found in Virgil manuscripts from the ninth century on, and a version of it is chapter 135 of Vatican Mythographer I.[115] How then has William come to ascribe it to Cato? I should suggest that he came upon a manuscript containing this note with a title such as 'De Origine Troiarum'. His prodigious memory recalled the *De Originibus (Romanorum)* of Cato, references to which he could have found easily enough in his wide reading.[116] He put two and two together, and his conjecture, although wrong, is by no means unintelligent.

The works of Caesar were to be found only in major European monastic libraries from Carolingian times on; William quotes three or four times from the *Gallic Wars*, and another apparent reference to pseudo-Caesar, *De Bello Alexandrino*, suggests that he knew the *Civil Wars*, since the two commentaries and doubtfully ascribed works usually travelled together in the same manuscript.[117] Suetonius, commoner, he quotes in the *Gesta Pontificum*,[118] and an interlinear note in William's collection of ancient military writings (Oxford, Lincoln College lat. 100; Frontinus and Vegetius plus Eutropius) shows once again how familiar he was with his texts. At f.85v, where Eutropius states that Domitian died 'anno etatis xxv', William

---

[113] Ed. H. Jordan, *M Catonis praeter Librum De Re Rustica quae extant* (Berlin, 1860); and in H. Peter, *Historicorum Romanorum Reliquiae* (Leipzig, 2 vols, 1914), I, pp. 55–97.

[114] Oxford, Bodl. Libr. Arch. Seld. B. 16, f. 7.

[115] 'Dardanus ex Ioue et Electra filia Athlantis natus ... in caelo ubi esse creditur Deus ingens nominatus est', found in Laon, Bibl. de la Ville 468, ff. 4–4v, and in Virgil MSS such as Paris, BN lat. 10307, ff. 96v–97. The former is reproduced in facsimile by J. Contreni, *Codex Laudunensis 468: a Ninth-Century Guide to Virgil, Sedulius and the Liberal Arts* (Turnhout, 1984). Vat. Mythogr. I in G. Bode, *Scriptores Rerum Mythicarum Latini Tres Romae Nuper Reperti*, I (Celle, 1834), p. 43. The same passage is quoted, although adapted more freely, in the late eleventh-century commentary on Ovid's *Fasti* printed by E. H. Alton, 'The Mediaeval Commentators on Ovid's *Fasti*', *Hermathena*, 20 (1926–30), 136–7.

[116] E.g. Servius, Macrobius, Gellius and Priscian. When these authors give a title, it is always simply 'De Originibus' or 'De Origine'.

[117] ?4. 28: GP, pp. 221, 268; 5. 14: GR II, p. 301; 6. 5: ibid., p. 312; *Texts and Transmission*, pp. 35–6.

[118] Calig. 1: GP, p. 188.

notes (correctly) 'dicit Suetonius xlv'.[119] The manuscript itself is interesting. Eutropius and Frontinus were copied together in manuscripts from the ninth century; William seems to have been the first to add Vegetius, whose inclusion is normal from the thirteenth century on.[120] Dr Janet Martin, noting the close textual affinity between this manuscript and John of Salisbury's quotations from Frontinus in his *Polycraticus*, has concluded that they were based on a common exemplar, and that the most likely place for both scholars to have found it would be Canterbury.[121] A copy of Frontinus figures in the early fourteenth-century library catalogue from Christ Church.[122]

The influence of Sallust on medieval historical writing has attracted recent scholarly interest, but long ago Marie Schütt attempted to demonstrate Sallust's influence on the literary form of William's *Gesta Regum*.[123] If her argument has not been thought entirely convincing, it is because a vital link is missing: she could not *prove* beyond reasonable doubt that William really knew Sallust. But he did. In the *Polyhistor* William states that 'Dimisi etiam quod Marius criminacione Metelli acquisierit consulatum, quoniam in Salustio copiose legitur'.[124] The reference is, of course, to the *Jugurthine War*, but this nearly always travelled with the *Catiline Conspiracy*, from which William seems to quote in his *De Miraculis B.V.M.*[125]

---

[119] Dom. 17. 3.
[120] *Iuli Frontini Strategematon*, ed. G. Gundermann (Leipzig, 1888), p. v. Gundermann did not realize that Vegetius was contained in the Lincoln College MS.
[121] J. Martin, 'John of Salisbury's Manuscripts of Frontinus and of Gellius', pp. 2–5; idem, 'John of Salisbury as Classical Scholar', in *The World of John of Salisbury*, pp. 180–4.
[122] M. R. James, *The Ancient Libraries of Canterbury and Dover* (Cambridge, 1903), p. 267. There is another copy in the later catalogue from St Augustine's abbey (ibid., p. 297), but this is the fourteenth-century Cambridge, St John's College 97, also containing William's *Polyhistor*.
[123] R. Latouche, 'Un imitateur de Salluste au Xe siècle: l'historien Richer', in idem, *Etudes Médiévales* (Paris, 1966), pp. 69–81; Southern, 'Aspects of the European Tradition of Historical Writing I', pp. 177–180; B. Smalley, 'Sallust in the Middle Ages', in *Classical Influences on European Culture A.D. 500–1500*, ed. R. Bolgar (Cambridge, 1971), pp. 167–175, esp. p. 172; Schütt, 'The Literary Form of William of Malmesbury's *Gesta Regum*'.
[124] PH, p. 118.
[125] *Cat.* 8. 4: *De Miraculis B.V.M.*, p. 160: '... illud memoriale sallustianum ... quod eorum qui fecere uirtutes, uirtus tanta habetur, quantum eam extollere potuerunt praeclara ingenia'; *Cat.* 8. 4; '... eorum, qui ea fecere, uirtus tanta habetur, quantum uerbis ea potuere extollere praeclara ingenia'; Jerome, *Vit. Hilarion.* (PL 23. 29) 'Eorum qui fecere uirtus, ut ait Crispus, tanta habetur quantam eam uerbis potuere extollere praeclara ingenia'. William may have known both of the earlier sources.

Most of the works mentioned above are of a kind obviously attractive to a historian and man of letters, but William also sought the more specialized and technical writings of classical authors. There are extracts from Vitruvius in the *Polyhistor*, and it has been suggested that these or their exemplar were copied from British Library Cott. Cleo. D. i, an eleventh-century English manuscript presumably made at and for St Augustine's Canterbury, where it was found by the fourteenth century.[126] We know from other evidence that William visited St Augustine's and ransacked its library, so that is seems likely that here he discovered and copied Vitruvius.[127]

At the beginning of William's collection of grammatical manuals (British Library Harl. 3969) he has provided his usual bibliographical introduction, in this case from Cassiodorus's *Institutes*. The extract concerns the agricultural writings of Gargilius Martialis, Columella and Palladius, but at the end William has made an addition of his own: 'Nota quod Palladius de Martiali et Columella plura testimonia sumit, sed eos in prologo tacitis nominibus reprehendit nimis difficulter locutos fuisse'.[128] I think that this is quite sufficient proof that William had read Palladius, *De Agricultura*, not an uncommon text in the twelfth century.[129] Pliny's *Natural History* he extracted copiously in the *Polyhistor*, mostly from books 1–16, but running up as far as book 32.[130] He ends with the remark 'De Plinio plura sed multa sunt et inania; plurima etiam ipse Plinius a Valerio, Valerius pene omnia que dixit sumpsit a Tullio; hic tamen non incommode posita puto, ut scias quid quisque mutuatus est ex altero'. Evidently he had a reasonably complete copy of Pliny. Finally, one should mention the *Polyhistor*'s extract from the *Mathesis* of Julius Firmicus. This text was a rarity in early Europe if only because of its unchristian presuppositions and purely specialist interest. Nevertheless it was known to a few other Englishmen of the twelfth century: Archbishop Gerard of York (d.1108), the author of the *Quadripartitus* (1114) and Daniel of Morley (c.1180).[131] Interestingly, in the first

---

[126] *Texts and Transmission*, p. 443. An English origin for Cott. Cleo. D. i is accepted by H. Gneuss, 'Manuscripts written or owned in England up to c.1100', ASE, 9 (1981), 22.

[127] See below, pp. 70, 73.

[128] London, BL Harl. 3969, f. 41. As William says, Palladius does not name the recipients of his criticism in his preface, but he does name his principal sources later in his work, passim; among them are the two writers listed by William, who has put two and two together. Evidently he had not only read Palladius, but had read him with his customary thoroughness.

[129] R. H. Rodgers, *An Introduction to Palladius* (University of London Institute of Classical Studies Bulletin, Suppl. 35, London, 1975).

[130] PH, pp. 45–61.

[131] Firmicus Maternus, *Mathesis*, ed. W. Kroll, F. Skutsch and K. Ziegler (Leipzig, 2 vols, 1897), II, pp. iii–v. On knowledge of his work in early Europe see V. Flint, 'World History in the early Twelfth Century; the "Imago Mundi" of Honorius Augustodunensis', in *The Writing of History in the Middle Ages*, p. 225 n. 1.

edition of his *Gesta Pontificum* William criticizes Archbishop Gerard 'qui etiam maleficiis dicitur inseruire, quod Iulium Firmicum secreto et pro meridianis horis lectitaret'. This passage was omitted from the second edition of 1135.[132] Was this because in the meantime William had acquired a copy for himself?

William was well acquainted with the commonest of the late antique writers, Macrobius, Martianus, Solinus and Boethius, as evidenced by his copies of and extracts from their works, and by references to them in marginal and other notes. Macrobius's *Saturnalia*, for instance, was for him a mine of historical and biographical information about ancient people and events.[133] We have William's own copy of Martianus, and something must be said of it. Cambridge, Corpus Christi College 330 consists of two manuscripts bound together by and for William.[134] Part I contains the text of Martianus in a Norman hand of c.1100. In its margins William himself wrote extracts from the gloss by Remigius of Auxerre. Part II, containing the Martianus gloss known as the 'Anonymus Cantabrigiensis', was written on the continent in the late ninth century, but was in England by the late tenth. It is not known where or how William acquired either part.

Perhaps the most interesting late antique author known to William is Aulus Gellius, extracts from whom are in the *Polyhistor*. Like Seneca's letters, the *Attic Nights* circulated after late antiquity in two parts.[135] The well-known ninth-century scholar Lupus of Ferrières knew books 1–7, but William is again one of the first to know both parts of this hitherto rare text. I have tried to demonstrate below that William used two exemplars, consisting of books 1–7 and 9–16 respectively, to compile a florilegium most of which was included in the *Polyhistor*, and which was also known to John of Salisbury. Like Macrobius, Gellius was used by William as a treasure-house of historical information which he could not find elsewhere. A comment from the midst of the Gellius passages in the *Polyhistor* illuminates this:[136]

> Ista que posui Agellius se sumpsisse affirmat ex ignotis nobis auctoribus, Quadrigario, Higino, Catone, Herodoto. Hiis autem supersedeo que de recencioribus mutuatus est: de Valerio reconcilia-cionem Publii Scipionis cum Tiberio Gracco, Cresi filio muto uocem datam, iudicium a Dolabella dilatum de muliere que confiteretur occisos a se uirum et filium, Sicinium Romanum Achillem uocatum; de Plinio esse homines effascinantes et esse alios qui uidendo interimant

---

132 GP, p. 259 n. 6.
133 7. 5: GR I, p. 196; CUL Dd. 13. 2 (See above, p. 52); Oxford, Bodl. Libr. Arch. Seld. B. 16; PH, pp. 103–4, 143–153.
134 See below, pp. 81–2.
135 See below, ch. 10.
136 PH, pp. 64–5.

Marsicorum scienciam; nam de taciturnitate Papirii pueri Macrobium Saturnaliorum narrasse quis nesciat? Proinde illa ponam que alibi me legisse non recolo.

One might just add that the Petronius quotation in the *Gesta Pontificum*, repeated in the *Commentary on Lamentations*, is most probably from Fulgentius Mythographus, although Petronius was known to John of Salisbury.[137] The passage allegedly from pseudo-Aurelius Victor, *De Viris Illustribus*, found in William's two major historical works, is also suspicious.[138]

We pass to grammar. It is perhaps not surprising that I can find no references in William's works to either Donatus or Priscian. His grammar-collection, which survives in a later copy, consists of obscurer works: Agroecius, pseudo-Caper and Cassiodorus, *De Orthographia*, together with the similar works of Alcuin and Bede.[139] Probably William did not put together this collection, but recopied a pre-existing one such as that which is found in Cambridge, Corpus Christi College MS 221, from the ninth and early eleventh centuries.[140]

III. GREEK AND ARABIC WRITINGS

Haskins and James were always interested in the knowledge of Greek possessed by twelfth-century scholars. William was hardly attracted by Greek history for its own sake; he viewed it from the Rome-centred perspective of Virgil and Dares Phrygius. But he was fascinated by Greek thinkers, writers and men of action, as evidenced by the contents of his *Polyhistor*. He knew the *Timaeus* in both versions, as shown earlier,[141] and quotes the most famous sentence from the *Republic*, 'that state is blest which

---

[137] *Sat.* 82: GP, p. 69 and Comm. Lam., f. 15; cf. Fulg. Met. 2. 15. The quotation is also in the *Florilegium Gallicum*: T. Brandis and W.-W. Ehlers, 'Zu den Petronex-zerpten des Florilegium Gallicum', *Philologus*, 118 (1974), 90, 101.

[138] GP, p. 397; GR I, p. 187.

[139] London, BL Harl. 3969.

[140] Cambridge, Corpus Christi College 221 consists of two volumes bound together at an unknown date. I, ninth-century and continental, has Alcuin and Bede; II, c.1000, possibly English, has Cassiodorus, Pseudo-Caper and Agroecius. Were the volumes bound in the reverse order, their contents would be in the same sequence as those in William's grammatical collection. Unfortunately William has so altered his texts that collation has not proved decisively whether or not Corpus Christi 221 was his source, though that seems likely; A. C. Dionisotti, 'On Bede, Grammars and Greek', p. 133 and n. 1.

[141] See above, p. 52.

has a philosopher for king and a king for philosopher', via Jerome.[142] In his *Commentary on Lamentations* he quotes Aristotle approvingly, from what source I do not know.[143] He probably knew the *Logica Vetus*, since marginal notes in the Selden manuscript suggest that he had read Boethius's commentaries on the *Categories* and *De Interpretatione*.[144] His extracts from Remigius's commentary on Martianus and his *Commentary on Lamentations* indicate that William could write Greek characters tolerably well and knew some vocabulary and simple sentences. More one cannot say, and that he knew much more than that is improbable.

The mention of writings other than Latin raises the question of William's contact with Arabic works in translation. Although his interest in this area has to be inferred from indirect evidence, there is little doubt of its existence. In his *Gesta Regum* William emphasizes Gerbert's fruitful contact with Arabic scientific doctrine, names an Arabic astrological work without providing any evidence that he had read it, and demonstrates his comparatively accurate knowledge of Islamic religion and history.[145] The same emphasis appears in the later part of the Selden collection, and there and in the *Commentary on Lamentations* are further accurate statements about the origins and nature of Islam.[146] In a collection of computistica which William had copied appears a series of treatises on the astrolabe which reflect, directly or otherwise, the influence of Islamic Spain.[147] But there is no evidence that he knew any of the translations made in his own time.

IV. LAW

Two kinds of ancient writing were of unusual interest to William: the first is law. It has long been known that William included in his collection of Roman historical writings the law–code known as the *Breviarium Alaricum*,

---

142 GP, p. 160, GR II, pp. 467, 520; Jerome, *Comm. in Ionam* 3. 6.
143 See below, p. 175.
144 Oxford, Bodl. Libr. Arch. Seld. B. 16, ff. 111v–112.
145 GR I, pp. 193–4; ibid., p. 194 'Alandreum in stellarum interstitio'. This almost certainly refers to the *Mathematica Alhandrei*, a work apparently written in eighth- or ninth-century Francia, of which William's is the earliest known citation: J. Millas Vallicrosa, 'Assaig d'Historia de les Idees Fisiques i Matematiques a la Catalunya Medieval', *Estudis Universitaris Catalans, Serie Monografica*, I. i (Barcelona, 1931), pp. 246–7. References to Islam are in GR I, pp. 71, 81, 92–4, 150, 211, 230, 245, 255; II, pp. 337, 395, 412.
146 On William's knowledge of Islam see below, ch. 9.
147 See below, p. 197, under 'De Horologio secundum Alkoran'.

an abridgement of the Theodosian Code.[148] James suggested that this text, rare and outdated by William's day, may have been known to Aldhelm, and argued that the source of William's knowledge of it, and the ancestor of his personal copy, was probably a manuscript from the Malmesbury library predating the seventh century. There is some textual evidence in support of this, for William's copy, though late, contains readings which place it close to the lost archetype of Mommsen's 'classis melior', which was at least as early as the seventh century. It is not so well-known that William was familiar with the Justinian Code, as indicated by two passages in the Selden manuscript. One is the prologue to his copy of the *Breviarium*, which reads thus:[149]

> Nunc quia quicquid de principibus Italiae et Romae potuimus inuenire curauimus non omittere, congruum uidetur leges Romanorum apponere, non eas quas Iustinianus fecit, esset enim hoc ingentis operis et laboris, sed eas quas Theodosius minor filius Archadii a temporibus Constantini usque ad suum sub titulo uniuscuiusque imperatoris collegit ...

The other is an addition made by William to one of the chronicles which he excerpted earlier in the book:[150]

> (On Justinian) Nam omnes constitutiones principum quae in multis uoluminibus habebantur intra xii libros coartauit idemque uolumen codicem Iustiniani appellari praecepit. Rursumque singulorum magistratuum siue iudicum leges quae usque ad duo milia pene libros erant extensae intra quinquaginta librorum numerum redegit, eumque codicem digestorum siue pandectarum uocabulo nuncupauit. Quattuor etiam institutionum libros in quibus breuiter uniuersarum legum textus comprehenditur composuit. Nouos quoque leges quas ipse composuit in corpus unum redactas nouellarum codicem uocauit.

Now these passages were written in 1129, at least ten years before Master Vacarius came to England.[151] By the early 1140s Gilbert Foliot was quoting extensively from the Code in his letters, and about two decades later he wrote to his uncle Bishop Robert of Lincoln that he had ordered a copy of

---

[148] See below, p. 200.
[149] Oxford, Bodl. Libr. Arch. Seld. B. 16, f. 140 (GR I, pp. cxxxvii–cxxxviii).
[150] ibid., f. 135.
[151] A. Saltman, *Theobald Archbishop of Canterbury* (London, 1956), pp. 175–6; R. W. Southern, 'Master Vacarius and the Beginning of an English Academic Tradition', in *Medieval Learning and Literature; Essays presented to R. W. Hunt*, ed. J. J. G. Alexander and M. T. Gibson (Oxford, 1976), pp. 259, 280.

the glossed Digest to be made for him.[152] Brooke stated that the basis of Gilbert's legal learning must have been laid in the 1120s or early 1130s, probably not in England, for 'there is no reason to suppose that it was possible to study the *Corpus* in England so early. Gilbert's early education may have been gathered in England; but we have seen hints of foreign connexions in his early life ... The pointers so far considered, for what they are worth, indicate Bologna'.[153] William's testimony makes all this questionable. He evidently knew the *Corpus* before Vacarius first popularized it in England, suggesting that copies were available locally, whether much utilized or not.

William was also a student of canon law. Oxford, Oriel College MS 42 contains the *Collectio Quesnelliana* of conciliar canons and papal decrees compiled at Rome at the turn of the fifth and sixth centuries.[154] William copied it in his own hand, and his annotations show that he took special pains to ensure an accurate text. Not only did he carefully correct his own transcription against the exemplar, but he compared this exemplar, which he describes as 'uetustissimus', with 'nouellis exemplaribus' of similar collections. He also supplemented some of the episcopal lists from other sources, such as Rufinus's *Historia Ecclesiastica*. As they are not otherwise available, I print the more interesting of them here:

[f. 2 in marg.] Horum [canonum] quecumque in nouellis canonibus et decretis sunt hoc signo R, quae desunt isto D.
[f. 2v, inserted at 'sub Constantino tot congregarentur'] episcopi; palam facit decimus liber Rufini qui coniunctus est .ix. libris aecclesiasticae historiae quos uir eruditissimus Eusebius Cesariensis edidit. Dubium enim non est.
[f. 3] In the list of bishops' names, between 'Alexander Alexandriae Aegypti' and 'Thebaides' William interlines 'Paphnutius teste Rufino'.
[f. 4v] After 'Nicholas' William adds 'Mirrensis teste auctore translacionis eius', after 'Eusebius Paritias', 'Spiridion teste Rufino'.
[f. 5] After 'Domnus Bosforensis', 'Alipius Gaudentius sicut in canonibus inuenitur'; following the list of Nicene bishops: 'De numero trecentorum decem et viii. seu quia propter uetustatem abolita sunt, seu quia, ut suprascriptum est, magis curauerunt serui Dei orientalium episcoporum nomina ponere cum quibus questio agebatur,

---

[152] A. Morey and C. N. L. Brooke, *Gilbert Foliot and his Letters* (Cambridge, 1965), pp. 63–6.
[153] ibid., p. 63.
[154] Edited by Quesnel, then by the Ballerini brothers, whose version is most accessible in PL 56. 359ff. They collated the Oriel MS and printed many of William's annotations. See P. Fournier and G. Le Bras, *Histoire des Collections Canoniques en Occident* (Paris, 2 vols, 1931–2), I, pp. 26–9.

quam occidentalium qui nullam de consubstantialitate Patris et Filii controuersiam habebant, desunt nomina nonaginta duo.

[f.7v in marg.)] Nota quod abhinc ad finem concilii Niceni tituli omnes inueniantur de Sardicensi fuisse concilio secundum nouella exemplaria.

[f.10] Hi canones sunt uel decreta Niceni concilii. Subscripserunt autem omnes episcopi sic: Ego episcopus illius ciuitatis et prouincie ita credo sicut suprascriptum est. Sciendum est autem quod in nouellis exemplaribus desunt cxvi. capitula, sed iste codex transcriptus est ex uetustissimo exemplari. Quocirca de ueritate scriptorum nec in isto primo capitulo Nicenorum canonum nec in omnibus sequentibus aliquis dubitare debet licet aliter in nouellis exemplaribus inueniatur.

[f.12v, lower marg.] 'Nota quod a vi. huius codicis capitulo usque huc omnia contra Pelagianos dicta sunt, nec habentur in nouis exemplaribus'. And again: 'Nota quod hiis iii. capitulis non habentur in nouellis exemplaribus'.

[f.32, top marg.] Commenting on a word in the top line of the text: 'Isidorus dicit quod hireiscunda est diuisio hereditatis'.

[f.38 in marg.] Nota quod ea quae suprascripta sunt de congreganda sinodo Calcedonensi et allocutio imperatoris in nouis exemplaribus non inueniuntur. Caetera omnia de ipsa sinodo inueniuntur, sensu eodem sed littera plerumque diuersa. Denique in ueteri exemplari non inuenitur in Simbolo Spiritum Sanctum procedere ex Patre et Filio, sed tantum a Patre sicut hodieque Greci dicunt. Latini uero dicimus ex Patre et Filio eum procedere, sicut in nouis exemplaribus scriptum est.

How old was William's 'uetustissimus' exemplar and where did he find it? What prompted him to copy such an old-fashioned collection whose unsystematic arrangement made it useless for the needs of his day? The answer to the first question is suggested by the other surviving manuscripts of the *Collectio Quesnelliana*, all continental and dating from the late eighth to early ninth century.[155] William's copy has not been collated, but the likelihood is that his exemplar was Carolingian. At the end of the Oriel manuscript are two letters which are not part of the *Collectio*. The first is from Abbot Thietmar of Monte Cassino to Charlemagne 'de priuatis eius moribus'; the second is the well-known circular letter sent by the Monte

---

[155] The latest list of nine MSS is in H. Mordek, *Kirchenrecht und Reform im Frankenreich* (Beiträge zur Geschichte und Quellenkunde des Mittelalters 1, Berlin, 1975), pp. 238–40.

Cassino monks to a number of German houses in 1072.[156] This version, addressed to Abbot Hartwig of Hersfeld, is known from only one other manuscript. William presumably found these two letters together in his exemplar, which is therefore likely to have been German. This does not tell us how he came upon it. It was presumably not already at Malmesbury, or he need not have recopied it. A loan from or visit to a house with closer continental connections than his own is a possibility, and Canterbury again springs to mind. As to why William found this ancient collection interesting, two reasons may be advanced. Firstly, his annotations indicate that he thought it textually accurate and authoritative. Secondly, it contained material which he knew from no other source, in particular some of the letters of Leo. Finally, what were William's 'new exemplars'? One would guess them to be some version of the pseudo-Isidorean Decretals, and that turns out to be the case. He was in fact referring specifically to the abbreviated version made by Archbishop Lanfranc, the form in which pseudo-Isidore was most accessible in early twelfth-century England.[157]

V. HISTORY

Discussion of the Selden Collection introduces the other class of ancient writings particularly beloved by William: history. This collection is a series of complete and excerpted works designed to provide a reasonably connected account of Roman history, from the siege of Troy to the Greek and German emperors of William's own day. It begins with Dares Phrygius, followed by excerpts from 'Cato', Justin and others, then Orosius. After these follows a long section put together from Eutropius, Jordanes and Paul the Deacon, along lines best explained by William himself in a prefatory note:[158]

> Sequentes x. libros de gestis Romanorum Eutropius ad Valentem imperatorem edidit. Quibus quia Paulus Montis Cassinensis monachus multa adiecit, curae nobis fuit nomina eorum separatim ponere ut quid a quo dictum sit lector possit intelligere. Sequentes etiam v. libros

---

[156] (i) Ed. MGH Epist. 2, pp. 509–14, and *Corpus Consuetudinum Monasticarum*, I, ed. K. Hallinger (Siegburg, 1967), pp. 139–175, listing 33 MSS. This copy is said to be derived from Trier, Stadtbibliothek 1202/501 (s. x, from St Maximin), and to be similar to BL Add. 22633 (s. xii, probably from Seligenstadt). (ii) K. Hallinger, *Gorze-Kluny* (2 vols, Rome, 1950 and Graz, 1971), I, pp. 450–1. It is printed in H. Weihrich, *Urkundenbuch der Reichsabtei Hersfeld* (Marburg, 1936), pp. 199–202, n. 113, not using the Oriel Coll. MS.

[157] This is demonstrated below, pp. 132–3.

[158] Oxford, Bodl. Libr. Arch. Seld. B. 16, f. 73 (GR I, p. cxxxiv).

usque ad Iustinianum idem Paulus ex pluribus auctoribus et maxime Orosio et Iordane contexuit, sicut in margine annotare curabimus. Paulo autem sicut Orosium preposuimus ita Iordanem subiecimus, ut ex utroque latere habeat lector integros quos iste putauit deflorandos. A Iustiniano autem usque ad Ludouicum collegit Haimo monachus.

We have already mentioned a number of ancient historians known to William: Caesar, Sallust, Suetonius, Josephus, Hegesippus, Eusebius/ Rufinus, Cassiodorus (*Historia Tripartita*). More interesting is the large number of later works of this character with which he was familiar. We might begin with the last chronicle excerpted in the Selden Collection, that by 'Haimo' of Fleury. This is in William's hand, and begins with a prologue by him:[159]

Precedentium gesta imperatorum Iordanes episcopus et Paulus dia-conus texuerunt. Sequentium acta Haimo monachus Floriacensis ex diuersis auctoribus collegit. Eius ergo semper sensum aliquando uerba ponemus, omissis quicunque de Longabardis, Francis, Gothis im-miscuit. Earum enim gentium alias propriis libris leguntur.

The first thing to say about what follows is that it is not Haimo (Aimoin), but the *Historia Ecclesiastica* of William's older contemporary Hugh of Fleury, in the second edition of 1110.[160] William continued it briefly to 1129, and an interpolation by him indicates that that was the year in which he copied this text.[161] How William came to write 'Haimo' for 'Hugh' is not clear. Probably he had before him a manuscript either with that name in it, or with the initial H., from which he conjectured, having heard of the earlier Fleury chronicler. He was not the only English writer to make this mistake: Ralph of Diss, later in the century, also refers to 'Haimo' meaning 'Hugh'.[162]

   Returning to our chronological order, let us see what early European historians William did know: Bede and Paul the Deacon have already been mentioned. He had read both Paul's Roman and Lombard histories, which were usually copied together, and also the 'interpolated version' of his *Vita*

---

[159] ibid., f. 135 (GR I, p. cxxxiv).
[160] Ed. B. Rottendorff, *Hugonis Floriacensis Monachi Benedictini Chronicon* (Münster, 1638); cf. A. Vidier, *L'historiographie à Saint Benoît-sur-Loire et les miracles de saint Benoît* (Paris, 1965), pp. 76–9. On knowledge of Hugh's work in twelfth-century England see Brett, 'John of Worcester and his Contemporaries', p. 118 and nn. William and John of Worcester were apparently the first to use him.
[161] See below, p. 177.
[162] *Radulfi de Diceto Opera*, ed. W. Stubbs (London, RS, 2 vols, 1876), II, p. xviii.

Gregorii, which he quotes in the biographical introduction to his own *Defloratio Gregorii*.[163] References in his two major historical works indicate that he knew Bede's *Historia Abbatum* and *Vita Cuthberti* as well as the *Historia Ecclesiastica*.[164] From here on we can conveniently divide William's historical reading into continental and English. I take the continental first.

Other Carolingian chronicles known to him were those by Freculf of Lisieux and Ado of Vienne, and the so-called *Continuatio Adonis* with some genealogical material and the *Visio Karoli Crassi* that went with it.[165] The identification of Oxford, Bodleian Library MS Lat. class. d. 39 as a later copy of a collection of materials for Carolingian history compiled by William enables us to add, in particular, Einhard and the *Annales Mettenses Priores*.[166] Yet more historical works, covering a chronological range from the early eighth until the late eleventh century, were excerpted by William for his unique edition of the *Liber Pontificalis*.[167] Its skeleton was constructed from two pre-existing versions of *Liber Pontificalis*, one reaching to 715, the other finishing c.795, plus a *Papstkatalog* which ended in 1087. For the earliest section at least William may have had a very early manuscript. Into this framework he interpolated from a wide variety of sources, some historical or literary, many documentary. Some, such as Einhard, the *Breviarium Alaricum* and the *Anglo-Saxon Chronicle*, we have met already. The most remarkable of his sources, however, was a collection of Latin inscriptions from churches in England, Rome and elsewhere, made for Bishop Milred of Worcester (745–775). William included excerpts from it in both of his major historical works as well as the *Liber Pontificalis*. A fragment of the tenth-century manuscript which he used, and which he may have procured for his monastery, still survives. Possibly in the same manuscript, but in any case illustrating the same interest of William's, is the otherwise unknown *Itinerarium Urbis Romae* originally made in the second

---

163 Both works are mentioned and extracted in Oxford, Bodl. Libr. Arch. Seld. B. 16; the *Hist. Lomb.* is also quoted in GR II, p. 486, and in *De Miraculis B.V.M.*, p. 87; not printed by Farmer, 'William of Malmesbury's Commentary on Lamentations', pp. 309–311. The extract falls between the introduction and the chapters.

164 *Vit. Cuth.*: GP, p. 267; *Hist. Eccl.*: GR and GP, passim; *Hist. Abbatum*: GP, p. 328.

165 Freculf: GR I, p. 24, AG, pp. 43–4; for Ado, the *Continuatio*, the genealogies and the *Visio* see below, pp. 148–50, 152–4.

166 ibid., pp. 144, 146–7.

167 For this work see below, ch. 6.

half of the seventh century, which he summarized in the *Gesta Regum*.[168]

More recent continental historians known to William were William of Poitiers and William of Jumièges on the Norman Conquest of England, Fulcher of Chartres and the *Itinerarium Bernardi* on Palestine and the first Crusade.[169] In the *Gesta Regum* he quotes from the lost History of Henry V's Italian expedition by David the Scot, and he knew Marianus Scotus's chronicle as well as the computistic treatise by Bishop Robert of Hereford based upon it.[170] William copied Robert's treatise into his own collection of astronomical and chronological writings.[171]

When we return to Insular historical works, there was very little still accessible today which was not known to William, and in addition he knew some works, or versions of works now lost. He had Eddi Stephen's *Vita Wilfridi*, and the way in which he attempts to combine Eddi's and Bede's account of the controversial bishop throws light on his historical method.[172] He knew 'Nennius' and perhaps Gildas as well; William calls him 'neque insulsus neque infacetus historicus'.[173]

Coming to the tenth and eleventh centuries, we find that William knew some royal genealogies, Frithegod's *Breviloquium Vitae Wilfridi*, Ethelweard, whose style he detested, Asser, perhaps in an abridged version, a lost

---

[168] GR II, pp. 404–8. This document, which survives only in William's extracts, was dated between A.D. 648 and 682 by G. de Rossi, *La Roma sotteranea christiana*, I (Rome, 1864), p. 146. The basis for his argument is the omission of certain information about some of the *loca sancta*. William's extracts were edited with commentary by R. Valentini and G. Zucchetti, *Codice Topografico della Città di Roma*, II (*Fonti per la Storia d'Italia* 88, Rome, 1942), pp. 133–153, who are more cautious about the date of William's source, arguing that William did not claim to be making a literal copy; the omissions therefore might be his and not the document's (ibid., p. 135). William however states only that he intends to alter the style of his source, not its information (GR II, p. 404). De Rossi's argument therefore, I believe, stands.

[169] William of Poitiers: GR II, pp. 285–300; William of Jumièges: GR I, p. 160ff; Fulcher: GR II, p. 402ff; *Itinerarium*: ibid., p. 423.

[170] David the Scot: GR II, pp. 498–9; Marianus: his Chronicle seems to be the source of the Easter Tables in Oxford, Bodl. Libr. Auct. F. 3. 14, William's collection of computistical treatises. Collation shows that the MS used was not London, BL Cott. Nero E. v, the late eleventh-century copy from Worcester. Robert of Hereford: GR II, p. 345; Stevenson, 'A Contemporary Description of the Domesday Survey', pp. 72–74.

[171] Oxford, Bodl. Libr. Auct. F. 3. 14; Stevenson, op. cit.

[172] GP, p. 6ff, 210ff. It is not true, as Hamilton stated (ibid., p. 222 n. 2) that William used MS C of Eddi (London, BL Cott. Vesp. D. vi). Collation of William's extracts with the edition of B. Colgrave (Eddius Stephanus, *Life of Wilfrid* [Cambridge, 1927]) shows that William's exemplar was better than either of the two extant MSS of Eddi's work.

[173] 'Nennius': GR I, p. 4ff; Gildas: ibid., pp. 5–6, 20; II, p. xix.

poem on Athelstan, and the Anglo-Saxon Chronicle.[174] The last suggests again William's rummaging through the *armaria* of the two great Canterbury houses. It has been shown that he used the so-called E-type version of the Chronicle, the ancestor of which was at St Augustine's by the mid eleventh century.[175] William seems not to have had the extant copy E, which was at Peterborough when he wrote. Until 1121 the annals in this manuscript were copied en bloc, whereas subsequent entries were made at intervals of time, thus at Peterborough. William does not use the Chronicle after c.1120, and therefore seems to have had the Canterbury archetype which ended in 1121, and which was still at Canterbury in the early twelfth century at least.

William's reading of history, especially English, shades off into biography and hagiography. It would be tedious to list here the number of these kinds of works which he is known to have read, but just one or two may be mentioned. For instance, in his *Vita Dunstani*, as Stubbs shows, he used the Life of Dunstan by the priest B., mainly following the version revised at St Augustine's Canterbury in the early eleventh century.[176] Again we are left in little doubt as to where William picked up his copy. But he did not go only to Canterbury. He also had the first edition of the Life, which he found at Glastonbury.[177] Here too he presumably discovered some of the sources for his *Vita S. Patricii*: Vita III (in the π-version associated with Glastonbury), W (the lost ancestor of *Vitae* II and IV), and Patrick's *Confessio*.[178]

[174] Genealogies: GR I, p. 18 and n. 1, II, pp. xxi–xxii; Frithegod: GP, p. 22; Ethelweard: GR I, pp. 1, 121; Asser: GR I, p. 109ff, and Whitelock, 'William of Malmesbury on the Works of King Alfred', pp. 78–93; Poem on Athelstan: GR I, pp. 145–6, and M. Lapidge, 'Some Latin Poems as Evidence for the Reign of Athelstan', ASE, 9 (1980), 62–71; *Chronicle*: GR I, p. 11ff, and *ASC*, pp. xx–xxi.

[175] ibid., pp. xx, xiv–xvii. But see C. Clark (ed.), *The Peterborough Chronicle* (Oxford, 2nd edn, 1970), pp. xxi–xxiii, and D. Dumville in *Peritia*, 2 (1983), 23–57.

[176] VD, p. xxix.

[177] ibid., p. xxxvii.

[178] L. Bieler, *The Life and Legend of St Patrick* (Dublin, 1949), p. 121ff; idem, *Four Latin Lives of St Patrick (Scriptores Latini Hibernienses 8*, Dublin, 1971), pp. 22–5. Bieler was not entirely certain about William's knowledge of W, but this is confirmed by J. Carley in his edition of John of Glastonbury, *Cronica* (Woodbridge, 1985), pp. xxvii, 281–2. On the other hand on p. 24 of his edition Bieler says that William knew Muirchu as well as the *Confessio*. But the only items in William which are in Muirchu but not in the *Confessio* are the words 'Haud procul' instead of 'non longe' (Bieler, op. cit. and n. 2). It is easier, on this basis, to conclude that William made the substitution independently for stylistic reasons, or that he found the passage at second hand, than that he had a copy of the very rare Muirchu.

VI. BELLES LETTRES

William loved 'literature' in the modern sense, for its own sake. He took immense pains over his prose style and was an avid if indifferent versifier. We noticed earlier his taste for Virgil and Cicero, and his censure of the obscure latinity of a Frithegod or Ethelweard. His perception of style was acute and sensitive. In the collection of Leo's sermons and letters which he copied into the Oriel manuscript, he correctly pronounces two sermons ungenuine, on the basis of their style.[179] On the other hand he was full of praise for some of his contemporaries: Osbern and Eadmer of Canterbury, Godfrey of Winchester and, above all, Hildebert of Le Mans.[180] He praises Godfrey in the *Gesta Regum*, and, in the preface to book II of the *Polyhistor*, announces that he will include some of his epigrams.[181] For some reason they do not appear in the two extant manuscripts. Hildebert is also praised in the *Gesta Regum*, and William, with typical good taste, included there two of the bishop's finest poems, on Rome and on the death of Berengar.[182]

In the *Vita Aldhelmi* William concluded his account of the saint's last hours with a Latin poem in his praise.[183] It is introduced without comment of any kind, and it seems natural to assume that it was William's own composition, especially as it is similar in many respects to other pieces of verse more certainly his. But what gives it a special interest is its first line, lifted verbatim from Hildebert's poem on the death of Bruno of Chartreuse. Other similarities appear later in the poem,[184] leaving little doubt that Hildebert's was the model for William's. Earlier in the *Gesta Pontificum* he quotes a single line from Hildebert, *Carm. Min.* 17.[185] Thus he knew at least four of the bishop's shorter poems. This makes it likely that he possessed some sort of 'collected edition'. Can it be identified?

---

[179] Farmer, 'Life and Works', p. 50. Oriel Coll. MS 42, f. 189v 'Non est de stilo Leonis pape hic sermo'; f. 192v 'Non congruit stilo Leonis'.
[180] Osbern: GR I, p. 166 (but William censures him on other grounds in VD, pp. 251–2, 322–3); Eadmer: GR I, pp. 1–2; Godfrey: GR II, pp. 513, 516; Hildebert: GR II, pp. 338–40, 402–3.
[181] PH, p. 101.
[182] The poems are *Carm. Min.* 18 and 36 in Scott, *Hildeberti Carmina Minora*, pp. 7–9, 22–4.
[183] GP, p. 382.
[184] Scott, pp. 18–19. Both poems give the date of the subject's death; both have a mythological reference (Hild., 1. 3 'Protea'; Wm., 1. 5 'Phebus', 'Laconas'); the last word of Hildebert's is 'adit' (but 'abit' in earlier editions), of William's, 'abit'. Scott attributes the version in GP to an anonymous versifier, but William would almost certainly have given some indication if it were not his own composition. Cf GP, p. 192.
[185] GP, p. 142 n. 4.

There are in fact three manuscripts containing the four *carmina minora* known to William.[186] One of them, Paris, B.N. Baluz. 120, is a modern transcript from several earlier continental manuscripts and therefore not relevant for our inquiry. The other two are Dublin, Trinity Coll. B. 2. 17 (Scott's D), and a copy of it, Hereford Cathedral P. I. 15 (He). D is dated about the middle or late twelfth century, its earliest known home Gloucester cathedral priory, where it was probably written, since He, copied from it late in the century, includes Hereford material (Gilbert Foliot's letters) and in the next century belonged to the Friars Minor there. D, then, although too late to have been known to William, does come from his *Kulturkreis*. A collation of the texts of *Carm. Min.* 18 and 36 in William's version and D leaves little doubt that William had access to the ancestor of D and He.[187] Like them it would have contained *Carm. min.* 1–43, that is, most of the certainly attributed shorter poems. It had good readings, judging from D, and probably came directly from the continent, since the latest dateable poem in it was written after 1114, and William had it before 1125.[188] D also contains Hildebert's *Vita S. Mariae Aegyptiacae* and Ivo's correspondence, but these items, especially the second, need not have been included in William's Hildebert manuscript; they could have been added from elsewhere by D's copyist. On the other hand William certainly knew Hildebert's *De Mysterio Missae*, an item not in D.

William was very much aware of the literary achievement of his contemporaries, and several of his statements show that he saw his own time as a renaissance of correct, antique latinity.[189]

VII. LITERARY TRAVELS AND CONTACTS

Having reviewed the main categories of William's wide and omnivorous reading, I wish to conclude by examining the question of where he obtained

---

186 The MSS are listed and described by Scott, pp. viii–xiv.

187 *Carm. Min.* 18: line 6 decus] dolor Wm.; forma] summa Wm.ZG; 13 cum] eum Wm.KZ; 24 factus] pauper Wm.; 28 nil] uel Wm.DCKW; 29 minimum] quenquam Wm.; 36 iste] Wm., ille DB; 40 prefuit] preminet Wm.; 44 posset] possit Wm.G; 45–8 *om.* Wm.G; 50 donat] ditat Wm.CG. *Carm. Min.* 36: 15 materiem] materiam Wm.D; 29, 30 *post* 22 *transpos.* Wm.DMR; 23–4 *om.* Wm. DMZ; 27 stanti] Wm., tanti D. This list includes all the variant readings of D and Wm. (the latter somewhat inaccurately recorded by Scott); the other MSS exhibit many more variants which separate them quite clearly from D and Wm.

188 *Carm. Min.* 37 was written between 1114 and 1118 (Scott, p. xxix). The first editions of GR and GP were completed by 1125: see above, pp. 3–4.

189 E.g. GP, p. 172, on Godfrey of Winchester: 'Quid omne diuinum officium, quod uenustate (uetustate MS) quadam obsoletum, natiua excultum uetustate fecit splendescere'.

his exemplars. This can frequently be answered either from textual evidence, or from information provided by William himself. From passages in his works we can deduce that he travelled widely and purposefully to track down books and documents, both for his historical work, and to augment the Malmesbury library.[190] We have already indicated, of course, that he found some books locally, such as the writings of Aldhelm and other Old English works, and perhaps the *Breviarium Alaricum* and *Codex Milredi*. But William himself bemoans the depleted and neglected state of the library as his predecessors left it, and the loss in particular of many ancient works by famous English writers.[191] The two Canterbury houses, so the evidence would suggest, were his principal target. He visited Christ Church not long after 1100, perhaps between 1109 and c.1115, talking with, and examining the writings of Eadmer and Alexander.[192] He may have been at St Augustine's between 1122 and 1125, the dates between which he had access to the copy of the Anglo-Saxon Chronicle from that house. He held Eadmer in high esteem and knew most of his works. In the *Gesta Regum* he quotes the first version of the *Historia Novorum*, completed soon after 1109, and the *Vita Anselmi*.[193] But by the time he completed the *Gesta Pontificum*, later in the same year, he had read more recent versions of both works, completed in about 1120 and 1122 respectively.[194] This seems to imply close contact with Canterbury, perhaps by means of a visit, during 1125. From the *Vita Wulfstani* we know that he visited Worcester cathedral between 1113 and 1124, and again between c.1124 and c.1142.[195] One of the two surviving manuscripts of his *Commentary on Lamentations*, dating from about the mid century, is from Worcester.[196] By 1125, on the completion of the first edition of the *Gesta Regum*, he had been to Oxford, where he investigated the archives of St Frideswide's.[197] But the evidence of the *Gesta Pontificum*

---

[190] See above, p. 51. For other statements of motive, see GP, p. 431 and GR I, p. 213.
[191] GP, pp. 361, 432.
[192] See above, pp. 46–7, 70.
[193] *Hist. Nov.*: GR I, pp. 1–2; II, p. 489ff; *Vit. Anselmi*: ibid., p. 377ff, GP, p. 74ff; Southern, *St Anselm and his Biographer*, p. 299; *De Excell. B. Mariae: De Miraculis B.V.M.*, pp. 52–5; Carter, 'The Historical Content of William of Malmesbury's Miracles of the Virgin Mary', p. 133; *Miracula S. Dunstani, Vita S. Oswaldi*: GR I, p. 167, GP, pp. 247–50, VD, pp. 303–4.
[194] GP, p. 123 et al.; Southern, op. cit., p. 304.
[195] VW, pp. ix, 1, 54.
[196] Oxford, Bodl. Libr. Bodl. 868; the text of the commentary, evidently the product of a monastic scriptorium judging by its script, format and decoration, is followed, in a less formal and slightly later hand, by a copy of a bull of Pope Alexander III in favour of Worcester, dated c.1170. There is also a thirteenth-century Worcester *ex libris*.
[197] GR I, p. 213.

shows that by the same date he had made a grand tour of England, visiting Thorney, Rochester, Sherborne, Crowland, Hereford, York, Carlisle, Shaftesbury, Bath, Durham, Wareham, Corfe, Gloucester, Bangor, Coventry and Winchester and perhaps Tavistock.[198] The *Antiquity of Glastonbury*, written between 1129 and 1135, enables us to add Glastonbury and Bury, where he found historical works which interested him,[199] and by the second edition of the *Gesta Regum*, c.1135, he had seen records at Milton Abbas.[200] In 1141 he represented his abbey at the Council of Winchester.[201] The evidence suggests a number of journeys through southern England, concentrating especially on religious houses and cathedrals in the neighbourhood of Malmesbury and the east, plus at least one long journey to the far north. There is no evidence that he went overseas, or that he was in direct contact with continental scholars, although Hildebert is a possibility. He did, however, have access to manuscripts written on the continent, although how he obtained them is a mystery.[202]

The evidence for William's contacts with fellow-scholars and book-lovers is thinner than for his visits to libraries. We would give much to know more, but William was extremely coy about his personal life and relations with others. Abbot Faricius of Abingdon, who died in 1117, had been a monk of Malmesbury before 1100.[203] William admired him and used his *Vita Aldhelmi* as a source for his own.[204] Did William know him personally? He was engaged on research for the *Gesta Regum* by 1118, and could therefore have visited Abingdon while Faricius was still alive. More exciting is the possibility that the well-educated Faricius taught him as a novice. Robert of Cricklade, prior of St Frideswide's, writing soon after March 1137, praises William's *De Miraculis, Commentary on Lamentations* and *Defloratio Gregorii*.[205] Although William visited St Frideswide's before 1125, Robert

---

[198] Thorney: GP, pp. 326–7; Rochester: pp. 133, 138; Sherborne: p. 177; Crowland: pp. 321–2; Hereford: pp. 298–9; York: pp. 208–9; Carlisle: p. 208; Shaftesbury: pp. 186–7; Bath: p. 194; Durham: p. 270; Wareham: pp. 363–4; Corfe: p. 364; Gloucester: pp. 273; Bangor: p. 326; Coventry: p. 311; Winchester: pp. 172–3; ?Tavistock: pp. 202–3.

[199] AG, pp. 1, 50.

[200] GR I, p. 154 n. 2; GP, p. 400.

[201] HN, p. 52.

[202] I refer, for example, to the exemplars for the second part of his copy of John the Scot's *Periphyseon* (See below, p. 91) and for the astronomical tracts in his collection of computistica (See below, p. 197), to Oxford, Bodl. Libr. Bodl. 852, brought from Jumièges to Malmesbury in his time (See below, pp. 79–80).

[203] GP, p. 192; D. Knowles, C. N. L. Brooke and V. London, *The Heads of Religious Houses England and Wales 940–1216* (Cambridge, 1972), p. 25.

[204] GP, pp. 192, 330–1.

[205] R. W. Hunt, 'English Learning in the late Twelfth Century', pp. 117–8. For the date, ibid., p. 117 n. 3, corrected in Knowles, Brooke and London, *Heads*, p. 79.

was not there until c.1140.[206] Nonetheless he was a canon of Cirencester, only about twelve miles from Malmesbury, and it is possible that he had met William when he wrote so warmly of his writings. We have already mentioned William's more certain contacts with the Canterbury scholars Eadmer and Alexander. Although linked by some common reading (probably via Canterbury), John of Salisbury and William almost certainly never met, since John was in France from about 1135 until after William's death.[207] Before that his movements are uncertain. Another interesting contemporary, whom William must certainly have met more than once, is John of Worcester, continuator, if not author, of the chronicle supposedly written by 'Florence'.[208] There are several pointers to close relations between the two men, the most important being the evidence for an exchange of information used in their respective historical writings.[209] We know that William visited Worcester at least once during John's lifetime. Cambridge University Library MS Kk. 4. 6, partly in John's hand, contains a copy of William's *Liber Pontificalis*.[210] Two of the three surviving copies of Bishop Robert of Hereford's computistic tract were written for John and William, although their precise relationship cannot be determined.[211] Probably both men made independent transcriptions of a Hereford manuscript. John himself travelled; between 1132 and 1139 he was searching for new material; in c.1134 he was at Winchcombe, about thirty miles from Malmesbury.[212]

It remains, then, to give a hand-list of the works known, with total or reasonable certainty, to William at first hand.[213] Despite the modifications which must be made to M. R. James's introductory sketch of William's reading, one at least of his dicta still stands: 'Only one writer of the century can be said to rival him in his literary equipment, and that is the somewhat younger John of Salisbury, the range of whose reading is co-extensive with William's, though naturally differing from it both by excess and defect'.[214]

---

[206] ibid., p. 180.
[207] W. J. Millor, H. E. Butler and C. N. L. Brooke (ed. and trans.), *The Letters of John of Salisbury*, I (London, 1955), pp. xii–xix.
[208] *The Chronicle of John of Worcester, 1118–1140*, ed. J. R. H. Weaver (*Anecdota Oxoniensia, Medieval and Modern Series*, 13 [1908]); VW, pp. xvii–xviii.
[209] Brett, 'John of Worcester and his Contemporaries', pp. 113–7.
[210] For the MS and this work in it see below, ch. 6.
[211] Oxford, Bodl. Libr. Auct. F. 3. 14 (William); Auct. F. 1. 9 (John).
[212] Weaver, p. 10.
[213] See below, Appendix I.
[214] James, *Two Ancient English Scholars*, p. 30. On the similarities and differences between John's and William's learning see above, pp. 6–10.

4

WILLIAM'S 'SCRIPTORIUM'

NOT ONLY A great historian, William was also, as we have seen, an omnivorous reader and an indefatigible collector of books for his abbey library. From his own statements and from textual evidence we know that he scoured the country between c.1115 and c.1140 looking for ancient volumes and rare works. The details of this large undertaking are mysterious and fascinating, provoking many questions. Did he purchase or otherwise obtain old or 'second-hand' copies? Did he have new copies made where the exemplar was held, or did he borrow the exemplar and have the copying done at Malmesbury? If the copying was done locally, how was it organized? What part did he himself play? Did he form a regular team of scribes to assist him? How did he set out his books? The mechanics of William's acquisition programme, seen in terms of these and related questions, are my concern in this chapter.

Let me first outline what has already been done in this direction. By the last century William's own hand had been recognized in more than one book. The starting point for these identifications was (as it still must be) the autograph copy of the *Gesta Pontificum*, Oxford, Magdalen Coll. MS lat. 172.[1] The work of Hamilton and Stubbs was corrected and amplified in 1938 by Neil Ker.[2] Since then William's hand has been found in other manuscripts which are listed in the 1964 edition of Dr Ker's *Medieval Libraries of Great Britain*.[3] Thus at the present time William's hand and its main characteristics are well known, although there is room for detailed work on his scribal habits and their changes during the course of his life. For instance, although

---

[1] Described by N. E. S. A. Hamilton, who used it as the basis of his edition of GP; ibid., pp. xi–xix. For other literature see below, p. 80 n. 26.
[2] Ker, 'Handwriting'.
[3] MLGB, p. 128.

William always wrote what may be described as a 'scholar's' hand,[4] he had both formal and informal versions of it (pls 1–2), using the latter alongside the former, for corrections and annotations. But he also wrote complete texts in the less formal style.[5] To what extent, then, was his formal hand an improvement developed in the course of long practice? I shall touch upon this question below, although the scanty evidence makes an assured answer impossible.[6] On the many scribes who helped William copy his books, and on the physical disposition of the books themselves, nothing has been written. Thus William's helpers and William's books, rather than William himself in his role as scribe, will be my main concerns here.

The nature of the evidence presents thorny problems. This chapter is quite deliberately not entitled 'William of Malmesbury and the Abbey Scriptorium' or something similar, for we are dealing at most with sixteen manuscripts, namely all those hitherto identified Malmesbury books dating from or before William's time. All but four can be directly associated with William, that is to say with his copying, supervision or acquisition. Indeed, this association has until now provided virtually the only criterion for identifying Malmesbury books from the first half of the twelfth century and earlier. As a consequence we are compelled to speak of 'William's' scriptorium (if 'scriptorium' at all), not the abbey's. It is to be hoped that the illustrations of the hands of William's main assistants and of the Malmesbury pressmark provided below (pls 3–5) will enable more manuscripts to be connected with the house.

How much can be learnt even of William's own copying programme from such scanty materials? Of the dozen manuscripts that can be connected with him, two, I shall show, are, for special reasons, of little assistance in our inquiry. The remaining ten are a diverse group in many ways, so that it is difficult to generalize confidently or reach sure conclusions from them. All that we can expect are impressions, and those fragmentary, potentially open

---

[4] Cf. the hands of other monastic scholars such as Orderic Vitalis and Guibert of Nogent: M. Chibnall (ed.), *The Ecclesiastical History of Orderic Vitalis*, I (Oxford, 1980), pp. 201–203, for a list of the manuscripts copied or annotated by Orderic, and references to the early but fundamental work by Delisle on Orderic as scribe; M.-C. Garand, 'Le Scriptorium de Guibert de Nogent', *Scriptorium*, 31 (1977), 3–29. On scholars' note-hands in general see T. J. Brown in Herrad of Hohenbourg, *Hortus Deliciarum*, ed. R. Green, M. Evans and others (London and Leiden, 1979), I, pp. 81–5.

[5] In particular Oxford, Magdalen College MS lat. 172 and part of Oxford, Lincoln College MS lat. 100.

[6] The earliest precisely dateable appearance of his 'formal' hand is in Oxford, Bodl. Libr. MS Arch. Seld. B. 16, written in 1129 (see below, pp. 92–3). However the original text of Oxford, Magdalen College MS lat. 172, written in or soon after 1125, is in his informal style. Some of the additions made to it between 1125 and 1135 are in his 'formal' hand, but none of them can be dated as early as the Selden manuscript.

to modification or contradiction by the future discovery of more of William's books.

What *is* certain is that William went some way towards developing a team of competent and experienced scribes to assist him. Among the fifty-one different hands (besides his own) found in these ten books, four collaborate with him more than once (scribes A-D; pls 6–18). These can reasonably be described as William's 'assistants'.

Let us begin with those early Malmesbury manuscripts least closely associated with William. The first (Oxford, Bodleian Library Marshall 19) is the most ancient surviving Malmesbury book, a ninth-century copy, in Carolingian minuscule, of Jerome (Philo), *De Interpretatione Nominum Hebraicorum*, sewn into an early limp leather wrapper.[7] On f. 1 a late eleventh-century hand has added the first two lines of the verses which also appear in Cambridge, Corpus Christi College 23, and which associate the two manuscripts with Malmesbury.[8] MS Marshall 19 was probably part of the ancient *fonds* of its library. We can be sure that William knew it, although it has none of his marks. It is a beautiful and important manuscript. So is the late tenth-century illustrated copy of Prudentius's works (Cambridge, Corpus Christi College 23), perhaps made at Christ Church Canterbury, but presented to Malmesbury in the same century.[9] William knew at least one of the works contained in it,[10] and must have known the book, but again it has no marks to connect it with him. What it does have of interest is a framed prefatory paragraph on Prudentius and his works extracted from Gennadius's *De Viris Illustribus*. William was in the habit of prefacing his collections with just such bio-bibliographical notices.[11] Perhaps he learnt this practice from some much earlier Malmesbury librarian, but I do not know of any books besides the Prudentius with these notices.[12] Third comes the meagre remains (a bifolium only) of a tenth-century English manuscript containing copies of inscriptions in Latin verse.[13] It is now

---

[7] *Summary Catalogue of Western Manuscripts in the Bodleian Library* (7 vols, Oxford, 1895–1953), 5265; B. Lambert, *Bibliotheca Hieronymiana Manuscripta*, II (Steenbrugge, 1959), p. 201.

[8] See below, pp. 113–14.

[9] The most recent account of its origin, including a full bibliography, is in E. Temple, *Anglo-Saxon Manuscripts 900–1066* (London, 1976), n. 48. For the verse inscription see M. R. James, *A Descriptive Catalogue of the MSS in the Library of Corpus Christi College Cambridge* (Cambridge, 2 vols, 1909–12), I, p. 44. 'Athelward', the donor of the book to St Aldhelm, was presumably the abbot of Malmesbury who reigned c.1033–44 (not 1040–50, as Temple: cf. Knowles, Brooke and London, *Heads*, p. 54).

[10] He knew Prudentius's *Peristephanon*; see below, p. 206.

[11] See above, p. 34.

[12] William knew Gennadius's work; see below, p. 203.

[13] Urbana, University of Illinois Library MS 128. See below, p. 128.

known that the original manuscript was a copy of a *Sylloge Inscriptionum* put together c.760 by Bishop Milred of Worcester, and that it was William's source for items reproduced by him in his *Gesta Pontificum*.[14] It was perhaps William himself who brought it to Malmesbury, where it was still to be found in John Leland's time.[15] Next we have an eleventh-century, continental copy of Gregory's *Pastoral Care* (Cambridge, Corpus Christi College 361).[16] This has an early fifteenth-century Malmesbury *ex libris*, but a hand which I believe to be William's has made some textual corrections and divided the work into three *partitiones*.[17] It certainly did not arrive in England or at Malmesbury before his time.[18]

Finally, we have an interesting collection of saints' Lives (Oxford, Bodleian Library Bodley 852), written at Jumièges and dateable from the list of abbots of that place contained in it.[19] The scribe responsible for most of the manuscript wrote all of the list to Abbot Robert III, who reigned c.1049–c.1072. Thus the book must have been written between these dates. The names of two more abbots were added by later hands. The last added name is Ursus (abbot 1106–1126), so the book must have come to Malmesbury after the beginning of his reign. It has a fourteenth-century Malmesbury *ex libris* and pressmark (pl. 3), and a slightly later inscription stating that William caused it to be made ('fecit scribi'), which is quite wrong. His hand does not appear in it, yet it seems probable that this book was at Malmesbury by his time and that he knew it. The writer of the Malmesbury *ex libris* also provided a table of contents which includes two items, the *passiones* of St Paternus and St Elphege, now lost.[20] They were probably gone when the book was acquired by the Bodleian Library (before 1618–20) and certainly by the middle of the seventeenth century when

---

[14] See below, pp. 126–30.

[15] It is annotated by Leland, who in his *Collectanea* reproduces a series of inscriptions from a MS which he found at Malmesbury. Some of these are in the Urbana fragment, and collation indicates that that was his source for them. See below, p. 128.

[16] James, *Catalogue of MSS in Corpus Christi College Cambridge*, II, pp. 193–4.

[17] Corrections, almost certainly William's, occur on f. 65 line 19 and f. 69 line 25 (both alterations to the form of the letter **g**; others may be his. The *partitiones* are marked at ff. 11, 32 and 102.

[18] Since a *Passio S. Mauricii* has been added to the last verso in a continental (probably Norman) hand of c.1100.

[19] *Summary Cat.* 2611; O. Pächt and J. J. G. Alexander, *Illuminated Manuscripts in the Bodleian Library Oxford*, I (Oxford, 1966), no. 439 and pl. xxxvi.

[20] F. v^v: 'In isto libro continentur uita sancti Aychadri abbatis; item uita sancti Philiberti abbatis; item passio sancti Paterni episcopi et martyris; item passio uel uita sancti Elphegi martyris; item uita sancti Wlganii confessoris. [Then a blank line.] Item Ieronimus ad Cromatium et Eliodorum episcopos de natiuitate beate Marie et de eiusdem consolacione usque ad ortum domini'.

Gerard Langbaine foliated it.[21] The same two works, though in reverse order, were in London, BL Cott. Vitell. D. xvii, ff. 1–22, before the fire of 1731.[22] This manuscript is now in ruins, charred, shrunken and remounted. It was obviously a Cottonian makeup, in which ff. 1–22 comprised a unit separate from the rest. Only three leaves from this part survive, apparently containing parts of the *Passio* and *Translatio* of St Elphege. The leaves have shrunk and have lost the outer margins and some of the text, but originally they must have approximated to the size of the leaves in MS Bodley 852. The hand of Vitell. D. xvii is Norman and of the late eleventh century; it is like the hands of the Bodleian manuscript, though not, apparently, identical with any of them. On such grounds Dr Ker tentatively identified the fragment as from the lost portion of MS Bodley 852.[23] There is further evidence to support both this and the proposition that MS Bodley 852 came to Malmesbury in William's time. The *Passio S. Paterni* once in Vitell. D. xvii was most probably the work by Fortunatus; the *Passio et Translatio S. Elphegi* was certainly that by Osbern of Canterbury.[24] William knew both of these works by 1125, mentioning them by name in the *Gesta Pontificum*.[25] Neither of them was uncommon, but it is surely reasonable to suppose that he knew them from the former Jumièges manuscript.

We proceed now to William's books, beginning with those which are least helpful for our present inquiry. This is not to say that the books so denominated are not of the greatest interest for other reasons. The first is the autograph of William's *Gesta Pontificum*, Oxford, Magdalen College MS lat. 172.[26] It throws little light on William's scriptorium because it is *sui generis*. Its edges have been trimmed, but it was always pocket-sized (106 leaves measuring 170×120–5 mm; bounding–lines c.140×85 mm). Although the parchment was well prepared, the makeup into quires is more than usually irregular,[27] no lines were ruled for writing on (hence there is no consistent

---

21 *Summary Cat.*, I, p. 103 no. 909. On Langbaine's foliation see ibid., p. xxiv.

22 T. Smith, *Catalogus Librorum Manuscriptorum Bibliothecae Cottonianae* (London, 1696), p. 94.

23 It is entered among the MLGB cards kept in the Bodleian Library, as Dr Ker was kind enough to inform me.

24 The only Life of Paternus recorded in the *Bibliotheca Hagiographica Latina* is Fortunatus's work (BHL 6477), edited in MGH Auct. Antiqu. 4, ii. pp. 33–7. Osbern's writings on St Elphege were edited, using this manuscript, by T. Wharton, *Anglia Sacra*, II (London, 1691), pp. 122–147.

25 GP, pp. 33, 399.

26 Ibid., pp. xi–xix; H. O. Coxe, *Catalogus Codicum MSS qui in Collegiis Aulisque Oxoniensibus hodie adservantur* (Oxford, 2 vols, 1852), II, p. 79; Ker, 'Handwriting', pp. 371–2.

27 Collation: 1¹⁰, 2¹², 3¹⁰ (wants 1 and 8), 4¹⁰ (wants 5), 5–7⁸, 8¹⁴, 9¹⁰, 10¹², 11⁸ (wants 6).

number of lines of text to a page) and the only decoration is a few plain red initials and others touched with red. William was responsible for the rubrication and probably for the painted initials as well. He wrote all of the text except for a twelfth-century pen-trial on the erased lower portion of f. 39v.[28] His hand varies much in size and formality, and there are erasures, cancellations, marginal and interlinear additions *passim*. On f. 1 the Prologue is in a tiny hand, whereas the opening of Book I (ending in the middle of the bottom line) is larger, and becomes larger still at the foot of the page. It is possible that all of f. 1 was copied over an erasure. Ff. 1v–10v are in a large, comparatively formal style; ff. 1 (beginning a new quire) to 44v are in a smaller and less formal one; ff. 45–104 are written in a tiny hand again. F. 43v is blank (f. 44 begins the section on Rochester).[29] None of the script is in William's most formal style; it grows less formal as it becomes smaller. Instructive for the workshop-technique of William as historian, the Magdalen manuscript is of less interest for his scribal conventions because of its informality. In spite of these features it does not represent, strictly speaking, a rough draft. It must have begun as a clean but working copy of the first edition of the *Gesta*, thus written after late 1125.[30] It was then revised sporadically over the next decade to provide the basis for the second recension of about 1135. It is thus only a rough draft of that edition.

Cambridge, Corpus Christi College MS 330 is unhelpful because in its essentials it predates William, and part at least was not made at Malmesbury at all. It consists of two separate books, now measuring 220×155 mm, after the trimming of all three edges.[31] The first is a copy of Martianus Capella's *De Nuptiis*, written c.1100 in one small hand of 'Norman' type.[32] The last five lines of the opening verses on f. 1 are in a different hand; the diagram on f. 35v was completed and inscribed in an early twelfth-century hand. It may have been made at Malmesbury by a Norman monk, but it certainly predates the period when William was intellectually active, and it is more likely that he acquired it elsewhere as an adult. He gave it an interlinear and marginal

---

[28] The pen-trial is 'Fateor inbecillitatem meam nolo spe pugnare' (Jerome, *Adv. Vigilant.* xvi; PL 23. 367B). Hamilton (GP, p. 121 n. 1) wrongly attributed it to William and is followed by Gransden, *Historical Writing in England c.550–c.1307*, p. 180. Facsimiles of his hand in this manuscript are given in GP as frontispiece, and in Gransden, pl. v.

[29] GP, p. 133.

[30] The date is established by Stubbs, GR I, pp. xix–xx.

[31] James, *Catalogue of MSS in Corpus Christi College Cambridge*, II, pp. 153–4; C. Leonardi, 'I Codici di Marziano Capella', *Aevum*, 34 (1960), 22–3, no. 30; T. A. M. Bishop, 'The Corpus Martianus Capella', TCBS, 4 (1967), 267; C. Lutz, 'Martianus Capella' in P. O. Kristeller (ed.), *Catalogus Translationum et Commentariorum*, II (Washington, 1971), pp. 371–2; below, p. 113.

[32] Bishop, art. cit., p. 267.

gloss extracted from that by Remigius of Auxerre,[33] at first copiously, but with waning enthusiasm; there are almost no glosses after f. 56. The second book, containing the *Glosae Cantabrigienses in Martianum*, was made on the continent in the late ninth century, although it was in England before the end of the tenth.[34] The fore-edges of the last quire (ff. 33–40) were cropped by a binder with loss of text, and the missing words have been made good by William between the lines, towards the outer margin on the recto and the inner margin on the verso. On f. 39 he does this only for the first few lines, and then is probably guessing. A few textual corrections elsewhere may be his. The last quire is in this condition because the written space gradually widens throughout the book: on f. 1 it is 130 mm wide; by f. 39 the width has increased to 145 mm. The fact that William was able to supply the shorn-off words proves that the damage was done at Malmesbury and in his time; had it occurred earlier he could only have repaired it with the aid of a separate, complete exemplar, an aid difficult to come by in the case of such a rare text as this. Furthermore, since the purpose of the heavy trimming of the second book was to make it conform to the dimensions of the first, we can assume that the two books were bound together in William's time. The first book was also cropped in the process, shaving the outermost letters of some of William's marginal glosses. This shows that he did the glossing before the binding together of the two books. Thus we seem to have a case of William's acquiring or discovering two separate, earlier manuscripts of Martianus, probably at different times: the first he supplied with glosses; later he had the second bound with it. The result was a handy teaching edition of Martianus Capella.

At last we come to the nine manuscripts which shed most light on William's scriptorium, notably because of the presence, in some of them, of the hands of William's identifiable collaborators. They are large and small, roughly- and highly-finished, of varying dates or undateable with any precision, written in a single hand or many. Nevertheless some comments can be made about them as a group. William's books are workmanlike; none is really badly written or carelessly laid out. The best of them are neat and plain, but not in any way splendid. Their decoration is chaste and unexceptional, ranging from plain minium initials to flourished ones in several colours. There is only one example of any artistic ambition, an initial in pen-outline painted with several colours,[35] and only a single example of the use of gold.[36] The quality of the parchment varies, but generally is not of

---

[33] *Remigii Autissiodorensis Commentum in Martianum Capellam*, ed. C. Lutz (Leiden, 1962–5), not mentioning this manuscript.
[34] Lutz in *Catalogus Translationum*, II, pp. 371–2.
[35] Oxford, Merton College MS 181, f. 137; see below, p. 95.
[36] Oxford, Bodl. Libr. MS Arch. Seld. B. 16, f. 1.

the highest; in the least finished products it varies in thickness, has imperfections such as holes, and has not been thoroughly prepared. The arrangement is always HHFF, ruled in drypoint from the hair side. This method of ruling was by the 1130s a conservative one: contemporary books at Canterbury and Worcester were already ruled in plummet.[37] Other details of layout, such as dimensions of written space, number of bounding lines, columns or lines per page, again vary, although they were nearly always carefully done. The scriptorial practices followed in these books were not always conservative. Small-format books in double columns were rarely produced in monastic scriptoria before the second half of the century,[38] but two of William's smaller books have this layout;[39] the Bodleian compu-tistical manuscript (Oxford, Bodleian Library Auct. F. 3. 14), small and in single columns, is the exception. In other ways this book shows scriptorial inexperience – lack of expertise in writing, the absence of a 'house-style', lack of co-ordination of the efforts of different scribes, little correlation between the demands imposed by the items to be copied and the physical features of the book. It may be one of the earliest of William's locally-manufactured books, although this is mere surmise. The makeup of these books into quires is often irregular (for reasons which will be pointed out); when it *is* regular the quires are in eights or occasionally tens. William did not use running titles, and among his books there is only one with quire-signatures and another with catchwords.[40] Three manuscripts have tables of contents by William[41] and there may have been more, but rebinding in modern times has disposed of every flyleaf except these three. The provision of titles to separate works and their subdivision into books and chapters is in general carefully done (Bodleian Library Auct. F. 3. 14 is again an exception), and William has sometimes provided the above-mentioned prefatory bibliographical notes about the authors and their writings.[42]

Let us begin a detailed account of William's scriptorium with three of his books which can be grouped together because they are the roughest of all, and because they all contain passages written by a single scribe (Scribe A; pls 6–8). Oxford, Bodleian Library MS Auct. F. 3. 14 has 164 leaves (modern numbering i–iii, 1–159, but three leaves are numbered '120'), measuring 250×170 mm (bounding lines 170×125 mm). It is the only one of the group

[37] N. R. Ker, *English Manuscripts in the Century after the Norman Conquest* (Oxford, 1960), p. 42. CUL Kk. 4. 6 is a plummet-ruled Worcester manuscript of William's time; see below, pp. 119–122.
[38] Ker, 'Handwriting', p. 375; idem, *English Manuscripts*, p. 42.
[39] Oxford, Lincoln College MS lat. 100; Oxford, Oriel College MS 42.
[40] Cambridge, Trinity College MS O. 5. 20 (1301); CUL Ii. 3. 20.
[41] Oxford, Bodl. Libr. MS Auct. F. 3. 14, f. ii^v; Oxford, Lincoln College MS lat. 100, f. 3; London, Lambeth Palace Library MS 224, f. [ii].
[42] See above, pp. 34, 78.

still in its medieval binding.[43] The flush, unbevelled oak boards are probably twelfth-century and the originals, but the leather and sewing have been renewed since then.[44] Its parchment was of poor quality and ill prepared, its ruling (in 32 long lines per page) was sometimes careless and the justification of the lines by its scribes uneven. Decoration is minimal: on ff. 1–6 are red and green initials, some in both colours with simple foliage; thereafter the initials are red or red-touched. There are diagrams outlined in red, green and blue on ff. 4, 5v, 6v–7v, 9v, 11, 13, 16, 17 and 19v (unfinished). The manuscript contains an interesting collection of computistical texts (Isidore, Helperic, Dionysius, Robert of Hereford and others), put together from several exemplars. Fourteen scribes worked on it (including William himself and two of his collaborators, Scribes A and D), and a separate rubricator, as follows:

William, f. ii[v] (verses and table of contents) and probably ff. 9v lines 23–6, 10 lines 11–15, 10v lines 1–9, 11v, 14 lines 9–10, 15v lines 1–5, 17 lines 9–24, 18 lines 30–41, 19v lines 4–11, 31 lines 1–22, plus smaller annotations and the verses prefacing Bede, *De Natura Rerum*, on f. 20v lines 12–16; he writes his informal script. Hand II ff. 1–1v line 13 (prologue and chapters). Hand III ff. 1v line 14–7v (end of quire); especially with this hand frequent changes of ink are noticeable. Hand IV ff. 8–19v (end of work). Hand V ff. 20–41v. Hand VI ff. 42–63v (end of quire). Hand VII ff. 64–69 line 4. Hand VIII ff. 69 line 5–116, 153 line 29–157v (end of work). Hand IX ff. 116v–120a. Hand X ff. 120va–130v (end of quire). Hand XI ff. 131–145. Hand XII ff. 145v–148v line 17 (end of work). Scribe D ff. 148v line 18–150 line 10. Scribe A ff. 150 line 11–153 line 38 (end of work). The rubricator writes in majuscules, mixed script or (in some instances) almost entirely in minuscules.

Here is an extraordinary repertoire of hands, mostly individualized and startlingly differentiated from each other, mostly unskilled although two or three really fine hands appear for short sections. With a single exception[45] they are uninfluenced by the 'Canterbury' style which derived from Bec,[46]

---

[43] *Summary Cat.* 2372; Ker 'Handwriting', pp. 374–5; Stevenson, 'A Contemporary Description of Domesday Book', pp. 72–84; C. W. Jones, *Bedae Pseudepigrapha* (New York, 1938), p. 126, and *Bedae Opera De Temporibus* (Cambridge, Mass., 1939), p. 154.

[44] Using the criteria listed by G. Pollard, 'Describing Medieval Bookbindings', in *Medieval Learning and Literature*, pp. 50–65.

[45] Hand XII, an elegant, pointed script, perhaps by a Norman scribe. It is like the hand of Scribe B1 found in some early twelfth-century Salisbury manuscripts: N. R. Ker, 'The Beginnings of Salisbury Cathedral Library', in *Medieval Learning and Literature*, pp. 23–24, esp. pl. v.

[46] On which see Ker, *English Manuscripts*, pp. 25–30.

and this is true of all the scribes of the other Malmesbury books from the early twelfth century. One hand at least resembles the script practised in England about the time of the Conquest.[47] Relative to its small size this book needed more scribes than any of the others, all of which (except for Lincoln College MS lat. 100) are larger than this. What conclusions may we draw?

I think that it is clear that William was not dependent upon an organized scriptorium for the making of this book. He was the initiator and supervisor, evidently deciding what was to go in it and supplying the exemplars; it is *his* collection. But he had to find his scribes from among those monks who were willing to help out, even for a leaf or column. We notice that changes of hand tend to coincide with the beginnings and ends of texts or quires; thus individual monks were assigned a quire or text, or perhaps asked merely to begin or finish one or the other. Some attempt has been made, as in others of the manuscripts, to make single works, or groups of them, correspond with quires, and this sometimes explains the irregularity of the quires; this manuscript, however, is mostly in eights.[48] We notice frequent changes in ink, the scribes apparently working in short bursts sometimes separated by long periods of inactivity. Lack of skill and organization are reflected in all these things. What William was up against is suggested by the Malmesbury *titulus* in the Mortuary Roll of Abbot Vitalis of Savigny, of 1122–3, in several hands, all poor to very poor, including that of one monk who had difficulty in writing his own name.[49] Its defects would lead us to give Bodleian Library Auct. F. 3. 14 as early a date as possible. In support of this is the fact that Scribe A, whose hand appears in three other manuscripts, here writes comparatively inexpertly. There is also some external evidence. In the *Gesta Pontificum* William describes Bishop Robert of Hereford's 'Excerptio de Chronica Mariani', which is contained in Bodleian Library Auct. F. 3. 14.[50] William uses the spelling 'Marimanus' which, as Stevenson long ago saw, must derive from the form 'Marinianus' used in MS Auct. F. 3. 14.[51] This means that we can almost certainly place the making of MS Auct. F. 3. 14 before 1125, the year in which the *Gesta* was completed.

---

[47] Hand X, which is large, rounded and widely-spaced with characteristically prominent ct and st ligatures; cf. the hands reproduced by T. A. M. Bishop, 'Notes on Cambridge MSS II', TCBS, 2 (1958), pls x–xi.
[48] Collation: at each end a bifolium, 1–11⁸, 12¹⁰, 13–14⁸, 15⁶, 16–17⁸, 18¹⁰, 19⁸, 20⁶.
[49] L. Delisle, *Rouleau Mortuaire du bienheureux Vital, abbé de Savigni* (Paris, 1909), pl. XXXVIII, no. 156.
[50] GP, p. 301.
[51] Stevenson, 'A Contemporary Description of Domesday Book', pp. 83–4.

Oxford, Bodleian Library MS Rawlinson G. 139 consists of 154 parchment leaves measuring 270×190 mm, after trimming by the binder.[52] It is ruled in double columns of 39 lines, within a written space of 200×145 mm. Ff. 153–4 were at first unruled, spare leaves, but ff. 153v–154v were not long after ruled in brown pencil with an irregular number of long lines, to receive additional text. This book is quired rather irregularly, its parchment is of poor quality, and its decoration (red and green initials) is of the plainest. It contains a collection of classical works: Cicero, *Partitiones Oratoriae* (ff. 1–10a) and *De Officiis* (ff. 10v–46va), pseudo-Quintilian, *Declamationes Maiores XIX* (ff. 46va–152) and a florilegium extracted from Aulus Gellius's *Attic Nights*, books 2–5 (ff. 152v, 153v–154v). These texts were written by seven scribes:

Scribe A ff. 1–10a (the whole of the *Partitiones*). Scribe D f. 6va lines 1–15. Hand III ff. 1v lines 25–39, 4b lines 8–12, 25–4va line 12, 4va line 36–6 line 4, 5b lines 5–39, 6va lines 1–15, 7a line 21–7b line 16, 7vb lines 9–39, 8va line 21–9a line 3, 9vb lines 11–39, 10a–20a line 13, 31a–71vb. Hand IV f. 20a line 14–30vb. Hand V f. 53va lines 7–39, 54vb lines 25–39, 55vb, 57a line 13–57b line 17, 66a lines 1–14, 71vb lines 1–22, 72–152. Hand VI f. 86a line 28–86b line 6. Hand VII ff. 152v, 153v–154v (the Gellius extracts). Two further hands annotate: (a) a very distinctive, late fourteenth-century hand, writing marginal notes in the early leaves; (b) William, writing marginal and interlinear corrections, comments and *nota*-marks in his informal hand, as far as f. 137v.

None of these scribes wrote particularly well. Scribe III eases into his main stint after a series of brief trial runs, and so does Scribe V, whose hand is very variable, changing its character slowly but markedly through his main stint, and deteriorating, presumably out of fatigue, towards the end. This man occasionally does an arrow through the lower loop of **g** on the bottom line of a page, as does the third of William's assistants (Scribe C), and one of the scribes of Oxford, Lincoln College MS lat. 100, described below.[53] N. R. Ker observed that this piece of exhibitionism was favoured by twelfth-century scribes from the south-west of England.[54] Since Scribe A wrote a little better

[52] *Summary Cat.* 15568. A preliminary discussion of this manuscript, with plates, is in R. M. Thomson, 'The Manuscripts of William of Malmesbury (c.1095–c.1143)', in *Manuscripts at Oxford: an Exhibition in Memory of Richard William Hunt*, ed. A. C. de la Mare and B. C. Barker-Benfield (Oxford, The Bodleian Library, 1980), p. 28 and figs. 15 and 17. Other details (of William's annotation, the binding and later ownership) not repeated here, are in idem, 'More Manuscripts from the "Scriptorium" of William of Malmesbury', *Scriptorium*, 35 (1981), 49–52.
[53] See below, pp. 87, 92.
[54] Ker, *English Manuscripts*, p. 7.

in this manuscript than he did in Auct. F. 3. 14, I tentatively date the making of Rawl. G. 139 between Auct. F. 3. 14 and the next manuscript to be discussed, in which his hand appears again, still further improved.

Oxford, Lincoln College MS lat. 100 is much the same size as MS Auct. F. 3. 14, although ruled in double columns.[55] Its ninety-five leaves measure 225×155 mm (all three edges trimmed), the bounding lines 180×115 mm. It is ruled with forty-four lines to a page. Again the only decoration is red initials, and the parchment is of poor quality and particularly ill-prepared: the hair side is yellow and polished, the flesh side rough, which has caused the ink to spread. There are six different hands including that of Scribe A, and a separate rubricator:

> William, ff. 3 (verses and table of contents), 91b line 7–93v (genea-logical tables), in his informal style (pl. 1). He corrects and annotates the main text, as do other hands. Hand II ff. 4–64va line 3. Hand III ff. 9vb lines 17–44, 10b lines 19–44, 24b lines 21–36, 25a line 12–25va line 32. Hand IV ff. 26vb lines 23–44, 27vb lines 27–44, 32b lines 5–44. Hand V ff. 64va line 4 (first verso of quire) – 72v. Scribe A ff. 73 (new quire) – 91b line 6.

The hands are rather more homogeneous than those in MS Auct. F. 3. 14, though none of them is as elegant as the best examples in that book. In Lincoln College lat. 100 there is no strict correspondence between hands, quires and texts, of which there are only three, Frontinus, Vegetius and Eutropius.[56] For its size it still required a comparatively large number of copyists, some of them not very calligraphic. William quotes Frontinus in the *Gesta Regum*; so he knew him by 1125.[57] While he need not have known the *Strategemata* through this very copy, that is likely and so we should be inclined to date it similarly to MS Auct. F. 3. 14, perhaps a year or two later, since Scribe A wrote much better in Lincoln College lat. 100 than he had in Auct. F. 3. 14 (pls 6, 8).

This scribe appears with William and Scribe B (Richard, the third of William's collaborators) in London, Lambeth Palace Library MS 224.[58] This is a large and ambitious book; its 215 leaves ([ii] + 210 + [iii]) measure 275×175 mm – the edges have been trimmed, but not much, since pricking

[55] Coxe, *Catalogus*, I, p. 47; Ker, 'Handwriting', p. 375; see below, pp. 57–8. Description and facsimile in R. W. Hunt et al., *The Survival of Ancient Literature* (Oxford, The Bodleian Library, 1975), no. 125 and pl. xxi.
[56] Collation: a bifolium, 1¹², 2–9¹⁰ (wanting the last leaves of quires 6 and 7), 10⁴ (wants 4).
[57] 4. 7. 4 in GR II, p. 488.
[58] M. R. James, *A Descriptive Catalogue of the Manuscripts in the Library of Lambeth Palace* (Cambridge, 1932), pp. 364–8; GP, pp. xi–xii; GR I, p. cxxxi; *New Palaeographical Society*, 2nd ser. (London, 1913–30), pl. 192; Schmitt, *Sancti Anselmi Opera* I, pp. 165*–171*; Ker, 'Handwriting', pp. 372–3.

and wide margins remain – and the bounding lines define an area of 210×130 mm. It is ruled in double columns of forty lines. Unfortunately the book cannot be dated; although a considerable improvement upon the three manuscripts just discussed, it is not as 'finished' as any others and this plus the fact that Scribe A, who wrote most of it, also wrote in the other three gives us reason for considering it as a transitional piece between the rougher and the more skillfully produced Malmesbury books of William's time. Lambeth Palace Library MS 224 has a table of contents in William's hand, and he wrote two substantial sections of text, as well as providing corrections and annotations throughout; we may therefore assume that he was again initiator and supervisor of this project, which was to collect between two covers Anselm's letters and major treatises. The last item in it in a hand of William's time (the *De Processione Spiritus Sancti*) does not figure in his table, and ends incompletely at f. 175va; subsequently a fourteenth-century hand completed this treatise and filled a further thirty-seven leaves with Anselmiana. William's drypoint ruling continues to f. 187v, the end of a quire, although it was ruled over in pencil by the later scribe. I assume that William prepared the original book for a larger number of Anselm's works than he at first had exemplars for, and that the *De Processione* was copied some time after the rest and after completion of the table of contents. The copying of this work was perhaps broken off on William's death, but that is conjecture.

In this book too the parchment is of poor quality and was ill prepared; nine scribes were required for it including William and perhaps one of the two rubricators:

William, f. [ii] (his verses and table of contents), ff. 86va lines 34–40 (extract from a letter), 125a–134vb (quire of 10, beginning a new letter, but ending in the middle of one), 155b line 17 (new letter) – 174b line 18 (ending the last letter of the collection). He corrected and annotated the letters. Apart from such notes and the material on f. [ii], all is in his formal style. The second hand is Scribe A's. Apart from the intrusions by other hands noted below, he wrote ff. 1–12va line 26, 32vb line 30 (beginning a new work) – 40va line 13 (end of the Prologue to the *Cur Deus Homo*), 63va (beginning a new work) – 85vb line 17, 87a (beginning a new work) – 121vb line 25 (ending a letter), 135a (new quire) – 149a line 7 (ending a letter). Hand III ff. 121vb line 27 (new letter) – 124vb (end of letter and quire). Hand IV ff. 11va lines 10–36 (this may be a separate hand), 34vb lines 7–21, 35va lines 18–40, 74b line 15 – 74va line 15, 80b lines 1–20, 82a lines 15–28, 85b lines 35–40, 85va lines 5–27, 85vb lines 17–35 (end of work), 96vb, 106b lines 18–35. Hand V ff. 86a–86va line 33 (end of work and of quire); col. b is blank except for the *incipit* of the next item, lines 39–40. Scribe B ff. 12va line 26–32vb line 26 (end of work), 40va line 16 (chapters of the *Cur Deus Homo*) – 63b (end of the work). Hand VII ff. 149a line

9–149va line 11 (two letters). Hand VIII ff. 149va line 12 (new letter) – 155b line 13 (end of letter). Hand IX ff. 174b line 23–174v line 21. This hand begins the *De Processione*. There are probably two rubricators of whom one, who does less ornamental work, may be Scribe A.

None of these hands is highly skilled, but all are better, and the total effect is more consistent, than in Bodl. Auct. F. 3. 14 and Lincoln College lat. 100 in particular. Scribe A wrote more carefully here than anywhere else (pls 6–9). The general impression is rather 'prickly', crisp and elegant. His rounded **d**, frequently employed, has a stylish recurve to the ascender, he uses only the ampersand, and a long-tailed, 'dagger' cedilla. In the other, presumably earlier manuscripts his hand is less individualized, his rounded **d** has no recurve, he uses both Tironian **et** and the ampersand, and a looped cedilla. Again there are evident signs of farming out; changes of scribe coincide with the ends of quires, with beginnings and ends of texts and (in this manuscript) of groups of letters. The makeup into quires is noticeably irregular.[59] But this manuscript, unlike the earlier ones, is nicely decorated, with four large, multi-coloured arabesque initials,[60] and plain, single-colour ones throughout.[61] Changes of colour in these minor initials sometimes coincide with changes of scribe, suggesting that the scribes carried out the simpler decoration themselves.[62] Titles, incipits and explicits are in red and purple majuscules.

Scribe B wrote in two other books. One is William's copy of John the Scot's *Periphyseon*, now itself divided between two separate manuscripts.[63] The prefatory letter containing biographical information about John was parted from the book in the seventeenth century, and is now London, British Library MS Royal App. 85, ff. 25–26v.[64] These two leaves, originally

[59] Collation: a bifolium, 1[10], 2–10[8], 11[4], 12[10], 13[8], 14[4], 15–16[8], 17[10], 18–21[8], two singletons, 22[12] (wants 9–11), 23[14] (wants 4, 5, 9 and 14), 24–5[8], 26[10].

[60] F. 1, 11–line **A** in purple, red and green, arabesqued; f. 40, 9–line **O**, red with purple foliage; f. 53v, 8–line **R**, purple with red foliage; f. 103, 5–line **Q**, purple with red foliage.

[61] On ff. 1–95 and elsewhere, red and purple alternate except on ff. 95v, 96v, 112v, 125–134v, 155–174, where green initials replace the purple, and ff. 149–153, on which the purple initials are replaced by blue.

[62] For instance the only long sections with green initials, ff. 125–134v and 155–174, are those written by William.

[63] Sheldon-Williams and Bieler, *Iohannis Scotti Eriugenae Periphyseon*, pp. 10–11, 19–21, 24–6; P. Lucentini, 'La nuova edizione del "Periphyseon" dell "Eriugena"', *Studi Medievali*, 17 (1976), 393–414.

[64] G. F. Warner and J. P. Gilson, *A Descriptive Catalogue of Western Manuscripts in the Old Royal and King's Collections in the British Museum* (London, 4 vols, 1921), II, p. 399. The letter is printed in several places, most recently by E. Jeauneau, 'Guillaume de Malmesbury, premier éditeur anglais du 'Periphyseon', in *Sapientiae Doctrina; Mélanges de Théologie et de Litérature Médiévales offerts à Dom Hildebrand Bascour O.S.B.* (Leuven, 1980), pp. 169–171.

a bifolium, have become separated and are glued on to paper guards in a volume which is a modern makeup. Both leaves have marks of vertical and horizontal folding: they are dark, stained and dirty, and have been repaired along the edges. The head and tail of f. 25 and all three edges of f. 26 have been trimmed. The leaves measure 325×c.230 mm, and the dimensions of the layout approximate closely to those of the rest of the book. F. 25 is blank but for a Greek alphabet written across the top, in upper and lower case with the Latin name supplied above each letter. William's letter to Peter occupies ff. 25va–26a line 2; f. 26v is blank. One early twelfth-century hand wrote the alphabet; a different one copied the letter. This hand wrote in dark brown ink to f. 25va line 20, finishing in a paler one. The letter opens with a ten-line initial **P** in red body-colour with simple foliage. The script which follows begins on line 3.

The rest of the original book is in Cambridge, Trinity College MS O. 5. 20 (1301).[65] This manuscript consists of two separate volumes, the second of which, beginning at p. 257, was at Malmesbury and bound with the first by 1365.[66] It is a twelfth-century copy of St Luke's Gospel, finely written in a single hand which is quite unlike any of those found in the books connected with William. The first volume was mainly written by him and by Scribes B and C. Scribe B, who copied nearly four-fifths of it, signs off at the end, naming himself as Richard (pl. 11). He wrote the whole of p. 57 (beginning a new quire) to p. 256a, the end of the text. His hand is unmistakeable; like William's (when writing formally) it is individual with strongly-marked characteristics, and consistent. He makes his **g** in the French fashion, and he could easily have been French. His work in Trinity College O. 5. 20 shows a marked improvement in quality over his stint in Lambeth 224, where he formed his abbreviation signs differently (pl. 10). The difference presumably reflects an interval of time between the making of the books, Trinity College O. 5. 20 being the later of the two.[67]

Pp. 1–16 (the opening quire) of Trinity College O. 5. 20 were written in a hand like, but inferior to Richard's, and William himself wrote pp. 46a line 4 to 56b, ending a quire in mid-sentence. Another hand has added catchwords in the lower margin at this point. From p. 50 onwards William has unwontedly stretched out words near the foot of each column, evidently trying to keep pace with his exemplar. Now precisely at that place in the text where his section ends there is a *signe de renvoi* in the margin of Reims,

[65] M. R. James, *A Descriptive Catalogue of the Western Manuscripts in the Library of Trinity College Cambridge* (Cambridge, 4 vols, 1900–1904), III, pp. 321–3.
[66] J. A. Weisheipl in *Oxford Studies presented to Daniel Callus* (Oxford, 1964), pp. 241–2.
[67] In Lambeth Palace 224 he uses rounded **d** frequently and not to save space, and the stroke joining his **c** and **t** in ligature curves inwards to the top of **t** less noticeably.

Bibliothèque Municipale MS 875, the earliest surviving copy of John the Scot's work.[68] From this manuscript, at an early stage, a two-volume version was made, dividing at this mark. The second section of his manuscript (all that follows the part written in his own hand) shared a common ancestor with the slightly later copy from Mont St Michel, now Avranches, Bibliothèque Municipale MS 235. This represents the redaction known as 'Periphyseon B' or the 'Supplementary Copy'. The first part of William's manuscript had as its exemplar a representative of 'Periphyseon C' or the 'Uncompleted Copy'.[69] This shows that he had access to two separate volumes, and further evidence suggests that he discovered the volume containing 'Periphyseon B' some time later, and that it contained the text of the complete work. Firstly, William was stretching out the words in his section in order to finish precisely at the end of the last column of a quire. There would have been no need to go to this trouble had the exemplar for the rest of the work already been at hand. Presumably this is why the catchwords at this point are not by William: they were doubtless only added when the second volume became available and copying could proceed. Secondly, a separate annotator was active in the first part of the manuscript, to the end of William's section, but did almost no work thereafter.[70] He added chapter–divisions as well as correcting and altering the text, with the aim of bringing this part of the manuscript into conformity with the 'Periphyseon B' redaction represented by pp. 57–256. William himself wrote marginalia, with gradually increasing frequency, only after p. 57. Finally, catchwords, mostly, it seems, by Scribe B, are only used after p. 56.

This has the largest format of all William's surviving manuscripts; its 128 leaves, probably untrimmed, measure c.365×240 mm (bounding lines 280×170 mm). It is ruled in double columns of 54 lines. The parchment has been well prepared, and is thick and even. The quiring is regular, in eights and tens.[71] Besides William, Richard and the scribe of pp. 1–16, only one other hand (Scribe C) wrote text, from p. 17 to p. 46a line 3; all wrote well.

[68] Sheldon-Williams and Bieler, p. 11.

[69] Jeauneau, 'Guillaume de Malmesbury', pp. 156–159. Another descendant of William's exemplar for this part of his *Periphyseon* manuscript is Oxford, Bodl. Libr. MS Auct. F. 3. 15, ff. 31–53v, written in north-eastern Ireland during the late twelfth-century: F. J. Byrne, *A Thousand Years of Irish Script* (Oxford, The Bodleian Library, 1979), pp. 14–15.

[70] On his work see T. A. M. Bishop, '*Periphyseon*: An Episode in the Tradition', TCBS, 7 (1980), 411–413.

[71] Collation: 1[8], 2–3[10], 4–13[8], 14–15[10].

Decoration is simple: large, plain, coloured initials open each book;[72] the minor initials are in minium or ink of the text touched with red.[73] The prefatory letter to Peter makes it clear that the letter itself was written after at least the first edition of the *Gesta Pontificum*, thus after 1125. In the *Gesta Regum, Gesta Pontificum* and the letter, John the Scot's work is referred to by a title found only in the later part of the Trinity College manuscript.[74] Thus 1125 can be taken as a reasonably certain *terminus post quem* for the copying of Trinity College MS O. 5. 20, even though the bifolium containing the letter could have been added later.

The fourth main hand in Trinity College MS O. 5. 20, Scribe C's, is found in two other manuscripts (pls 13–15). One of these is Oxford, Bodleian Library MS Arch. Seld. B. 16, the well-known collection of Roman history, whose copying was shared by this very competent scribe and William.[75] Internal evidence dates its manufacture to the year 1129.[76] It has been noticed that in this manuscript (and in the third, Oxford, Merton College MS 181) Scribe C sometimes wrote a **g** on the lowest line of a page with an arrow through the enlarged lower loop.[77] He did not do so in Trinity College O. 5. 20. In these two manuscripts, also, his hand is steadier than in Trinity College MS O. 5. 20, and these features might lead us to suggest that the Trinity College manuscript predates them by a few years.

The Selden manuscript too was carefully made. Its 222 leaves measure 315×200 mm after trimming (bounding lines 230×140 mm). The parchment is white, of good quality and, although varying in thickness, was well prepared. The quiring is irregular but mostly in eights and tens.[78] The book is ruled in double columns of 48 lines. William started and ended it (ff. 1a–73a line 14, 135a–222vb) (pl. 2), as well as correcting and annotating throughout; Scribe C wrote a substantial portion in the middle (ff. 73a line 15 – 134vb). One good rubricator did the whole. Decoration is simple but attractive: on f. 1 is a gold initial; the rest are mostly red, plus green more or

---

[72] P.1, 14–line **S** in dark, metallic red with foliage, followed by red display-script in a mixture of upper- and lower-case letters; p. 38, red and green **C** and red explicit and incipit; p. 79, large, plain red **I** followed by majuscule script in ink of text, red-touched, explicit and incipit in red, mixed script; p. 132, large purple **P** with floreated descender, explicit and incipit in red, mixed script; p. 184, red **N** with some foliage, followed by majuscules and preceded by explicit and incipit as for p. 79.

[73] There are no red initials to Book V.

[74] Sheldon-Williams and Bieler, pp. 20–21.

[75] *Summary Cat.* 3362; GR I, pp. cxxxi–cxl; Ker, 'Handwriting', pp. 373–4; T. Mommsen, *Theodosiani Libri XVI*, I (Berlin, 2nd edn, 1954), pp. lxv–lxvii, cxxxii; see above, pp. 62–3, 66–8.

[76] See below, p. 177.

[77] Stevenson, 'A Contemporary Description of Domesday Book', pp. 78–9.

[78] Collation: 1–2[10], 3[8], 4–5[10], 6–8[8], 9[6], 10–17[8], 18[10], 19–25[8], 26[10], two singletons and a bifolium.

less alternately, and one or two fawn and blue. Some have simple foliage, occasionally in two colours. This was a book peculiarly William's, since he was responsible not only for arranging the collection of chronicles in it,[79] but for correcting, abbreviating and writing introductions to them. Behind this manuscript must lie, in fact, not only a number of separate exemplars, but a rough draft of the whole.

Scribes B and C collaborated again, this time as members of a large band which copied Oxford, Merton College MS 181, a collection of commentaries on the Old Testament sapiential books.[80] This manuscript has an early fourteenth-century pressmark on f. [ii]v, apparently in the same hand as the pressmark in Lambeth Palace MS 224 (pls 4–5), and William's hand has been noticed on a scrap of leaf used in its binding.[81] But there are other and stronger reasons for connecting it with the Malmesbury scriptorium and with his copying programme. After all, the binding-leaf could have been added to the book at a later date, even though it is sewn into the last quire. This leaf, f. 231 (wrongly numbered 230 in modern pencil), is ruled in double columns (bounding lines 215×135 mm) of 43 lines. It contains part of Rufinus's version of Eusebius's *Historia Ecclesiastica*, in William's formal hand. The initials have not been filled in, and the text breaks off halfway down the first column of the verso. One cannot say why William did not complete it. His hand, however, is found elsewhere in the Merton College manuscript, in the form of corrections and nota marks,[82] of which his are distinctive and individual. It is the presence of Scribes B, C and D (found also in Bodleian Library Auct. F. 3. 14 and Rawl. G. 139) that clinches the early Malmesbury connection (pls 12, 15, 18). As a result we are able to say with confidence that William, as usual, arranged the collection of material in this manuscript and supervised its execution. It consists of 233 leaves which after trimming measure 270×180 mm (bounding lines 210×140 mm). Although ruled throughout in double columns, other details such as the number of lines per page vary, as does the quiring.[83] Otherwise it is a fine

---

[79] The contents are: Dares Phrygius, excerpts from Justin etc., Orosius, a conflation of Eutropius, Jordanes and Paul the Deacon, an edited text of Hugh of Fleury's *Historia Ecclesiastica*, and the *Breviarium Alaricum*. And see above, pp. 57, 62–3, 66–8.

[80] Coxe, *Catalogus*, I, p. 73. The contents are: Bede on Proverbs, Jerome and Alcuin on Ecclesiastes, Origen (Jerome), Honorius Augustodunensis and Bede on the Song of Songs and John the Deacon, *Vita Gregorii*.

[81] MLGB, p. 128.

[82] On ff. 1, 2va line 20, 14, 28, 47va, 80va(?). Other notes may be by him.

[83] Ff. 1–97v 40 lines per page; after f. 91 the number drops to 38, after f. 111v to 34, although f. 111v was originally ruled for 38 (The new ruling is in plummet). From f. 112 35 lines per page. On ff. 221–9 the original ruling has been redone in pencil. Collation: a bifolium, 1⁸, 2¹⁰, 3–12⁸, 13⁶, 14–17⁸, 18¹⁰, 19–26⁸, 27¹⁰, 28⁶ (wants 4), 29⁴ (wants 4), 30⁴ (wants 1).

book: the parchment good, the text well written. But it needed an extraordinarily large number of hands, no less than thirteen including Scribes B, C and D, and two rubricators:

Hand I ff. 1–6. Hand II ff. 6v–54va line 16 (end of work). Scribe B ff. 54v line 22 – 87vb line 3 (end of work). Hand IV ff. 87vb line 11 – 90va line 21, 147vb–149vb line 21, 155a line 11 – 155vb. Scribe D ff. 90va line 22 – 94b line 23, 100vb–111va, 120va line 19 – 120vb lines 1–6. Hand VI ff. 94b line 24 – 100va. Hand VII ff. 111vb–117b line 22. Hand VIII ff. 117v line 22 – 120va line 13 (end of work), 137a lines 1–27. Hand IX f. 117vb. Scribe C ff. 120vb line 7 – 136va (end of work), 196va line 15 – 220va (end of work). Hand XI ff. 137 line 28 – 147va, 149vb line 21 – 155a line 10. Hand XII ff. 131va lines 4–14, 165a–196va line 14. Hand XIII ff. 221a–229b line 11 (all of the last work). This looks a somewhat later hand than the rest. There are three rubricators, all of whom use a mixture of upper- and lower-case letters: R. I to f. 87; R. II (this is Hand XII) ff. 87v–220v; R. III ff. 221–229.

Six of the scribes began or ended separate texts, but in this manuscript there is little correspondence between the stints of the scribes and the beginnings and ends of quires or works. In part the number of scribes simply reflects the length of the book, 456 columns averaging about 37 lines of writing each. But there does not on this occasion seem to have been the same necessity to divide up the unbound manuscript for copying. Six scribes each wrote more than one stint. The copying seems to have been done quickly. Scribe B (Richard) writes in the mature and confident style which he had developed by the time of his stint in the Trinity College manuscript. Thus Merton College MS 181 was probably written about the same time as Trinity College O. 5. 20 and Bodleian Library MS Arch. Seld. B. 16. If I am right about this, then it seems that even by the mid 1130s William had sometimes to employ a high proportion of the local monks for the making of a large book. Scriptorial work was not, at Malmesbury, a highly specialized activity. In this it resembles Salisbury cathedral at a slightly earlier date.[84] Merton College 181 is however by far the most lavishly decorated of all the manuscripts, with nineteen major initials, some in more than one colour and

---

[84] Ker, 'The Beginnings of Salisbury Cathedral Library', pp. 23–4, 26–8, 33–4 etc.

with coloured display-script.[85] The **C** on f. 137 is the exception noted earlier, a particularly well-executed initial in pen-outline, with four colours on a painted ground.

With this manuscript we complete our account of William's collaborators. We might summarize it thus: Scribe A appears in Bodleian Library Auct. F. 3. 14, Rawl. G. 139, Lincoln College lat. 100 and Lambeth Palace 224; Scribe B (Richard) appears in the Lambeth manuscript, Trinity College O. 5. 20 and Merton College 181; Scribe C writes in the Trinity and Merton College manuscripts, and in Bodleian Library Arch. Seld. B. 16; Scribe D, a minor figure, writes in Bodleian Library Auct. F. 3. 14, Rawl. G. 139 and Merton College 181 (pls 16–18). All four appear in manuscripts with William, and thus their connection with each other is confirmed by their connection with him.

There remain for discussion two highly-finished manuscripts, one written in hands found nowhere else and annotated by William, the other written entirely by William himself. Cambridge, University Library MS Ii. 3. 20 is the unique copy of his *Deflorationes Gregorii*.[86] It consists of 135 leaves measuring 300×220 mm, ruled with plummet in double columns of 39 lines, within a space of 230×150 mm. It was provided with plain red and green initials. Construction is mainly in regular quires of eight.[87] Uniquely among William's books, this has quire-numbers, somewhat unusually situated at the foot of the first recto of each quire.[88] They seem to be by the main scribe

[85] F. 1, red and purple **P**, flourished; f. 17v, red **P**, flourished; f. 40, purple **H**, followed by majuscules in ink of text; f. 54v, blue **M** with red decoration, and purple **emini** in rustic capitals, followed by majuscules in ink of text; f. 55, purple **V** with red foliage and majuscules in ink of text; f. 87v, green **D**; f. 88, red **V**, a little flourished; f. 111v, red **B** with green foliage, and green **I** with red dots; f. 116, red **A**, some foliage; f. 120v, red **Q**, green foliage; f. 131v, red **S** with green foliage; f. 137, green **C** with outline foliage in red, green and blue and pale yellow wash filling, 8 lines high, followed by red and green majuscules; f. 151v, red **S** with green foliage, followed by majuscules in ink of text; f. 163v red **D** with red and green foliage, followed by majuscules in ink of text; f. 181, red **G** with red and green foliage, followed by majuscules in ink of text; f. 197v, green **C** with red and green foliage, followed by majuscules in ink of text; f. 207, red **I** with red and green foliage, followed by majuscules in ink of text; f. 207v, green **O** with red ornament and majuscules in ink of text; f. 220v, green and red **F**; f. 221, initial omitted. Minor initials: ff. 1–54, alternating plain red and purple; ff. 55–87, small minium or red–touched initials; ff. 88–220v, alternating plain red and green.
[86] H. R. Luard et al., *A Catalogue of the Manuscripts preserved in the Library of the University of Cambridge* (Cambridge, 6 vols, 1861 etc.), I, pp. 507–9; Farmer, 'William of Malmesbury's Commentary on Lamentations', pp. 308–311, printing the preface and chapters.
[87] A⁴ (lacks 1; 2–3 paper), 1–16⁸, 17⁸ (lacks 6, 7), B² (lacks 2; 1 is a sheet of paper glued to a parchment stub).
[88] Ker, *English Manuscripts*, p. 50.

of the text. This was written by one hand to f. 130a, and completed by another, probably that of a west-countryman,[89] who did all of the rubrication. The first scribe had not allowed sufficient space for this, and his successor's large, sprawling script was often forced to overflow down the centre column or a margin. This again shows a lack of professionalism, though both scribes wrote well. William's contribution was to correct the text throughout, in the margins and between the lines, presumably from the exemplar, and to write the rubricator's guides. All of this is in his informal hand. It is noteworthy that the main scribes did not correct.

This is, I think, William's clean copy of a work written expressly for the local community. It does not look like a presentation-volume, but that does not mean that it necessarily stayed at Malmesbury until the Dissolution. There is no trace of the abbey's pressmark, and Dr N. R. Ker drew my attention to the fourteenth-century chapter-numbers in Arabic numerals, added in the lower margins by 'a rather scratchy sort of hand' reminiscent of 'what one finds in a good many Lanthony books'.[90] The *Defloratio* evidently did not circulate very widely. It was however known to Robert of Cricklade by c.1137,[91] and was probably written not long before, following William's period of immersion in historical composition. There is certainly some internal evidence for dating the manuscript to the late 1130s: the fact that its two scribes do not appear in William's other known books; the good standard and comparative homogeneity of their writing; the book's regular construction and clean parchment. But these features may be explained rather by the book's purpose than by its date.

When all is said and done, although Scribes B and C wrote well, William himself was the best of the Malmesbury scribes of his time, in terms of the scholarly purpose for which his books were designed. Oxford, Oriel College MS 42[92] is all by William except for the rubrics.[93] It is one of the small-format books in double columns, its 222 leaves measuring 245×165

---

[89] It is like that of Scribe C; similar hands appear in books from Worcester, Winchester and nearby; for instance, Ker *English Manuscripts*, pl. 20.

[90] In a letter to the writer, August 1980. According to a modern bookplate pasted inside the front cover, the manuscript was owned by Richard Holdsworth, Master of Emmanuel College, who died in 1664. At the top right-hand corner of f. 2 is the name of a sixteenth-century owner, 'Thomae Turneri', and the same hand, doubtless Turner's, has written an alphabetical index on f. 1ᵛ. The same name occurs on f. 211 of London, BL MS Cott. Nero D. IV (the 'Lindisfarne Gospels'); R. A. B. Mynors, *Durham Cathedral Manuscripts* (Oxford, 1939), p. 17.

[91] See above, p. 74 and n. 205.

[92] Coxe, *Catalogus*, I, pp. 14–16; see above, pp. 64–6, citing earlier literature.

[93] The rubricator may be the corrector of Cambridge, Trinity College O. 5. 20 (see above, p. 91). There are some twelfth-century notes to Leo's sermons, perhaps by Scribe A.

mm after trimming (bounding lines 180×115 mm).[94] The first quire (ff. 1–7v) is ruled with 30 lines per page; thereafter the number is 36. This book is utterly different from the other one entirely by William, the Magdalen College manuscript of the *Gesta Pontificum*. The materials and their preparation are excellent, the quires regular,[95] and the decoration – alternating plain red and pale blue initials – is very neat and uniform. The contents and their arrangement are of great interest and merit a much closer examination than can be offered here.[96] They consist of the *Collectio Quesnelliana* of early Church councils, followed by Leo's letters and sermons. William has compared and combined different exemplars to obtain a correct and complete text; he has annotated and cross-referenced the *concilia* and Leonine works; he has given variant readings. William quoted Leo in his Commentary on Lamentations, written about 1135–7,[97] and this may mean that the Oriel College manuscript was made before then. I should not want to put it much earlier. Of all the books discussed in this chapter, this one shows to best advantage William's own fully-developed combination of scribal and book-making ability, linked directly to his precise and intelligent scholarship.

---

[94] The leaves are now numbered iv + 221. There are paper guards *passim*. Ff. i–ii and 221–2 are modern paper. Ff. iii–iv are two separate leaves now made into a bifolium on paper guards. They are blank except for the late medieval Oriel College *ex dono* on f. iv.

[95] Collation: 1⁸ (wants 2), 2–9⁸, 10¹⁰, 11⁸, 12¹⁰, 13–26⁸, 27¹⁰ (wants 1). The last leaf was once the back pastedown.

[96] See above, pp. 64–6.

[97] Comm. Lam., f. 125vb.

THE EARLIEST BOOKS FROM
THE LIBRARY OF MALMESBURY ABBEY

MALMESBURY ABBEY WAS one of that select group of English houses which could trace its history back to the golden age epitomized and chronicled by Bede.[1] To Bede's older contemporary Aldhelm (d. c.709) belongs most of the credit for setting the recently founded community on its feet and for making it a by-word throughout the British Isles for the pursuit of divine and secular learning.[2] During his abbacy Malmesbury eclipsed the reputations of the Irish schools and of Hadrian's Canterbury. At only one other point in its long history did the abbey attain a comparable reputation for learning, when it housed William, whose career, intellectual interests and writings were consciously modelled upon the examples of Bede and Aldhelm.[3]

To judge from the quotations in his own works, Aldhelm's library – in secular literature at least – was more extensive than Bede's.[4] One assumes

---

[1] On the early history of Malmesbury, see A. Watkin, *Victoria County History of Wiltshire*, III, p. 230; Knowles, Brooke and London, *Heads*, pp. 54–5; GP, pp. 345–57 and 361–443.

[2] M. L. W. Laistner, *Thought and Letters in Western Europe* (London, 2nd edn, 1957), pp. 151–6; James, *Two Ancient English Scholars*, pp. 9–15; C. J. Godfrey, *The Church in Anglo-Saxon England* (Cambridge, 1962), pp. 201–6; P. Riché, *Education et Culture dans l'Occident Barbare* (Paris, 2nd edn, 1961), pp. 421–6; and M. Winterbottom, 'Aldhelm's Prose Style and its Origins', ASE, 6 (1977), 39–76. On the dating of Aldhelm's career, see now M. Lapidge and M. Herren, *Aldhelm: the Prose Works* (Woodbridge, 1979), pp. 1–10.

[3] See above, pp. 9, 18–20, 44–5.

[4] On Bede's library see Laistner, 'The Library of the Venerable Bede', and now P. Hunter Blair, 'From Bede to Alcuin', *Famulus Christi*, ed. G. Bonner (London, 1976), pp. 239–60. On Aldhelm's reading, see R. Ehwald, MGH, Auct. Antiqu. 15 (Berlin, 1919), pp. 11–537, *passim*; Ogilvy, *Books known to the English, passim*, but esp. under Cicero (*Cat.* and *Verr.*), Claudian, Donatus, Gellius, Juvenal, Lucan, Orosius, Ovid, Persius, Phocas, Pliny, Pompeius, Priscian (*Inst. de Nom.* only), Seneca(?), Servius, Solinus, Suetonius and Terence. But both Ehwald's and Ogilvy's information is to be regarded critically. On both Bede and Aldhelm see M. Manitius, 'Zu Aldhelm und Beda', *Sitzungsberichte der phil.-hist. Klasse der kaiserlichen Akademie der Wissenschaften zu Wien*, 112 (1886), 535–634, also printed separately (Vienna, 1886), and M. Roger, *L'Enseignement des lettres classiques d'Ausone à Alcuin* (Paris, 1905), pp. 290–301.

that Aldhelm brought books to Malmesbury for his teaching and that some of them remained at the abbey after his death. In 1931 M. R. James tried to show that one or two of Aldhelm's books were still available to William.[5] Some of the books, too, which John Leland found at Malmesbury in the first half of the sixteenth century, must have been ancient, to judge from their titles.[6] There can in fact be little doubt that, from the twelfth century on, Malmesbury's was one of the great monastic libraries of England. Can we learn anything of its prehistory? In other words, is there any possibility of reconstructing the abbey's pre-Conquest collection, or at least of compiling a list of early manuscripts which could at one time or another have been found at the house? This is a hazardous undertaking and at first sight the prospects of success look bleak: only five Malmesbury manuscripts earlier than the twelfth century find a place in Ker's *Medieval Libraries of Great Britain*;[7] works quoted by Aldhelm need not have been known to him from books at Malmesbury; demonstrably ancient manuscripts used by William could have come, and often did come, from elsewhere, sometimes to be returned after copying;[8] and Malmesbury books listed by Leland, however early they might be, could have entered the library there at any time before the sixteenth century. More fundamentally, there is little evidence that institutional libraries involving corporate ownership of books and standardized procedures for their housing, borrowing and maintenance existed in England prior to the late eleventh century. Before that time books seemed to have changed hands and places much more freely than was the case from c.1100 until the Reformation.[9] Malmesbury itself had a chequered history between the times of Aldhelm and William, even becoming a college of secular clerks between c.950 and c.965.[10] Thus the chances of a book used by Aldhelm still being available to William need to be carefully considered. And *e converso*: King Athelstan (924–39) was a generous donor to the abbey and, although William does not mention books among his gifts, the king certainly gave them to other houses and one would expect him to have given them to Malmesbury as well.[11]

---

[5] James, *Two Ancient English Scholars*, pp. 12–14.

[6] See below, pp. 100–111.

[7] MLGB, p. 128. But two, perhaps three, additions can now be made to this; see below, pp. 102–4, 105–7, 110–11.

[8] This is true, for instance, of his use of London, BL Cott. Tib. A. xv, a probably Canterbury book dated c.1000, of the version of the *Anglo-Saxon Chronicle* from Canterbury and of a lost exemplar for the second part of his manuscript of John Scotus Eriugena's *Periphyseon*; see above, pp. 70, 91, and below, 159–163.

[9] Cf. the remarks by M. B. Parkes in ASE, 5 (1976), 170–1.

[10] GP, p. 403.

[11] ibid., pp. 396–403. Cf. S. Keynes, 'King Athelstan's Books', in *Learning and Literature in Anglo-Saxon England; Studies presented to Peter Clemoes*, ed. M. Lapidge and H. Gneuss (Cambridge, 1985), pp. 143–201.

Such a formidable array of pitfalls enforces caution; and yet, when we examine Leland's lists, the manuscripts known to William and internal evidence in a few extant manuscripts, and when we consider these sources of information in conjunction with Aldhelm's quotations and other background material, the connections that can be made enable us to draw up an unexpectedly long and interesting list of ancient, rare and important books which were, or may have been, at the abbey in pre-Conquest days. The list will, of course, constitute no more than an unrepresentative fragment of the total collection as it was at any particular time, but it seems worth offering as a basis on which more may yet be built.

In his *Collectanea* John Leland listed twenty-four books which he found at Malmesbury, giving the author and usually the title of the first or main item of contents. Five of these books are mentioned again in his *De Scriptoribus*, evidently for their exceptional rarity and possibly for their age, for Leland describes them as 'multo praestantiora' than Aldhelm's relics and a psalter 'literis Saxonicis longiusculis scriptum', which he was shown during his visit.[12] The latest dateable items of the twenty-four contained works by twelfth-century authors: Faricius of Abingdon, William of Malmesbury, Robert of Cricklade and Grossolanus of Milan. There are six of these, including one mentioned in the *De Scriptoribus*, and we may exclude them from our enquiry. The other eighteen are all worthy of consideration and I proceed roughly in order of Leland's list.

He begins with Juvencus, an author certainly more popular before the Conquest than later and much used by Aldhelm.[13] The eight surviving Insular manuscripts include one each from the seventh, eighth and ninth centuries, two from the tenth century, one from c.1000 and one each from the eleventh and thirteenth centuries.[14] Three, including the single post-Conquest example, have known provenances. The earliest, Cues, Hospital-bibliothek, 171, a mere fragment, may have been written in Northumbria, but, if so, passed early to the continent. It was certainly there well before Leland's time.[15] Of the two remaining possibilities, one is the most important of all Juvencus manuscripts, Cambridge, Corpus Christi College 304. This copy, assigned to the early eighth century, was written in uncials,

---

[12] Leland, *Collectanea*, IV, p. 157, and *De Scriptoribus*, I, pp. 100–1.

[13] Ed. J. Huemer, CSEL 24; see also *Clavis*, no. 1385. On knowledge of Juvencus in Anglo-Saxon England, see Ogilvy, *Books known to the English*, p. 190.

[14] Cues, Hospitalbibliothek 171 (?Insular, s. vii); Cambridge, Corpus Christi College 304 (?Italy, s. viii); CUL Ff. 4. 42 (Wales, s. ix); London, BL Roy. 15 A. xvi (continental, s. ix; in England by s. x²); Oxford, Bodl. Libr. Barlow 25 (?English, s. x); Paris, Bibliothèque Sainte-Geneviève 2410 (English, s. x/xi); CUL Gg. 5. 35 (St Augustine's Canterbury, s. xi med.); and Oxford, Bodl. Libr. Bodl. 527 (Waverley, s. xiii).

[15] CLA, VIII, no. 1172; left to the Cues Library by Nicholas of Cues (d.1464).

probably in Italy.[16] M. R. James tentatively identified it with the 'Juvencus in Romana scriptura' which figures in the twelfth-century library catalogue from Christ Church, Canterbury.[17] This, however, bore a distinguishing mark resembling HL, probably on its opening leaf, and, as James noted, there is no trace of such a mark in the Corpus Juvencus.[18] At the head of its f. 1 is an erased early inscription consisting of a single word of about eight to ten capitals. James distinguished S at the end and A at the beginning. Were he right, ALDHELMUS would be an attractive conjecture which would fit the space well enough. In fact, however, James's 'initial letter' is more likely to be a V and is in any case the *second* letter, not the first.[19] Thus the inscription is more likely to have read IVVENCUS. The book was certainly in England c.1000, when annotations were made both in Anglo-Caroline and Anglo-Saxon minuscule, but its exact provenance is still a mystery. The other possible candidate for identification with Leland's Malmesbury book is Cambridge, University Library Ff. 4. 42.[20] It was made in the ninth century at an unidentified centre in Wales but may later have come into the possession of an English centre, for it has Latin glosses in Anglo-Caroline script of c.1000 by a scribe whose writing is found in other English manuscripts.[21] At present a Malmesbury provenance cannot be demonstrated for either of these manuscripts; it seems inherently less likely for the Welsh book, for there is no evidence of any significant cultural links between Wales and Malmesbury.

Next on Leland's list is 'Opera Fortunati carmine scripta', an entry which he repeated in the *De Scriptoribus*. This copy was probably early, since most

[16] CLA, II, no. 127; James, *A Descriptive Catalogue of the Manuscripts in the Library of Corpus Christi College, Cambridge*, II, p. 101; F. A. Rella, 'Continental Manuscripts acquired for English Centres in the Tenth and Early Eleventh Centuries', *Anglia*, 98 (1980), 107–16, at 110 (To Rella's list should be added Oxford, Bodl. Libr. Marshall 19; see below, p. 113), and H. Gneuss, 'Manuscripts written or owned in England up to 1100', ASE, 9 (1981), 1–60.

[17] James, *The Ancient Libraries of Canterbury and Dover*, p. 11, no. 152, and cf. pp. xxxii–iii; see also H. Thoma, 'The Oldest Manuscript of Juvencus', *Classical Review*, 64 (1950), 95–6.

[18] Marks survive in this position, for instance, in Cambridge, Corpus Christi College 260, Trinity College B. 14. 3 and R. 15. 22, and New Zealand, Wellington, Turnbull Library 16; and in many other manuscripts not included in the surviving fragment of the twelfth-century catalogue.

[19] My own examination convinced me of the S at the end, but not the A at the beginning. Later the inscription was studied under ultra-violet light by Professor R. I. Page and Dr M. Lapidge, who reported the fact that James's 'initial letter' was in fact the second letter of the inscription, and more likely to be a V. I am grateful to them for this information.

[20] Bishop, 'The Corpus Martianus Capella', p. 258.

[21] London, BL Cott. Vesp. D. xv, ff. 102–21, and BL Harl. 3376; see Bishop, art. cit.

of those extant were written between the ninth and eleventh centuries,[22] and since in England Fortunatus was well known – and probably best known – for at least a century and a half before the Conquest.[23] There is some positive evidence that William did not know his verse.[24] This seems odd for an omnivorous reader with such pronounced antiquarian interests, and the Fortunatus may therefore have been a late-comer to the abbey. On the other hand, Fortunatus's *Vita Paterni*, a work noted by Leland, was known to William,[25] and Leland's reference is probably to the copy once in London, British Library Cott. Vitell. D. xvii, burnt in the fire of 1731. This manuscript was originally bound up with Oxford, Bodleian Library Bodl. 852, written at Jumièges in the mid-eleventh century but at Malmesbury after 1106, probably acquired by William.[26] The relics of St Paternus had been given to Malmesbury by Athelstan.[27]

Of the next item, 'Beda super Canticum Abacuc', Laistner and King comment that 'MSS of it are few and it rarely appears in medieval catalogues'.[28] They list twelve manuscripts, of which six are English. All of these except one have known provenances, and all are of the twelfth century except for their common ancestor, Cambridge, Pembroke College 81, made in southern France during the second half of the ninth century, at Bury abbey by c.1150.[29] The only English manuscript of uncertain origin is London, Lambeth Palace Library 237, a post-medieval make-up of three volumes. Bede, *Super Habacuc*, is in the first volume, from the twelfth century. While there is no positive evidence to connect this volume with Malmesbury in particular, it was almost certainly written in south-west England, and is closely related to a copy of similar date from Gloucester abbey.[30] Less can be said of the next entry in Leland's list, 'Bedae allegorica expositio super Leviticum et Tobiam'. Laistner and King comment that the popularity of *De Tobia*, especially in the twelfth century, is astonishing, and

[22] *Fortunati Opera*, ed. F. Leo, MGH, Auct. Antiqu. 4. 1, pp. v–xiv.
[23] Ogilvy, *Books known to the English*, p. 140, is now thoroughly superseded by R. W. Hunt, 'Manuscript Evidence for Knowledge of the Poems of Venantius Fortunatus in Late Anglo-Saxon England', ASE, 8 (1979), 279–295.
[24] GP, p. 316.
[25] ibid., p. 399.
[26] See above, pp. 79–80.
[27] GP, pp. 398–9.
[28] M. L. W. Laistner and H. H. King, *A Hand-List of Bede Manuscripts* (Ithaca, N.Y., 1943), pp. 121–3. Now edited in CCSL 119B, p. 379ff.
[29] The manuscript was probably copied from a Corbie exemplar (information from Dr D. Ganz). It bears the Bury *ex libris* of c.1200 and figures in the earliest part of its composite library catalogue from the second half of the twelfth century.
[30] CCSL 119B, pp. 379–80.

they list seventy-four manuscripts of it.[31] None of the surviving English ones includes (pseudo-)Bede on Leviticus.[32]

I deal next with a group of items, 'Claudii tres libri super Matteum', 'Cassiodorus de Anima', 'Exameron Basilii' and 'Gregorius Nicenus de conditione hominis', which can be connected with Malmesbury only on Leland's testimony. To judge from other library catalogues and surviving copies all of these were especially popular in the twelfth century, and probably the Malmesbury examples were typical stately folios of that date. Aldhelm quotes Basil's work,[33] but the *Hexameron* was too common for that to be significant. Gregory of Nyssa is included in the twelfth-century section of Lambeth 237.

Interspersed with this group are some items which look more promising. 'Sententiae Xysti', interprete Rufino, qui contendit hunc fuisse Xystum pontificem Romanum' denotes Rufinus's translation of the *Sentences of Sextus*, a rare work surviving in twelve manuscripts of which no fewer than six, interestingly enough, are from England.[34] Glastonbury had a copy in 1247 and Leland records two others, at Faversham and the London Carmelite priory.[35] No less than five of the extant manuscripts from England are later than the twelfth century (two being of known provenance), so that we might well think that not much can be made of this item of Leland's. The remaining English manuscript is the third part of Lambeth 237, dating from the early tenth century. It was written on the continent but was in west or south-west England by the middle of the same century, since it is annotated by the hand identified as Dunstan's.[36] It may therefore be the copy recorded in the thirteenth-century Glastonbury catalogue. Leland's rendering of the alleged pope's name as 'Xystus', rather than 'Sixtus' or 'Sextus', seems at first sight against the connection; since this form occurs in only two of the extant manuscripts, Paris, Bibliothèque Nationale, lat. 2676 and 113, both continental and of the ninth and eleventh centuries respectively, it might indicate that Leland saw an early continental manuscript at Malmesbury. But Lambeth 237 remains a possibility, for Leland renders the name thus for

---

[31] Laistner and King, *Hand-List*, pp. 78–82.

[32] F. Stegmüller, *Repertorium Biblicum Medii Aevi* (Madrid, 11 vols, 1950–1980), no. 1649.

[33] Ed. Ehwald, p. 263 (*De Virg. Prosa*), in the version of Rufinus.

[34] Rufinus, *The Sentences of Sextus*, ed. H. Chadwick (Cambridge, 1959); reprinted CCSL 20, pp. 257–9; see also *Clavis*, no. 198h. Cambridge, St John's College 168 is from Witham; Cambridge, Sidney Sussex College 94, from York Franciscans. Unassigned are CUL Add. 584, Cambridge, Gonville and Caius College 351, London, BL Roy. 2 F. ii and Lambeth Palace Library 237.

[35] For the Glastonbury catalogue see T. W. Williams, *Somerset Medieval Libraries* (Bristol, 1897), p. 63, and, for the manuscripts seen by Leland, *Collectanea*, IV, pp. 6 and 53.

[36] Rella, 'Continental Manuscripts', p. 113, no. 22, and T. A. M. Bishop, 'An Early Example of Insular-Caroline', TCBS, IV. 5 (1968), 396–400, esp. p. 399, and idem, *English Caroline Minuscule* (Oxford, 1971), no. 3.

the Faversham and London copies also. He follows this entry with 'Questiones Albini super Genesim. parvus libellus', meaning Alcuin's *Interrogationes et Responsiones in Genesim.* Thirteen manuscripts of this work are known, five each from the ninth and tenth centuries, two from the twelfth century and one from the thirteenth.[37] The two English examples are late: Lambeth 148, twelfth-century from Lanthony, and BL Roy. 8 E. xvi of the early thirteenth century. But it is the description of the book rather than its contents that arouses interest, for Leland's words suggest that it contained *only* the item he mentions. Such a book would resemble Malmesbury's extant ninth-century copy of Jerome, *De Nominibus Hebraicis*, of which more later. It might not have been as early as that, but early it would certainly have been. By the twelfth century a single volume would scarcely have been wasted on this work alone. It is followed in Leland's list by another ninth-century author, 'Dionysius, interprete Ioanne Scoto', referring to the standard collection of pseudo-Dionysius's works in John Scotus Eriugena's translation, accompanied by the glosses and preface of Anastasius the Librarian and other matter.[38] This collection does not seem to have reached England before c.1100, after which it became very popular.[39] William of Malmesbury had it[40] and one imagines that Leland's volume must have had some connection with William. Two other books containing works of Alcuin appear in the *Collectanea* list and we may mention them to dismiss them. One, 'Albinus super Ecclesiasten', if early, might conceivably have been the ancestor of the copy in Oxford, Merton College 181, made for William of Malmesbury in the 1120s or 1130s and given to Merton before 1344.[41] The other, 'Epistolae Albini', from which Leland quotes elsewhere in the *Collectanea*, refers to the apograph of BL Cott. Tib. A. xv and the exemplar of its last section, made by William of Malmesbury, now lost.[42] In

---

[37] Stegmüller, *Repertorium*, no. 1085; PL 100. 515–66; prologue in MGH, Epistolae 4, p. 122ff (Ep. 80).
[38] MGH, Epistolae 7, pp. 430–4; see J. Cappuyns, *Jean Scot Erigène* (Brussels, 1933), pp. 150–61 and H. F. Dondaine, 'Le Corpus dionysien de l'université de Paris au XIIIe siècle' (*Storia e Letteratura* 44, Rome, 1953), esp. pp. 35–66.
[39] The earliest known English manuscript, from which all others apparently derive, is Oxford, St John's College 128, from the first quarter of the twelfth century, provenance unknown. Collation with William's quotation suggests that his manuscript too derived from this one. I have examined the St John's College manuscript for a possible Malmesbury connection, but could find no positive evidence. The historiated initial on f. 9v might assist in localizing the manuscript. It is an O enclosing *Christus super aspides*, in tinted outline style, the drapery showing 'nested V-folds'. Later English manuscripts are Cambridge, Trinity College B. 2. 31; Oxford, Bodl. Libr. Laud misc. 639, Ashmole 1526 and e Mus. 134.
[40] The evidence is set out below, p. 150.
[41] On this MS see above, pp. 93–5, and F. M. Powicke, *The Medieval Books of Merton College* (Oxford, 1931), p. 112.
[42] See below, pp. 172–3. Cf. MLGB, p. 128, where Leland's manuscript is identified with Oxford, Bodl. Libr. Wood Empt. 5, of the early thirteenth century.

other words, the manuscript seen by Leland almost certainly dated from the early twelfth century.

There remain four works in Leland's list and they are the most interesting of all. I begin with one already studied by James, 'Junilius ad Primasium papam'. The work meant is Junilius's *Institutes* or *De Partibus Divinae Legis*, dedicated to Primasius, bishop of Hadrumetum.[43] James noted that this work was quoted by Aldhelm,[44] who also made Leland's mistake as to the office held by Primasius: 'Iunillius, instituta regulari ... Primasio, sedis apostolicae pontifici scribens'.[45] James thought that this error must stem from Aldhelm's manuscript of Junilius, and that this manuscript was the one seen by Leland. This suggestion, in itself plausible, can be supported with additional evidence. Twenty-one of the twenty-three known manuscripts of Junilius are early, dating from the seventh to the eleventh century. But we may even have the remains of the Malmesbury copy.

BL Cott. Tib. A. xv, ff. 175–180, is a fragment of Junilius in early eighth-century Anglo-Saxon minuscule, written, according to Lowe, 'probably in a southern centre'.[46] The six leaves, containing *Inst.* I.9–II.17 and 22–4, were much damaged in the fire of 1731 and are now mounted separately. Their correct order is ff. 177, 179, 180, 176, 175 and 178 and they now measure c.230×160 mm. There are two obstacles to be tackled before considering some positive arguments for identifying these leaves as the remains of the Malmesbury book. First of all, Lowe compared the script of the present manuscript with that of BL Cott. Charter Aug. ii. 18, dated 704–5 and now proved to have been written in London.[47] The resemblance is

---

[43] See James, *Two Ancient English Scholars*, p. 13. The work is in PL 68. 15–42; see *Clavis*, no. 872, and Stegmüller, *Repertorium*, no. 5328. There is a critical edition by H. Kihn, *Theodor von Mopsuestia und Junilius Africanus als Exegeten* (Freiburg, 1880), pp. 467–528, based on thirteen manuscripts. Another ten were added by M. L. W. Laistner, 'Antiochene Exegesis in Western Europe', *Harvard Theological Review*, 40 (1947), 19–31. For the dates of the earliest manuscripts see CLA, II, no. 189 (addition), III, no. 348 (s. viii/ix), and VII, no. 965 (s. vii/viii). Cf. also Avranches, Bibl. Mun. 109 (s. xi), ff. 138–150, Laon, Bibl. de la Ville 273, and Oxford, Bodl. Libr. Laud misc. 159 (Lorsch), ninth-century manuscripts containing Wicbod, *Quaestiones in Octateuchum ex Dictis Sanctorum Patrum Augustini, Ambrosii, Hilarii, Eucherii et Junilii* (on which see J. Contreni, *The Cathedral School of Laon from 850 to 930* [Munich, 1978], pp. 37–8 and 45; Stegmüller, *Repertorium*, no. 8376, citing Paris, BN nouv. acq. 762). Salisbury Cathedral Library 115 (s. xi ex), ff. 20–41v contains a work entitled 'Pauca problemata et enigmata ex tomis Canonum', which proceeds through the biblical books with extracts from Jerome, Augustine, Ambrose, Isidore, Gregory, Eucherius, Cassian, 'Petrus' and Junilius.

[44] James, *Two Ancient English Scholars*, p. 13; Laistner, 'Antiochene Exegesis', pp. 26–7.

[45] Ed. Ehwald, pp. 81–2 and n. 1 (*De Metris*).

[46] CLA, II, no. 189.

[47] Earlier transcriptions and discussions are now superseded by P. Chaplais, 'The Letter from Bishop Wealdhere of London to Archbishop Brihtwold of Canterbury', in *Medieval Scribes, Manuscripts and Libraries*, pp. 3–23.

not however close and we can with greater justice assign the script of Cott. Tib. A. xv to south-west England. In a recent article Malcolm Parkes has studied the handwriting of St Boniface and of an associate whom Parkes calls 'Glossator B', describing him as 'a kind of amanuensis ... working under supervision, amplifying the glosses of Glossator A' (whom Parkes identifies as Boniface).[48] This man and the scribe of the Spangenberg Servius[49] form a group which Parkes connects with south-west England. Dr Parkes himself suspects Malmesbury as a likely place of origin for the Servius;[50] it is a pity that Aldhelm's quotations from Servius are not extensive enough to permit a comparison. Characteristics of the handwriting of this group are: an upright **g** with a long, horizontal head-stroke, the tail occasionally brought back to form a loop; **tio** in a ligature; **fi** ligature with the **i** traced across the head-stroke of **f**; and **g** in ligature with a following letter at the beginning of a word. The Cotton Junilius fragment has Glossator B's form of **g** and his **g** and **tio** ligatures, but not the others. It has the form for **fi** used by Glossator A (**f** plus **i** subscript).

Another consideration is that a copy of Junilius, described as 'vetustus', appears in the Glastonbury library catalogue of 1247.[51] One has therefore to make a case for identifying the Cotton fragment with Leland's Malmesbury book rather than with the Glastonbury one. The compiler of the Glastonbury catalogue distinguished between books which were 'vetustus' and those which were 'vetustissimus', which suggests that the local Junilius was perhaps not as old as the eighth century. Nor is there any evidence that this book survived until the Dissolution, as was the case with the Malmesbury example. But what tips the scales decisively in favour of Malmesbury, I believe, is the fact that Leland called what he saw there 'fragmenta' and the Cotton leaves were in that state even before the fire of 1731. In his catalogue entry for Cott. Tib. A. xv Thomas Smith described a 'Fragmentum theologicum', characteribus uetustis, et a festinante scriba exaratis'.[52] That this was the Junilius is proved by Wanley's annotation of 'Saxonicis cursoriis' after 'characteribus' in Oxford, Bodleian Library, Gough Lond. 54, his copy of Smith's *Catalogus*.

Aldhelm's quotation from Junilius does not tell us much. Collation with Kihn's edition shows that Aldhelm's exemplar was not related to his manuscripts A, D, E or L, but that leaves another nine possibilities. Kihn did not use the Cotton fragment, which does not overlap with Aldhelm's quotation. It is not related to A, D or L either (it does not overlap with the

---

[48] M. B. Parkes, 'The Handwriting of St Boniface; a Reassessment of the Problems', *Beiträge zur Geschichte der deutschen Sprache und Literatur*, 98 (1976), 161–179, esp. 177.

[49] CLA, Suppl., no. 1806.

[50] So Dr Parkes informs me.

[51] Williams, *Somerset Libraries*, p. 75.

[52] Smith, *Catalogus Librorum Manuscriptorum Bibliothecae Cottonianae*, p. 21.

excerpts in E), nor to B, H, M, P or R. Thus all that can be said is that there are no insuperable textual obstacles to its identification with Aldhelm's manuscript and that there is a balance of probability in favour. It was apparently written early in the eighth century, by which time Aldhelm was an old man; unfortunately the *De Metris*, in which he quotes Junilius, cannot be closely dated.[53] To sum up: there is good if not conclusive evidence that the Cotton Junilius is a fragment of the Malmesbury copy, and some reason to connect it with Aldhelm.

The next work, mentioned in both of Leland's books and therefore thought by him particularly noteworthy, is the *Peri Hermeneias* doubtfully ascribed to Apuleius. The two most recent editors of this work[54] together list ten manuscripts, all continental, four from the ninth century, two from the tenth, three from the eleventh and one from the twelfth. Again this gives us grounds for presuming that the book which Leland saw was an ancient one. Neither editor mentions the copy in Cambridge, Corpus Christi College 206, a tenth-century manuscript written in a puzzling mixture of continental Caroline script with many Insular abbreviations.[55] Its opening leaf, originally left blank to receive special treatment, was written in England c.1100, in a fine hand uninfluenced by newly introduced continental fashions but accompanied by a striking 'Norman' initial outlined in red, tinted with violet, red and green and displaying a lion and dragon, foliage and interlace. This was obviously done in a well-established scriptorium and at this date one thinks of Canterbury, in particular St Augustine's.[56] It is perhaps worth noting that William certainly knew other items in Corpus Christi 206: Boethius's Trinitarian works (although they were not uncommon at the time), and probably Alcuin's *Dialectica*, much rarer.[57] There is therefore a possibility that this was the manuscript that Leland saw at Malmesbury, but it is a remote one.

The next item, 'Grammatica Euticis', survives in thirty manuscripts dating from the ninth century to the eleventh.[58] The only specimen of English

[53] Lapidge and Herren, *Aldhelm*, pp. 12–13.

[54] A. Goldbacher, 'Liber *peri hermeneias* qui Apuleii Madaurensis esse traditur', *Wiener Studien*, 7 (1885), 253–277, and P. Thomas, *Apuleii Opera*, III (Leipzig, 1908), pp. 176–194.

[55] James, *Catalogue of Manuscripts in the Library of Corpus Christi College*, I, pp. 495–498, and Leonardi, 'I Codici di Marziano Capella', pp. 21–2, no. 29. Neither notices that the first recto was written later than the rest of the manuscript.

[56] Since a Norman style of script was adopted at Christ Church soon after the Conquest, whereas Anglo-Caroline was written at St Augustine's well into the early 1100s: C. R. Dodwell, *The Canterbury School of Illumination 1066–1200* (Cambridge, 1954), pp. 6–8, 25–6.

[57] See below, pp. 197, 200.

[58] C. Jeudy, 'Les manuscrits de l'*Ars de Verbo* d'Eutychès et le commentaire de Rémi d'Auxerre', in *Etudes de civilisation médiévale IXe–XIIe siècles: mélanges offerts à E.-R. Labande* (Poitiers, 1974), pp. 421–436.

provenance is one of the ninth-century sections of St Dunstan's 'Classbook' from Glastonbury,[59] and even that originated in Brittany. Leland records another copy at St Augustine's, Canterbury.[60] In 1247 Glastonbury had two copies of this work, both described as 'vetustissimi',[61] but it was evidently not well known in England, nor thought useful after the early eleventh century.[62] We may be fairly confident, therefore, that the book which Leland saw was part of the pre-Conquest library at Malmesbury, that it was continental and probably not older than the ninth century. Ogilvy credits Aldhelm with a reference to Eutyches, but it is a dubious one.[63]

I have left until last the most complicated case of all, yet also the most important and interesting. In his *Collectanea* Leland refers to an item as simply 'Tertullianus'. M. R. James was misled, and has misled others, into thinking that this referred to a collection containing Tertullian's *Apology* and some works of Lactantius put together by William of Malmesbury and known from late manuscripts.[64] Had James looked at Leland's *De Scriptoribus*, however, he would have seen that this was wrong, for there Leland refers to a 'Tertulliani librum de Spectaculis, de Ieiunio'. The two references enable the manuscript to be identified as another example of the 'Corpus Corbeiense' of Tertullian's works, originally compiled in the fifth century and containing *De Resurrectione Mortuorum*, *De Trinitate* (now attributed to Novatian), *De Spectaculis*, *De Praescriptione Haereticorum*, *De Pudicitia*, *De Monogamia* and *De Ieiunio*.[65] This collection is known to have existed in two manuscripts: one, probably of the ninth century, described in two eleventh-century catalogues from Corbie, the other listed in the early ninth-century (833) catalogue of Cologne cathedral library. Two folios from the second of these manuscripts were not long ago discovered doing duty as endleaves in the sixteenth-century register of a German baronial family. The script apparently resembles the work of the scribes under Hildebald, bishop of Cologne 785–819.[66]

The Cologne manuscript, dismembered by c.1563, was probably used by

[59] Oxford, Bodl. Libr. Auct. F. 4. 32; ed. R. W. Hunt, *St Dunstan's Classbook from Glastonbury* (Umbrae Codicum Occidentalium 4, Amsterdam, 1961).
[60] Leland, *Collectanea*, IV, p. 7.
[61] Williams, *Somerset Libraries*, p. 75; also Leland, *Collectanea*, IV, p. 154, though this is Dunstan's book yet again.
[62] Ogilvy, *Books known to the English*, pp. 137–8.
[63] Ed. Ehwald, p. 195 (*De Metris*); cf. Roger, *L'enseignement*, p. 329 n. 4.
[64] James, *Two Ancient English Scholars*, p. 20; cf. above, p. 42. The 'Codex Luganensis' of Tertullian's modern editors, to which William's text of the *Apology* is related, is now Oxford, Bodl. Libr. Lat. theol. d. 34.
[65] *Tertulliani Opera*, I, ed. E. Dekkers et al., CCSL 1, p. vii and n. 3.
[66] G. Lieftinck, 'Un fragment de *De Spectaculis* de Tertullien provenant d'un manuscrit du 9e siècle', *Vigiliae Christianae*, 5 (1951), 193–203, esp. p. 196, and E. Dekkers, 'Note sur les fragments récemment découverts de Tertullien', *Sacris Erudiri*, 4 (1952), 372–383.

the second editor of Tertullian, Mesnart (1545), and perhaps by the third, Ghelen (1550).[67] However, on his title-page Ghelen claimed to have had recourse to 'complures veteres e Gallicanis Germanisque bibliothecis conquisitos ... codices, in quibus praecipuus fuit unus longe incorruptissimus in ultimam usque petitus Britanniam'. On the verso he added further details of this manuscript: 'Tandem ex ultima Britannia Ioannes Lelandus, uir antiquarius et feliciori dignus ualetudine, communicauit exemplar in Masburensi coenobio gentis eius uetustissimo repertum'.[68] It is astonishing that the modern editors of Tertullian and Novatian have, because of Ghelen's generally untrustworthy editorship, from time to time doubted the very existence of this manuscript, without checking Leland's works.[69] But let us proceed further.

In 1579 Jacques de Pamele (Pamelius) published the third edition of the works of Tertullian and Novatian, using, *inter alia*, 'liber manuscriptus Anglicus quidam, quem thesauri loco penes se adseruabat Ioan. Clemens Anglus'.[70] In the *Notarum Explicatio* he refers to 'Anglicus codex antiquissimus Ioan. Clementis Angli, e quo VII castigati sunt libri'. The seven works are those in the 'Corpus Corbeiense' and Pamele, using this manuscript, was able to correct some faults of Mesnart and Ghelen. The latest editor of Novatian says: 'On ne saurait rien dire avec certitude sur le rapport mutuel de ces trois manuscrits, ne serait-ce que parce que nous ne savons pas exactement de quelle manière les éditeurs se sont servis des ressources qui étaient á leur disposition'.[71] Again, it is astonishing that the continental editors of Tertullian and Novatian have not troubled to identify the Englishman John Clement. He is not hard to track down. A distinguished Oxford graduate, protégé of Sir Thomas More and royal physician, he was the owner of a fine library,[72] which was catalogued in 1554–5 as part of proceedings to recover property seized during his exile from England in the reign of Edward VI. Among the authors listed in this catalogue is Tertullian.[73] Since these books were sequestrated in England,

---

[67] Lieftinck, 'Fragment', pp. 198–9; Dekkers, 'Fragments', pp. 379–382.
[68] *Novatiani Opera*, ed. G. F. Diercks, CCSL 4, p. 3.
[69] Dekkers, 'Fragments', p. 381, and *Novatiani Opera*, p. 3.
[70] Dekkers, 'Fragments', pp. 374–5, and *Novatiani Opera*, pp. 4–7.
[71] ibid., p. 7.
[72] A. B. Emden, *A Biographical Register of the University of Oxford, A.D. 1501–1540* (Oxford, 1974), pp. 121–2; *Dictionary of National Biography*, IV, p. 489; E. Wenkelbach, *John Clement: ein englischer Humanist und Arzt des sechzehnten Jahrhunderts*, Studien zur Geschichte der Medizin 14 (Leipzig, 1925); G. Mercati, 'Sopra Giovanni Clement e i suoi Manoscritti', *La Bibliofilia*, 28 (1926), 81–99, reprinted in Mercati's *Opera Minori*, IV, *Studi e Testi* 79 (Rome, 1937), 292–315; and A. W. Reed, 'John Clement and his Books', *The Library*, 4th ser., 6 (1926), 329–339; R. W. Hunt, 'The Need for a Guide to the Editors of Patristic Texts in the 16th Century', *Studia Patristica*, 18 (1982), 365–371.
[73] Reed, 'John Clement', p. 339. But Reed says that 'in all instances the books appear

they must have been in Clement's possession before his first flight to the continent, which was in July 1549. In the autumn of 1560 or thereabouts he transferred to Antwerp and then to Malines, where he died in 1572. I assume that his ancient copy of the 'Corpus Corbeiense' of Tertullian's works was Leland's, passed on to him either by Leland himself or by Ghelen after he had finished with it. For one thing, the only alternative interpretation, that *two* ancient English manuscripts of this rare collection were owned by two contemporary English scholars who lent them to successive continental editors, seems remote and unlikely. Secondly, Leland and Clement had for a time at least been friends. They were at St Paul's School together under Lily and, when in 1526 Clement married Thomas More's step-daughter, Leland, then in the Duke of Norfolk's household, composed an appropriate epithalamium.[74] After 1530, certainly, one assumes that relations between the two men must have become somewhat strained, since Leland supported the religious policies of Henry VIII, while Clement remained faithful to the principles of his benefactor. What happened to their copy of Tertullian after Pamele had used it is not known.

In other words, Ghelen's 'codex Masburense' did in fact exist and did contain the 'Corpus Corbeiense', and we have the word of Ghelen and Pamele that it was very ancient. Can we find out any more about it? The copy of the 'Corpus Corbeiense' which appears in the Cologne catalogue apparently did not contain any authors' names ('sed auctorem ignoramus' runs the entry) and Novatian, *De Trinitate*, and Tertullian, *De Spectaculis*, were lumped together under the title 'De Fide'.[76] John Clement's manuscript, which I take to be Leland's from Malmesbury, distinguished the two works as in the tables of contents reproduced by the Corbie catalogues.[77] So the Malmesbury manuscript was, in this respect at least, more closely related to the Corbie copy than to the Cologne one. Were the manuscripts from Malmesbury and Corbie indeed one and the same? The two Corbie catalogues in which the Tertullian appears date from the first half and third quarter of the eleventh century respectively. But Tertullian is absent from a third Corbie catalogue of c.1200.[78] One assumes that it left the house (if it

---

to be printed editions unless they are described as written' (p. 337).

[74] Wenkelbach, *John Clement*, pp. 17–18 and 55–8 and n. 55.

[75] Presumably it was, as usual, disbound and 'marked up' for the printing process and then discarded afterwards.

[76] Dekkers, 'Fragments', pp. 374–5.

[77] ibid.

[78] L. Delisle, *Le Cabinet des manuscrits de la Bibliothèque Impériale* (Paris, 3 vols, 1858–81), II, p. 428 (first catalogue), 428–32 (second) and 432–40 (third). On their dates see C. de Merindol, *La Production des Livres peints à l'Abbaye de Corbie* (Lille, 3 vols, 1976), I, pp. 70–1. Dr D. Ganz informs me that the titles of works in the second catalogue were taken from tables of contents apparently written in the ninth century.

was not destroyed outright) during the intervening period and there is therefore a real possibility that it came to England and thus to Malmesbury. One is tempted to see it as yet another of William of Malmesbury's continental acquisitions, although there is no evidence for his knowing these particular works of Tertullian. The most likely alternative hypothesis would be that the Malmesbury manuscript was a *gemellus*, early copy, or even the ancestor of the Corbie book and that it was at Malmesbury well before the Conquest.

With this we leave Leland's list, but it does not include all the notable manuscripts that he found at Malmesbury. Elsewhere in the *Collectanea* and also in *De Scriptoribus* he quotes a series of verse inscriptions ascribed to Bede and others, which he says he found in an ancient volume from Malmesbury abbey.[79] Michael Lapidge was able to show that William of Malmesbury knew this collection, which was originally made in the eighth century by Bishop Milred of Worcester.[80] Recently a bifolium from the Malmesbury manuscript came to light in the library of the University of Illinois, Urbana.[81] It is written in tenth-century Anglo-Saxon square minuscule and is annotated by Leland.[82] How long it had been at Malmesbury before William's time cannot as yet be determined; it may have been another of his acquisitions.[83]

Let us sum up before proceeding to other kinds of evidence. In the Cotton Junilius fragments we have perhaps identified the remains of one of Aldhelm's books. Several others, Juvencus, Fortunatus, Rufinus, Alcuin *Super Genesim*, Apuleius and Eutyches, were probably ancient and part of the pre-Conquest library at Malmesbury, although this cannot be proven. The Tertullian was certainly ancient, probably from the ninth century, perhaps written and for a time kept at Corbie, in which case it came to Malmesbury during the twelfth century. Finally, a tenth-century copy of Bishop Milred's collection of epigrams by English and other authors was at Malmesbury by William's time. To William we turn now.

---

[79] Leland, *Collectanea*, III, pp. 114–118, and *De Scriptoribus*, p. 134. See the bibliography cited below, pp. 125–8.

[80] M. Lapidge, 'Some Remnants of Bede's Lost "Liber Epigrammatum"', EHR, 90 (1975), 798–820.

[81] L. Wallach, 'The Urbana Anglo-Saxon Sylloge of Latin Inscriptions', in *Poetry and Poetics from Ancient Greece to the Renaissance: Studies in honor of James Hutton*, ed. G. M. Kirkwood, Cornell Studies in Classical Philology 38 (Ithaca, N.Y., 1975), pp. 134–151, and D. Schaller, 'Bemerkungen zur Inschriften-Sylloge von Urbana', *Mittellateinisches Jahrbuch*, 12 (1977), 9–21. For further bibliography see below, pp. 126–9.

[82] The annotations are visible on the photograph reproduced by Wallach, p. 135. See below, p. 128.

[83] Lapidge, 'Some Remnants', p. 820, and below, p. 128.

In the lecture in which he connected Aldhelm's quotation from Junilius with the Malmesbury copy seen by Leland M. R. James drew attention to William's copy of the rare *Breviarium Alaricum*.[84] He noted that Aldhelm claimed to be teaching Roman law at Malmesbury and asked what text he could have used, concluding that at this period it could hardly be other than the *Breviarium*.[85] Thus he conjectured that William copied an ancient manuscript available to Aldhelm. As I have pointed out above,[86] the textual evidence supports James's suggestion, for William's copy, in spite of its comparatively late date and William's heavy editing, is the closest to the lost archetype of the 'classis melior', which must have predated the second half of the seventh century, the date of its earliest surviving descendant. The question arises: how is it that, in spite of the existence of many early continental copies of the *Breviarium*, William's should be the closest of all to the archetype? That this archetype left the continent early, having had time to produce only one or two descendants there, is certainly an attractive hypothesis. The late seventh century and Aldhelm's lifetime would suit admirably.

I mentioned earlier William's copy of Tertullian's *Apology* and three works of Lactantius.[87] The *Apology* had some circulation in England after c.1100,[88] but the only other trace of these particular Lactantius items in pre-Conquest England is Aldhelm's quotation from one of them, the *De Opificio Dei*.[89] The extreme rarity of Lactantius manuscripts makes it likely that William's exemplar was, or was derived from, the manuscript used by Aldhelm. This is not contradicted by the meagre textual history of William's copy.[90]

---

[84] James, *Two Ancient English Scholars*, pp. 13–14.
[85] See also A. S. Cook, 'Aldhelm's Legal Studies', *Journal of English and Germanic Philology*, 23 (1924), 105–113.
[86] See above, pp. 62–3, and below, p. 200.
[87] See above, p. 42 and notes.
[88] Three English Tertullian manuscripts are known apart from the copies of William's collection (Oxford, Balliol College 79 and the German Gotha, Forschungsbibliothek membr. I. 55): Oxford, Bodl. Libr. Lat. theol. d. 34 (see above, note 64) and Add. C. 284 (s. xii); London, BL Roy. 5 F. xviii (Salisbury, c.1100). Ogilvy, *Books known to the English*, p. 250, produces virtually no evidence for knowledge of Tertullian's works before the Conquest, though to argue from Ogilvy's silence is dangerous.
[89] James, *Two Ancient English Scholars*, p. 20; Ehwald, p. 197 (*De Metris*). Lactantius was listed by Alcuin among the authors in the library at York (Ogilvy, p. 191).
[90] William's copy shares a common ancestor with Paris, BN lat. 1664 (s. xii) and Monte Cassino, Archivio della Badia 595 (c.1100): *Lactantii Opera*, I. i, ed. S. Brandt, CSEL 19, pp. xlvii–liii. The Paris manuscript gives accents and breathings to the Greek, a remarkable feature in a twelfth-century western manuscript. They must surely have been present in the archetype and are a fair guarantee of its antiquity.

A more certain relic of the pre-Conquest Malmesbury library was the old copy of Aldhelm's *De Metris* described by both Faricius and William in their Lives of the saint.[91] Faricius called it 'quodam antiquissimo codice in eiusdem [*scil.* Malmesburiensis] ecclesiae reperto'. Ehwald suggested that it must have resembled extant early manuscripts containing the *De Metris* alone, such as Brussels, Bibliothèque Royale 9581–95, of the tenth century. In his *Gesta Pontificum* William mentions a Bible in the possession of his church, allegedly once owned by its patron.[92] Not knowing the basis for this attribution one has to be sceptical of it, although we can at least accept William's testimony that the book was a venerable one. The *De Metris*, Bible and *Breviarium* are the only works known to William through ancient manuscripts of certain Malmesbury provenance. The handful of other early and interesting manuscripts which it can be demonstrated he knew could have come from elsewhere, since he visited many other libraries, some more than once.[93] We do, however, possess one of William's own ancient books. This is Cambridge, Corpus Christi College 330, his edition of Martianus Capella.[94] It consists of two volumes bound together by William himself. The first, which does not interest us, is the text of Martianus written c.1100, with Remigius's gloss added by William; the second contains commentaries on Martianus in late ninth-century Carolingian minuscule. It was in England by the tenth century, but, again, where William found it cannot be said. The odds are that it was a local book.

This brings us to the third class of evidence, features in extant books. Oxford, Bodleian Library Marshall 19 is the ninth-century copy of Jerome, *De Nominibus Hebraicis*, mentioned earlier.[95] It was written by one Theudbert for the church of St Medard, Soissons, but it was at Malmesbury by the late tenth century, for a hand of that date has inscribed at the head of f. 1 the opening line of the *ex libris* verses, mentioning Aldhelm, found in Cambridge, Corpus Christi College MS 23, also from the house. The line was repeated just below by a hand of the late eleventh century. The book, however, has the thirteenth-century pressmark of Christ Church, Canterbury. It is one of the two certain attributions to the pre-Conquest Malmesbury library. Cambridge, Corpus Christi College 23, a splendid illustrated copy of Prudentius's works written c.1000, is the other.[96] The

[91] *Acta Sanctorum Maii*, VI, pp. 84–93 (25 May), esp. p. 87 and GP, p. 344; see R. Ehwald, 'De Aenigmatibus Aldhelmi et Acrostichis', *Festschrift Albert von Bamberg* (Gotha, 1905), pp. 1–26, esp. pp. 13–14.
[92] GP, p. 378.
[93] For this evidence see above, pp. 73–5.
[94] Bishop, 'The Corpus Martianus Capella', pp. 267–8, and above, pp. 81–2.
[95] See above, p. 78.
[96] See above, p. 78; Temple, *Anglo-Saxon Manuscripts 900–1066*, no. 48, with bibliography.

verses at the beginning show that it was given to the house by Abbot Aethelweard (c.1033–44). Two other manuscripts with claims, BL Cott. Otho B. x. f. 51 + Otho C. i, part I (Gospels in English)[97] and Cambridge, Corpus Christi College MS 361 (Gregory, *Pastoral Care*),[98] date from the first half and middle of the eleventh century respectively. The first, badly burnt in the 1731 fire, is connected fairly firmly with Malmesbury from early on by the addition to it c.1050 of an Old English translation of Pope Sergius's confirmation of Aldhelm's foundation. The second is written in a Norman hand, and at the end the *Passio S. Mauritii* was begun by a continental, probably Norman hand of c.1100. It presumably came to England and Malmesbury not long after this, since it has some annotations probably by William as well as a fifteenth-century Malmesbury *ex libris*.

Finally I must discuss the recent attribution to Malmesbury by Dr P. Lucas of another great illustrated Anglo-Saxon manuscript, Oxford, Bodleian Library Junius 11 (the 'Caedmon Genesis').[99] This manuscript has been traditionally assigned to Christ Church, Canterbury, on stylistic grounds, and because it fits the entry of 'Genesis anglice depicta' in Prior Eastry's early fourteenth-century library catalogue.[100] The stylistic parallels are, however, not compelling in themselves, and Lucas argues that the catalogue description suits just as well a manuscript such as BL Cott. Claud. B. iv – though this suggestion would carry more weight if Claud. B. iv had been at Christ Church rather than at St Augustine's in the later Middle Ages.[101] Lucas then mounts four positive arguments for a Malmesbury origin and provenance for Junius 11. Firstly, some of its illustrations are by the artist of Cambridge, Corpus Christi College MS 23. 'This identification makes it likely that both manuscripts were produced at one place ... Since the provenance of the "Corpus Prudentius" is Malmesbury ... it seems most probable that the two manuscripts were produced there'. Both of these inferences are questionable. Considering the peripatetic operations of illuminators in the twelfth century at least, one cannot assume that two manuscripts originated in the same scriptorium simply because they were

[97] N. R. Ker, *Catalogue of Manuscripts containing Anglo-Saxon* (Oxford, 1957), no. 181.

[98] See above, p. 79.

[99] The attribution was first argued in his edition of the Old English *Exodus* (Methuen's Old English Library, London, 1977), pp. 1–6. Cf. Temple, *Anglo-Saxon Manuscripts*, no. 58. Some of my criticisms made below were also made by D. Jost, reviewing Lucas's edition in *Speculum*, 54 (1979), 829–830. Lucas has since advanced the same arguments in a more elaborate form in 'MS Junius 11 and Malmesbury', *Scriptorium*, 34 (1980), 197–220.

[100] Dr Temple has been criticized for her tendency, in *Anglo-Saxon Manuscripts*, to attribute a number of manuscripts to the Canterbury scriptoria or libraries on insufficient evidence; see L. Brownrigg, 'Manuscripts containing English Decoration 871–1066, Catalogued and Illustrated: a Review', ASE, 7 (1978), 258–266.

[101] Temple, *Anglo-Saxon Manuscripts*, no. 86.

illustrated by the same artist. The work of the 'Alexis Master' of the St Albans Psalter or of the artist of the Lambeth Bible are cases in point.[102] And then, a Malmesbury *origin* is not proven for Corpus Christi 23. Since it was donated by the abbot c.1033–44 its presence there is guaranteed only from that time and it may have come from elsewhere. Secondly, Lucas notes a 'very close and exclusive correspondence between features of some of the illustrations in MS Junius 11 and features of some of the carved medallions (c.1170–80) on the voussoirs of the entrance arch of the south porch of Malmesbury abbey'. He refers in particular to three medallions in the porch's Genesis cycle (Noah's ark, Adam delving and Eve spinning, and Adam and Eve hiding from God) which show inconographical details otherwise found only in Junius 11.[103] Any conclusions from this, however, must be exceedingly muted, because of Lucas's double 'some of', because of the late twelfth-century date of the carvings and because some of them show iconographical affinities with BL Cott. Claud. B. iv, Corpus Christi 23 and other manuscripts.[104] The most that this evidence could be expected to support would be the presence of Junius 11 at Malmesbury in the twelfth century. But I think it more inherently likely that the carvers' team used a pattern-book containing an eclectic repertoire of Old English iconographical schemes. Thirdly, the 'Aelfwine' whose portrait was added to p. 2 of Junius 11 is identified as the abbot of Malmesbury c.1043–6, although Lucas admits that 'this name was quite common among the Anglo-Saxons'.[105] It so happens that an Aelfwine was prior of Christ Church, Canterbury, at some time between 1052 and c.1074,[106] but since the portrait is of an untonsured man, perhaps he was not a member of the clergy at all. Finally, Lucas notes that the book was exposed to thick smoke before it was sewn and bound, an operation which he dates c.1050.[107] He therefore connects the smoke-stains with the fire which destroyed 'totum coenobium' at Malmesbury 'in the time of Edward the Confessor', that is, between 1042 and 1066.[108] But his authority on this point, William of Malmesbury, speaks of two fires 'quae

---

[102] R. M. Thomson, *Manuscripts from St Albans Abbey 1066–1235* (Woodbridge, 2 vols, 1982), I, pp. 5–6, 31–36.
[103] Lucas, 'MS Junius 11 and Malmesbury', pp. 215–219.
[104] On the correspondences, see now M. Q. Smith, *The Sculptures of the South Porch of Malmesbury Abbey* (Malmesbury, 1975), based on, and sometimes correcting K. J. Galbraith, 'The Iconography of the Biblical Scenes at Malmesbury Abbey', *Journal of the British Architectural Association*, 3rd ser., 28 (1965), 39–56.
[105] In fact 71 instances of it (not including this one) are given in W. G. Searle, *Onomasticon Anglo-Saxonicum* (Cambridge, 1897), pp. 27–29.
[106] Knowles, Brooke and London, *Heads*, p. 33.
[107] Lucas, *Exodus*, p. 4, based on the opinion of the late G. Pollard. Interesting details of the manuscript, not affecting the question of its provenance, are given by P. Lucas, 'On the Incomplete Ending of *Daniel* and the Addition of *Christ and Satan* to MS Junius 11', *Anglia*, 97 (1979), 46–59 (the binding is discussed pp. 50–1).
[108] Lucas, *Exodus*, p. 4.

totum coenobium temporibus Elfredi et Aeduuardi regum consumpserunt'.[109] Had William meant the Confessor he would have said so; an Edward paired with Alfred can only mean the latter's son who reigned 899–924, and this puts both of the Malmesbury fires earlier than the manufacture of Junius 11.[110] In any case, Barbara Raw has recently and conclusively redated the present binding of Junius 11 to the early thirteenth century.[111] The character and date of its earlier binding are totally unknown and unknowable.[112] Four weak arguments do not support each other or constitute a single strong one. These particular arguments do not make much of a case for a Malmesbury provenance for Junius 11 and no case at all for its origin there. On the contrary, some of the new facts adduced by Lucas add support to the case – such as it is – for Christ Church Canterbury.

William and the extant books add a few items to the pre-Conquest library. The *Breviarium* used by William was certainly venerable and possibly Aldhelm's; so perhaps was William's Lactantius exemplar, and the copy of Aldhelm's *De Metris* still at the abbey in the twelfth century could have dated from the eighth or the ninth century. Oxford, Bodleian Library Marshall 19 is the best-attested case of an ancient manuscript which was also at the abbey early on and the Corpus Prudentius shows that the house was acquiring splendid books during the period of monastic reform. Some of the other old and valuable books available to William may have been local, such as the second part of Corpus Christi 330, but this cannot be proven.

Few generalizations can be made on the basis of such a brief list of sometimes uncertain attributions, but the variety of important and interesting books which we have discovered is noteworthy: rare patristic works, late antique secular literature, early copies of English and Carolingian writings. The presence of such works was due to a number of factors: the early origins of the house, the learning of Aldhelm and William, and probably Malmesbury's relative provinciality after the early twelfth century, permitting the survival of books which would have been discarded as outdated in centres with a more continuous intellectual vitality. Had we more evidence, we would probably find the Malmesbury library to have been most like those at Durham and Glastonbury, comparable ancient centres. The loss of nearly all of its books has undoubtedly deprived us of one of the greater libraries of pre-Reformation England.

---

[109] GP, p. 363.

[110] On the date of Junius 11, see Brownrigg, 'Manuscripts', p. 255 n. 2. Moreover William says that a beam, miraculously lengthened by Aldhelm, was not harmed by the fires, although since then 'annis et carie uicta defecit'. This seems to imply a substantial lapse of time between the later fire and William's day.

[111] B. C. Raw, 'The Construction of Oxford, Bodleian Library, Junius 11', ASE, 13 (1984), 197–9.

[112] G. Pollard, 'Some Anglo-Saxon Bookbindings', *The Book Collector*, 24 (1975), 130–159, does not treat Junius 11. Note his cautionary comments on the dating of early bindings on p. 137.

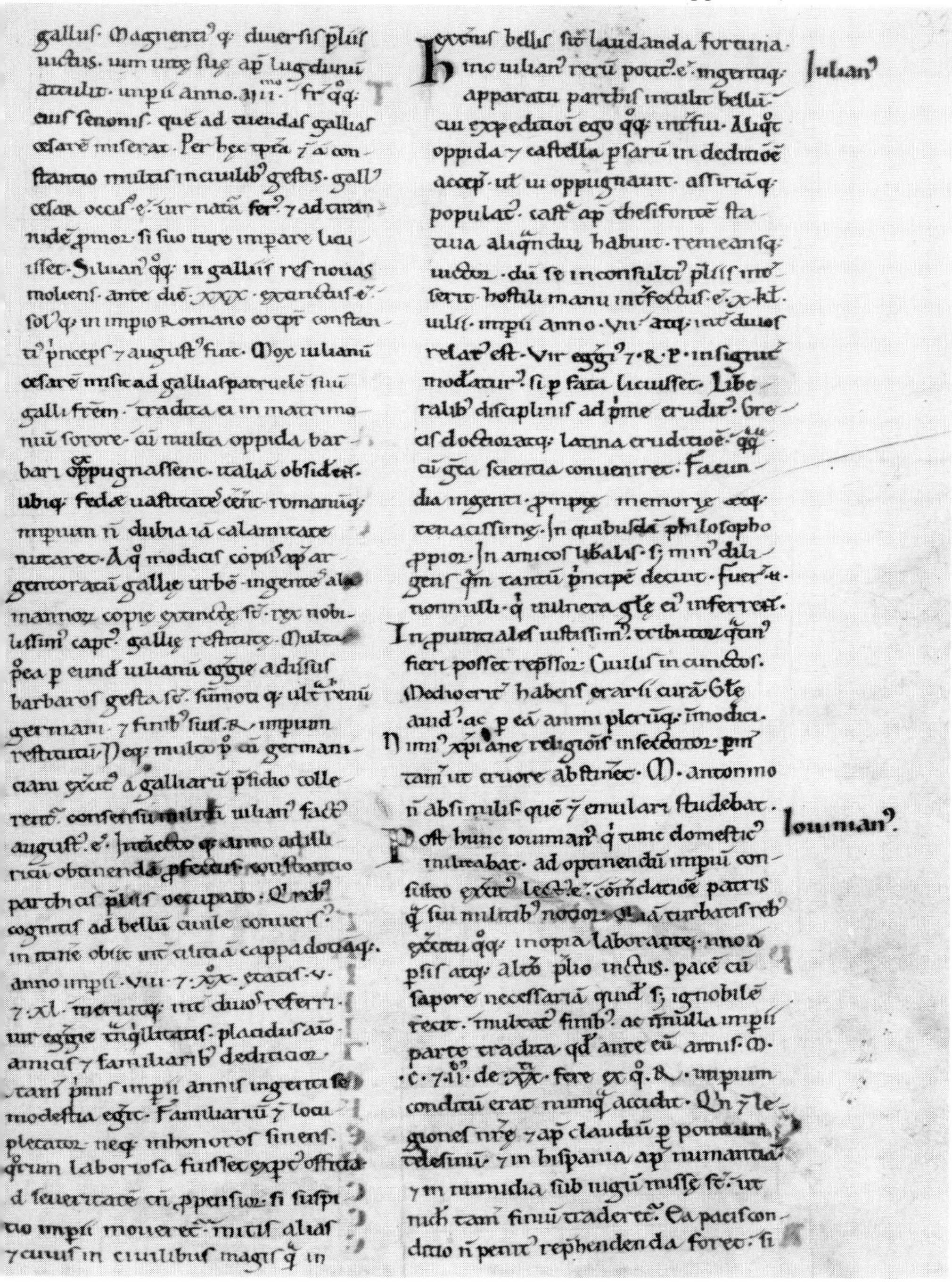

Plate 1. William's hand, 'informal' version. Oxford, Lincoln College MS lat. 100, f. 92. The body of the script occupies about one third of the interlinear space, and William apparently writes with his pen held away from him, i.e. at ninety degrees to the line. Note the widely-spaced letters and words, the 'dash' form of the abbreviation signs, 'CesaR' col. a line 7, the form of -**NT** col. a line 16, -**ae** in 'fedae' col. a line 17, and the sign for 'enim' col. b line 20.

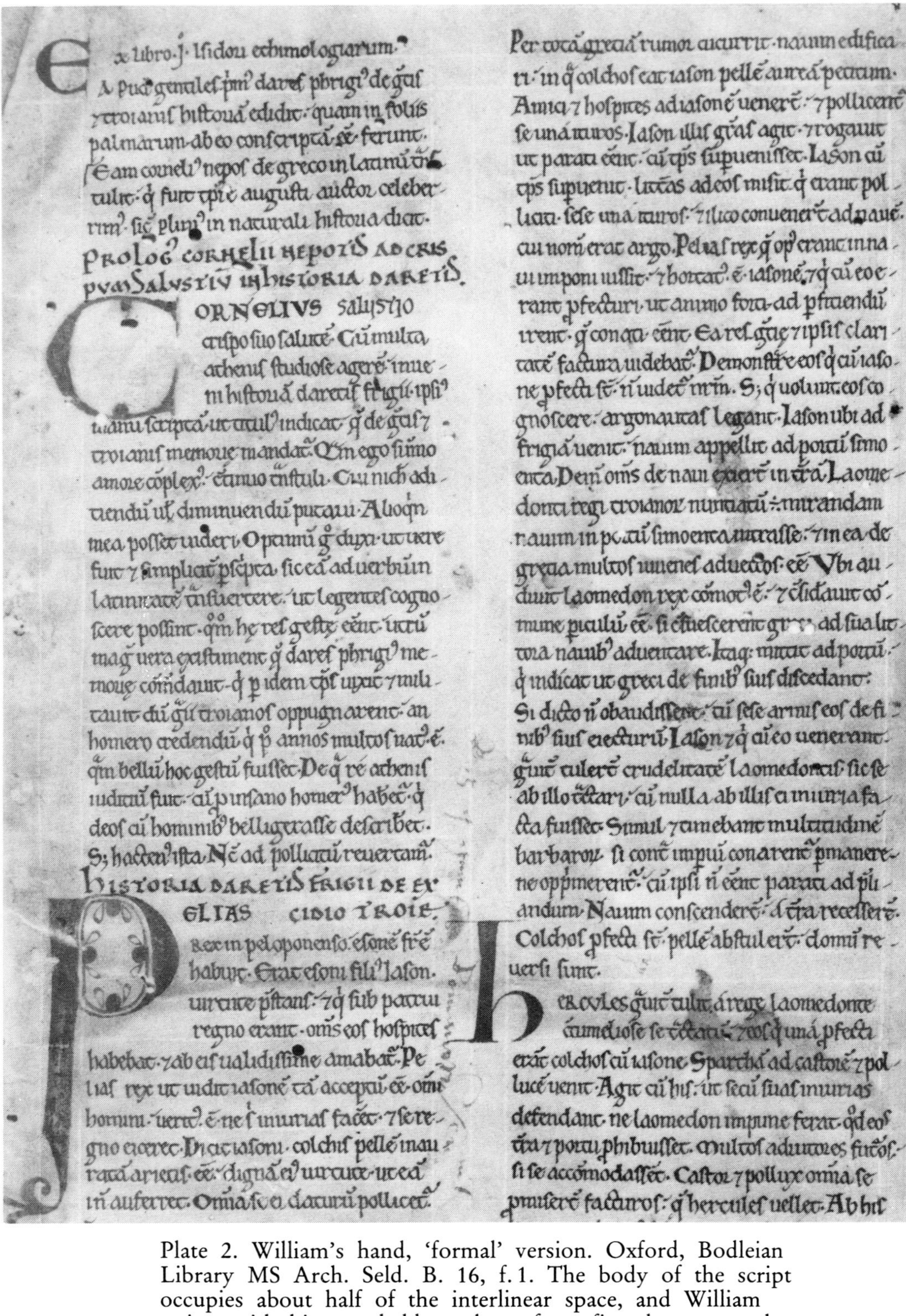

Plate 2. William's hand, 'formal' version. Oxford, Bodleian Library MS Arch. Seld. B. 16, f. 1. The body of the script occupies about half of the interlinear space, and William writes with his pen held at about forty-five degrees to the line. The angling is plainly visible in the lower bowl of **g** and the curled abbreviation-signs. The script is compressed horizontally, and regular. Note the elaborate **g**.

Plates 3–5. Malmesbury Abbey *ex libris* inscriptions and press-marks, c.1400 (See above, p. 77).

Plate 3. Oxford, Bodleian Library MS Bodl. 852, f. 1. *Ex libris* and press-mark.

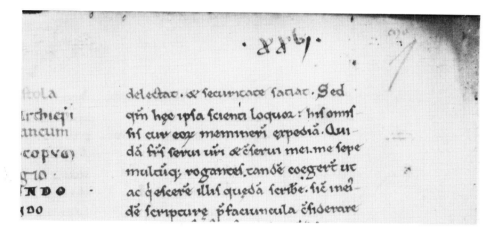

Plate 4. London, Lambeth Palace Library MS 224, f. 1. Press-mark and faint traces of *ex libris* ('Malmesbur').

Plate 5. Oxford, Merton College MS 181, f. [ii]v. Press-mark, erased *ex libris* ('Malmesbur') and table of contents.

Plates 6–9. The development of Scribe A's hand (See above, pp. 83–9).

Plate 6. Oxford, Bodleian Library MS Auct. F. 3. 14, f. 150v. The script is clumsy and irregular and only Tironian **et** (7) is used. Note the form of the cedilla (line 5), and the form and frequency of rounded **d**.

Plate 7. Oxford, Bodleian Library MS Rawl. G. 139, f. 2. The script is smaller, slightly more compressed and regular, and two forms of cedilla are used (the 'dagger' form col. a line 9).

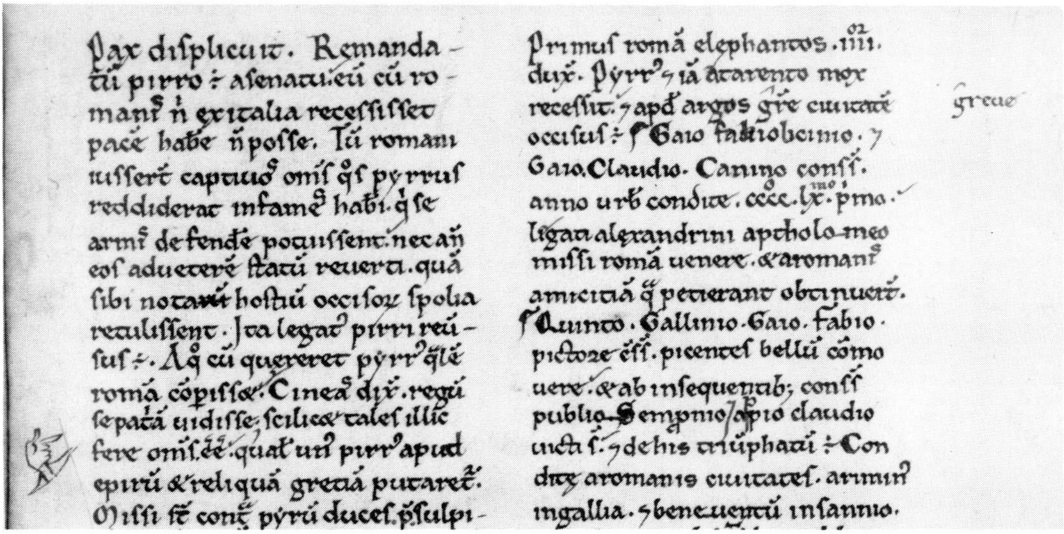

Plate 8. Oxford, Lincoln College MS lat. 100, f. 73. The general appearance is as in Plate 7. Both Tironian **et** and the ampersand are used (note 'comperiss&' and 'scilic&', col. a lines 12, 13), and the form of rounded **d** is gaining character. The correction to col. b line 3, in the outer margin, is by William.

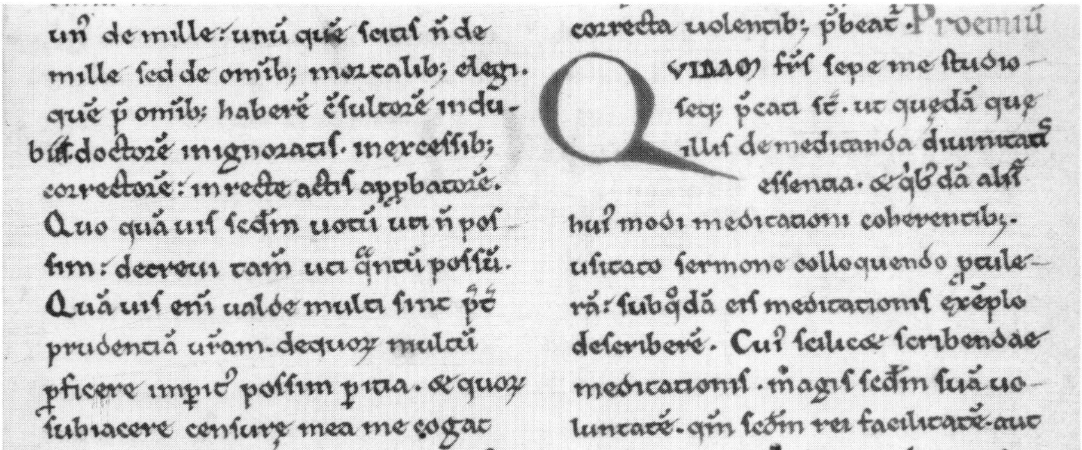

Plate 9. London, Lambeth Palace Library MS 224, f. 1. The script is more regular and 'prickly', only the ampersand is used and the form of rounded **d** is individualized. Note the long-tailed cedilla (e.g. col. a line 11), **ae** in 'scribendae' (col. b line 9) and 'scilic&' and 'asserer&' (col. b lines 9, 16).

Plates 10–12. The hand of Scribe B ('Richard'; see above, pp. 88–91, 93–4).

Plate 10. London, Lambeth Palace Library MS 224, f. 12v. Note the characteristic, 'continental' form of **g**, and the smoothly-curving abbreviation-signs.

Plate 11. Cambridge, Trinity College MS O. 5. 20, p. 256, showing Richard's colophon. Note the hooked form of his abbreviation signs and the form of his **ct** ligature, e.g. line 9 'recte'. The correction to line 1, in the outer margin, is by William.

carmen ostendit. ita in uanitate
uanitatu uanitatis magnitudo mon
stratur. Tale qd ce in psalmis scriptu
Verumtamen uniuersa uanitas. om
nis homo uiuens. Si uiuens homo
uanitas. e. q mortuus uanitas uani
tatu. Legim in exodo glorificatum
uultu moysi intantu ut filii isrl eu
aspicere n possent. Qua glam paulus
apls ad comparatione euangelice gle
dicit esse in glam. Na nec glorificatu
fuit qd claruit in hac parte ppter ex
cellente glam. Possunt g ce nos hunc
mundu. celu. terra. maria. ce omnia q
in hoc circulo continent bona quide
pse dicere. sed ad dnm coparata. ee p
nichilo. Et quomodo igniculu lucerne
uidens. creatus esse ex lumine. ce pea
orto sole n cernere qd lucebat. stella
rum quoq; lumina nibare uiderem
solis abscondi: ita aspiciens elementa
ce reru multiplice uarietate admiror
quide opu magnitudine: Recogitas
aute omnia ptransire. ce mundum
suo fine senescere. soliq; dm semp ee
id qd fuerit. copellor dicere n semel
sed bis. Vanitas uanitatu. ce omnia
uanitas. In ebreo p uanitate uanita
tu. abal. abalim. scriptu. e. qd excep
tis. lxx. interpretib; oms similiter
transtulerunt. asbea. sabei. qd nos
possum uapore fumi. ce aura tenue
que cito resoluitur appellare. Ca
duca itaq; ce nichil uniuersitas ex
hoc uerbo ostenditur. Que eni ui
dentur temporalia st. que aute n
uidentur eterna st. Siue qa uani
tati creatura subiecta. e. ce ingemiscit
ce parturit. ce prestolatur reuelatio
nem filioru dei. Et nc ex parte cog

noscim. ce ex parte pphani. Tam diu
omnia st donec ueniat qd pfectu e.
Quid sup est homini in omni
labore suo q laborat sub sole?
Post generale sententia qd uana sunt
oia ab hominib; incipit: qd frustra in
mundi isti labore desudent. cgregant
diuitias. erudientes liberos. ambientes
ad honore. edificia cstruentes. ce in medio
ope subita morte subtracti audiunt.
Insipiens hac nocte auferent omnia tua
a te. que aute pparasti cui erit? Maxi
me cuin ex omni labore nichil secum
ferant. sed nudi redeant in tra unde
sumpti sut ri.
Generatio uadit ce generatio aduе
nit. ce terra in selm stat. Aliis mo
rientib; nascuntur alii. ce quos uideras
n uides. incipies uidere eos q non erant.
Qd uani hac uanitate qua terra ma
nere. que causa hominu facta. e. ce
ipsu homine dnm terre in puluerem
repente dissolui? Aliter. Prima ge
neratio iudeoru recedit. ce succedit ge
neratio de gentib; cgregata. Terra
aute tam diu stat: qua diu synagoga
relicta. omnis eccla intueat. Du aute
pdicatu fuerit hoc euangeliu in toto
orbe. tunc erit finis. Imminente u con
summatione. celu ce terra transibt. Et
signanter n ait. terra in selis stat: sed
in selm. Porro laudaui dnm n in
uno. sed in seculis seculorum.
Oritur sol ce occidit sol. ce in locu
suum ducit. ce oriens ipse sibi. Sol
ipse q in luce mortalib; dat. e. interitu
mundi ortu suo cotidie indicat ce oc
casu. Qd postq ardente rota oceano
tinxerit. p incognitas nobis uias ad
locu unde exierat regreditur. expletoq;

Plates 13–15. The hand of Scribe C (See above, pp. 91–4).

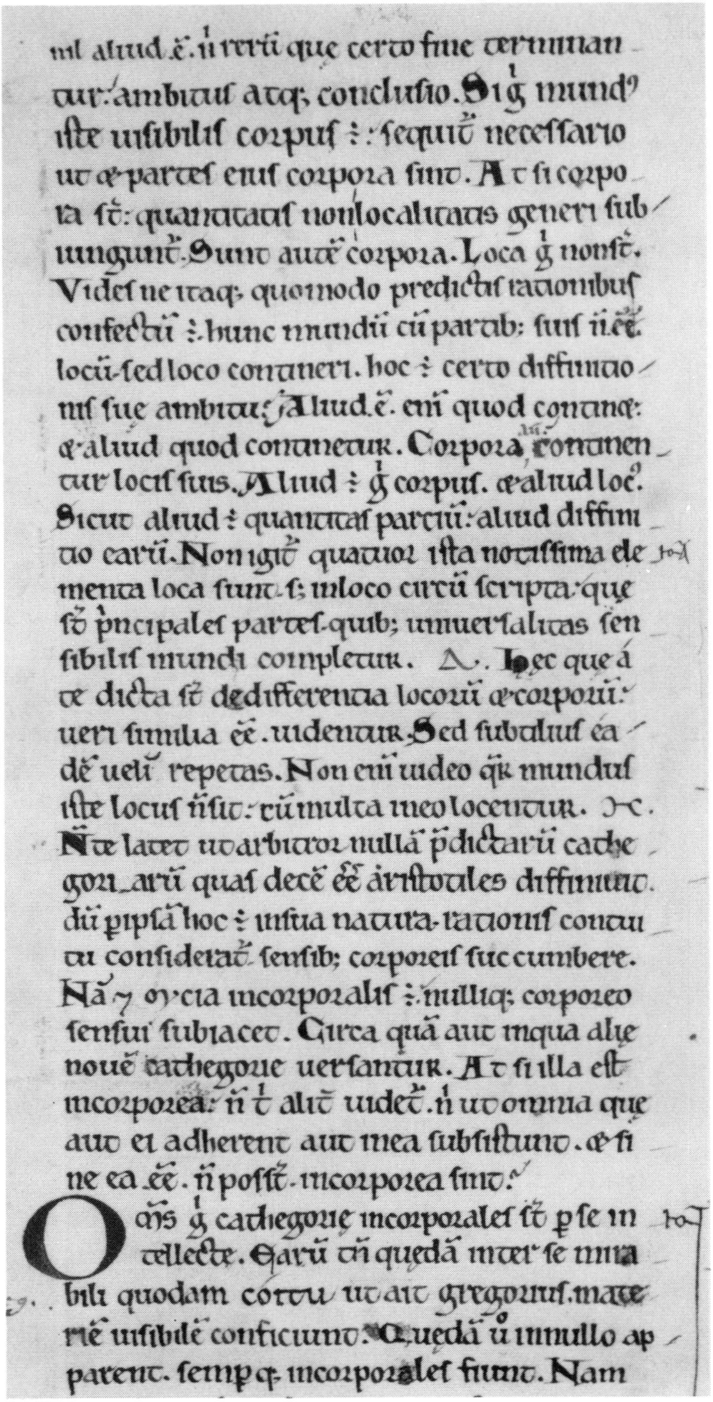

Plate 13. Cambridge, Trinity College MS O. 5. 20, p. 17, col. a. Note the form of **g**, 'contin&' in line 10, and '-tinetuR', line 11.

EVTROPIVS [con]fortuacensis.

INCIPIT EVTROPI-
mi maximo p[er]petio au-
gusto eutropius.

Res romanas exvo-
luntate mansuetudi-
nis tue ab urbe condi-
ta ad nram memoriam que in negotiis
uel bellicis uel ciuilibus emineba[n]t
p[er] ordinem temporum breui narra-
tione collegi stri[c]tim additis etiam
his que in principium uita egregia
extiterunt ut tranquillitatis tue possit mens diuina letari prius se illus
trium uirorum facta in administrando
imp[er]io secutam quam cognosceret
lectione. Incipit liber i. pauli.
paulus. eutropii DE GESTIS ROMANII.

PRIMVS IN I-
talia ut quibusdam
placet. regnauit
ianus deinde sa-
turnus. iouem si-
liium egregia fu-
gientis in ciuitate
que exeius nomine saturnia dicta
est cuius ruine hactenus cernunt
in finibus tusciee. haud p[ro]cul ab urbe.
Hic saturnus quia in italia latuit
abeuis latebra latium appellata e[st].
Ipse [et] enim adhuc rudes populos.
domus edificare. terras incolere.
plantare uineas docuit. atq; humanis moribus uiuere. cu antea seni-
seris glandium tantum modo ali-
mentis uitam sustentarent. [et] aut

q[ue] na anni referuntur euoluti.
Regnante tam latino. qui latina lingua
correxit. [et] latinos de suo noie appellauit. troia a grecis capta est. cu apud
hebreos. labdon tertium sui principat[us]
ageret. annum. [et] apud assirios tauta-
nes. apud egyptios thous regnaret. ex-
pletis a mundi principio annis. iiii. xcviii.
a diluuio annis mille .d. cclxxvii. a
natiuitate abraham. occc. xxxv. que fuit xl
tercio anno nini regis assiriorum annis
scccxxxv. a natiuitate moysi anno
.cccc.x. ante urbe aute conditam annis
.cccc.iiii. ante primam quoq; olimpiade
annis. cccc.vi. Capta igitur troia
eneas uenerit [et] achise filius ad italiam
uenit. anno tercio post troie excidium
cu turno dauiniitas coz regis filio di-
micans eum interemit. eiusq; sponsa
lauiniam latini regis filiam in coniugium accepit. De cuius eciam noie lau-
uium oppidum quod construxerat
appellauit. Regnauit q[ue] eneas latinus
annis tribus. Quo uita decedente
regnum suscepit ascanius qui [et] iulus
eiusdem enee filius. quem apud troia
ex creusa coniuge genuerat. [et] secum
in italia ueniens adduxerat. Qui ascanius derelicto nouercee sue lauiniee
regno. albam longam condidit [et] siliu
um postumum fratrem suu enee ex lau-
nia filium summa pietate educauit.
Deinde ascanius iulium filii sui perea
uit. a quo familia iulioz exorta est.
Paruulu qui nec du regendis ciuib;
idoneus erat. Ascanius cu xxxviii.

& aspect̄ cui̅ʼ spectiosus. Quappropter con
surgeuces despcemur dn̅i uo digni eſt ꝫ nega̅
ciamur sponso sermone sapiencia ꝩpo gllo
thi̅ cui eſt imperium in secla seculoꝝ.

EXPLICIT LIBER ORIGENIS SUP
CANTICA CANTICORUM.

INCIPIT LIBELLUS SUP CANTICA
CANTICOLIU. Qui vocat̄
Sigillu̅ Scē MARIE.

QVIA poꝑulus deū
ec eſtuſ decreui̅ in ui-
nea dn̅i ꝑ denario por
tare nolo ut tam ut ſterilis ficulnea
in uacuu̅ occupare-ſꝫ, ut oliua fruc
tifera domui dei aliquid decoris
adicere-ut merear in ea quandoꝗ
mansione perpe. Igitur quia ut in
sciti collegiu̅ gꝑanter suscepit quiē
misi libellu̅: dabo opam ꝑ clauem
dauid uob̅ reserare. de quibʼ uide-
mini dubitare. Ad glam itaꝗ filii di & ad honorem genitricis sue hic
libelluſ edat̄: & nomen et sigillum
Scē MARIE imponat̄. Ipse autem in-
tellectu̅ tribuat. cuiuſ sapientia om
nem sensuum eruperat.

actua
uita

ITAQꝫ.
INTRAVIT ihc in qꝫdda̅ castellu̅. In
stello ē. turris alta̅ inqua co̅tʼ hoſ
ppugnacula-mur̅ʼ u̅ exteri. q̅: ui-
la cuub̅ interi. Hoc castellu̅ fuit
spe̅ sci sacellu̅: scilicet glosa di geni
uirgo maria. q̅ inꝗ angloꝝ ꝫcodia
to undiꝗ munita. Inꝗ̅ turiſ alta u̅
licet humilitas pingens adceli cul
na. Vnde dt. Respexit dn̅i humi
litate̅ ancille sue. Mur̅ʼ u̅ exteri
eiſ castitas fuit. q̅ cetiſ uirtutab
interiʼ munitione̅ pbuit. Hoc castell
dn̅i munitur. quando mutero ligna
humana̅ natura̅ sibi copulauit.
mulier qda̅ martha nomine e-
pit illu̅ indomu̅ sua̅. Et huic era
soror noie maria. Per martha̅ acti
uita: per maria̅ co̅teplatiua desig
ꝗn utiniꝗ ppetua uirgo maria
ꝙpo excellenti excoluisse pdice-
Omnia naꝗ: euangelii opa impen
et passue uite ministeria. Apa
naꝗ: regno,ppt nos exule̅.& in hu
mundo hospite.suscepit multi su̅
hospiciu̅.& emnis uirtutu̅ cospic

Plate 15. Oxford, Merton College MS 181, f. 120v. Scribe C
writes col. b. Note the ornamental lower bowl of **g** in the
bottom line.

mil̃. ad dextrā manū cephei dextrā alā. sinistrā ad pedes eq̃ porrigit. Intē pisces
requū caudāq; capcorn. aqrī? collocat̃. aqā in urnā fundens. q̃ effusio ad
magnū pisce decurrit. In parte aut̃ humillima zodiaci iuxta sagittariū
atq; aqlā. capcorn̄ in cōmissura hiemalē circli ac sinistri sit̃. ē. habent p se sa
gittariū i cōmissura zodiaci atq; lactei circlor sub delfino ēstrictū. Est &
sagitta q̃dā sola sub cigno. iuxta aqlā iacens. Sup capcornū ū cap̃ delfin?
ē. posit̃. p caudā serpentis. q̃ a serpentario tenet̃. Sub ipso aut̃ serpenta
rio scorpione dicunt̃ ēē locatū. ita ut pedib serpentarii tangat̃. & habe
subtc̃ ad australē plagā centaurū bestiā. q̃si manu ad arā ferent̃e.
hec ara a quibdā sacrariū uocat̃. & est cont̃ summitatē caude scorpii ad

Plate 16. Oxford, Bodleian Library MS Auct. F. 3. 14, f. 149. The general appearance is that of a formal charter-hand. Like Scribe B, this man used a 'continental' form of **g** and hooked abbreviation signs. Note the height of some of the ascenders in relation to the body of the script, high-backed **a**, the eccentric rounded **d** (line 2) and long flourish to end the ampersand (bottom line).

sed etiā ad opiniones eorum q̃ audiunt
accommodanda est oratio. Hec primum in
telligam?; hominū duo gña ēē. altm indoc
tum & agreste. quod ante ferat semp
utilitatem honestati. alterū expolitum.
qd reb omnib; dignitatem ante ponat.
Itaq; huic gñi laus. honos. gła. fides.
iustitia. onīsq; uirtus. illi aut̃ quest?
emolumentum. fructusq; pponit̃. atq;
etiam uoluptas. que maxime est uirtuti
inimica. boniq; natam fallaciū imitan

Plate 17. Oxford, Bodleian Library MS Rawl. G. 139, f. 6v. Here the ascenders are somewhat shorter and the **a** is normal.

ñ qui intellexerit eam; Unde & plura te-
mereb; noxia creata · ut dum uitamus
ea · ad sapienciam erudiamur; Et qual'
ƺ studii fuit salomonis scire sapientiam · errorem & stulticiam · ut in ap-
petendis aliis · & aliis declinandis · ue-
rac' sapiencia pbaretur·

Et agnoui quod in huiusmodi morta-
gorib; afflictio sps · & pturbatio
animi · eet · eo quod in multa sapiencia
multa sit indignatio · Et qui addit
scienciam · addit dolorem; Quanto
magis qui sapienciam fuerit consuet'·
tanto plus indignatur subiacere sen-
tiis · & pcul eet aurtutib; quas requi-
rit · Dolet ignoranciam · dum que-
rit scienciam · Intelligit se ex parte
agnoscere · & ad plenum intellegendi
lumen rerum occultarum se ñ posse
puenire inde · Ideo addit dolorem·
qui addit scienciam ·

Dixi in corde meo · uadam & affluam
deliciis & fruar bonis · & uidi quod
hoc quoq; eet uanitas · Hic contio-
natoris in communi sentencia uul-
gi loquitur · quia tamen uanam ostendit · Et · ē sensus · Postquam
in multitudie sapiencie & adiec-
cione sciencie dolorem · & laborem·
eet comphendi · & nichil aliud ñ cas-
sum laborem · & inane certamen·
cstitui me ad leticiam · ut letus fru-

Plate 18. Oxford, Merton College MS 181, f. 91, col. b. In
general a more orthodox book-hand. The ascenders are
shorter again, and the body of the script has been enlarged
to occupy about half of the interlinear space. The form of
the ampersand has changed.

PART II

STUDIES OF THE WRITER
AT WORK

6

WILLIAM'S EDITION OF
THE *LIBER PONTIFICALIS*

WILLIAM IS MOST commonly thought of as a national historian, and it is upon his achievement in writing the history of England from Bede until his own day that his reputation has always rested.[1] But he had wider historical perspectives, and they are important. Even in the *Gesta Regum* there are lengthy asides upon the histories of the Carolingian Empire, of France and Normandy, of papal-imperial relations and the crusading movement.[2] He was also fascinated by the civilization of Antiquity, and Oxford, Bodleian Library MS Arch. Seld. B. 16 contains his collection of chronicles of imperial history from the earliest days of Rome until the reign of Louis the Pious.[3] To these interests and the works which they produced we can now add the history of the papacy, illustrated by a unique edition of the *Liber Pontificalis* which William compiled. To state this is to credit him with another major work, of similar scale to the *Gesta*, although formally much more primitive. It is also to credit him with a major piece of research and writing which predates at least the final drafting of the *Gesta Regum* and *Gesta Pontificum*.

In 1910 Wilhelm Levison, with his customary learning and precision, described and discussed a hitherto unnoticed version of the *Liber Pontificalis* which had been compiled in England soon after 1119.[4] It is transmitted in two manuscripts. As found in the first, Cambridge University Library Kk. 4. 6, ff. 224–280 (C), dating from the 1130s, this version consists of three main sections, each interpolated from a variety of sources. To 715 the basis was a Class 2 manuscript of the *Liber Pontificalis*, perhaps a gemellus of B[1],

---

[1] GR I, pp. ix–lxv, cxv–cxlvii, II, pp. xv–cxlii; Darlington, *Anglo-Norman Historians*, pp. 3–11; Farmer, 'Life and Works', pp. 39–54; R. W. Southern, 'Aspects of the European Tradition of Historical Writing, IV', pp. 253–256; Gransden, *Historical Writing in Medieval England, c.550–1307*, ch. 9; above, pp. 15–18, 22–6.

[2] GR I, pp. 69–72, 110–117, 137–140, 230–232, 246–253; II, pp. 285–294, 342–344, 390–461, 498–512.

[3] On this MS see GR I, pp. cxxxi–cxl, and above, pp. 57, 62–3, 66–7 etc.

[4] W. Levison, 'Aus Englischen Bibliotheken II', *Neues Archiv für ältere deutsche Geschichtskunde*, 35 (1910), 333–431.

the incomplete late seventh-century copy from Bobbio. From 715 until 772 (plus an isolated reference c.795) the main source was a Class E manuscript of the *Liber*. From 741 until 1087 the compiler used a (probably Italian) *Papstkatalog* of a familiar type.[5] After that he apparently made up his own brief biographies, concluding with the Acts of Calixtus II's Council of Reims, 1119. The second manuscript is London, British Library Harl. 633 of the late twelfth century, in which the *Liber Pontificalis* occupies ff. 4–71 (L). To Stephen II (757) this version has nothing in common with C, being based on a *Liber Pontificalis* manuscript of Class D very similar to two Beauvais copies from the ninth and twelfth centuries, both of which end with Stephen's reign.[6] There are a few interpolations to this section of L. From 757 until 1119 L depends upon the same exemplar as C. However from the reign of Paschal II the compiler of L's *Liber Pontificalis* had access to another set of papal biographies, which took his account on to 1133.

Our interest is in the lost exemplar of the *Liber Pontificalis* version which is common to these two manuscripts (CL). Levison showed convincingly that it was used by William of Malmesbury; I intend to demonstrate that he was in fact its compiler. But first its exact nature must be ascertained by a comparison of C and L. Of the quite different first sections in both versions, that in C obviously belonged to CL: firstly, because this section was known to William of Malmesbury by 1125; secondly, because the number and the sources of the interpolations in it make it of a piece with the rest of CL; and finally, because a clumsy process of grafting is detectable in L at the point where it ends its dependence on a D manuscript and changed to CL. No less than three separate lives of Pope Stephen II occur here: two were already in CL as a consequence of its own employment of two different sources; the third is from D.[7] Thus the compiler of L's *Liber Pontificalis*, for admittedly obscure reasons, discarded CL to 757 in favour of a complete Class D manuscript.[8] On the other hand there are three passages in L alone which undoubtedly reproduce CL. One is a Life of Hadrian I based on a Class E manuscript of *Liber Pontificalis*, interpolated from Einhard. Since a Class E manuscript and extracts from Einhard were used at about this point in C but not in L, and since the Life of Hadrian is interpolated in the same fashion as the rest of CL, Levison was surely correct in identifying it as part of CL.[9]

---

[5] It most nearly resembles Duchesne's Type III, of which all the examples cited by him are Italian and all diverge after 1087; L. Duchesne, *Le Liber Pontificalis*, II (Paris, 1888), pp. xix–xx.
[6] Levison, pp. 402–3; Duchesne, *Le Liber Pontificalis*, I (Paris, 1886), pp. cxciii–cxcv.
[7] Levison, pp. 405–6.
[8] Obscure, because his D-class MS gave him, if anything, rather less information than the interpolated B-class MS which constituted the earliest portion of CL; cf. Duchesne, *Liber Pontificalis*, I, pp. clxxxviii–ix, cxciv–cxcv.
[9] Levison, pp. 384 and n. 2, 406 and n. 4, 407.

The second passage occurs at the end of the Life of Paschal II which is common to both manuscripts. At this point in C there are two sentences: 'Quapropter Henricus filius superioris Henrici, qui Hildebrandum expulerat, in ecclesia sancti Petri papam cepit et sacramentum ab eo exegit, quod in magna Cronica descripsimus. Epistolas etiam illius alibi descriptas, quoniam ad alias tendimus, rescribere omittimus'.[10] After 'exegit' this was written over an erasure, and the few letters not quite expunged show that the scribe or his director changed plans in the course of copying, and that the exemplar (CL) at this point continued as found in L, giving the text of the oaths taken by Paschal and Henry V, followed by the papal 'pravilegium' of the same day, the Acts of the Lateran Council of 1112, and eleven letters of the same pope.[11] Finally, a letter of Gelasius II in L but not in C probably belonged to their common exemplar.[12] In short, CL is substantially represented by the surviving manuscript C.

Levison had no difficulty in showing that William of Malmesbury made extensive use of CL in his *Gesta Regum* and *Gesta Pontificum*, both completed in 1125. Not surprisingly he raised the question of whether William was himself its compiler, but he decided against this. Although one at least of CL's interpolations, the privilege of Pope Sergius to Aldhelm, shows a clear Malmesbury interest, others are connected with the claims of Canterbury, and Levison finally opted for a Canterbury origin for CL.[13] On the other hand he thought that he could recognize William's own hand among those in the Cambridge manuscript, and suggested that the 'Magna Cronica' named in the passage quoted earlier was William's lost '(tres libelli) quibus Cronica dedi uocabulum'.[14] In attempting to demonstrate that William was after all the compiler of CL I shall employ four main lines of argument; firstly, the correction of a handful of (understandable) errors and omissions made by Levison will by itself tip the scales in favour of Malmesbury against Canterbury; secondly I shall show that William made even more use of CL in his works than Levison thought; thirdly, it can be demonstrated that the technique used in the compilation of CL, particularly the selection and arrangement of the interpolated material, is precisely that employed by William in those works certainly his; finally, the weightiest and most decisive point, I will show that William knew complete and independent versions of many of the pieces of which extracts were interpolated into CL. In this respect it will be seen that those interpolations that originated from Canterbury were nonetheless known to William and used by him independently of CL.

[10] ibid., p. 395 and n. 3.
[11] ibid., pp. 409–411.
[12] ibid., pp. 396 n. 4, 412.
[13] ibid., pp. 418–421.
[14] ibid., pp. 421–424; GR II, p. 525.

Let us begin with the manuscript itself. Here Levison was wrong, for it has no connection either with Malmesbury or with William. The main hand of the *Liber Pontificalis* section is found in a group of contemporary manuscripts from Worcester, and the hand which corrects and annotates the text is that identified as John of Worcester's.[15] It is found in the same group of Worcester manuscripts, most notably in Oxford, Corpus Christi College 157, containing the chronicle of 'Florence' of Worcester with John's continuation.[16] Thus we should expect the 'magna cronica' containing documents of Paschal II to be 'Florence of Worcester's', and indeed those very documents are found there.[17] Levison realized this, but rejected any connection between C and 'Florence', because he did not know of the manuscript's Worcester origin, and because he knew that Florence had died in 1118, at least a year before the compilation of CL.[18] Now, however, it is realized that Florence's role in the writing of the Worcester chronicle is indeterminate, and certainly less than was generally supposed in 1910. The whole work may even be John's. It is certain that in the section before 1118 at least one source of later date was used, Eadmer's *Historia Novorum*, as completed after 1122.[19] Thus C was copied under the direction of John of Worcester, and it was doubtless he who ordered the omission of the papal documents, which he had already transferred from CL into his own chronicle.

Before considering the texts interpolated into CL, we must explore the possibility that William knew one at least of its basic sources in an independent version. This is the *Papstkatalog*. The Catalogue used in CL had one outstanding peculiarity in that it erroneously identified Gerbert with Pope John XV, a confusion repeated by William in his *Gesta Regum*.[20] There he states that 'unde in uetusto uolumine, quod in manus meas incidit, ubi omnium apostolicorum nomina continebantur et anni, ita scriptum uidi: Iohannes qui et Gerbertus menses decem; hic turpiter uitam suam finiuit'. William's quotation is virtually identical with the relevant CL entry. As Levison himself stated, William's 'uetustum uolumen' could hardly refer to the complete CL, at the most five or six years old when he wrote the *Gesta*

---

[15] Ker, 'Handwriting', 375–6.
[16] MLGB, p. 209 and n. 4; Weaver, *The Chronicle of John of Worcester*, pp. 7–9.
[17] Oxford, Corpus Christi College MS 157, pp. 368–370.
[18] Levison, p. 422.
[19] R. Darlington in VW, pp. xvi–xviii and notes; Brett, 'John of Worcester and his Contemporaries', pp. 104–112.
[20] Levison, p. 389; GR I, pp. 193 and n. 3, 195. It is easy to imagine how the confusion might have arisen; cf. Duchesne's List III (*Liber Pontificalis*, II, p. xx, *ad loc.*):
    'Iohannes sed. m. x., qui turpiter finiuit uitam suam.
    Siluester sed. an. IIII m. i d. viii.'

Regum passage. All that is known of William's scholarship suggests that when he called a book 'uetustus' he was expressing an honest and well-founded opinion.[21] Moreover his description of this book's contents does not in any way fit CL; rather it suits the original Catalogue before either its incorporation into CL or interpolation with biographical data. Such a volume could have been forty years old or more when William used it. On this line of reasoning, as Levison admitted, 'man könnte weiter vermuten, Wilhelm selbst habe diese Quelle erweitert und mit dem Liber Pont. verbunden . . .'.[22] However, he went on to describe this suggestion, I believe too harshly, as a 'ziemlich willkürliche Vermutung', without presenting – as he was surely obliged to – an alternative interpretation for William's words. Instead he pointed to the Canterbury affinities of so many of the interpolations in CL, and on that basis decided against William of Malmesbury's authorship. Despite this, the fact remains that William quite obviously knew the Catalogue used in CL as well as CL itself.[23] That becomes a strong argument for William's authorship of CL once we have disposed of Levison's other objections, if not before.

Turning now to the interpolations, I want first to clear the ground of material which, for one reason or another, offers little help in identifying CL's compiler or his provenance. For instance, some of the CL extracts were known independently by William but were too commonly available for this to carry any weight; other sources were not used by him (on available evidence) independently of CL; for others again the textual tradition is too thin for any conclusions to be drawn as to CL's or William's source for them, while a further handful are at the opposite end of the spectrum, widely dispersed, surviving in many manuscripts and still awaiting a critical edition without which we cannot make use of them here. In the first category are Gregory's *Dialogues*, Bede's *Ecclesiastical History*, Sallust's *Jugurthine War* (merely a *Sprichwort* in CL), Einhard's *Vita Karoli*, Orosius, Paul the Deacon's *Historia Romana* and *Historia Langobardorum* (though the reminiscence in CL may be at second hand) and Jordanes's *Romana*. Einhard and Jordanes are perhaps uncommon enough in England at this

---

[21] See above, pp. 64–6.
[22] Levison, p. 418.
[23] Oxford, Bodl. Libr. MS Auct. F. 3. 14, William's computistic collection, has Paschal tables (ff. 120–132v) adapted from the Chronicle of Marianus Scotus. On ff. 120–120v and 130–132v the lists of popes in the outer margins have had lengths of reigns added, sometimes over erasure, to conform to the CL Catalogue. The additions begin with John XII, for Marianus had provided lengths of reigns up to his predecessor. The popes' names are in the main hand of the tables to Calixtus II (f. 120), but names and lengths of reigns continue to the death of Anacletus (1138; f. 120v). The CL Catalogue seems to be the source until Paschal II. In other words, the additions to the list of popes in MS Auct. F. 3. 14 appear to have been made from the completed CL, not from the original Catalogue employed in it.

period to be significant. William quoted Einhard in the *Gesta Regum* and in his collection of materials on Roman history in Bodleian Library, MS Arch. Seld. B. 16.[24] In the same manuscript also appear Orosius and the Roman Histories of Paul and Jordanes. CL quotes one passage from the *Anglo-Saxon Chronicle*, unfortunately at a point where all extant versions are identical.[25] William knew the E version of the *Chronicle*, and just possibly others as well.[26] Then there are those works extracted in CL but otherwise unused by William as far as we know. These are: an anecdote about Pope Cornelius, the Merovingian *Vita Aniani*, Hilduin's *Vita S. Dionysii*, the *Vita Remigii* by Hincmar,[27] Sigibert of Gembloux's chronicle, and the Acts of the Councils of Clermont (1095) and Reims (1119). It is perhaps curious that we have no evidence of independent use by William of Sigibert, if indeed he did know his work. Certainly William had access to the works of several recent and contemporary continental historians: William of Jumièges, William of Poitiers, Fulcher of Chartres and Hugh of Fleury. The Sigibert extracts in CL occur as part of a Life of Pope Leo I, otherwise conflated from the *Liber Pontificalis*, Paul the Deacon, Jordanes and perhaps the *Vita Aniani*. A few sentences from this conflated Life are prefixed to the edition of Leo's letters and sermons in Oxford, Oriel College MS 42, written by William, probably c.1135.[28] They were doubtless taken directly from CL, since they occur in company with other material from the same source. The Acts of Urban II's Council of Clermont are given in CL and by William in the *Gesta Regum*, from the same version.[29] One cannot in this instance know whether William's exemplar was independent of CL or not, but what is important is that the version of the Acts common to William and CL is entirely different from that which was current at Canterbury from c.1100.[30] If the compiler of CL were a Canterbury man, one would expect him to have used the version of the Clermont Acts which was available locally; however, one must

---

[24] GR I, p. 70; Oxford, Bodl. Libr. MS Arch. Seld. B. 16, f. 139.

[25] Levison, p. 385; *ASC*, p. 37 *s. a.* 799.

[26] See above, p. 70; K. Sisam, 'Anglo-Saxon Royal Genealogies', *Proceedings of the British Academy*, 39 (1953), 287–348, esp. 318–320.

[27] These three *vitae* are in Cambridge, Corpus Christi College MS 9, a late eleventh-century Passional from Worcester. The CL extracts were not, however, taken from this book, for its texts have been abbreviated to facilitate their division into lessons, and the passages in CL are among those omitted.

[28] Oxford, Oriel College MS 42, f. 90v; cf. Levison, pp. 369–70.

[29] ibid., p. 393 and n. 4; GR II, pp. 391–3.

[30] R. Somerville, *The Councils of Urban II; I: Decreta Claromontensia* (Annuarium Historiae Conciliorum, Supplementum nr. 1, Amsterdam, 1972), pp. 53, 83–8, 91. Somerville's *stemma* requires modification in the light of the conclusions proposed here. Instead of C, L and (X) (William's exemplar for the GR extract) deriving from b independently of one another, C and L should be seen as deriving from (X) via our CL. It is unclear whether William's GR text derives directly from CL or (X).

entertain the possibility that the surviving Canterbury version was not the only one known there in the early twelfth century. As for the Council of Reims, we should hardly expect William to have quoted its Acts in any context except one similar to CL; they were widely and quickly disseminated and their textual transmission has yet to be studied in detail.[31] For what they are worth, there are some scraps of evidence to suggest that William had some Reims material independently of CL. The collection of Pope Leo's letters in Oriel College MS 42 was put together by him from several sources.[32] One of the letters (Ballerini 138, Jaffé 512) is otherwise known only in four manuscripts, all containing the same collection of the False Decretals, put together at Reims in the wake of the 1119 Council.[33] The exemplar for part of William's manuscript of John the Scot's *Periphyseon* was derived from Reims, Bibl. Mun., MS 875 of the ninth century,[34] and the exemplar of a collection of computistic texts found in another of his books, Oxford, Bodleian Library, MS Auct. F. 3. 14, may have been a Reims manuscript.[35] His account in the *Gesta Regum* of the vision of Charles the Fat reproduces a text written c.901 and displaying obvious Reims interests.[36] A permissible conclusion from all this seems to be that William had one or more friends who were willing to transcribe Reims material for him and to get it to Malmesbury.

Finally, there are eight papal documents, the nature of whose textual tradition prevents their use as evidence in this enquiry. Two of them seem to derive either from Eadmer's *Historia Novorum* or its source, which is of some significance, as will become clear shortly, but that is all that can be said for the moment. It remains only to say that the equivocal material so far considered adds up to perhaps one sixth of all the CL interpolations. We must now turn to the other five sixths which can be used in our argument.

---

[31] I owe this information to Dr Martin Brett; cf. the references given by Levison, p. 39 n. 1.

[32] They are outlined by A. Chavasse, *Sancti Leonis Magni Tractatus Septem et Nonaginta* (CCSL 138), p. xxviii.

[33] So I was informed by the late Professor S. Williams; cf. S. Williams, *Codices Pseudo-Isidoriani* (Monumenta Iuris Canonici, Series C: Subsidia 3, New York, 1971), nos 39, 53, 55 and 75.

[34] Though not directly; Sheldon-Williams and Bieler, *Iohannis Scotti Eriugenae Periphyseon* I, pp. 10–11, 18–21, 24–5; Bishop, '*Periphyseon*: An Episode in the Tradition', pp. 411–426.

[35] Oxford, Bodl. Libr. Auct. F. 3. 14, copied from the same exemplar as Avranches, Bibl. Mun. 235, ff. 58–69v; cf. J. Contreni, 'The Study and Practice of Medicine in Northern France during the Reign of Charles the Bald', *Studies in Medieval Culture*, 6–7 (1976), 45.

[36] GR I, pp. 112–116, not, as Stubbs thought, copied from Hariulf's *Chronicon Centulense*; W. Levison, 'Die Politik in den Jenseitsvisionen des frühen Mittelalters', in his *Aus Rheinischer und Fränkischer Frühzeit* (Düsseldorf, 1948), p. 243 and n. 2.

The bulk of the CL interpolations can be linked, with varying degrees of certainty, to William independently of their use in CL. I take them in roughly chronological order. CL contained a series of documents connected with the Council at Rome in 680.[37] Some of Pope Agatho's synodical letter given in C is also quoted by William, but he provides a clause not in C. This may mean that he knew the Acts of the 680 Council independently of CL, a matter of some importance for our argument, since no other English manuscripts of this Council are known.[38] But the copyist of C was extraordinarily careless, and it is possible that the clause given by William was also in CL, but omitted in C through scribal inadvertence.

The next set of extracts is more important, although the case for William's independent knowledge of their source is not easily proven. As Levison pointed out, the discovery of the Cambridge manuscript added nothing to the establishment of the text of *Liber Pontificalis*. Nonetheless at least one of the major interpolations has considerable importance for the study of early Christian Rome; this is the series of papal inscriptions and epitaphs taken from a lost *Sylloge Inscriptionum*.[39] The series has been studied by Levison, Duchesne and Silvagni, the last of whom has provided the best critical edition.[40] Forty-one extracts are given in C, of which nine are known only from this manuscript, or from one other closely related one, to be described shortly. The latest extract is the epitaph of Pope John VII (d.707), which gives a reasonably precise date for the compilation of the original *Sylloge*, since if it had verses from later reigns they would certainly have been included in CL.

Three years after his study of the Cambridge *Liber Pontificalis*, Levison published a brief Papal Chronicle, which he found in Canterbury Cathedral, Cart. Antiqu. A. 42, a roll written in the late thirteenth century.[41] The Chronicle itself, however, stops at 964. It is a compilation from several sources, among them CL. Ten of the *Sylloge* inscriptions in CL are reproduced, abbreviated, in the Canterbury roll, which adds one more, the epitaph of Sabinian, d.606. Because of this addition, Levison thought that the compiler of the Papal Chronicle used the *Sylloge* extracted in CL, as well as CL itself. However he did not sufficiently reckon with the extreme carelessness of C's main scribe, first properly exposed by Silvagni.[42] This

[37] Levison, 'Aus Englischen Bibliotheken', pp. 375–6.
[38] ibid., p. 376.
[39] ibid., pp. 350–366.
[40] ibid.; L. Duchesne, 'Le Recueil èpigraphique de Cambridge', *Mélanges d'Archéologie et d'Histoire*, 30 (1910), 279–311; A Silvagni, 'La Silloge Epigrafica di Cambridge', *Revista di Archeologia Cristiana*, 20 (1943), 49–112.
[41] W. Levison, 'Eine Geschichte der Päpste aus Canterbury', *Neues Archiv*, 38 (1913), 645–664; cf. N. R. Ker, *Medieval Manuscripts in British Libraries*, II (Oxford, 1977), p. 312.
[42] Silvagni, pp. 53–4, 56–7, 75–6.

man, surely illiterate, committed hundreds of the grossest misreadings and omissions in his transcription of CL. This is why John of Worcester's hand figures so prominently in C, erasing and correcting. However, *pace* Levison,[43] collation with L, with William and with standard editions of the various texts interpolated into CL suggests that John rarely corrected from C's exemplar if at all. His corrections are mostly unauthoritative, dictated by his own grammatical sense. Thus it may be that C's scribe simply omitted Sabinian's epitaph, in which case John would have been unable to restore it. We conclude that it is at least as likely that the compiler of the Canterbury Papal Chronicle lifted his inscriptions from CL, as that he took them from the original *Sylloge*. Mechanically, of course, the former procedure would have been much the simpler one. Even on this reckoning, though, we have to assume a copy of CL at Canterbury before the late thirteenth century, and this still favours Levison's case for a Canterbury origin for CL.

William was interested in the inscriptions in CL, for he copied one of them, Leo's epitaph, into his collection of that pope's works in Oriel College MS 42. Presumably he took this directly from CL, as it occurs in company with other CL material, including the extract from the Life of Leo mentioned earlier.[44] Can we show that he knew the complete *Sylloge* which supplied the CL extracts? Not long ago Michael Lapidge showed that William knew a *Sylloge Inscriptionum* contained in a lost codex made for Bishop Milred of Worcester (745–775), probably c.750.[45] William copied three of its inscriptions into his *Gesta Pontificum*, and these and many more were transcribed by Leland who found the manuscript, significantly, at Malmesbury. Naturally one would like to know whether this *Sylloge* is identical with the one used in CL, but there is no overlap of contents between the transcriptions and the Cambridge manuscript. On the other hand, this is no argument *against* possible identity, for of the twenty-nine extracts in Leland, twenty-four were English (many mentioning Bede or contemporary fellow-countrymen), two are of unknown provenance, while the remaining three were from Vercelli, Picardy and Rome. It is reasonable, in terms of Leland's known antiquarian interests, to think that he deliberately selected from the *Sylloge* inscriptions relating to England. On the other hand, the fact that it contained at least one Roman inscription suggests that it

---

[43] Levison, 'Eine Geschichte', p. 337.

[44] Oxford, Oriel College MS 42, f. 90v. Collation (done by Silvagni though not with complete accuracy) shows C and Or. to be closely related although neither is copied from the other. Their text is quite distinct from the versions in the other three manuscripts collated; see Silvagni, no. 3.

[45] Lapidge, 'Some Remnants of Bede's lost "Liber Epigrammatum"', pp. 798–819, esp. pp. 812 (no. 20) and 813 (no. 21), 814, 819–20 (no. 29); cf. above, p. 111; P. Sims-Williams, 'Milred of Worcester's Collection of Latin Epigrams and its Continental Counterparts', ASE, 10 (1982), 21–38.

might have contained more. Incidentally, one would not expect the CL compiler to have copied this particular Roman inscription because it is not a papal one. The date of Milred's codex (c.750) is not too far removed from the *terminus post quem* of 707 for the *Sylloge* used in CL.

The matter is worth pursuing further, although it is involved. Recently there came to light a bifolium from a tenth-century English *Sylloge*, the so-called 'Urbana fragment', after its present home.[46] The fragment contains sixteen inscriptions of which a number are associated with Rome, and of which nos 14 and 15 correspond to Lapidge's nos 9 and 10. In spite of its date, and in spite of some variants between its texts 14 and 15 and Leland's versions of them, this is a remnant of his exemplar, for it bears his annotations.[47] Its survival enables us to say that the 'Codex Milredi' did contain a number of Roman as well as English inscriptions. But again, none of the Urbana inscriptions is in C, for only one of them is papal, and that has no indication of its *locus*, which may explain why CL's compiler omitted it, if he knew it.

There is one further piece of evidence which perhaps brings the 'Worcester *Sylloge*' (represented by Leland's extracts and the Urbana fragment) and the *Sylloge* extracted in CL closer together. Four of the inscriptions in the Urbanensis were also contained in the lost 'codex Bertinianus' (B*) used by André Duchesne for his 1617 edition of Alcuin's works. This ninth-century manuscript contained an extensive corpus of Alcuin's own verse, together with much other poetry by contemporary and earlier poets known and unknown.[48] Dieter Schaller explains: 'Geht man davon aus, dass der Codex Bertinianus den poetischen Nachlass Alcuins überlieferte, ist es nicht sehr verwunderlich, wenn sich hierunter auch Texte befunden haben, die er zwar nicht verfasst, aber doch vielleicht aus Interesse mit eigener Hand aufgezeichnet hat oder deren Aufzeichnung durch andere

---

[46] Wallach, 'The Urbana Anglo-Saxon Sylloge of Latin Inscriptions', pp. 134–151; Schaller, 'Bemerkungen zur Inschriften-Sylloge von Urbana', pp. 9–21.

[47] D. J. Sheerin, 'John Leland and Milred of Worcester', *Manuscripta*, 21 (1977), 178–180; cf. Schaller, p. 12, 17–20, esp. p. 19 n. 42. The collation is as follows: Lapidge no. 9, Wallach no. 14 no variants except line 3 *medeliferi* Lap., *medelli ueri* Wall. Both versions read *hic nobis Christum* at line 4 for *hic etiam nobis*, as in Florence, Bibl. Laurenziana, MS Lat. plut. LXVI 40, and both omit the last line of the version in the Florence manuscript. Lapidge no. 10, Wallach no. 15: the first six lines of Wallach are not in Lapidge, since Leland did not copy them. Line 8 *commendes* Lap., *commendens* Wall.; *hic* Lap., *haec* Wall.; line 12 *celestia* Lap., *caelestiae* Wall.; *premia* Lap., *pignora* Wall. In all cases Lapidge's reading is as the printed text of Leland's *Collectanea*, III, pp. 114–5, while Wallach's can be checked against the facsimile on p. 135 of his art., which also shows that Leland himself interlined the correction of 'medelliferi' for the scribe's 'medelli ueri' in line 3 of Wallach no. 14.

[48] Schaller, pp. 13–17.

er bei sich verwahrte'.[49] In support of this proposition he notes the close stylistic links between three of the inscriptions included in the Urbanensis and B* and some of Alcuin's genuine verse. Clearly Alcuin modelled his style on these earlier Roman inscriptions, *inter alia*. Perhaps he knew them from Milred's own manuscript. But what is really significant for our case is that a distich found in C was also included in B*.[50] Moreover Levison gave further examples which showed that the *Sylloge* used in CL was known to Alcuin and influenced his poetic style, a conclusion endorsed by Schaller.[51]

I conclude, then, that the inscriptions in CL derive from a tenth-century copy of the 'Codex Milredi', a *Sylloge* containing Roman, continental and English inscriptions put together by Bishop Milred of Worcester c.750 and available to Alcuin a few decades later. Of course this conclusion is far from proven; only an overlap of verses between Leland's extracts and the Urbana fragment on the one hand and the CL collection on the other would constitute a watertight case. Nonetheless Dr Sims-Williams has been able to strengthen it by demonstrating that CL and the extant representatives of the 'Codex Milredi' share an identical relationship to the same group of known congeners – mainly *Syllogae* extant in manuscripts of the ninth century.[52] I think, therefore, that we can regard the conclusion reached here as at least plausible. Now we have to connect our putative *Sylloge* with William. This is not difficult, for it is certain that he knew the 'Codex Milredi', and if that is identical with the 'Sylloge Cantabrigiensis' then he must have known that too independently of CL. Moreover in the *Gesta Regum* William summarizes the description of Rome from a lost *Itinerarium Urbis Romae* shown by De Rossi to have been made between 649 and 767 or perhaps 682.[53] It has been suggested that this *Itinerarium* would have been most appropriately included in a *Sylloge* manuscript, as with the extant example from Einsiedeln.[54] One cannot help but be struck by the similar dates of the CL *Sylloge* and William's lost *Itinerarium*. Perhaps it is pushing hypothesis too far to suggest that one of Bishop Milred's main sources for his codex may have been an early eighth-century manuscript containing inscriptions

---

[49] ibid., p. 15.

[50] ibid., p. 16.

[51] Levison, *England and the Continent in the Eighth Century*, p. 162 and n. 2; Schaller, p. 16 n. 28.

[52] P. Sims-Williams, 'William of Malmesbury and *La Silloge Epigrafica di Cambridge*', *Archivum Historiae Pontificiae*, 21 (1983), 9–33.

[53] GR II, pp. 404–408; de Rossi, *La Roma Sotteranea Christiana*, I, p. 146; cf. Valentini and Zucchetti, *Codice Topografico della Città di Roma*, II, pp. 133–153; above, p. 69 and n. 168.

[54] De Rossi, pp. 153–4; D. A. Bullough, 'Roman Books and Carolingian Renovatio', in D. Baker (ed.), *Renaissance and Renewal in Christian History* (Studies in Church History, 14, Oxford, 1977), pp. 35–6 and n. 25.

from Roman churches and a topographical description of the city.[55] Milred's codex, or rather a copy of it, then became William's source for material in CL and in the *Gesta Regum* and *Gesta Pontificum*.

We are on much surer ground in considering the next source excerpted in CL, the *Breviarium Alaricum*. Three imperial edicts were copied from it into CL, and survive in C.[56] Two of these are also in Oxford, Oriel College MS 42, William's Leonine collection;[57] we should, *prima facie*, expect these to have been copied from CL. But then, William had a complete text of the *Breviarium*, copied with his own hand into Bodl. MS Arch. Seld. B. 16. It is a distinctive and textually valuable version, dependent upon a very ancient exemplar.[58] Levison himself noticed the number of readings shared by the CL edicts and William's copy of the *Breviarium*.[59] With the help of the two texts in Oriel College MS 42 and Mommsen's edition of the Theodosian Code we are able to undertake some meaningful collation. The results are clear: C and Oriel College MS 42 derive independently from CL; CL and Bodl. MS Arch. Seld. B. 16 are dependent upon the same exemplar. Where was this exemplar kept? Bodl. MS Arch. Seld. B. 16 was made in 1129, and so its exemplar was then at Malmesbury. M. R. James showed that Aldhelm probably knew the *Breviarium*, and Mommsen demonstrated that William's exemplar was earlier than the seventh century.[60] So William was probably recopying an ancient and deteriorating manuscript from his local library. Here then is our first indubitable evidence that William knew the complete text of a work which was extracted in CL, and from the same manuscript.

Levison commented that the presence of the papal privilege for Malmesbury in CL in itself proved nothing, for there are also documents in favour of Wearmouth, Evesham and Canterbury in it. There is some force in this, but of far greater moment is the fact that these last and many other documents in CL not so far mentioned were extracted from a small group of manuscripts, nearly all of them from Canterbury, but known also to William. Let me begin with British Library, MS Cott. Tib. A. xv, an early eleventh-century manuscript containing letters of Alcuin, and others relevant to the rights and privileges of Christ Church Canterbury, where the book was doubtless made and kept.[61] CL contains four letters recognized by Levison to be from this manuscript, among them the papal letter to Abbot

---

55 Sims-Williams ('William of Malmesbury', pp. 31–3) points out that this is impossible to prove on the evidence currently available.
56 Levison, 'Aus Englischen Bibliotheken', pp. 373–4.
57 Oxford, Oriel College MS 42, ff. 123–123v, 139–139v.
58 Mommsen, *Theodosiani Libri XVI*, I, pp. lxv–lxvii, cxxxii.
59 Levison, 'Aus Englischen Bibliotheken', p. 374.
60 See above, pp. 33, 62–3.
61 On this manuscript see below, pp. 159–163.

Ceolfrid of Wearmouth.[62] All of them are in William's *Gesta Regum*, and there and in the *Gesta Pontificum* William extracted a series of letters by Alcuin and others from the Cotton manuscript. This is in itself enough to show that William was acquainted with the Cotton manuscript independently of CL. However, I have sought to demonstrate below that he made his own transcript of Cott. Tib. A. xv, and that it was from this transcript that he extracted into the *Gesta Regum* and *Gesta Pontificum*.[63] Into it he worked textual 'improvements', some stylistic, some historical. The most notorious of the latter was the substitution in the Wearmouth letter of the words 'Beda presbyter' for the Cotton text's 'N'.[64] This substitution is found in the CL copy of this document, and textual readings shared by the transcriptions in CL and William's major historical works indicate that the CL versions were taken from William's copy of the Cotton manuscript, not directly from the manuscript itself. Conversely, the four letters in the *Gesta Regum* and in CL were copied into the *Gesta* from William's transcript of the Cotton manuscript, not from CL. This illustration undoubtedly strengthens the case for William as the compiler of CL, particularly as it provides a partial explanation of the Canterbury interest displayed in that work. This is just as true of the remaining extracts in CL.

Let us take, for instance, a group of four documents (three quoted, the fourth mentioned only) which Levison recognized as derived from a collection of pseudo-Isidorean Decretals.[65] He particularized the collection as 'Lanfranc's', since one of the four CL documents, Jaffé 19965, is found only in the *Collectio Lanfranci*. In fact only a single manuscript of the *Collectio*, Cambridge, Trinity College B. 16. 44, includes this Decree.[66] Working before Z. N. Brooke's study of Lanfranc's Collection, Levison was unaware of this, and since his own collation showed that the CL copy was not derived from the one in the Trinity manuscript, but from an entirely different recension (now known to be that of the Collection in Five Parts), its presence does not show that CL's compiler used the *Collectio Lanfranci*.[67] Nonetheless, in spite of his deficient evidence, it would be

---

[62] Levison, 'Aus Englischen Bibliotheken', pp. 377, 383, 385, 389.

[63] Below, pp. 159–165.

[64] GR I, pp. 62 and n. 2, 63; below, pp. 172–3.

[65] Levison, 'Aus Englischen Bibliotheken', pp. 374–5, 378.

[66] Williams, *Codices Pseudo-Isidoriani*, p. 79; Z. N. Brooke, *The English Church and the Papacy* (Cambridge, 1931), pp. 232–5.

[67] Levison, 'Aus Englischen Bibliotheken', p. 375 and n. 1, referring to H. Boehmer, *Die Fälschungen Erzbischof Lanfranks von Canterbury* (Studien zur Geschichte der Theologie und der Kirche, VIII/1, Leipzig, 1902), pp. 161–3. Boehmer's MS 3, with which the C text often agrees, is London, Lambeth Palace 171, f. 7, c.1300, part of a record of the 1076 Council of Winchester. His MS 2 is Ivo, *Decr.* 7, 22(2). For the Collection in Five Parts see Fournier and Le Bras, *Histoire des Collections Canoniques en Occident*, I, pp. 421–431. The text on f. 1 of Oxford, Bodl. Libr. MS

surprising if Levison's conclusion were not correct, since Z. N. Brooke showed that Lanfranc's was by far the commonest version of pseudo-Isidore known in England during the twelfth century.[68] Two other documents in CL, the Decree of Nicholas II resulting from the Lateran Council of 1059, and the Acts of the Council of 1060, were probably copied from that source; they certainly do not appear in pseudo-Isidorean collections which are unrelated to Lanfranc's.[69] Five documents, then, in CL, came from a manuscript of the *Collectio Lanfranci*. None of them is quoted by William, but at least it can be shown that he too knew the *Collectio*. To prove this we must return to his own manuscript of canon law and Pope Leo's works, Oxford, Oriel College 42. The first part of this manuscript contains the *Collectio Quesnelliana* of early Church Councils and papal decrees,[70] copied, so William writes in a marginal note, from a 'uetustissimum exemplar'.[71] This exemplar he compared with 'nouella exemplaria', indicating by marginal signs texts present in or absent from the newer collections, describing more complex variants by longer notes. There are forty such indications, most of which apply to any reasonably complete pseudo-Isidore collection. However, among them are thirteen documents marked as lacking from the 'modern copies'. These documents are all found in normal pseudo-Isidore manuscripts, but are omitted from the *Collectio Lanfranci*. Turning to William's collection of Leo's letters in the same manuscript, we find a similar situation. Chavasse has shown that most of the letters were rearranged by William from the *Collectio Quesnelliana*, another two, as we saw, came from the *Breviarium Alaricum* via CL, while eight were taken from a False Decretals manuscript.[72] One of these, apparently

---

Hatton 93 (10th-cent., from Worcester), is an early 12th-cent. addition. It is textually similar to Boehmer's MSS 2 and 3, but has been corrected by a contemporary hand to bring it closer to C.

[68] Brooke, *The English Church*, pp. 231–7; H. Fuhrmann, *Einfluss und Verbreitung der pseudoisidorischen Fälschungen*, II (MGH Schriften, 24/2, Stuttgart, 1973), pp. 419–422.

[69] Levison, 'Aus Englischen Bibliotheken', pp. 390–1; Williams, *Codices Pseudo-Isidoriani*, p. 78. But these documents are also in London, BL Cott. Claud. E. v, and Eton College MS 97. The first of these contains a copy of Pseudo-Isidore made in northern France c.1100 and completed at Canterbury c.1125, using a text of the *Collectio Lanfranci*. The documents in question occur, of course, in this later part. The Eton College manuscript was made either at Exeter or in Normandy in the early twelfth century, and was certainly at Exeter by 1327 (Ker, *Medieval Manuscripts in British Libraries* II, p. 711 and n. 2). It contains a version of Pseudo-Isidore related to, but more complete than the *Collectio Lanfranci*. See below, n. 114.

[70] See above, pp. 64–6.

[71] Printed above, p. 65.

[72] Chavasse, op. cit., p. xxviii; eight letters are from the False Decretals, not nine as he says.

from Reims, we discussed earlier, leaving seven to be accounted for.[73] The question is, why did William take so few letters from the False Decretals, any reasonably complete specimen of which could have given him many more?[74] The answer is, of course, that what he used was a manuscript of the *Collectio Lanfranci*, which contains twenty-eight Leonine letters (about one quarter. of the normal pseudo-Isidorean total), twenty found also in the *Collectio Quesnelliana*. One letter from Lanfranc's Collection was not used by William, presumably by inadvertance, but as four of his Leonine letters are in the same order as they are in the *Collectio Lanfranci*, there can be little doubt that this was his source. Here then is a *fons* for CL which Levison thought flowed from Canterbury; in fact it could just as well lead back to Malmesbury.

Next I take the group of eleven letters of Paschal II contained only in L, whose concern is the primacy of Canterbury and relations between Anselm and Henry I.[75] Both their contents and textual tradition naturally point to Canterbury. Two must be eliminated from our discussion, one found only in L and nowhere else, the other found otherwise only in collections of Anselm's correspondence.[76] All the rest are known from one or both of the famous Canterbury books, BL Cott. Cleo. E. i and Claud. E. v. All were copied by Eadmer, five of them by William. Once again collation of these texts has produced some surprises.[77] First of all, Cleo. and Claud., closely related, depend upon a common ancestor, Claud. through an intermediate copy. This intermediate copy was Eadmer's source, since the readings of his text agree in most cases with Claud. against Cleo., but are better than either. Eadmer's lost source was also, apparently, the source of the nine letters of Paschal II in L. And what of the five letters copied by William? The collation shows – quite overwhelmingly in two cases – that he was not dependent upon (C)L, but like it upon either Eadmer or Eadmer's source – the number of variants is too few, and Eadmer's texts too accurate to permit further

---

[73] See above, p. 125.

[74] See above, p. 66. A complete Pseudo-Isidore collection contained 102 Leonine items: S. Williams, *Master-List of the Collectio Pseudo-Isidoriana* (Lille, 1964), pp. 14–19. Two closely-related manuscripts containing collections affiliated with the *Collectio Lanfranci* are BL Cott. Claud. E. v and Eton College MS 97 (see above, n. 69). But they contain 51 Leonine letters, among them several not used by William. Cf. R. Somerville, 'Lanfranc's Canonical Collection and Exeter', *Bulletin of the Institute of Historical Research*, 45 (1972), 303–306.

[75] Levison, 'Aus Englischen Bibliotheken', pp. 410–411.

[76] 'Visis litteris uestris' to Robert of Normandy, printed by Levison, op. cit., pp. 427–8; 'Consulta illa' to Anselm (Jaffé no. 5909), ed. Schmitt, *Sancti Anselmi Opera Omnia*, Ep.223.

[77] Jaffé nos 5910, 5868, 5956, 5928, 6073 are in Claud.; 5908, 5930, 5955, 6547 in Cleo. and Claud. William has 5956, 5928, 6073 (together and in the same sequence as in Eadmer), 5930 and 6547.

particularization. For other documents in the *Gesta Pontificum*, in particular the notorious Canterbury forgeries, William was certainly copying from Eadmer, although even in these cases he compared Eadmer with Eadmer's own exemplar and sometimes emended accordingly.[78] There is no un-equivocal evidence for the use of Eadmer in CL, and it would be surprising if there were, since CL's compilation probably took place before or simultaneously with the writing of the *Historia Novorum*.

I mentioned earlier the copies of the mutual oaths of Paschal II and Henry V, the 'pravilegium' of 1111, and the Acts of the 1112 Lateran Council, suppressed in C but present in L. This collection of documents had a very wide distribution, and a good deal of work is necessary before the ancestry of the CL version can be pinned down.[79] Nonetheless it is at least possible to establish the independence from CL of William's copies of the same documents in the *Gesta Regum*. Collation shows that William's version, while closely related to both John of Worcester's and CL's, came from CL's exemplar, whatever that was.[80] The most decisive proof of this is a lengthy and important clause in William's and other versions but omitted by L and John.[81] Since L's copyist was not careless like C's one can reasonably regard this omission as the deliberate policy of CL's compiler.

Levison was, as I have already suggested, too dismissive of the Malmesbury privilege in C. Apart from its share of copyist's errors and some omissions which may have been deliberate, it represents a text close to that found in the Malmesbury cartularies.[82] William's copy, in the fifth book of his *Gesta Pontificum*, comes from a similar local source. But what must be said against Levison, I believe, is that behind the manufacture of such a papal History, with its English emphasis, it is easier to imagine a Malmesbury compiler who included Canterbury documents – he could hardly avoid doing so – than a Canterbury writer using a Malmesbury privilege. The

---

[78] Cf. GP, pp. 50–1, where the notes indicate changes made by William in his autograph: p. 50 n. 1 *promissa* as Cleo. and Eadmer, changed to *promissio* as Claud.; p. 50 n. 4 *annuentes* as Cleo. and Eadmer, changed to *annuimus* as Claud.; p. 51 n. 4 *habetote* as Eadmer, changed to *habeto* as Cleo. and Claud.

[79] I am obliged to Dr Martin Brett for advice on this point. See Brett, 'John of Worcester and his Contemporaries', p. 116 and n. 1, with bibliographical references.

[80] John of Worcester's text is close to CL, but contains some readings in common with other manuscripts.

[81] GR II, pp. 499–504. The sentence missing from L and John is p. 502 lines 6–7: 'exceptis nimirum illis qui uel in archiepiscoporum uel in Romani pontificis solent dispositione consistere'.

[82] Levison, op. cit., p. 377. I have collated C and William's copy (GP, pp. 367–370) with J. S. Brewer (ed.), *Registrum Malmesburiense*, I (RS, London, 1879), pp. 343–4, and with Oxford, Bodl. Libr. MS Wood Empt. 5, ff. 57–60, a thirteenth-century Malmesbury cartulary.

inclusion of Pope Sergius's letter to Abbot Ceolfrid of Wearmouth hardly needs justification, but as we saw earlier it is partly explained by its presence, along with other papal letters, in BL Cott. Tib. A. xv, one of the sources mined by CL's compiler. Even the Evesham document has more than local implications and is, indeed, addressed to an archbishop of Canterbury and copied into Canterbury cartularies.[83] In fact, using the Evesham documents and others, we can turn Levison's argument upon its head. The Evesham forgery, the forged account of Pope Formosus's partition of the dioceses of Wessex, and the Acts of the Council of Clermont discussed earlier each survive in Canterbury recensions as well as other, quite different ones. Levison noted, and further collation has confirmed that while the Evesham forgery was copied into contemporary Canterbury cartularies, the CL version reflects, not the Canterbury tradition, but the rather different Evesham one.[84] So also with the Formosus document. It is found in BL Cott. Cleo. E. i from Canterbury, but the CL text represents a different tradition found among houses in the south-west of England.[85] As we saw earlier, William and CL share a recension of the Clermont Acts quite different from the Canterbury one.[86] The conclusion from this seems inescapable; a Canterbury compiler would have reflected the textual tradition local to his house for some at least of these documents; since CL's compiler does not reflect Canterbury tradition where one would expect him to, he did not work at Canterbury, or at least not at Canterbury only.

So far, I have been concerned to establish William's independent knowledge of many of the texts interpolated into CL, and I believe that the weight of evidence accumulated by pursuing this line of argument is overwhelming. Any uncertainties which remain ought to be quickly effaced by a brief consideration of the method employed by CL's compiler, a method entirely familiar to anyone who has studied William's method in those compilations already known to be his, and in his great Histories. The most important shared characteristic is this: that behind the scissors-and-paste work can be discerned a process of continuous ratiocination, the efforts of a considering intelligence accustomed to the exercise of historical judgement. That is to say, although CL is essentially a compilation, it is in

---

[83] Levison, p. 378. It is in both Cleo. and Claud.
[84] I have collated both of the Evesham sources, London, BL Cott. Vesp. B. xxiv, ff. 76–76v, and J. D. Macray (ed.), *Chronicon Abbatiae de Evesham* (RS, London, 1863), pp. 171–2, and two Canterbury ones, BL Cott. Cleo. E. i (which Levison mentions) and Claud. E. v (which he omits).
[85] Levison, pp. 386 and n. 3, 387–8; BL Cott. Cleo. E. i, ff. 45v–6, Faust. B. vi, ff. 98–9, both from Canterbury, and Add. 15530, ff. 112–112v, from Winchester. It is printed from the latter in W. De Gray Birch, *Cartularium Saxonicum* (London, 3 vols, 1883–92), II, no. 614.
[86] See above, p. 124.

no way a mechanically or mindlessly constructed one. This is best illustrated by the compiler's treatment of the Christian inscriptions in it, carefully studied by Silvagni. He was able to distinguish, more clearly than Duchesne before him, between the mistakes of the ignorant copyist, and the retouching and rearrangement of the learned, although sometimes mistaken compiler. This compiler emended the texts of some of the inscriptions, removing what to him were barbarities in the diction, and making intelligible the textual corruptions, always working sensibly although quite unauthoritatively.[87] This was the consistent and well-documented practice of William, to the dispair of modern editors.[88] He never copied without correcting and retouching. The compiler also tried to match the inscriptions to the reigns of appropriate popes, and to assign them to particular buildings or parts of buildings. His exemplar evidently gave him little help, and he was often reduced to conjecture. The results were faulty, but it is important to realize that the chain of reasoning behind this process can be reconstructed, precisely because it *was* a rational, not a haphazard activity. Again this is typical of William's *modus operandi*, and one can observe another example of it in William's use of Alcuin's letters in his *Gesta*.[89] Thirdly, one might consider the variety of the sources from which extracts were added to the basic substructure of CL: papal letters, privileges, conciliar acta, chronicles, inscriptions, hagiography and pastoral exhortation. Similar variety characterizes the sources utilized in the *Gesta* and in the *Antiquity of Glastonbury*; it is a distinctive feature of William's historiography.[90] Finally, not all of the interpolations into CL were in the form of undigested lumps; in several passages, notably the Lives of Popes Leo I, Stephen II, Hadrian and Leo III, a number of sources, mostly identified explicitly, were woven together.[91] These are examples of historical portraits built up from the collection of minute pieces of information contained in disparate texts. I would compare with this technique William's attempt to reconstruct the history of England in the century after Bede, or his cautious account of the earliest history of Glastonbury abbey.[92]

If CL was put together by William at Malmesbury, then one is forced to reconsider the date of its compilation. Certainly this was later than 1119, but how much later? I have been assuming that it was completed in that year or soon after, but this needs justification. So long as CL was assigned a

---

[87] E.g. Duchesne, 'Le Recueil', pp. 281–3; Silvagni, pp. 53–4.
[88] The views of modern editors are documented above, p. 33 n. 117.
[89] See below, pp. 168–71.
[90] Southern, 'Aspects of the European Tradition of Historical Writing IV', p. 255; above, pp. 16–17.
[91] Levison, pp. 369–371, 381–3, 385–6, 406–7.
[92] GR I, pp. 67–9, 74–102; for the *Antiquity* see idem, pp. 23–9, or AG, pp. 168–172.

Canterbury provenance, then 1125, the date by which William had incorporated extracts from it into his *Gesta*, was the *terminus ante quem* for its manufacture. However this becomes questionable once CL is seen as William's own work, for it is at least possible that his extracts in the *Gesta Regum* and *Gesta Pontificum* were made from materials later used in CL, not from a pre-existent CL itself. In that case the only *terminus ante quem* for its manufacture would be the date of Oriel College MS 42, which does unquestionably contain parts of the completed work, and that manuscript can only be dated vaguely and uncertainly to c.1135.[93] A date after 1125 for CL's composition has something to recommend it, for it breaks up the 'log-jam' which seems to have William working simultaneously upon CL and his two major Histories. We must then scrutinize more closely the CL material in the *Gesta*. It is indeed true that nearly all of it could have come from CL's sources rather than CL itself, but there is a notable exception. William's account of the reign of Urban II in the *Gesta Regum* includes not only the Clermont Acts as in CL, but also the information which flanks it there, in the same sequence.[94] In other words, William reproduces virtually the whole account of Urban's reign as given in CL. It is still conceivable that William put this together in the *Gesta Regum* before it was done in CL, but that seems the less natural explanation. Moreover, if CL were compiled after 1125, one would expect it to end later than 1119, and to include relevant material of a later date such as William had included in the *Gesta Regum* or *Gesta Pontificum*, for instance the Canterbury forgeries. I am led, therefore, to proceed in the opposite direction, while recognizing the improbability that CL was compiled close to the final stages of composition of the two *Gesta*, and to suggest that it was put together by 1119 or very soon after.

William, then, compiled a surviving edition of *Liber Pontificalis* between 1119 and 1125; this discovery opens up entirely new avenues of research. We can now recognize those sources used in CL but not quoted elsewhere by William as nonetheless known to him, and can thus include them in the already extensive reading-list with which he is credited.[95] More importantly, it should now be possible to date more precisely his visits to other houses, especially Canterbury, and to give a more detailed account of his bibliographical activities there. Of course a whole flood of new light is shed upon William's historical method, as the penultimate paragraph has suggested in an introductory way. One mystery, however, is deepened.

---

[93] See above, pp. 96–7.
[94] GR II, pp. 390–3; Levison, pp. 392–4.
[95] See below, Appendix I. The additions from this source are: two *Liber Pontificalis* manuscripts and the *Papstkatalog*, the *Sylloge* as part of the *Codex Milredi*, Sigibert, the *Vitae Aniani, Dionysii* and *Remigii*, without taking account of the documentary material.

William was a young man when he began his major works, and we have not until now found any writings by him which predate them. One would like to know something of his education, his early intellectual development, and of the preparations which he made for this immense task. Now we have a work which predates the final drafts of the two *Gesta*, although not their first beginnings, which were prior to 1118. But the *Liber Pontificalis* is no minor work, or that of a tentative beginner. Its scope is comparable to William's English Histories, even though its form is less highly-wrought and its content more derivative than theirs. Our picture of William the historian is thus still that of a giant who reaches his full stature with mysterious suddenness. And that is not likely to be a correct picture.

7

WILLIAM'S CAROLINGIAN SOURCES

WILLIAM'S *GESTA REGUM*, completed in 1125, is of course primarily a history of England; primarily, but not solely, and certainly not in any narrow sense. On the contrary, William felt it necessary to at least summarize, in a series of digressions, the history of those people who, by invasion, intermarriage or diplomatic intercourse, became part of England's history. So, he dealt with the continental Saxons and Scandinavians briefly, the Frankish, German and French royal families and the Normans in greater detail.[1] The excursuses became more frequent as, on nearing his own time, his vision grew even more pan-European, encompassing the First Crusade, the later stages of the Investiture Controversy and the appearance of new monastic Orders.[2] More frequent also become the notorious and baffling fables and folk-tales, apparently (but only apparently?) introduced as light relief.[3] William justified these excursuses in various ways. Only one of them claims our attention here, and that is his prolonged treatment of the revived Empire of Charlemagne and his successors. The subject attracted him, not merely because of his perception of the various links between these monarchs and the English ones; he was also interested in the notion of 'empire', which he saw as an entity with an unbroken existence stretching from classical antiquity to his own day. Its history is summarized and interpreted by him in one of his best-known collections, the partly autograph Oxford, Bodleian Library MS Arch. Seld. B. 16, written in 1129.[4] This double interest is made abundantly clear in the introduction to his first section on the Franks in the *Gesta Regum*:

[1] GR I, pp. 8–9 (Saxons); 75–6, 219 and II, pp. 317–320 (Danes, but William does not seem to have had much information on their early history outside England); I, pp. 69–72, 110–7 (Franks); I, pp. 230–6, II, pp. 342–4 (Germans); I, pp. 139–40 (French); I, pp. 137–9, and II, pp. 285–297, 320–2 (Normans).
[2] GR II, pp. 390–463 (Crusade); 322–6, 489–492, 489–509 (Investitures); 380–5 (Cistercians).
[3] GR I, pp. 193–206, 231–5, 253–60; II, pp. 295–7, 344–5; cf. the comments by B. Ward, 'Miracles and History; a Reconsideration of the Miracle-Stories used by Bede', in Bonner, *Famulus Christi*, pp. 70–6.
[4] For its contents and date see above, pp. 62–3, 66–7, and below, p. 176.

... Quoniam ad id locorum uenimus ut Karoli magni mentio ultro se inferret, uolo de linea regum Francorum, de qua multa fabulatur antiquitas, ueritatem subtexere; nec multum a proposito elongabor, quia progeniem eorum nescire dampnum duco scientiae, *cum et confines nobis sint, et ad eos maxime Christianum speciet imperium.*[5]

There follow three pages on the history of the Frankish royal house, from its misty origins to Charlemagne, and thence to the end of his line and the resuscitation of the Empire by Otto the Great, from whom 'modernus Henricus ... lineam trahit'.[6] In his next book, prompted by the meagre excuse of Ethelwulf's marriage to Judith, daughter of Charles the Bald, William intrudes a further seven pages *De successoribus Caroli Magni*, from Louis the Pious to Louis the Child.[7] Both sections are based mainly upon annalistic and genealogical sources.

As Bishop Stubbs demonstrated, in his treatment of the Carolingians William is not at his most reliable, and his account contains errors and confusions.[8] Stubbs managed to identify some of William's sources, but confessed himself in the final analysis beaten: 'Our author's habit of paraphrasing or reproducing the matter borrowed from the earlier authorities, renders it impossible in every case to refer his statements to their primary source; nor is the amount of information which he adds to the current foreign history of early times sufficiently important to make it worth the trouble'.[9] The sources of William's information about the Franks are indeed difficult to identify for the reason Stubbs gives, but they *are* worth some trouble, not indeed for any great gain in our understanding of ninth-century Francia, but because of the light shed on William's historical method.

Fortunately we are not dependent upon the *Gesta Regum* alone for our knowledge of William's Frankish sources and his treatment of them. There exists a manuscript which throws unsuspected light upon the Frankish sections of the *Gesta Regum* and upon William's technique as a historian. Until 1977 it was London, Sion College MS Arc. L. 40.2/L. 21, and while there was fully described by N. R. Ker,[10] although he did not succeed in identifying all of the items in it. It is now Oxford, Bodleian Library MS Lat. class. d. 39 (hereafter referred to as B). Written almost entirely in one expert English hand of about 1175, the manuscript has no indication of provenance.

---

[5] GR I, p. 69.
[6] ibid., p. 72.
[7] ibid., pp. 110–7.
[8] GR II, pp. xxi–xxvii.
[9] GR I, p. 69 n. 2.
[10] N. R. Ker, *Medieval Manuscripts in British Libraries*, I (Oxford, 1969), pp. 278–9.

However, as Dr Ker noted, a book with the same main items of contents in the same order appears in the library-catalogue of Christ Church, Canterbury, compiled by Prior Henry of Eastry at the beginning of the fourteenth century.[11] Bodleian Library MS Lat. class. d. 39 could be the same book, though it does not bear a Canterbury press-mark.

It contains Suetonius's *Vitae Caesarum* (ff. 1–125), a *Genealogia Regum Francorum* from Faramund to Pippin II (ff. 125–125v), the *Annales Mettenses Priores* from Pippin II to the death of Pippin III (ff. 125v–136v), Einhard's *Vita Karoli* (ff. 136v–150v), another genealogy from St Arnulf to Lothar I (f. 150v), the *Visio Karoli Crassi* (ff. 150v–152v), a *florilegium* of twenty-eight extracts from Aulus Gellius's *Attic Nights* (ff. 153–9), and, in another but similar and contemporary hand, the poem *Cesar tantus eras* (ff. 159–159v). William knew Suetonius, Einhard, the Gellius *florilegium* and *Cesar tantus eras*,[12] and we shall see that he also knew the Metz *Annals* and *Visio Karoli*. None of these works was very common in twelfth-century England; the *florilegium* and poem in particular merit further comment. It is certain that both William and John of Salisbury used the Gellius *florilegium* copied (incompletely) in B, and it is even possible that William was its compiler.[13] At all events he excerpted from it into his own much more copious florilegium, the *Polyhistor*.[14] As for *Cesar tantus eras*, so popular on the continent, William's text in the *Gesta Regum* is strikingly different from all other known versions in its readings and order of lines.[15] It is therefore significant that the B text (not used in the *Monumenta* edition) follows William's version but for four variants: *tollit* (with three late German manuscripts) for William's *tollat*, *ac* (a scribal slip) for his *ad*, *lenis* (with Vat. lat. 3827) for his *laetus*, and *numina*, incorrectly with seven *Gesta Regum* manuscripts against *lumina* of the remainder.[16] The seven manuscripts with the defective reading represent all three editions of the *Gesta*, and thus the variant probably arose from a change of mind by the author himself. *Numina* we may conjecture as his first choice, the **n** soon after cancelled with a sublinear point and the **l** written over it, William's usual practice as revealed by the autograph of his *Gesta Pontificum*.[17] A provisional

---

[11] James, *The Ancient Libraries of Canterbury and Dover*, p. 44, no. 24.
[12] For Suetonius see above, p. 58; for Einhard, see below notes 31 and 46; for Gellius see below, pp. 185–195; *Cesar tantus eras* is in GR I, p. 235.
[13] See below, pp. 185–195, but note the objections raised by Janet Martin, described on p. 194.
[14] Extant in London, BL MS Harl. 3969, and Cambridge, St John's College MS 97; ed. as PH.
[15] MGH Poetae 4. 2, pp. 1074–5.
[16] GR I, p. 235 n. 2; '. . . defecta . . . lumina' appears to be an echo of Statius, *Thebais*, xii. 325.
[17] Oxford, Magdalen College MS lat. 172. William's corrections and alterations are faithfully recorded by Hamilton in his edition of GP.

explanation of these interesting facts might be that B's scribe or compiler had access to some of William's books, and perhaps copied *Cesar tantus eras* from the *Gesta Regum* itself.

But the manuscript bears evidence of a more intimate connection with William than this. Scattered throughout it are marginal notes in the hand of the main scribe of the text. They were undoubtedly copied from his exemplar, and since they are certainly by a single author, they show that the exemplar contained most if not all of the items in B. In short, B is a copy of a single manuscript with the same contents. The notes are as follows:

1. f. 17 Verbum Ciceronis est adulantis Cesari in oratione pro M. Marcello: Itaque illam tuam preclarissimam et sapientissimam uocem inuitus audiui; satis te diu uixisse uel nature uel glorie. Satis si ita uis, naturae fortasse. Addo etiam si placet, glorie. At quod maximum est, patrie certe parum (Cicero, *Pro Marcello*, 25).
2. f. 79 Verba Orosii sunt: Verum hec Suetonius dixerit hec [*sic*] Claudium egisse, quia Ɔ tumultuantes Iudeos coherceri et comprimi iusserit, uel etiam Christianos uelut cognate religionis homines uoluerit expelli, nequaquam discernitur.
3. f. 80 Hic est Felix qui in Actibus apostolorum legitur apostolum Paulum eripuisse a Iudeis.
4. f. 139v Ex Albini epistola: Antiqui Saxones et omnes Fresonum populi, instante rege Karolo premiis et minis, ad fidem Christi conuersi sunt (Alcuin, Ep. 7).
5a. f. 140v Ex A(lbini) epistola: Duces regis mille partem Hispaniae tulerunt a Sarracenis, quasi ccc milia in longum per maritima (*ibid.*).
5b. Ludouicus etiam filius eius Hispanias ingressus, Barcilleam ciuitatem que rebellabat iterum subegit (Hugh of Fleury, *Historia Ecclesiastica*[18]).
6. f. 141v Rex Karolus cum exercitui irruit super Sclauos ... eosque subegit (Alcuin, Ep. 7).
7. f. 142 Auari quos nos Hunos dicimus ... inuaserunt (*ibid.*).
8. f. 143v Greci cum classe ... ceteri fuerunt (*ibid.*).
9. f. 144 Ex decretis ... (Ivo of Chartres, *Panormia* 8. 135).
10a. f. 147 Ex Hammonio: Sub eius imperio sunt multa et precipue he monasteria facta ... piissimus imperator insigniuit (Hugh of Fleury[19]).
10b. In Gallia monasterium sancti Pauli Cormaricense de medietate possessionum quas habebant canonici de sancto Martino, hortante Alcuino, unde hodieque pro anima ipsius Alcuini fiunt ibidem elemosina multa cotidie.

[18] Rottendorff, *Hugonis Floriacensis Monachi Benedictini Chronicon*, p. 173.
[19] ibid., p. 175.

11. ff. 147–147v Ex Hammonio: Cognati Adriani pape ... anno incarnationis dcclxxxiiii (ibid.[20]).

William wrote this sort of note, amplifying the main text from other sources, in his various collections, for example in the already-mentioned Bodleian Library MS Arch. Seld. B. 16.[21] I believe that he wrote the originals of these notes too. Let us give our attention to the sources that they quote. Orosius and the book of Acts were too commonly quoted to be significant.[22] But Cicero's *Pro Marcello* is a different story. The three *Orationes Caesarianae (Pro Marcello, Pro Ligario, Pro Rege Deiotaro)* travelled together, and they are included in the late copy of William's great edition of Cicero's speeches and philosophical writings.[23] There is a possibility that they were added to the collection after William's time, and I have not found any citation from them among his other works.[24] Still, William was the greatest English Ciceronian of the twelfth century, the *Orationes Caesarianae* had some circulation at that time, and one would expect him to have known them.[25] More convincing are the four notes from Alcuin's letter 7. This letter is only transmitted in two early eleventh-century English manuscripts, and the readings of these extracts point to one of them, British Library Cott. Tib. A. xv, probably from Christ Church Canterbury.[26] William knew this manuscript, made a copy of it, and extracted from it in the *Gesta Regum* and *Gesta Pontificum*.[27] In fact, he quoted letter 7, including the passages given in notes 4, 5a and 6, in the *Gesta Regum*.[28] Hugh of Fleury, quoted in notes 5b, 10a and 11, William used in the same work,[29] and he summarized his

---

[20] ibid., p. 177.

[21] See above, pp. 63, 66–7.

[22] For what it is worth, William copied Orosius in Oxford, Bodl. Libr. MS Arch. Seld. B. 16, ff. 11–71.

[23] CUL Dd. 13. 2; see above, pp. 50–4, R. W. Hunt et al., *The Survival of Ancient Literature*, p. 76, no. 135, and *Texts and Transmission*, pp. 59, 65–7, 77, 80–2, 95. None of the known early MSS of the *Caesarians* is English, though they were in Normandy by the mid twelfth century.

[24] Mynors, *Catalogue of the Manuscripts of Balliol College Oxford*, p. 377.

[25] The stocks of John of Salisbury, his main rival in this sphere, continue to fall; see above, pp. 6–10, and J. Martin, 'John of Salisbury as Classical Scholar', in *The World of John of Salisbury*, pp. 179–201.

[26] Citing the edition of E. Dümmler, MGH Epistolae 4. Note 4 Fresonum *with* London, BL Cott. Tib. A. xv (Dümmler's A1) *and* GR: Frisonum A2; note 6 irruit *with* A1 *and* GR: inruit A2.

[27] See below, pp. 159–165.

[28] GR I, p. 92.

[29] GR I: most of p. 69 line 13 until 70 line 5 (Rottendorff, p. 104ff); p. 71 line 8, the epithet of 'Tudites' for Charles Martel (ibid., p. 162); p. 72 line 1, the description of Pope Leo's assailants as Hadrian's 'consanguinei' (ibid., p. 172); most of p. 110 lines 1–16 (ibid., pp. 179–180).

Historia in Bodleian Library MS Arch. Seld. B. 16.[30] There he calls him *Haimo*, as in notes 10a and 11 (although they seem to suggest the form *Hammonius*). In fact all three extracts are substantially as in the Selden manuscript, f. 139, where the last is accompanied by a reference to Einhard, against whose text it is written in B.[31] We come to note 9, presenting an extract from a letter fraudulently ascribed to Pope Hadrian, exactly as given in Ivo's *Panormia*. The *Panormia* was introduced into England about 1100, and rapidly became popular.[32] In the second half of the twelfth century there was a copy at Cirencester, not far from Malmesbury (Oxford, Jesus College MS 26), and a house with which William had had some contact.[33] He knew a number of the bishop's writings, and in the *Gesta Regum* gives a resumé of this very extract, which he puts into the mouth of Pope Gregory VI.[34] Finally, there is the curious note 10b, concerning Alcuin's patronage of Cormery, a dependent cell of St Martin's abbey actually founded by his predecessor Abbot Itherius.[35] The erroneous description of the St Martin's community as *canonici*, and the mention of the daily alms, suggest that the basis of this note was a late and presumably oral communication. A variant of it is found in some manuscripts of the *Gesta Regum*,[36] either in the text or as a marginal note – the latter doubtless reflecting the situation in William's autograph. His note runs 'Iacet in Francia apud Sanctum Paulum de Cormarico, quod coenobium Karolus magnus eius consilio construxit; unde hodieque quatuor monachorum uictus et potus pro eiusdem Alcuini anima

---

[30] See above, p. 67. William used Hugh's second edition of 1110.

[31] The equivalent to this note and the reference to Einhard in the Selden MS runs: 'Denique ista et multa preterea monasteria sub eo facta: monasterium Sancti Philiberti, Sancti Maxentii, Concas, Murate, Magniloco, Nursiacum, Sancti Saluii, Nobiliacum, Sancti Theofridi, Sancti Pascentii, Dorosa, Solemniacum, monasterium puellare Sanctae Mariae, item Sanctae Radegundis, monasterium Deuera, monasterium Deuta in pago Tholosano, monasterium Valida in Septimania, Sancti Aniani Galimme, Sancti Laurentii, monasterium in Rubine, monasterium Caunas. Et alia quibus ueluti gemmis tota decoratur Aquitania. Haec ideo de Carolo dicimus, omissis omnibus eius gestis quae in ipsius uita leguntur, ut ostenderemus quomodo et quantum imperatores Constantinopolitani perdiderint Romanae urbis imperium ...'.

[32] Z. N. Brooke, *The English Church and the Papacy*, pp. 94–5, 244–5.

[33] William and Robert of Cricklade, canon of Cirencester and then prior of St Frideswide, seem to have known each other. Robert certainly knew some of William's works; see above, p. 74 and n. 205.

[34] GR I, pp. 250–1.

[35] On Cormery see J.-J. Bourassé 'Le cartulaire de Cormery précédé de l'histoire de l'abbaye et de la ville de Cormery', *Memoires de la Société Archéologique de Touraine*, 12 (1861), and A. Kleinclausz, *Eginhard* (Paris, 1942), pp. 160, 197–8. Alcuin already claimed to be its founder (MGH Epist. 4, p. 309); compare Ardo, *Vita Benedicti Aniani*, MGH Scriptores 15, p. 210.

[36] GR I, pp. lv and 69 n. 1.

quotidianae infertur elemosinae in eadem ecclesia'. This note, too, contains erroneous information, namely that Alcuin founded Cormery and that he was buried there. None of the contents of either note is found in any other known written source. On the other hand, each note has specific information not in the other, excluding the possibility of either being adapted from the other. They are best accounted for as the work of one man, each reflecting with different emphases information which he carried only in his head. It is also perhaps worth noting the use in both of 'hodieque' for 'hodie', a peculiarity of William's.

My earlier suggestion, that B derives from a group of William's books, must consequently be modified. Rather, it was copied from a single one compiled or acquired for or by William and bearing his annotations. With this in mind, we can profitably examine the Carolingian chronicles in it, and their relationship to the similar material in the *Gesta Regum*. These chronicles make up a compilation which, as the numerous cross-references show, was the work of one man. It begins with the conflation of an otherwise unknown regnal list and genealogy:

(f. 125) Incipit genealogia regum Francorum. Anno ab incarnatione Domini CCCXXIIIJ regnauit primus rex Francorum Faramundus annis v. Successit filius eius Clodio annis vi. Filius Clodionis Meroueus annis xiiii. Ab hoc omnes reges Francorum Merouingi uocati sunt. Childericus filius Merouei regnauit annis xxiiii. Clodoueus filius Childerici annis xxx. Hic primus fidem Christi suscepit. Lotarius filius Clodouei regnauit annis li. Chilpericus filius Lotharii annis xxiiii. Lotarius filius Chilperici annis liiii. Dagobertus filius Lotharii annis xxxiiii. Clodoueus filius Dagobertus annis xvi. Clotarius filius Clodouei annis iiii. Theodoricus filius Lotharii annis xviii.

Medio tempore Botgisus illustris (f. 125v) dux Francorum ex filia Chilperici regis filii Lotharii primi genuit Arnulfum sanctissimum Metensis urbis episcopum. Arnulfus genuit Angisum. Angisus genuit Pipinum, de quo ita historia narrat. (Here begin the *Annales Mettenses Priores* with a new line and painted initial.)

The regnal list distantly resembles one published by Holder-Egger from Le Havre, Bibl. Mun. MS 1 of the eleventh century.[37] There is also a slight resemblance to some early entries in the Rouen *Annals*.[38] These parallels, although not close, emphasize that the list is probably dependent upon a late source, and certainly upon a corrupt and confused one. Botgisus or Botgisel

---

[37] O. Holder-Egger in *Neues Archiv*, 16 (1890–1), 602–6.
[38] A. Le Prévost and L. Delisle, *Orderici Vitalis Historia Ecclesiastica* V, (Société de l'histoire de France, Paris, 1855), appendice; F. Liebermann, *Ungedruckte Anglo-Normannische Geschichtsquellen* (Strassburg, 1879), p. 31ff.

is given as St Arnulf's father in a genealogy discussed by Bonnell and copied later on in B, but this example is unique in making his wife Chilperic's daughter rather than the daughter of his son Lothar. It too is probably based upon a late and unauthoritative source. Neither the list nor this genealogy were used in the *Gesta Regum*. There William reproduces a quite different genealogy for the Arnulfings, the so-called *Domus Carolingiae Genealogia*, in a redaction made at the abbey of St Wandrille.[39] However his statement about Meroveus, 'a quo omnes post eum reges Merouingi sunt', has an analogue in the regnal list, and his date of 424 for Faramund's accession an obvious resemblance to its 324.[40] More important than the discrepancy, which could easily be due to a scribal slip, is the fact that, so far as I am aware, no other source assigns Faramund a date remotely similar to these.

Then follow the *Annales Mettenses*. Until the year 717, they are rendered verbatim except for small omissions which might have been accidental. In the course of the entry for 717 summarizing begins, with some unfortunate results. The events of 725 and 731 were somehow telescoped under 721, and the years 732–746 misread as 722–736. The entry for 738 was omitted altogether. In the margin of f. 133, opposite the entry for 731 (741), is a note by the scribe, beginning with a coloured initial as the entries in the text: 'Anno Domini DCCXXVIIII Aquitanos Karolus iterum tributarios fecit'. This is based on the *Annales Mettenses*' entry for 738, except that 'Aquitanos' should read 'Saxones'. Heavy summarizing begins at 754,[41] and continues to 768, where the extract ends. This last, summarized section reads as follows:

(f. 136) . . . et [Pipinus] Papiam obsedit, usquequo ipsum Haistulfum ad deditionem compulit, et se omnia redditurum Romanis que eripuerat sa(f. 137)cramento firmare fecit. Sed reddeunte Pipino Franciam, Haistulfus spreto sacramento nichil Romanis reddidit, sed insuper Romam graui obsessione afflixit. Quo per litteras pontificis cognito, Pipinus iterum Italiam aduolat, iterum Haistulfum ad redditionem ereptarum ciuitatum in scripto compellit. Quam redditionis cartam excellentissimus Pipinus per Fulradum uenerabilem abbatem et consiliarium ipsius Romam Sancto Petro cum clauibus ciuitatum misit. Post non multum uero tempus Haistulfus in uenationem pergens diuino nutu percussus est, cui Desiderius quidam successit, quem postea Carolus magnus a regno expulit, sicut sequens liber declarabit. Pipinus uero reuertens Franciam xiii. annis postea

---

[39] GR I, p. 71 lines 1–8; MGH Scriptores, 2, pp. 308–9.
[40] GR I, p. 70.
[41] The entry for 754 is reasonably intact until p. 47 line 10 of the edition by B. von Simson, MGH Script. in usum schol. (1905).

uixit, et regno Francorum undique dilatato ix. kal. Octobris obiit, et apud Sanctum Dionisium sepultus est.

It is a surprise to find no direct textual relationship between this and the only other known English version of the *Annales*, the early twelfth-century copy from Durham.[42] Rather, this version shows a close connection with the important late twelfth-century manuscript from St Arnulf's Metz, now Berlin (West), Staatsbibliothek MS. Lat. 141.[43] This manuscript presents the *Annales Mettenses Iuniores*, a conflation of the *Annales Priores* in a form already somewhat abbreviated, and the Chronicle of Regino of Prüm. The B version drew on the same slightly abbreviated form of the *Annales*, but is not interpolated from Regino.[44] It thus depends upon the same manuscript of the *Annales* as the Berlin text, and that manuscript could hardly be other than a Metz one. Let us now return to William. Could he have known the version of the *Annales Mettenses* found in B? Though skeletal, his account of the rise of the Carolingians in the first Frankish section of the *Gesta Regum* seems certainly based upon the *Annales*:[45] the sum total of its information is found in the *Annales* and only there (in particular the date of 687 for Pippin II becoming count of the palace), and its emphases reflect those of the relevant section of the *Annales*. It is, then, surely significant that William's use of the *Annales* in the *Gesta Regum* is confined to the years covered by the extract in B, that is, the period up to the death of Pippin III. Thereafter, his main source is Einhard, whose text follows the *Annales* in B.[46] It is also worth noting a curious mistake, unusual for William, in his account of Pippin III's reign, where he refers to Desiderius, meaning Aistulf.[47] Supposing William to have used B's version of the *Annales* makes it possible to see how he might have made this slip, which was certainly easier to make from a cursory glance at the summary rather than the full text of the relevant events.

Next in B comes Einhard, much used by William in the first Frankish section of the *Gesta Regum*, and then the following genealogy:

---

[42] Durham Cathedral Library MS C. iv. 15; Von Simson, pp. v–vi.
[43] V. Rose, *Verzeichnis der lateinischen Handschriften der königlichen Bibliothek zu Berlin* (Berlin, 1893), I, pp. 317–321; Von Simson, pp. ix–xi; F. Grat, J. Veilliard and S. Clemençet (eds), *Annales de Saint-Bertin* (Société de l'Histoire de France, Paris, 1964), pp. xxxix–xli.
[44] Specimen readings: (Von Simson) p. 1 line 6 gestorum] om. B as the Berlin MS (Von Simson's B1); p. 3 lines 15–16 uirtutum ... dubitatione] om. as B1; p. 4 line 1 Itaberga] Luberga B, cf. Iuberga B1; line 8 potestatis] etatis B and B1; line 19 Osterliudos] -liudo B and B1; p. 5 lines 21–2 uisi sunt] fuerunt B and B1; p. 6 line 1 seuitia] ob seuitiam B and B1.
[45] GR I, pp. 70 lines 21–30 (Von Simson, pp. 1–21), 71, most of lines 9–27 (Von Simson, pp. 21–55).
[46] GR I, pp. 70 lines 10–11, 71 lines 9–10 (Einhard, ch. 2?), 15–16 (Einhard, chs 3, 15, 23, 28, 30).
[47] GR I, p. 71.

147

(f. 150v) Prosapia regum qui a beato Arnulfo usque in hec tempora geniti constant, uel quot tempora regnum Francorum ampliauerunt, uel gubernauerunt, hic annotata habentur. Bothgisus illuster uir genuit Arnulfum, sanctissimum uirum episcopum urbis Metensium. Beatus quoque Arnulfus genuit Angisum. Angisus genuit Pipinum maiorem domus. Pipinus genuit Karolum ducem. Karolus genuit Pipinum regem, Pipinus quoque rex genuit Karolum regem famosissimum et primum regem Francorum et imperatorem Romanorum. Karolus imperator genuit Ludouuicum imperatorem *qui regnauit annis xxvi.* Hludouuicus imperator genuit *Ludouuicum et Karolum et* Hlotharium imperatorem, qui nomen quidem imperatoris annis xv. obtinuit sed monarchiam regni cum fratribus sortitus est. *Lotharius genuit Ludouuicum qui regnauit* [blank].

With the exception of certain interpolations, distinguished by italics, this reproduces a well-known genealogy discussed by Bonnell and others.[48] For the *Monumenta* edition, two manuscripts were used, in both of which this genealogy follows a text of Einhard, as here. Thus a manuscript containing Einhard plus this genealogy was presumably one of the physical constituents of the Frankish compilation in B. At this point, too, one should note the Metz interest shared by this genealogy, the earlier one and the *Annales*. Probably all of these and Einhard were extracted from a single manuscript of Metz provenance or ancestry.

Next comes the *Visio Karoli*, an account of the emperor's alleged vision written at or near Reims about 900, which William copied verbatim in the second Frankish section of the *Gesta Regum*.[49] Unfortunately this work survives in a great many manuscripts, and as most have not been collated, no sure deductions can be made about the relationship between this copy and the one in the *Gesta Regum*. Nevertheless, it must be significant that there are only four variants between the two, all of which seem to represent stylistic 'improvements' made to the *Gesta* version, according to William's

---

[48] Printed in MGH Scriptores 13, p. 246, no. 3, using Paris, BN MS lat. 4955 and London, BL MS Egerton 810 (c.1200, from Germany); H. E. Bonnell, *Die Anfänge der karolingischen Hauses* (Berlin, 1866); E. Hlawitschka, 'Die Vorfahren Karls des Grossen', in W. Braunfels (ed.), *Karl der Grosse*, I. (Düsseldorf, 1965), pp. 51–82.

[49] GR I, pp. 112–116. Stubbs (GR II, pp. xxxi–xxxii) wrongly thought that William took this passage from the chronicle by Hariulf of Saint-Riquier; cf. W. Levison, 'Zur Textgeschichte der Vision Kaiser Karls II', *Neues Archiv*, 27 (1902), 493–502; R. Poupardin, 'Le royaume de Provence sous les Carolingiens', *Bibliothèque de l'Ecole des Hautes Etudes*, 131 (1901), 324–332. William was not the only Englishman who knew it. It is summarized in the *Chronicon fani Sancti Neoti*, written at Bury abbey in the early twelfth century: D. Dumville and M. Lapidge (eds), *The Anglo-Saxon Chronicle*, 17 (Woodbridge, 1985), pp. lvi–lviii.

usual practice.[50] There is thus good reason to think that the *Gesta* text derived from B's exemplar.

We come to the last and most perplexing section of the Carolingian compilation in B. Like the Frankish sections in the *Gesta Regum*, it is a pastiche of which the elements are not easily isolated. It will be simplest to give it *in extenso* with commentary.

(f. 152v) Post K[arolum] magnum ut supradictum imperauit in omni imperio patris Ludouicus annis xxvi.

The date is as in the genealogy printed above, where it is apparently an interpolation.

Post eum diuiserunt filii eius regnum. Et Karolus quidem in ea parte Gallie que nunc proprie *Francia* dicitur, et in *Britannia* minori et in Flandria et in Normannia et in Andegauiensi prouintia et *Aquitania et Wasconia et Burgundia* regnauit, et diuisit eas ducibus suis sicut usque hodie diuise sunt.

The italicized words recall part of the so-called *Continuatio Adonis*, another St Wandrille product, copied verbatim in the second section on the Franks in the *Gesta Regum*:[51]

Carolus uero medietatem Franciae ab occidente, et totam Neustriam, Brittanniam, et maximam partem Burgundiae, Gothiam, Wasconiam, Aquitaniam ...

In the B passage, however, those geographical names unintelligible to the twelfth century ('Neustria', 'Gothia', 'medietatem Franciae ab occidente') have been updated or omitted, and the nationality of the compiler and his audience indicated by the addition of 'minori' to 'Britannia'. The next passage introduces a new source:

Ludouicus alter L[udouici] filius regnauit in Saxonia et in omni Germania preter aliquam partem que iacet iuxta Alpes. Hanc enim tertius filius Ludouici accepit Lotharius, et ex nomine suo Lotharingiam quasi Lotharii regnum uocauit, et totam Italiam cum imperio Romanorum. Regnauit xv. annis, et monachus factus in extremo uite migrauit.

---

[50] See below, pp. 165–8. William could never resist these, even when he claims, as here, to be rendering the original verbatim (GR I, p. 116).
[51] GR I, pp. 110–112; MGH Scriptores 2, pp. 324–5. Its title, bestowed by d'Achery and Pertz, is misleading. As far as I am aware, it is not found in any manuscript appended to Ado's *Chronicle*. It is an independent work.

The passage 'et ex ... uocauit' recalls the *Historia Francorum Senonensis*,[52] 'Regnauitque ... migrauit' Ado of Vienne, used by William in the *Gesta Regum*.[53] But the whole section resembles the first nine lines of the second Carolingian excursus in that work:[54]

> ... quorum Lotharius ... regnauit annis quindecim in ea quae iacet iuxta Alpes parte Germaniae, et nunc Lotharingia, quasi regnum Lotharii, dicitur, et in tota Italia cum Roma. In extremo uitae ... seculo renuntiauit ...

The compilation in B continues:

> Post eum filius eius Ludouicus eodem annorum numero [eius filius Ludouicus iii. annis *interlined by the scribe*], ea potestate functus est. At uero Karolus frater Lotharii ut superius dixi rex Francie optime litteratus fuit. Quo poscente, Iohannes Scottus Ierarchiam Dionisii de Greco transtulit in Latinum. Sed et Anastasius bibliothecarius Romanae sedis ad personam eius fecit glosas eiusdem Ierarchie, sed et Passionem beati Demetrii.

The source for the passage 'Quo ... Ierarchie' would have been a copy of the standard collection of John's Dionysian translations, which included Anastasius's glosses and prefatory letter addressed to Charles the Bald. William possessed just such a manuscript.[55] In the *Gesta Regum* and in the letter to Peter prefixed to his manuscript of John the Scot's *Periphyseon*, William recalls some of this passage: '[Regis] ergo rogatu Ierarchiam Dionisii de Graeco in Latinum ... transtulit'.[56] The knowledge that Anastasius also translated a *Passio Sancti Demetrii* for Charles the Bald could only have come from the author's prefatory letter.[57] This rare item survives in only two manuscripts, Brussels, Bibliothèque Royale MS 8690–8702, and Alençon, Bibliothèque Municipale 10, both of the twelfth century, the latter from Saint-Evroult.[58] From such a centre it could easily have been transmitted to England.

---

52 MGH Scriptores 9, p. 367.
53 PL 123. 135–6; cf. GR I, p. 69 line 13 to 70 line 5 (PL 123. 95), along with Hugh of Fleury; p. 110 line 5 'annis quindecim' (PL 123. 135).
54 GR I, p. 110.
55 MGH Epistolae 7, pp. 430–4, no. 13; see above, pp. 43–4, 104.
56 GR I, pp. cxliv, 131.
57 MGH Epistolae 7. 5, pp. 438–9.
58 The Alençon MS contains a recension of the canons of the Council of Clermont, 1095, related to that used by William and Orderic Vitalis; Somerville, *The Councils of Urban II: 1. Decreta Claromontensia*, p. 88.

Cuius filiam Aþulfus rex Anglie a Roma rediens uxorem duxit nomine Iuditham. Porro Ludouicus rex Germanie genuit Ka(f. 153)rolum istum cuius uisio superius scripta est, qui cum regno patris sui accepit etiam imperium patrui, anno Dominice incarnationis DCCCLXXX-IIII, et posteriori anno obiit.

The mention of Ethelwulf's marriage to Judith is found in the *Gesta Regum*; its source is apparently Asser.[59] The information on Charles the Fat's assumption of the imperial title and death appears to be based on the *Anglo-Saxon Chronicle*, although the dates have become confused.[60] The *Chronicle* was used by William in the Frankish and other sections of the *Gesta Regum*.[61] After this, a new paragraph opens the last section of the Frankish compilation in B, based largely, perhaps entirely upon a single source.

Ludouicus nepos Ludouici senioris apud Ferrariis qui locus est in pago Senonensi et uxor eius, nullo presente metropolitano, a quibusdam episcopis sunt consecrati et coronati. Supererant duo filii Rotberti Andegauorum comitis, qui fuit Saxonici generis uir. Senior ex his Odo uocabatur, Rotbertus alter. Ex his maiorem natu *Odonem Franci et Burgundiones Aquitanicique proceres, congregati in unum*, licet reluctantem tutorem Karoli pueri regnique eligere g u b e r n a t o r e m, quem unxit Galterius archiepiscopus Senonum. K a r o l u s s i m p l e x i n c a r c e r e p o s i t u s, *Radulfum nobilem filium Ricardi Burgundionum ducis, quem ex sacro fonte susceperat, una cum consilio Hugonis magni filii supradicti Rotberti et procerum Francorum*, i n r e g n u m *sullimauit. Vnctus uero est in regem ipse Radulfus iii. idus Iulii, Suessionis ciuitate.* P o s t m o r t e m R a d u l f i r e g i s, p e r W i l l e l-m u m a r c h i e p i s c o p u m a b A n g l i a r e d u c t u s e s t *Ludouicus filius Caroli simplicis in Franciam* et *xiiii. kalendas Iulii unctus est in regum apud Laudunum.* Post translationem uero regni Francorum in progenie Hugonis magni ducis, Rotbertus piissimus rex filius Hugonis regis Aurelianis consecratus est in regem. Cuius filius Hugo [*meaning Henricus*] iuuenis Compendii est unctus et in regem sullimatus.

The italicized passages in this section reproduce verbatim the *Historia Francorum Senonensis*, a chronicle of Frankish history written at Sens in

---

59 GR I, p. 109; W. Stevenson (ed.), *Asser's Life of King Alfred* (Oxford, rev. ed., 1959), p. 9. The same information could have been obtained, with great difficulty, from the *Anglo-Saxon Chronicle* (*ASC*, pp. 43–4, 51). William was certainly using other parts of Asser at this point in the *Gesta*.

60 *ASC*, pp. 51–2, years 885, 887.

61 GR I, p. 72 lines 5–7 (*ASC*, p. 37, year 799); see above, p. 70.

1015 or soon after.[62] The widely-spaced passages come from the same source, though not verbatim. But it is particularly interesting that several more passages not found in the printed text of the *Historia* also show an obvious connection with Sens, and indeed the homogeneity of the language in this section would suggest a single author or source for the whole. It is possible that we have here a fragment of a lost Sens chronicle from the early eleventh century which was used as a basis for the extant *Historia Francorum Senonensis*.[63] The *Historia* itself was well-known in France and Normandy by about 1100, and in fact the earliest surviving manuscript of it, of about that date, has recently been identified as English.[64] Even so the Sens material in B, as with the *Annales Mettenses*, seems an eccentric and exotic component in the repertoire of an Anglo-Norman historian.

The portion of the Frankish compilation in B which follows the *Visio* is thus shown to be itself a mosaic put together from a number of sources, not all perhaps identified. The manufacturer of this portion was certainly English and working in the first half of the twelfth century. This is shown by his revision of certain geographical names, already noted, by his use of Asser and the *Anglo-Saxon Chronicle*, by his knowledge of Anastasius's *Passio Sancti Demetrii* prologue, known only from twelfth-century manuscripts, and of John the Scot's Dionysian translations which seem not to have reached England before about 1100.[65] It is not difficult, in the light of what we have so far learned about B and its Frankish compilation, to show that the compiler was William of Malmesbury. First of all, most of the B compilation or its elements were used in the *Gesta Regum*: some details from the regnal list, a summary of the same part of the Metz *Annals*, Einhard, the *Visio*, and, most crucially, a few passages from the concluding

---

[62] MGH Scriptores 9, pp. 364–9; F. Lot, 'Les derniers Carolingiens', *Bibliothèque de l'Ecole des Hautes Etudes*, 87 (1891), appendice 7, pp. 338–345; idem, 'Découverte du MS original de l'Historia Francorum Senonensis', *Bulletin de la Société Archéologique de Sens*, 38 (1936), 389–382, reprinted in his *Travaux* (Geneva, 1968), I, pp. 520–3.

[63] A. Fliche, 'Les sources de l'historiographie sénonaise au XIe siècle', *Bulletin de la Société Archéologique de Sens*, 24 (1909), 149–206; R.-H. Bautier et al., *Odorannus de Sens, Opera Omnia* (Sources d'histoire médiévale 4, Paris, 1971), pp. 45–6, raising the possibility of a lost work used for the *Annales de Saint-Colombe*, the *Historia Francorum Senonensis* and Odorannus's *Chronicle*.

[64] J. Ehlers, 'Die Historia Francorum Senonensis und der Aufstieg des Hauses Capet', *Journal of Medieval History*, 4 (1978), 22 n. 1 and facsimiles. Professor B. Bischoff, responsible for suggesting the provenance, dates the MS to about 1100 or the first half of the twelfth century. From Ehlers's facsimiles, I should be inclined to make 'about 1100' the upper limit for this flamboyant example of late English caroline.

[65] All English MSS of this collection seem to depend upon Oxford, St John's College MS 128, c.1100, of unknown provenance. William's extracts from Anastasius's letter (GR I, p. cxlvi) are related to this MS.

section, itself the concoction of an Englishman working in the early twelfth century. Conversely, texts known to William and quoted in the *Gesta* appear in various forms in the B compilation: Ado of Vienne, the *Continuatio Adonis*, a manuscript of John the Scot's Dionysian translations, Asser and the *Chronicle*. So far all is plain sailing, but we must take account of the fact that items used in one work are not found in the other. The maker of the B compilation omitted most of the St Wandrille material quoted in the *Gesta Regum*, and yet, as Levison showed, this material (the *Domus Carolingiae Genealogia* and *Continuatio Adonis*) was almost certainly available to him in the same manuscript which supplied him with the *Visio*, and towards the end of his work he included some reminiscences of one part of it, the *Continuatio*.[66] This means that he excluded most of it deliberately, in preference to the similar Metz genealogies. Why he preferred the one to the other is not as clear as why he would have avoided including both. This remains a problem whether William was the compiler or not. On the other hand, in the *Gesta* William shows no knowledge of the two Metz genealogies. One can understand why he would have omitted the first, which is only a summary of the second. If he did know the second, then he apparently preferred the St Wandrille alternative, again for reasons not clear to us. Perhaps it makes good sense to see William, identifiable as B's compiler, faced with a choice between similar material from two different manuscripts, and deciding to include the Metz items in one book, the St Wandrille ones in another.

My general conclusion is, then, that Bodleian Library MS Lat. class. d. 39 was copied from a book of the same contents written by or for William of Malmesbury, who provided it with marginal annotations. This I consider to be beyond reasonable doubt. The further conclusion, that he was also responsible for the compilation on Frankish history in it, is based essentially on a high degree of coincidence between texts known to William and used in the compilation, and to that extent falls short of absolute proof. Nevertheless, I think it highly likely that he *was* the author of the compilation, and that he put it together before 1125, since so much of it appears in the *Gesta Regum*. We should not, however, rule out the possibility that William had only the *sources* of the compilation at hand by this date. On the whole, the balance of probability seems to me to marginally favour the former alternative. In comparison with his collections of Roman history, of canon law and Pope Leo's works, this one seems less mature and rather hastily constructed.[67] It is more akin to William's edition of the *Liber Pontificalis*,

---

[66] Levison, p. 500 and notes.
[67] Oxford, Bodl. Libr. MS Arch. Seld. B. 16 and Oriel College MS 42; see above, pp. 62–7, 92–3, 96–7.

put together shortly after 1119, from similarly heterogeneous sources.[68] Like it, I would want to see this work as a product of his comparative youth. Possibly it was his engagement in this sort of enterprise that prompted Queen Matilda to request the production of the *Gesta Regum*.[69]

We are now ready to tackle the important question of what William's treatment of the Franks in the B compilation and in the *Gesta Regum* tells us about his historical technique. First of all, a historian's work is conditioned by the available sources, and one can now give a precise account of William's Frankish materials. For his general outline, he relied upon the chronicles of Ado of Vienne and Hugh of Fleury, and the Metz Annals, with some snippets from the *Anglo-Saxon Chronicle*, Asser and perhaps some unidentified written sources.[70] On Charlemagne himself he had Einhard, and for the later Carolingians chronicles from Sens and St Wandrille, the *Visio Karoli Crassi* and the writings of John the Scot and Anastasius Bibliothecarius. Finally, he had a regnal list and an assortment of genealogies. Moreover we now know something of the form in which some of these works were available to him. A manuscript from Metz or a transcript of it supplied him with the *Annales*, two genealogies and probably Einhard, another, which Levison thought originated ultimately from St Bertin,[71] contained the *Visio* and St Wandrille items, and we should probably add another for the Sens chronicle. How long some of these books had been in England cannot be said, but I am inclined to see them as recent entrants, perhaps sought by William himself, with Norman religious houses as the main agencies of transmission. This would be consistent with the other evidence of William's involvement in such a process, and we should probably imagine the books making the journey in both directions, that is coming, being copied and then returned.[72]

This reminds us that sources are not, strictly speaking, 'available' to a historian; they must be recognized and a decision taken to use them. On the one hand, some of these sources were rare in England at this date, and William must have put some effort into obtaining them, whether or not he sought them from overseas. On the other hand, he was selective in the employment of what he had, both in the B compilation and in the *Gesta Regum*. He used Alcuin's letters, for instance, in his two major Histories,

---

[68] See above, ch. 6.

[69] ibid., pp. 15, 34–5; Könsgen, pp. 201–214.

[70] I cannot identify the sources for GR I, pp. 71 lines 31–3 ('et ab imperatoria ... temperans'), 110 lines 13–14 ('Carolum ... exosculabatur') and 15–16 ('et Wasconia'), 116 line 23 to 117 line 13.

[71] Levison, p. 500 and notes.

[72] For William's involvement in such a process see above, pp. 43–4, 65–6, 74, 90–1. In this connection it is interesting that the text of Suetonius in B is of the Z family, descended from a Norman parent (information from Professor R. H. Rouse).

but to illuminate the history of post-Bedan England, not the reign of Charlemagne.[73] The chronicles of Ado of Vienne and Hugh of Fleury, both used in the first Frankish section in the *Gesta Regum*, hardly appear at all in the compilation. One can, I think, reconstruct the reasoning which governed this process of selection. Neither in the *Gesta* nor in the compilation was William committed to providing the fullest possible account of the Franks. In the *Gesta Regum* Frankish history represented a deviation from his main theme, and so could be appropriately and briefly covered with the aid of general chronicles which were not necessarily either contemporary or authoritative. The B compilation was also no more than a compendium, therefore of a skeletal, annalistic character, with the exception of Einhard's *Life* and the *Visio*. The former was surely there because of the importance of its subject; the latter William probably included because his materials for that period were so thin, and because of his lively interest in political prophecy.[74] But the compilation was intended to be more authoritative than the *Gesta Regum*'s asides, so William tried to use contemporary sources, possibly available to him in what he thought of as early manuscripts.

This labour of selection suggests that William evaluated his sources according to rational criteria. There are two particular cases which bring his critical judgement into sharper relief. Firstly, one notes that, both in the B compilation and in the *Gesta Regum*, he discarded the Metz Annals for the period covered by Einhard's *Life*. The obvious reason was that Einhard provided more intimate (and therefore, for William, more weighty) information about Charlemagne's character and rule. In common with other historians of his time, moreover, he regarded literary form as one yardstick of *auctoritas*; a biography was, therefore, inherently more trustworthy than a set of annals.[75] The second case occurs in the first Frankish section of the *Gesta Regum*, in which he makes extensive use of Hugh of Fleury's *Historia* for his description of the origins of the Frankish people. One prominent feature of Hugh's account, however, he significantly omits. This is Hugh's reference, shared with many other chroniclers from Fredegar on, to the Franks' Trojan ancestry.[76] That William ignored it deliberately is beyond doubt, for this must be what he meant in the opening sentence of this section, in which he introduced the Franks, 'de qua multa fabulatur antiquitas', but of whom he will 'ueritatem subtexere'.[77] One is forcibly

---

[73] See below, pp. 158–173.

[74] This interest can be illustrated from GR I, pp. 72–4, 125–6, 162, 164, 181–2, 185–7, 274–8.

[75] See above, pp. 19–20.

[76] Rottendorff, p. 104; J. M. Wallace-Hadrill, *The Long-Haired Kings* (London, 1962), pp. 79–83.

[77] GR I, p. 69; R. Ray, 'Bede's *Vera lex historiae*', *Speculum*, 55 (1980), 1–21.

reminded of his famous description of Arthur, 'de quo Britonum nugae hodieque delirant; dignus plane quem non fallaces somniarent fabulae, sed ueraces praedicarent historiae . . .'.[78] Why William rejected the Trojan origin of the Franks is suggested by a slightly later passage:[79]

> Nepos Faramundi fuit Meroueus, a quo omnes post eum reges Merouingi uocati sunt. Eodem modo et filii regum Anglorum a patribus patronymica sumpserunt: ut filius Edgari, Edgaring; filius Edmundi, Edmunding, uocentur; et ceteri in hunc modum; communiter uero Athelingi dicuntur. Naturalis ergo lingua Francorum communicat cum Anglis, quod de Germania gentes ambae germinauerint.

Both the Franks and English were Germanic, of the same ethnic and linguistic stock; therefore, if one hailed from Troy, so did the other, and William was obviously not prepared to accept this. He knew, from Dares and Virgil, that the descendants of the Trojans were the *Romani*, a race entirely distinct from the Germans.[80]

William may have had the *Gesta Regum*'s needs in mind when he made the B compilation, but they cannot have been his whole, or even his principal justification for its manufacture. The relationship between the *Gesta Regum* passages and the compilation is too loose for the latter to have been conceived solely as *praeparatio* for the former. At least two other reasons can be advanced for the making of the compilation. Firstly, as with William's other collections, it was doubtless produced as much for the edification of others, meaning in particular the Malmesbury community, as for William's own needs. But even his own needs were wider than the terms of reference for the *Gesta*. His historical interests were not confined to England's past, let alone its ecclesiastical heritage. He was by temperament a universal historian, who not only read all the historical works which he could find, but who liked to make up his own handbooks from them, upon topics which especially fascinated him. This he did for the history of the papacy to his own time in his papal chronicle based upon the *Liber Pontificalis*. He did it on the theme of 'empire', as mentioned earlier, in the Selden manuscript. And he did it, I suggest, for the Carolingians in the collection which we have studied here. It is worth emphasizing the breadth of William's historical vision. It has become fashionable in recent years to account for the extraordinary phenomenon of Anglo-Norman historiography in terms of a reaction by English monks to the assault upon their

---

[78] GR I, p. 70.
[79] He gives the Trojan origins of the Romans, after Dares and others, in Oxford, Bodl. Libr. MS Arch. Seld. B. 16, ff. 1–7v.
[80] See above, pp. 47–8, 57, 61, 66.

traditions by the Norman prelates.[81] William certainly registered this reaction, in his *Gesta Pontificum*, his *Antiquity of Glastonbury*, and his saints' Lives. But this did not constitute the mainspring or *point de départ* of his historical interest and output. It conditioned only the *form* of some of his works, and the commissioning and patronage which lay behind them. What the mainspring was is not so easy to say. I suggest, however, that it is not to be discovered by scrutiny of William's English environment or of England's past alone. Rather, we must analyse more intently the development of historical awareness among western European *literati* generally during the early twelfth century.[82]

[81] Southern, 'The Place of England in the Twelfth-Century Renaissance', pp. 160–162; idem, 'Aspects of the European Tradition of Historical Writing IV', 249–250; Gransden, *Historical Writing in England c.550–c.1307*, pp. 105–132, 169–170. But note the comment on William's pan-European interest on p. 170.

[82] Haskins, *The Renaissance of the Twelfth Century*, has a chapter (8) entitled 'Historical Writing', containing the challenging sentence 'One of the best expressions of the intellectual revival of the twelfth century is to be seen in the writing of history' (p. 224). Not many studies of the period have taken this further. Cf. the remarkable statement of R. W. Southern, 'Aspects of the European Tradition of Historical Writing II: Hugh of St Victor and the Idea of Historical Development', TRHS, 5th ser., 21 (1971), 163, 'The intellectual climate of the twelfth century was not generally favourable to historical thought'. The writing of history is not discussed at all by Morris, *The Discovery of the Individual 1050–1200*, although he has a section entitled 'The Return to the Past'. We clearly need a detailed study of twelfth-century historiography in relation to other contemporary intellectual and cultural phenomena.

8

WILLIAM AND THE LETTERS OF ALCUIN

IN TRYING TO piece together a coherent account of English secular and ecclesiastical history in the century after Bede, William was forced back upon the *Anglo-Saxon Chronicle*, supplemented by such miscellaneous sources as he could find either in his local library or in the course of his extensive bibliographical travels.[1] Among them, charters and letters occupy an important place, and for a good many of these William is a valuable textual witness. This is true for letters of Aldhelm, Boniface and, to a greater extent than has been realized, of Alcuin.[2]

In the first book of the *Gesta Regum Anglorum* William uses twelve of Alcuin's letters. Five of these reappear in the *Gesta Pontificum*, plus a further four.[3] I propose to study this material with two goals in view: firstly, to identify and describe the manuscript or manuscripts which William used and to assess his contribution to the reconstruction of Alcuin's text; secondly, to analyse and discuss the editorial treatment to which William subjected these letters in the process of incorporating them into his two major historical works.

---

[1] The most comprehensive account of William's sources is still that by William Stubbs in GR II, pp. xv–xxxviii. For William's reading and travels in general see above, ch. 3.

[2] On William's use of Boniface and Aldhelm see above, pp. 44–5. William's extracts from Alcuin's letters were noted and sometimes collated by E. Dümmler, *Alcuini Epistolae*, MGH Epistolae 4.

[3] In GR I: p. 68 – Dümmler p. 167, no. 114, p. 177, no. 121; p. 73 – p. 55, no. 19, p. 89, no. 43, p. 147, no. 101, pp. 42–3, no. 16; pp. 73–4 – p. 180, no. 122; p. 74 – p. 47, no. 17; p. 75 – p. 33, no. 8, p. 147, no. 101 again; p. 82 – p. 375, no. 230; p. 86 – p. 412, no. 255; p. 92 – p. 32, no. 7; p. 93 – pp. 145–6, no. 100; in GP: p. 17 – p. 374, no. 230 again; p. 18 – pp. 412–3, no. 255 again; p. 19 – p. 190, no. 128; p. 209 – p. 43, no. 16 again; p. 246 – p. 177, no. 121 again, p. 167, no. 114 again; p. 247 – p. 374, no. 230 again; pp. 255–6 – p. 72, no. 31; pp. 256–7 – p. 431, no. 273; pp. 267–8 – pp. 57–8, no. 20; p. 268 – pp. 42–3, no. 16 again.

Long ago Bishop Stubbs stated that William must have used two extant manuscripts of Alcuin's correspondence, British Library Cott. Vesp. A. xiv (Dümmler's A2) and Cott. Tib. A. xv (A1).[4] A2 was made for Archbishop Wulfstan, perhaps at York;[5] the provenance of A1 is uncertain. Stubbs argued solely on the basis of the particular letters contained in the *Gesta Regum*, some of which are found in no other MSS but A1 and A2. It is odd that he did not take into account the letters in the *Gesta Pontificum* or collate William's extracts with the most recent edition available to him, that of Jaffé and Wattenbach.[6] But even on the basis of which letters are quoted in the *Gesta Regum* there was no positive reason for supposing William to have known A2, and the suspicion that he did not is confirmed by a scrutiny of the *Gesta Pontificum* letters and a collation of all of them with the *Monumenta* edition. In that edition Ernst Dümmler made somewhat desultory use of William's extracts without himself adding anything to Stubbs's argument.

It is true that, of the total of sixteen letters quoted by William in his two major works, eight are found only in the Cotton MSS.[7] But four of them are found only in A1, and a further three are not in A2; none of the sixteen is found in A2 alone.[8] Moreover, the readings of William's extracts from the ten letters found in *both* A1 and A2 clearly favour a relationship to the first manuscript rather than the second.[9] If any further proof be wanting that William, if he knew either of these manuscripts at first hand, knew A1 and not A2, it is provided by three non-Alcuinian, papal letters quoted by him in

---

[4] GR II, pp. xxvii–xxviii.

[5] N. R. Ker, 'The Handwriting of Archbishop Wulfstan', in *England before the Conquest; Studies in Primary Sources presented to Dorothy Whitelock*, ed. P. Clemoes and K. Hughes (Cambridge, 1971), pp. 316, 326–7.

[6] Since Dümmler's edition was not completed when Stubbs wrote, he used the edition begun by Jaffé and completed by Wattenbach and Dümmler, *Monumenta Alcuiniana, Bibliothecae Rerum Germanicarum*, VI (Berlin, 1873), pp. 132–897. In GP Hamilton cites from the edition of Froben (1777).

[7] Nos 7, 8, 16, 100, 101, 122, 255, 273.

[8] Only in A1: nos 100, 101, 122, 255; in A1 and other MSS but not in A2: nos 31, 121, 230.

[9] No. 7 (GR I, p. 92): Fresonum Wm.A1: Frisonum A2; irruit Wm.A1: inruit A2; subegit sue dicioni Wm.A1: suae subegit dicioni A2; irruerunt Wm.A1: inruerunt A2; dissensionis Wm.A1: disentionis A2; Carolum Wm.A1; Korolum A2; mittendos Wm.A1: mittendas A2. No. 8 (GR I, p. 75): maiestatem Wm.A1; magestatem A2. No. 16 (GR I, p. 73): Eboraco Wm.: Eboraca A1: Euboracia A2. No. 20 (GP, p. 267): episcopo Wm.A1: epīs A2; Alcuinus Wm.A1*: Alcuine A2; dominus Wm.A1*: domnus A2. No. 114 (GR I, p. 68): exaltatione Wm.A1: exultatione A2. For letters used by William and also contained in A2 I have compared Dümmler's edition with that of C. Chase, *Two Alcuin Letter-Books* (Toronto, 1975).

the *Gesta Regum*, for these are otherwise known only from the MS A1.[10] Thus all of the sixteen Alcuinian letters quoted by William are in A1; four are found nowhere else.

We may take it as established, then, that William did not know A2, but A1 or a manuscript very like it. To establish the precise connection between his exemplar and A1 entails a detailed comparison between the readings of his extracts and of the letters in the Cotton MS. First, a proviso must be made by way of warning. The ways in which William presented the letters vary from a brief summary in his own words to verbatim quotation of the best part of a complete letter. The majority of instances fall somewhere between these extremes, being quotations of reasonable length, verbatim but for some stylistic 'improvements'. William's editorial method will be studied later on; here I mention it only to point out that it is a task of some delicacy to recognize and disentangle his deliberate alterations from readings which he must have adopted from his exemplar. In general, however, enough of his quotations are given verbatim to enable some precise conclusions to be reached about the manuscript or manuscripts which he used.

Briefly, in the case of extracts from fourteen separate letters, the evidence is either not against or positively in favour of William having copied directly from A1.[11] But there are five cases in which he clearly knew a better text, perhaps the exemplar of A1. As this is a matter of importance, I give the evidence as follows;

Letter 100 (GR I, p. 93;) religioni Wm.: religione A1; plenam Wm.: post piam A1; Ethelredi Wm.: Aedilfredi A1.
Letter 101 (GR I, pp. 73 and 75; otherwise in A1 only): eram Wm.: *om.* A1; esse Wm.: *om.* A1; de uobis Wm.: uobis A1; missorum Wm.: missurum A1; nece Wm.: neci A1; essem Wm.: esset A1.

---

[10] GR I, pp. 62–3, printed in C. Haddan and W. Stubbs, *Councils and Ecclesiastical Documents*, III (Oxford, 1871), pp. 248–50; GR I, pp. 172–3, 191–3, printed in *Memorials*, pp. 396–7, 397–8.

[11] See note 9 above. In addition see: No. 17 (GR I, p. 74): accidit partibus Wm.A1 et al.: acc. in part. QTSI; trecentis Wm.A2K1Q: tricentis A1 et al.; quadraginta Wm.S1AKQ: quinquaginta *rell.*; Britonum Wm.AQ: Brettonum *rel.*; Britones Wm.AQ: Brettones *rell.*; dignatus Wm.K2; dignata *rell.* No. 19 (GR I, p. 73): Wiorenses Wm.: cf. A; sequi Wm.AKD: sequere TQS1; discant nunc Wm.A: discunt T: discant *rell.*; Bedam Wm.: Baedam A1TK1S1D: Boedam A2: Bedan Q: Bedum K2; habet Wm.KTQ: habeat A: habent S1D. No. 20 (GP, pp. 267–8): Higbaldo Wm.A: hugibaldo S1; episcopo Wm.A1*S*: epīs A2; Alcuinus Wm.: Alcuinus A1*: Alchuine A2S1; dominus Wm.A1*: domnus A2S1; eum Wm.A2S1: illum A1*. No. 121 (GR I, p. 68): desunt A1*TK2: detis K1: date Wm.; libellos Wm.K1: libelli A1*TK2; industriam Wm.A1*TK1: industria K2; Eboraca Wm.A1*: Euboraca *rell.*; emissiones Wm.A1*K1: emissionis TK2. No. 122 (GR I, pp. 73–4): no significant variants.

Letter 128 (GP, pp. 18–19) quod si Wm.: si A1*[12]; possit Wm.: posset A1*; ut Wm.: *om.* A1*; resarciatur Wm. A1*: resarcietur A2 et al.; coepiscopi Wm. A2 (*after corr.*): coepiscopis A1*; ut fiat Wm.: deliberare A1*: *om. rell.*

Letter 230 (GP, pp. 17–18; also in A1 and H): Wm. gives full *titulus* as in H.

Letter 255 (GR I, p. 86, GP, p. 18; otherwise in A1 only): Audita prosperitate Wm.: Audiatque prosperitatem A1; suscepti Wm.: suscepi A1; (GP) Ethelardo archiepiscopo Wm.: illi A1; multo Wm.: *om.* A1.

It has long been recognized that A1, an extensive corpus of letters (125 of Alcuin, 24 of Dunstan), was transcribed from a group of at least three smaller collections, plus a scatter of single letters.[13] Now the letters quoted by William occur in all three main sections of A1. If he knew its exemplar, therefore, that exemplar must have contained virtually all the letters in A1. That would be to put A1 at two removes from the group of separate manuscripts from which its contents derive, an unlikely solution, since some of A1's Dunstanian letters date from the 990s – or not much earlier than the date of the manuscript itself[14] – and since it does not explain why some of William's extracts seem dependent upon A1, while others improve upon it. In fact it can be shown that William did know A1, and not an exemplar of the whole of it. If we examine the five letters for which his extracts give better readings than A1, it will be seen (using Dümmler's table)[15] that they all come from the third section of that manuscript. We might then conclude that William, besides knowing A1 itself, had access to the exemplar of this section of it only. This would make him an important witness for the text of these five letters.

This hypothesis can be tested by a consideration of two of the three papal letters mentioned earlier.[16] They, too, are found in this last section of A1, from which Stubbs printed them, giving William's variants in his notes. Does William's text suggest that for these letters, also, he used the exemplar of this part of A1, rather than A1 itself? Indeed, this appears to be the case. One of the letters has a very few variants from A1, some of which look like

[12] A1* was the siglum used by Dümmler for Thomas Gale's transcript of A1 (Cambridge, Trinity College O. 10. 6), used to supplement those portions of A1 made illegible by damage from the 1731 fire.

[13] Dümmler, pp. 10–11, citing T. Sickel, *Alcuinstudien*, I, *Wiener Sitzungsberichte*, 79 (1875).

[14] On the date of A2 see Ker, art. cit., p. 316, who describes it as having been a new book when Wulfstan used it (before 1023). The latest precisely dateable letter of Dunstan in A1 is of 991, no. XXVI in *Memorials*, p. 397.

[15] Dümmler, pp. 10–11.

[16] See above, note 10; I refer to the second and third documents.

William's habitual 'improvements'. Two of them, however, correct A1's text.[17] The evidence of the other letter requires more elaborate consideration. Of the many variants in William's version, three are almost certainly interpolations made by him from Glastonbury sources. I shall discuss these later.[18] Six other variants represent improvements on the text of A1; some might be William's work, but some at least seem to reflect a better exemplar. Three others might be William's mistakes, and three are equivocal.[19] Thus for these two letters and for the five Alcuinian ones just mentioned, William is as important an authority as A1 itself.

I said earlier that the provenance of A1 is at present unknown. Without doubt the clue to the original home of this important though much damaged manuscript lies in the fullest possible study of its physical disposition and contents. Nevertheless it may be worthwhile making some provisional deductions as to where William might have found it and the exemplar of its last section. This section contains twenty-two letters of Alcuin, followed by twenty-four concerning Archbishop Dunstan.[20] At first sight it might seem that we have to do with two sections based on two separate exemplars. However the two sets of letters are united by a common concern, as has long been known.[21] That overriding concern is the affairs of the See of Canterbury. Again, the fact that all of William's extracts from this section, both Alcuinian and tenth-century, have better readings than A1 suggests that he was using a single, earlier manuscript of this complete section. Fairly certainly this exemplar was written at Christ Church, although whether William found it there is no more than probable. What of A1 itself? The fact that it was copied not long after the latest of the Dunstanian letters in it again

---

[17] GR I, pp. 191–3: matris nostrae ecclesiae Wm.: nostrae *om.* A1; necnon et Leofstanum Wm.: et *om.* A1; perpetrauerint Wm.: perpetrauerit A1; stabilis Wm.: *om.* A1; uel de inimicis Wm.: de *om.* A1.

[18] GR I, pp. 172–3; Stubbs, *Memorials*, pp. 396–7. After 'Glastingaburgh' Wm. adds 'quae totius Britanniae prima, et ab antiquis primoribus ad proprietatem et tutelam Romani pontificis pertinere dinoscitur'; after 'uillas' Wm. adds 'sed et ecclesias de Brente, de Piltune, quas, Ina rege dante operam, cum aliis ecclesiis quas iuste et canonice possidet, scilicet, Soweie, Stret, Merlinc, Budecale, Sapewice'; after 'proprietatibus' Wm. adds 'ecclesiis, capellis'.

[19] I give the variants here, since Stubbs's collation (*Memorials*, pp. 396–7) is incomplete: propter quod eidem Wm.: p. q. eodem A1; habitationem Wm.: habitatione A1; nocuus Wm.: nociuus A1; cui propinquus Wm.: cum p. A1; a beato Wm.: in b. A1; A1 *adds* fidelium *after* omniumque; ideo Wm.: ideoque A1; admonemus Wm.: monemus A1; amore Wm.: timore A1; nil de Wm.: nihil ab A1; si haec feceris Wm.: s. h. non feceris A1; proditore Wm.: traditore A1.

[20] Dümmler, p. 11, and Stubbs, *Memorials*, pp. 355ff.

[21] Dümmler, p. 11, citing Sickel, op. cit.

points in the direction of Canterbury.[22] When we add to this the information that William is known to have made extensive use of the Canterbury libraries preparatory to the writing of his two major Histories, the evidence that here he found both A1 and the exemplar of its third section seems at least worthy of consideration.[23]

Doubtless more than one process intervened between William's location of these manuscripts and his copying of extracts from them into the *Gesta Regum* and *Gesta Pontificum*, but it is hard to describe those processes accurately. Leland saw a copy of Alcuin's letters at Malmesbury.[24] By itself, of course, this tells us little, not even whether what he saw was a book dating from William's time. However, elsewhere in his *Collectanea* Leland gives extracts from sixty-five letters of Alcuin and Dunstan, citing a 'vetus codex'.[25] The letters, their order and readings show that Leland's manuscript was either A1 or a copy; Stubbs assumed the first alternative.[26] This cannot be the case, for Leland's extracts share a handful of readings with William against the Cotton MS.[27] Especially significant are the readings shared by Leland and William for letters found in the third section of A1, and these further support our argument that William knew the exemplar of that portion of it. It is notable, therefore, that the lengthy additions in William's text of the second papal letter mentioned above are not found in Leland's version.[28] In the case of three other variants between William and A1 for this letter, Leland sides twice with William and once with A1.[29] The source of William's additions is, in fact, not hard to find. All of the information in them is found in his own *Antiquity of Glastonbury* and is based upon alleged privileges of King Ine.[30] We shall see below that William felt no compunction about treating his texts in this way.

I conclude that Leland's 'vetus codex' is identical with the manuscript of 'epistolae Albini' which he found at Malmesbury. This was a transcript of A1 and the exemplar of its last section made by William, into which he had

---

[22] See above, note 14. A Christ Church provenance for A1 is favoured, on similar grounds, by C. Hohler, 'Some Service Books of the Later Saxon Church', in *Tenth Century Studies*, p. 74.

[23] See above, p. 73.

[24] Leland, *Collectanea*, IV, p. 157.

[25] ibid., II, pp. 392–404.

[26] *Memorials*, pp. 366 n. 1, 381 n. 1.

[27] Letter no. 17: Gildi A1: Gildae Wm.Lel. No. 100: religione A1: religioni Wm.Lel. No. 101: uobis A1: de uobis Wm.Lel. No. 114: Aelberthus A1: Egbertus Wm.: Aelberthus Lel., the 'Ae' cancelled with sublinear points and 'Eg' written above. See below, notes 28 and 29.

[28] Leland, *Collectanea*, II, p. 404.

[29] Proper quod eidem Wm.Lel.: p. q. eodem A1; habitationem Wm.: habitatione A1Lel.; nocuus Wm.Lel.: nociuus A1.

[30] AG, pp. 92–103; GR I, pp. 36–9. The privilege given by William *in extenso* is spurious; see P. H. Sawyer, *Anglo-Saxon Charters* (London, 1968), no. 250.

already worked some textual modifications. Thus, consistently with what is otherwise known of his *modus operandi*, William made up his own collection of Alcuin's and Dunstan's letters, extracting from it in his two Histories.[31]

William seems to have carried out the preparatory work for the *Gesta Regum* and *Gesta Pontificum* simultaneously. The first edition of the *Gesta Regum* was completed early in 1125, and he then wrote up the *Gesta Pontificum*, finishing the first edition before the end of the same year.[32] I wish firstly to compare the five extracts from letters of Alcuin which occur in both of these works. In two cases the *Gesta Pontificum* passages are somewhat longer than their counterparts in the *Gesta Regum*; in three, the extracts are virtually identical in both works. In one case of the three the *Gesta Regum* extracts are split in two in the *Gesta Pontificum*, and the halves quoted in entirely different contexts, some fifty pages apart. In another case the *Gesta Pontificum* quotation omits the last clauses given in the *Gesta Regum* version. In the third instance there is exact identity as to the extent of the passage. This would lead to the reasonable presumption that William copied these three quotations into the *Gesta Pontificum* directly from the *Gesta Regum*; but such is not the case, for each *Gesta Pontificum* extract contains readings close to or identical with Alcuin's text, but which William had modified in the *Gesta Regum*.[33] We might then conclude that William went afresh to his complete letter-collection for the *Gesta Pontificum*. But against this would have to be weighed the similarities between the three *Gesta Regum* and *Gesta Pontificum* extracts, both in their extent and in their modifications from Alcuin's text. Two solutions are possible: Either William, in making the *Gesta Pontificum* extracts, referred simultaneously to *both* his Alcuin manuscript and the *Gesta Regum*, or he employed, for both works, a collection of extracts already made by him from the complete manuscript. The second alternative seems to me the more likely, by virtue of its neatness and practicability. One would assume that into this collection of extracts William had already worked some summarization and stylistic

---

[31] William liked to make collections of texts either complete, abridged or summarized; for instance, in London, BL Harl. 3969, which contains his collection of grammatical handbooks, he omitted from his version of Alcuin, *De Orthographia*, what Alcuin had lifted from Bede's work of the same name, also included in William's collection. See above, pp. 13–14, 61.

[32] GR I, pp. xix–xx, xliv–xlv; on p. 83 William refers to his forthcoming ecclesiastical history in a way so specific as to suggest that it was already at least at the planning stage. It is now known that work on the GR was well advanced by 1118; on the other hand the many references in the GP to particular books of the GR show that William had completed GR before the final writing of GP took place.

[33] No. 16: populum GPAlc.: terram GR. No. 114: eruditus GPAlc.: educatus GR; praeesse GP: et praeesse Alc.: et praeesset GR. No. 121: excellentiae GPAlc.: sapientiae GR.

improvements, which thus reappear in both of his Histories. Here he took these processes further, sometimes in the *Gesta Regum*, sometimes in the *Gesta Pontificum*. If I am right about this, we have a valuable glimpse into the workshop of William as philologist and historian, into the elaborate preparations which must have been necessary for the almost simultaneous, certainly contiguous writing of his two massive works. We are also given an indication of the care which we should expect to find bestowed on his use of such literary evidence. William notoriously rarely quotes verbatim – he admits this himself, justifying his alterations on the grounds of concision and stylistic consistency[34] – and he has been stigmatized as careless in the use of his sources.[35] Yet here, at least, he seems to have deliberately shunned the simplest of all possible procedures – simply to recopy his *Gesta Regum* extracts into the later work – in favour of recourse to the primary material. We would do well, on the basis of this hint, to explore all other possibilities before denouncing William as slipshod.

William did not see fit to absorb the information conveyed by Alcuin's letters into his own text, as he did, for instance, in the case of Bede; rather, he draws attention to them by introductory and interpretative comment, and by quoting from them verbatim and at some length explicitly distinguishes their text from his own. This raises the question of the extent to which William was the slave of his sources. In fact he was not mechanically dependent upon their *ipsissima verba*. In most cases William quoted a mere fraction of a lengthy letter. In nearly all instances the quotation is a compact block of text, not a conflation of passages from various parts of a letter, although sometimes this is the case.[36] Sometimes the quotation is from the beginning of a letter, but just as often it is from the main body.[37] In one case William quotes verbatim from near each end of a letter, summarizing the intervening contents in his own words.[38] The impression created by these considerations is that William was master of his material, able to select from the raw mass just so much as he found relevant and interesting. This impression is reinforced by a study of the alterations which he made to Alcuin's words. We shall now examine these, keeping in mind two important questions: What were the principles according to which William made these alterations, and did his alterations do violence to Alcuin's text?

---

[34] GR I, p. 2; II, p. xvi.
[35] ibid. II, pp. xxxiii–xxxviii; Carter, 'The Historical Content of William of Malmesbury's Miracles of the Virgin Mary', pp. 140–165.
[36] Cf. nos 20 (GP, pp. 267–8), 230 (ibid., p. 247).
[37] Cf. nos 101 (GR I, p. 73), 17 (ibid., p. 74), 128 (GP, p. 15), 31 (ibid., pp. 255–6).
[38] No. 20 (GP, pp. 267–8).

In the first place, William made omissions, in the interests of concision, even within the block of material which he quoted, leaving out words, clauses or even whole sentences. Most of what he omitted was rhetorical. Alcuin's biblical apostrophes are a good example; they add nothing to the contents or message, and William understandably dropped them. For instance, in the passage which follows, William omitted the words in Italics:

> Laus et gloria *domino* Deo *omnipotenti*, qui dies meos in prosperitate bona conseruauit; ut in filii mei karissimi exaltatione gauderem, *et aliquem, ego ultimus aecclesiae uernaculus – eius donante gratia, qui est omnium bonorum largitor – erudirem ex filiis meis*, qui *dignus haberetur dispensator esse misteriorum Christi et* laborare uice mea in aecclesia, ubi ego nutritus et eruditus fueram; et praeesse thesauris sapientiae, in quibus me magister meus dilectus Aelberhtus archiepiscopus heredem reliquit.[39]

The remainder of William's omissions consist of historical information not germane to his theme, such as the internal affairs of the Carolingian Empire or personal messages from Alcuin to his addressees. To present relevant information, shorn of unnecessary (but not all) rhetoric: That, in brief, appears to have been William's aim in making his abridgements. I do not think that there is any case in which his omissions distorted the content or meaning of the passages quoted. This is worthy of note.

But William did not only omit; he wrought changes in syntax, in words and word-order. Some of these were made necessary by his omissions, and they are in support of the same goal: to summarize by pruning Alcuin's rhetoric. But most of William's abbreviation was carried out by simple omission. His alterations were more usually for purely stylistic purposes. It is well known that William was a careful literary craftsman and critic of style.[40] The autograph of his *Gesta Pontificum* shows how he worked over even his final draft, polishing and repolishing with no other end in mind but to achieve the best possible rhetorical effect. He is frequently and explicitly critical of earlier Anglo-Latin writers, even of his patron Aldhelm.[41] Bede is the one exception who calls forth William's warmest and least patronizing praise.[42] By implication, William seems to have considered Alcuin a good stylist, and yet many of his alterations to Alcuin's text can be explained only by dissatisfaction and a desire to improve. Often it is easy to discern the reason for a particular change, but it must be said that in some cases I, at

---

[39] No. 114 (GR I, p. 68).
[40] GP, p. 22; GR I, pp. 1, 121.
[41] GP, p. 344, on Aldhelm's sermons.
[42] GR I, pp. 1, 61–7.

least, cannot tell why William preferred a particular word, expression or word-order to another. A certain proportion of these may, of course, be simple scribal slips.

William's stylistic alterations, I believe, can be seen as attempting to achieve three goals: increased conformity to the ideal of his own time (the ideals associated with monastic *Reimprosa*), a closer approximation to classical canons as he understood them, and greater clarity and simplicity. It is arguable that William himself would not have differentiated the first two goals; he saw his own age as recovering the literary ideals of antiquity, and probably thought of his own style as one modelled upon the precepts of the antique grammarians and the great Roman prose-writers known to him – Caesar, Sallust and Cicero.[43] Still, although it is important that this be understood, the differentiation can be made clearly and legitimately.

I deal first with William's attempts to bring Alcuin's prose into conformity with the ideals of early twelfth-century monastic writing. For instance, in Letter 101 Alcuin has 'melius uisum est mihi', which William has changed to 'melius mihi uisum est', apparently to achieve greater fluency and sonority from the closer conjunction of the **m**'s and **i**'s, and from the firmer final cadence. In the same letter William, who disliked alliteration as much as Alcuin and his English contemporaries favoured it, changed 'peregrinatione permanere' to 'peregrinatione remanere'. In Letter 17 William reversed 'Gildi Brettonum sapientissimi' to 'Gilde sapientissimi Britonum' in order to retain the pattern of 'Britonum ... principum ... episcoporum ... populi', very much in the fashion of his day. Very similar is his change of 'rapinas' to 'rapinam', thus adding one more to the series of four nouns ending in '-am'. In parenthesis, I draw attention to William's substitution of 'Gilde' for Alcuin's 'Gildi' in the passage quoted above, for this is an alteration which does not properly fall into any of the three classes defined earlier. It might be described as a 'philological' change. William obviously thought 'Gild(a)e' the proper genitive form of 'Gildas', surely following the evidence of other manuscripts, either of Gildas himself or of one of his *vitae*.[44]

William's obviously classicizing alterations are less frequent. In Letter 17 he changed 'perdiderunt' to the more poetic and (from a twelfth-century viewpoint) more noticeably classical 'perdidere'. In this connection another

---

[43] See above, pp. 19–20.
[44] Bede also uses the form 'Gildus/ Gildi' (*Hist. Eccl.* i. 22); the alternative 'Gildas/ Gildae' is given in the title to the *De Excidio*, which William may have known independently of Bede (GR I, p. 20; see above, p. 69), and in the Lives by the monk of Ruys and Caradoc: *Gildae De Excidio Britanniae* ..., ed. H. Williams (*Cymmrodorion Record Series*, 3, pts 1 and 2 [1900–1]). It is interesting to note that Leland, in his transcript of this letter, has 'Gildae' (*Collectanea*, II, p. 399), suggesting that William had already made the alteration in his complete transcript of A1 and its partial exemplar.

fascinating glimpse of him at work is provided by the autograph of the *Gesta Pontificum*. Alcuin opens Letter 17 with 'audiens' plus accusative. William did the same for the extract in his autograph, but later lined it through and substituted the more classical 'Cum audissem'. This assures us of the deliberateness of what William was about. He also tries, laudably, to simplify and clarify Alcuin's sometimes tortuous sentence structure. 'Striving after effects' was one of William's criticisms of early English writers – 'Angli pompatice dictare solent', he wrote of them on one occasion.[45] By inserting particles, by small omissions and grammatical changes and by toning down needlessly strong words, William aimed at a less stilted effect and increased comprehensibility.

Taking into consideration all of these 'improvements', it can still be said that William gives us essentially Alcuin's words and meaning. But there is another, quite different class of alteration, which we may term historical, leading to an altogether different conclusion. There are not many of these, but they are of such a serious nature that I shall discuss them individually.

The easiest to deal with occurs in Letter 16, where Alcuin's 'Euboraca ciuitate, in ecclesia beati Petri principis apostolorum, que caput est totius regni' has been changed to 'Euboraca ciuitate, que caput totius regni est'. The effect is to prevent the legitimate inference being drawn from Alcuin's word-order, that it is the church of York, not York itself, which is 'head of the whole realm'. William's reproduction in the *Gesta Pontificum* of the notorious 'Canterbury forgeries',[46] his preference for Bede's account of the Wilfrid affair as against Eddi's,[47] and his relations with such advocates for Canterbury as Anselm and Eadmer all predisposed him to find this inference repugnant;[48] this in spite of the fact that Alcuin, if this was his intended meaning, was referring only to Northumbria, not the whole of England. William has at least interpreted Alcuin's meaning, if not altered it altogether. I assume that he was motivated by a prudent consideration of his audience, among whom would surely be the Canterbury monks. If one wished to go further, it would be to say that William himself was to some extent involved and partisan in the great dispute between the two sees.

The next alteration is more problematic. In Letter 114, where Alcuin refers to his master Archbishop Ethelbert (founder of the famous York library), William has substituted 'Egbertus' for the 'Aelberhtus' of his manuscript. In the extract from Letter 121 which follows 114 in the *Gesta*

---

[45] GP, p. 344.
[46] ibid., pp. 46–62, GR II, pp. 346–8; Southern, 'The Canterbury Forgeries', pp. 193–226.
[47] GP, pp. 211–244.
[48] See above, pp. 46–7, 73.

Regum he inserts the words 'Egberti archiepiscopi' after Alcuin's 'magistri mei'. This is wrong, but it is important to understand, if possible, how William came to make his error. First of all it must be realized that William was interpreting, not contradicting his source. William always expanded or contracted the Old English *ash*, which in this case would have given him a choice of 'Albertus', 'Ethelbertus' or 'Egelbertus'; no doubt he considered these alternatives. Secondly, searching for Alcuin's 'magister', he would have had the choice of 'Ethelbertus' or 'Egbertus', since Alcuin had been taught by both.[49] It is interesting to note that Leland's extract from this letter has 'Aelberthus' in the text, the first syllable cancelled by sublinear points and 'Eg' written above it.[50] Of course this might be due to Leland's having collated his 'vetus codex' with a manuscript of the *Gesta Regum*; but I think it more likely that he is faithfully reproducing an emendation already in his exemplar, which I have tried to show was William's personal copy. Thirdly, William had some information about Egbert other than that in Alcuin's letters. He prefaces the extracts from Letters 114 and 121 with these remarks:

> Plures post [Paulinum] tantae urbis praesules, simplici episcopatus nomine contenti, nihil altius anhelauerant; at uero Egbertus inthronizatus, animosioris ingenii homo, cogitans quod 'sicut superbum est si appetas indebita, ita ignauum si debita negligas', pallium multa throni apostolici appellatione reparauit. Hic, omnium liberalium artium armarium, ut ita dicam, et sacrarium fuit, nobilissimamque bibliothecam Eboraci constituit; cuius rei testem idoneum aduoco Alcwinum, qui ... in epistola ad Eanbaldum, tertio loco Egberti successorem, ait ...

In the *Gesta Pontificum*, where this passage and the subsequent extracts are repeated,[51] William adds that Egbert was the brother of King Eadbert of Northumbria; perhaps by simple inadvertence, he calls the king Egbert also. The passage shows that William was unaware of the two Archbishops Eanbald whose reigns were contiguous. He did know of an archbishop between Egbert and Eanbald (I and II conflated), even if he did not know that his name was Ethelbert; he should have known his name and dates, and of the two Eanbalds, since they were recorded in the version of the *Anglo-Saxon Chronicle* which he used.[52] In the *Gesta Pontificum*, however,

---

[49] Godfrey, *The Church in Anglo-Saxon England*, pp. 213–4.
[50] *Collectanea*, II, p. 397.
[51] GP, p. 246.
[52] William used a manuscript of the so-called 'E-Type'; see above, p. 70; *ASC*, pp. 28, 33–4, 37.

he calls this man Cena, the name given him in the letters of Boniface.[53] The second conclusion which can be drawn from the above passage is that William, not surprisingly, did not know of Alcuin's poem in praise of York, or he would have known whom to credit with the foundation of the library.[54] There is, in fact, no positive evidence that William knew any of Alcuin's verse.

The problem then is: Where did William obtain his information about Egbert's relationship with King Eadbert, his assumption of the pallium, his supposed foundation of the York library and reputation for learning? The *Anglo-Saxon Chronicle* could have provided him with the first two items, and if this was his only source, then he has fleshed it out quite creditably on the basis of inference, to arrive at a judgement about Egbert's character and motives. That this archbishop was a learned man and possessor or founder of a good library he could have deduced from the correspondence between him and Boniface[55] – his reference to Archbishop Ethelbert as 'Cena' suggests that he may have had access to this exchange of letters. It was presumably on the basis of this information that he credited Egbert with the origins of the famous library, about which he must have heard at one or more removes from Alcuin's poem. All this led him to reject the testimony of the *Chronicle* and expand the 'Aelberhtus' in A1 to 'Agelberhtus' = 'Egbertus', rather than to 'Ethelbertus'.

William's third alteration occurs in the extract from Letter 230 given in the *Gesta Pontificum*.[56] William gives some sentences from the opening paragraph of this long letter, but then occurs a sentence which is not found there. At first sight this looks like a rather careless summary of the rest of the letter, but it is, in fact, an extract from Letter 128, from which a longer passage is quoted earlier in the *Gesta Pontificum*.[57] William, then, has conflated two separate letters, without warning his readers. I assume that he did so deliberately, and the question must then arise, was he justified in so doing?

Letter 230 was written in 801 to Archbishop Aethelheard of Canterbury, who was about to embark on a journey to Rome. The background to this was a letter of King Coenwulf of Mercia to Pope Leo III, seeking the reinstatement of Gregory I's original plan for two English provinces, with the southern see based in London.[58] Letter 128 was written to Aethelheard in

---

[53] GP, p. 246.
[54] Ed. Dümmler, MGH Poet. 1, p. 169ff., and P. Godman (Oxford, 1983). William's ignorance is not surprising, given its evidently restricted distribution. Only two, continental, manuscripts are known to have existed, both now lost.
[55] M. Tangl, *Die Briefe des heiligen Bonifatius* (Berlin, 1916), nos 75, 91.
[56] GP, pp. 246–7.
[57] ibid., pp. 18–19.
[58] Haddan and Stubbs, *Councils*, II, pp. 521–3; GR I, pp. 86–9.

797 consoling him and urging him to repent for the state of the church of Canterbury, 'divided asunder not by rational consideration, but by a certain lust for power'. This refers to Offa's raising of Lichfield to metropolitan status in 778, a grievance raised by Aethelheard in Rome, where he was confirmed as primate over all the dioceses traditionally subject to his see.[59] At the Council of Cloveshoe in 803 it was declared that Offa had obtained a division of the province by false pretences; Canterbury had its honour restored, and the then archbishop of Lichfield apparently resigned or was demoted.[60]

William introduces the extracts from these letters in the context of his treatment of the succession of the archbishops of York. After introducing Eanbald (he means Eanbald II), he continues:

Ipse est Eanbaldus, qui cum Ethelardo archiepiscopo Cantuariensi mutuis probitatis offitiis inuasionem, quam Offa rex Mertiorum super Cantuariensem ecclesiam fecerat, ad nichilum redegit. Quod Albinus significare uidetur in epistola ad eundem Adelardum, ita dicens: [Letter 230] Audiens salutem et prosperitatem uestram et conuentum cum Eboracensi archiepiscopo filio meo Eanbaldo, satis mihi placuit speranti ex uestre colloquio sanctitatis unitatem sanctae ecclesiae recompaginari, [Letter 128] quae partim discissa est non rationabili consideratione sed quadam potestatis cupiditate.

On the presumption that these letters were the only source for William's preceding interpretative statements, he has again used their skeletal information imaginatively. I think that it can also be said that he was perfectly justified in conflating the two letters, which relate after all to the same set of circumstances.

What has this study taught us? Surely a good deal about William's attitude to his sources. It has illustrated the care which he took to make accurate or at least intelligible versions of them – in fact his text of Alcuin is very faithful, apart from his deliberate alterations. In this connection we have established his importance as a witness for five Alcuinian, plus two other early letters. At the same time William was able to accomplish the dangerous task of editing by omission, alteration and conflation without substantially altering the sense of the original. He knew what he wanted his texts to do for him and he was master of their content. On the other hand he had no compunction about interpreting ambiguities in Alcuin's meaning or in the manuscript-readings, in the light of other historical data available to him. As an attitude to source-material and as a means of using this fragmentary information to construct a coherent account of events, this is impressive, but

[59] Godfrey, op. cit., pp. 266–7.
[60] ibid., p. 267; Haddan and Stubbs, III, pp. 542–4.

we have shown that on at least one occasion it got William into trouble. This was because he failed to reconcile his texts and culpably cut the Gordian knot by simply disregarding the testimony of one of them, the *Chronicle*, probably regarding Alcuin's *auctoritas* as weightier.

At this point something should be said of the third papal letter quoted by William and also found only in A1. This is a letter of Pope Sergius to Abbot Ceolfrid of Wearmouth-Jarrow, written about 700.[61] William's text seems to have been copied from A1, where it appears in the first section (that is, part of the manuscript for which William did not have the exemplar), but there is one major variant. Whereas A1 contains an invitation to the abbot to send the 'religiosum Dei famulum N. uenerabilis monasterii tui' to Rome, William has 'religiosum Dei famulum *Bedam*, uenerabilis monasterii tui *presbyterum*'. Bishop Stubbs noted that Bede was not ordained priest until after Sergius's death and that he was not one of the mission of Wearmouth monks who went to Rome in 700 and brought back a papal privilege.[62] Still, he thought it conceivable that the pope, having heard of Bede's learning, may have invited him, 'and that the pope's death may have prevented him going'. He concluded: 'That Malmesbury garbled the letter, as has been supposed, is in the highest degree improbable'. Having in mind, however, the way in which William used Alcuin's letters, altering names and conflating passages as he felt necessary, we should be less certain than Stubbs that William was not responsible for the expansion of N. to 'Bedam' and the insertion of 'presbyterum' in the text of Sergius's letter. Indeed, since he almost certainly copied the letter from A1, it is difficult to account for these variants in any other way.[63]

This important modification is found in two other versions. One is in Cambridge University Library MS Kk. 4. 6, an extensive miscellany prepared for and annotated by the chronicler John of Worcester, with whom William was acquainted.[64] The text of the *Liber Pontificalis* in it was first associated with William by Levison, and I have shown above that the Cambridge copy was made from a version modified and interpolated by him.[65] Among the many added texts which point to William's workmanship is Sergius's letter.[66] This part of the Cambridge manuscript was written by a

---

[61] Godfrey, pp. 248–250.

[62] GR I, p. 62 n. 2.

[63] The only alternative explanation would be that he collated A1 with another manuscript containing this reading. This is not impossible, but the 'presbyterum' suggests that we are dealing with an interpolation based on guesswork, rather than an authoritative reading from an early manuscript.

[64] Ker, 'Handwriting', 375–6; idem, MLGB, p. 206; E. A. McIntyre, 'Early twelfth-century Worcester Cathedral Priory, with special reference to the Manuscripts written there' (D. Phil. thesis, Oxford, 1978). See above, pp. 75, 122.

[65] ibid., ch. 6.

[66] CUL MS Kk. 4. 6, ff. 270–270v.

very careless scribe, but once his errors are eliminated, it can be seen that this copy of the letter is derived from A1, except that it shares two variant readings with William, including the reference to Bede.[67] The other version is an extract in Leland's *Collectanea*, made from his 'vetus codex' of Alcuin's and Dunstan's letters.[68] This, too, derives from A1, but has the same two agreements with William found in the Cambridge manuscript. My conclusion is that both Leland's and the Cambridge text derive from A1 via William's complete transcript of it and its partial exemplar, and that in this transcript William had already made his major alteration.

'Garbling', however, would be the wrong word to describe what William actually did. I would hope that this study has to some extent exonerated William from charges of dishonesty or carelessness. Just as he felt free to 'improve' Alcuin's style, so he felt justified in interpreting (rather than altering) his information. So here: 'N.' cried out for expansion. Whom else but Bede would the pope single out among the monks of Wearmouth-Jarrow for a special invitation to Rome? Although William overplayed his hand by the insertion of 'presbyterum', he may, for ought we know, have been right in his interpretation. William demands, not our blame, but our understanding; our task is not to judge his use of sources against twentieth-century ideals but to understand his vision of history.

---

[67] The other shared reading is: ut expedire nostrae saluti Cambr.Wm.: u. e. saluti nostrae A1.
[68] *Collectanea*, II, pp. 396–7.

9

WILLIAM AND
SOME OTHER
WESTERN WRITERS ON ISLAM

IN HIS BOOK *Western Views of Islam in the Middle Ages* R. W. Southern distinguished between an 'Age of Ignorance', extending to the early twelfth century, and the 'Century of Reason and Hope' which succeeded it.[1] Typical of views widely current in the earlier period are those expressed in the *Song of Roland*, in which the Saracens are polytheists and idolaters, Mohammed being one of their several gods.[2] However, from c.1120, notable advances were made in western knowledge of the Islamic religion and of its prophet-founder. Among several reasons for this, the Crusades and travels associated with or facilitated by them may be singled out as especially important. So also were the increasing and increasingly amicable contacts between Eastern and European scholars in frontier-areas such as Spain and Sicily.

And yet William, a monk who never travelled outside England, was the Westerner who, according to Southern, first presented a reasonably accurate account of Islam and Mohammed. Remarkably, as Southern puts it, '[he] ... was the first ... to distinguish clearly between the idolatry and pagan superstitions of the Slavs and the monotheism of Islam, and to emphasize against all current popular thought that Islam held Mahomet not as God but as His prophet.'[3] In support of this, Southern quotes a passage from William's *Gesta Regum*:

[1] R. W. Southern, *Western Views of Islam in the Middle Ages* (Oxford, 1962); these are the titles of the first two chapters.
[2] W. W. Comfort, 'The Saracens in the French Epic', *Publications of the Modern Language Association of America*, 55 (1940), 628–659; N. Daniel, *Heroes and Saracens; a Re-interpretation of the Chansons de Geste* (Edinburgh, 1984).
[3] Southern, pp. 34–5.

[Henricus III] erat imperator ... bellicosissimus, quippe qui etiam Vindelicos et Leuticios subegerit, ceterosque populos Sueuis conterminos, qui usque ad hanc diem soli omnium mortalium paganas superstitiones anhelant; nam Saraceni et Turchi Deum Creatorem colunt, Mahomet non Deum sed eius prophetam aestimantes.[4]

The purpose of this chapter is to draw attention to other passages, found in William's unprinted works, which enlarge and refine our knowledge of his views on this subject; in combination they illustrate the intensity of his interest (prompting the question why), and his insistence that the popular tradition was wrong. They also enable some account to be given of the sources of his new and surprising knowledge.

The first passage, a brief one, is found in William's *Commentary on Lamentations*, written c.1136.[5] Similar to the *Gesta Regum* extract already quoted, it runs thus;

Denique quamuis Christianorum et Iudeorum et Sarracenorum secte habeant de Filio compugnantes sententias, omnes tamen Deum patrem Creatorem rerum et credunt corde et confitentur ore.[6]

This is an interesting statement on two grounds: in the first place, it indicates that William's knowledge of the Islamic religion was even more precise than the *Gesta Regum* passage permitted one to assume. In the second, this accurate knowledge is accompanied by an unusually sympathetic attitude. William actually categorizes Christians, Jews and Moslems together as 'secte'; in the *Gesta Regum* extract he explicitly distinguishes them as a group from the inferior 'pagani'. The Moslems and Jews are by implication heretics rather than members of religious systems entirely different from Christianity. The same term was used, and the same view held, by Peter the Venerable in his *Liber contra Sectam Saracenorum*, written in the late 1140s.[7] But William could express an accommodating attitude even to pagans, as witness the following extract from the same commentary:

Vnde Aristotiles pulchre *atque haut scio an inferius aliquo Christiano* precepit, ut uoluptatum non principium sed finem attendamus.[8]

---

[4] GR I, p. 230.
[5] See Farmer, 'William of Malmesbury's Commentary on Lamentations', p. 289; R. W. Hunt, 'English Learning in the Late Twelfth Century', pp. 117 and n. 3, 118. Hunt's date for Robert's mention of William (1138 or later) is to be slightly corrected (to 1137 or later) by reference to Knowles, Brooke and London, *Heads*, p. 79.
[6] Comm. Lam., f. 78v.
[7] J. Kritzeck, *Peter the Venerable and Islam* (Princeton, 1964), pp. 141–9.
[8] Comm. Lam., f. 58v. I have not been able to identify the source of William's quotation.

William was therefore prepared to look for points of contact between Christianity and other religions, both in theology and, in the case especially of the ancients, in ethics.[9] The latter attitude was shared by some other litterateurs and humanists of William's time, notably by Hildebert of Le Mans,[10] whose verse William read and admired.[11]

The second passage is much longer, and it is on this that I wish to concentrate discussion, beginning with the manuscript in which it is found. Oxford, Bodleian Library MS Arch. Seld. B. 16 has been associated with William at least since Stubbs's time.[12] Mostly in William's own hand, it contains a compendium of material designed to form a continuous history of the Roman emperors. Its main contents, in order of appearance, are Dares Phrygius, Orosius, Eutropius, Jordanes, Paul the Deacon, what purports to be a digest of Aimoin of Fleury's *Historia Francorum*, and the *Breviarium Alaricum*.[13] To most of these William has provided his habitual introductory comments and interpolations, and the sections not in his hand have been annotated by him. The portion claiming our attention is the 'digest of Aimoin'. It opens with an introduction as follows:

> Precedentium gesta imperatorum Iordanes episcopus et Paulus diaconus texuerunt. Sequentium acta Haimo monachus Floriacensis ex diuersis auctoribus collegit. Eius ergo semper sensum aliquando uerba ponemus, omissis quecumque de Longabardis, Francis, Gothis immiscuit. Earum enim gentium gesta alias propriis libris leguntur.[14]

The reader acquainted with Aimoin's work will raise his eyebrows at this passage, for the *Historia Francorum* has very little to say about the Eastern emperors at all, and concentrates, as its title suggests, on the history of Merovingian Gaul, breaking off at A.D. 652.[15] Yet William's lengthy account continues to the reign of Louis the Pious, with some scrappy additions and regnal lists to his own time. In fact a careful examination of it soon shows that it has nothing to do with Aimoin; it is rather a summary of Hugh of Fleury's *Historia Ecclesiastica*, in the second edition of 1110.[16] This edition concluded with the reign of Louis the Pious, so that the regnal lists

---

[9] Cf. the view expressed in the prologue to his own *Polyhistor* (PH, p. 37; transl. James, *Two Ancient English Scholars*, pp. 26–7).
[10] von Moos, *Hildebert von Lavardin*, pp. 94–116, 240–289.
[11] GR II, pp. 402–3.
[12] ibid., I, pp. cxxx–cxl; see above, pp. 92–3.
[13] ibid., pp. 63–4, 66–7.
[14] MS Arch Seld. B. 16, f. 135; printed in GR I, p. cxxxiv.
[15] PL 139. 617–798.
[16] See above, p. 67 and notes.

which follow are William's own addition. I have discussed the possible reasons for William's error above.[17] As to the date of the manuscript, although the latest king in the regnal lists is Louis VI, crowned in 1108, an earlier passage indicates that William was writing nearer to the time of his death:

Sicilia Sarracenis paruit usque abhinc xlii. annos, quando eam Normanni subiecerunt, anno Dominicae Incarnationis millesimo centesimo minus xiii.[18]

This passage was therefore written in the year 1129. It occurs shortly after the section devoted to the reign of the emperor Heraclius. It was at this point in his narrative that Hugh of Fleury inserted a long account of the career of Mohammed, noticed by Dr Daniel as the first appearance in the West of the 'Khorasan' version.[19] William has abbreviated this account, at the same time making some additions of his own. So that a proper comparison can be made, I print Hugh's version followed by William's. William's additions to Hugh's account are italicized.

Hugh of Fleury

Hac preterea tempestate Saraceni, qui et Turci dicuntur, Machomet pseudopropheta eis ducatum praebente, a suis sedibus exierunt, et imperium Heraclii grauiter deuastare coeperunt. Porro iste Machomet, Saracenorum et Arabum princeps et pseudopropheta, fuit de genere Ismael filii Abrahae. Qui cum in primaeua aetate sua esset mercator, pergebat frequenter cum camelis suis ad Aegyptum et Palaestinam, et conuersabatur cum Iudeis et Christianis, a quibus tam Nouum quam Vetus Testamentum didicit; sed et magus perfectissimus effectus est; et cum hac illacque discurreret, contigit ut Chorozaniam ingrederetur prouinciam. Cuius prouinciae domina Cadiga nominabatur; quae cum diuersa species, quas secum Machomet attulerat, miraretur, coepit ei praefata mulier familiarius adhaerere. Quam Machomet incantationum suarum praestrictam phantasmate, coepit astu paulatim in errorem inducere, dicens ei quod ipse esset Messias, quem esse uenturum adhuc Iudaei expectant. Suffragabantur uerbis eius tam incantationum praestigiae quam calliditatis eius ingenium copiosum; qua opinione non solum potens mulier decepta est, sed et omnes Iudaei, ad quos fama eius pertingere poterat, ad eum cum Saracenis cateruatim confluebant, attoniti tanta nouitate rei; quibus coepit nouas leges fingere, et eis tradere, adhibens ipsis legibus testimonia de utroque

[17] ibid., p. 67.
[18] MS Arch. Seld. B. 16, f. 137.
[19] Rottendorff, pp. 149–150; N. Daniel, *Islam and the West; The Making of an Image* (Edinburgh, 1960), pp. 12, 324 n. 11.

Testamento. Quas leges Ismaelitae appellant suas, eumque suum legislatorem esse fatentur. Praefata quoque mulier, uidens hominem Iudaeorum et Saracenorum pariter contubernio uallatum, existimabat in illo diuinam latere maiestatem; et cum esset uidua, assumpsit eum sibi maritum; sicque Machomet totius prouinciae illius obtinuit principatum. Demum uero Arabes ei adhaerentes, regnum Persidis infestare coeperunt, ac demum orientalis imperii fines usque Alexandriam, contra Heraclium inuadere. Post haec uero Machomet coepit cadere frequenter epileptica passione; quod Cadiga cernens oppido tristabatur, eo quod nupsisset impurissimo homini et epileptico; quam ille placare desiderans, demulcebat eam, dicens quia 'Gabrielem archangelum loquentem mecum contemplor, et non ferens splendorem uultus eius, utpote carnalis homo, deficio, et cado'. Credidit ergo mulier, et omnes Arabes et Ismaelitae, quod ex ore archangeli Gabrielis illas susciperet leges, quas suis discipulis dabat, eo quod Gabriel archangelus saepe a Deo mittatur hominibus sanctis.[20]

William of Malmesbury

Nec minus Turchi Muameth pseudopropheta duce imperium Romanum populantur. Hic Muameth Ismahelita genere in arte negotiationis iuuentam suam triuit et cum mercatoribus Iudeis et Christianis conuersatus, utrorumque legem adprime addidicit. Itaque discursu mercaturae cuidam mulier Cadigam nomine que Corozaniae prouinciae principabatur, notior factus, magicis prestigiis quorum peritus erat, quod ipse esset Messias quem Iudei expectant, facile persuasit. Qua opinione muliercula decepta, in eius coniugium concessit. *Nec dubitandum est multis eum effecisse miraculis, ut tot fidei suae populos conciliaret, cum usque hodie omnes illae nationes eum non Deum ut quidam putant sed ut summum Dei prophetam colant*, utanturque legibus quas ipse composuit, adhibens ex utroque Testamento uerisimilia testimonia. Tunc ergo confluentibus ad eum Iudeis et Sarracenis et Arabibus (*quo nomine uocantur communiter Idumei et Moabitae et Ammonitae*), quia miraculis suis animos eorum dementauerat (*Iudei quippe sicut Apostolus ait signa querunt* [I Cor. 1.22]), illis ergo fretus et regnum presidis et orientale imperium Heraclii usque Alexandriam infestare cepit. Is cum frequenter epilemptica passione caderet, idque immodicae mentis mulier permolestum esset, dicebat ille non se infirmari, sed a sensibus corporis abduci, ut liberius cum Gabrihele loqueretur archangelo, qui sibi leges illas quas ceteris promulgaret, asserebat e caelo. *Recepta est haec opinio apud gentes barbaras, et adhuc credunt leges illas esse angelicas.*[21]

---

[20] Rottendorff, pp. 149–150.
[21] MS Arch. Seld. B. 16, f. 136v.

Hugh's account is a mixture of little-known fact and current, well-established fiction.[22] Obligingly, he tells his readers what his main source for it was:

Verum multa, quae secuntur, ab Anastasii Romani bibliothecarii libro decerpsi, quem ... de Greco transtulit in Latinum ... Prefatus autem Anastasius suis temporibus ea, quae in Greca continebantur historia ab Octauiano Augusto usque ad Michaelem, qui Nicephoro successit, rationabili prosecutus oratione Latino transtulit eloquio, in quo opere nobis multa quae hactenus nesciebamus, aperuit, *ibique de Muhamet pseudopropheta pauca quidem locutus est, sed quibus temporibus fuerit lucide designauit.*[23]

Hugh seems to imply that before he read Anastasius's *Historia Tripartita*, he did not really know when Mohammed lived; he also appears to suggest that he had access to other information about him. A comparison of his treatment of Mohammed's life with Anastasius's indicates that this is so. Since Anastasius's account is lengthy, and readily accessible in De Boor's edition, I will not print it here *in extenso*, but merely summarize the chief points of agreement and difference between it and Hugh's.[24] Hugh's account is shorter than Anastasius's, and it is to his credit that he has completely omitted some of the more fabulous tales told in his main source, such as Khadija's friendship with the adulterous pseudomonk, the conversion of ten Jews, and Mohammed's preaching of the erotic delights of paradise. Hugh has retained from Anastasius the term 'pseudopropheta' applied to Mohammed, his Ishmaelite ancestry, his mercantile profession and conversation with Jews and Christians, his marriage, his assumption of a messianic role, his epileptic fits and explanation of them. All else is added, and even in his presentation of those facts which he shares with Anastasius, Hugh departs markedly from his predecessor's sequence of events. Thus Hugh, less correctly, has Mohammed meet with the Christians and Jews, accept a

---

[22] To the fictional class belong the references to Mohammed's use of magic and his epilepsy (Southern, pp. 30–1; Daniel, *Islam and the West*, pp. 27–8). Some of the true facts were known to earlier and other contemporary writers, such as Mohammed's marriage to Khadija, his contacts with Christians and Jews, and his early career as a merchant (Southern, pp. 29 and n. 26, 30–1; Daniel, *Islam and the West*, pp. 80–90). For a few other matters (in particular the mention of Khorasan) Hugh seems to be our earliest western authority.

[23] MGH Scriptores 9, p. 357.

[24] *Theophanis Chronographia*, ed. C. de Boor (Leipzig, 2 vols, 1883–1885), II, pp. 208–210. It should be noted that Hugh was not the only, nor the first western writer to be influenced by Anastasius's account of Mohammed's career. Anastasius's words were reproduced almost verbatim by Landolf Sagax in his *Historia Miscella*, written in southern Italy shortly before 1023; *Landolfi Sagacis Historia Miscella*, ed. A. Crivellucci (*Fonti per la Storia d'Italia*, Rome, 2 vols, 1913), II, pp. 132–4.

version of their 'law' and proclaim himself Messiah, before meeting Khadija. Khadija herself he describes not merely as a rich widow, but also (and less accurately), as a person of authority in Khorasan. All the detail found in Anastasius but omitted by Hugh comes into the category of legend; conversely, some at least of Hugh's additions are factual – these include Mohammed's conversations with Jews and Christians and interest in their scriptures, and the origin of the Koran, containing elements of the Old and New Testaments. The major exceptions are the mention of Mohammed's magical powers and epileptic fits, part of the *koinê* of western writers about Islam in Hugh's day, and his vague and overstated account of Mohammed's campaigns. Oddly, in a separate passage, Hugh places the date of Mohammed's death about a decade too late, although Anastasius should have set him right about this.[25] Nonetheless, thanks to his main source, Hugh's dating of Mohammed's career is streets ahead of that proposed by most other contemporary authors.

Where did Hugh obtain his information correcting and supplementing Anastasius? It is not possible to say precisely. Much of his additional material is not found in any known earlier source, Eastern or Western. He may have spoken with travellers or crusaders who returned from the East; an oral rather than written tradition seems to lie behind the new details.[26]

The relationship between William of Malmesbury's account and Hugh's is similar to Hugh's with Anastasius's. William has abbreviated heavily, again mostly to the advantage of his version. He omits principally two kinds of material: mere rhetorical verbiage, of which Hugh is inordinately fond and which serves only to pad out and slow down his narrative, and the marvellous element, which, although still present in William's version, is much reduced as a prime explanation of Mohammed's actions and successes. Mohammed's interpretation of his epileptic fits is not only seen as a ploy to calm his wife, but, less simplistically, as related to the prophet's earlier-developed religious ideas and magical powers – powers whose efficacy William did not doubt.

William makes three small additions to Hugh (the italicized sections in the passage quoted earlier), the second of which, taken from Bede, we may at once dismiss as illustrative only of William's book-learning, and of the common desire among western scholars to fit the Islamic peoples into the

---

[25] Rottendorff, p. 153; De Boor, II, p. 208.
[26] Daniel, *Islam and the West*, p. 342 n. 9; Southern, pp. 30 n. 26, 31 n. 28.

Old Testament ethnographic framework.[27] The first is an explanation by William of the tremendous number of believers in Islam in his own time, nothing short of miraculous. William was impressed and worried by this fact. He enlarges on it in his *Commentary on Lamentations*:

> (Glossing Lam. 1:14 – Vigilauit iugum iniquitatum mearum ... infirmata est uirtus mea) Hi mores sepe Christianos exercitus gentilibus fecerunt cedere, ut etiam abhinc plus ducentis annis, Thurci et Sarraceni dominacione sua illa premerent loca quae fuerant Dei natiuitatis et passionis conscia. Hi mores ad quantulos nos redegerunt, qui eramus quondam gens etsi non multa, at certe multis eruditione et affabilitate preferenda. Profecto illud in nobis uidetur impletum quod psalmista Iudeos denotauit dicens: Disperge illos in uirtute tua, et destrue eos protector meus Domine (Ps. 58.12).[28]

The spread of Islam plainly puzzled William, as its past victories over Christianity troubled him. In the early pages of the *Gesta Regum*, discussing Charlemagne and his times, he quotes a letter of Alcuin lamenting the Saracens' domination of Africa and the Middle East ('Asia Major') and describing the recovery from them of some of the Spanish coast by Charles's generals.[29] This is followed by William's own reflections upon the advance of Islam, eventually checked by the Frankish rulers and reversed by the crusaders and others of his own day:

> In his uerbis ... poterit curiosus animaduertere quantum iam annorum effluxerit ex quo Saraceni Affricam et Asiam Majorem inuaserint. Et profecto, nisi Dei clementia ingenitum robur Francorum imperatorum animasset, pridem Europam subiugassent; adeo contemptis imperatoribus Constantinopolitanis Siciliam et Sardiniam et Baleares insulas, et pene omnes terras quae pelago cinguntur, praeter Rhodum et Cretam et Ciprum, occupauerunt: sed nostris diebus per Northmannos Siciliam, per Pisanos Corsicam et Sardiniam, per Francos et omnis generis ex Europa Christianos magnam partem Asiae, et ipsam Ierusalem, relinquere coacti sunt.

---

[27] William's source is the *Nomina regionum atque locorum de Actibus Apostolorum* appended to Bede, *Super Acta Apostolorum Expositio* (*Clavis*, nos 1357, 1359); PL 92. 1035. The *Nomina* is always found in MSS of the *Expositio*, sometimes in MSS containing both the *Expositio* and *Retractatio*, but never in MSS of the *Retractatio*: M. L. W. Laistner, *Bedae Venerabilis Expositio Actuum Apostolorum et Retractatio* (Cambridge, Mass., 1939), pp. xvii–xli. Oxford, Jesus Coll. MS 68 is a mid twelfth-century MS of the *Expositio* and *Nomina* from Cirencester, not far from Malmesbury.

[28] Comm. Lam., f. 34v.

[29] GR I, p. 92.

Later on in the same work, in his account of the Council of Clermont in 1095, he reports Pope Urban II as lamenting Christian territorial losses to Islam and the comparatively small number of Christians in the world.[30] In his Selden Collection he saw Mohammed's miracles as important to the expansion of Islam; in his Commentary he saw in it God's judgement on the unfaithful Christians.

The third of William's additions again refers to contemporary Islam, and the belief in the heavenly origin of the Koran. This is the only specific piece of factual information which he adds, and it is of course correct. There is no need to suppose that William was dependent on a written source for this detail. Together with the other minor modifications to Hugh's account it could have resulted from his conversations with returned crusaders, presumably the same men who supplied him with scraps of information about the first Crusade recorded in the Gesta Regum.[31]

One must ask whether the statements about Islam contained in William's Gesta Regum and Commentary on Lamentations are dependent on his knowledge of Hugh of Fleury. He knew Hugh's work by 1129, well before he wrote the Commentary. He would have needed to know it before 1125 if it was the source for the passage in the Gesta Regum. There is no proof of this, and in any case William had access to other sources of information about Mohammed: he was, as mentioned, in contact with returned crusaders, and he had access to some Arabic writings in translation.[32]

There remains the intriguing question of why he was so interested in Islam. After all, the long passage on Mohammed occurs in the midst of the gesta of the Roman emperors, to which it is not highly relevant, at least in such detail. The shorter passages from the Gesta Regum and Commentary on Lamentations are also gratuitous pieces of information, so far as the main themes of each work are concerned. His interest was not overtly polemical; Hugh's account is much more of a 'smear' than William's. True, William does mention Mohammed's use of magical deception, but on the whole his account is temperate and unrhetorical. I think that his interest in Mohammed is largely to be explained in terms of his historical sense. He seems to have recognized that in Mohammed's career lay the origins of an important religion and significant historical developments involving very large numbers of people; these developments, by giving rise to the Crusades, had impinged upon the Western Europe of William's day and, to a historian of his quality, demanded an explanation. In support of this I note the sentence in his description of Mohammed's career in which he defends the

---

[30] ibid., II, pp. 393–8.
[31] ibid., II, pp. cxviii–cxxvii.
[32] William's interest in Arabic scientific writings is documented above, p. 62.

genuineness of the prophet's magical or miraculous powers by adducing the very large number of his followers in William's own time. I also note that from this point on, in his abbreviation of Hugh's chronicle, which purports to be a history of the Roman emperors, William devotes a disproportionate amount of space to the expansion of Islam. Doubtless the long account of the first Crusade which William wrote into the earlier *Gesta Regum* – again departing from his main theme – prompted him to ask questions about the nature and origins of Islam, a religion of tremendous motivating power. Mohammed, he soon saw, was himself the explanation, and he also saw that the earlier accounts of him available and current in the West were unsatisfactory. As his explicit criticisms of them show, he thought it important that they should be corrected, and he certainly succeeded in improving on them.

This exploration of the treatment of Mohammed's career by some Western writers from the tenth century to the second quarter of the twelfth century illustrates the importance of establishing the sources of information available to such men, and the relationships between their various accounts. In this connection it draws attention to a methodological flaw in Dr Daniel's fine study. Organized on topical lines, rather than on chronological, as is Southern's shorter essay, the work does not enable one to map the temporal development of Western knowledge of Islam; it presents a static rather than dynamic picture.[33] It also fails to trace connections between the accounts of Western writers. Thus, for instance, a passage of Mohammed quoted from Vincent of Beauvais was lifted verbatim by Vincent from Hugh of Fleury.[34] This exploration also calls in question the neatness of Southern's division between the ages of ignorance and reason. Anastasius the Librarian knew nearly as much about Mohammed as did William of Malmesbury; he knew

[33] The same writer's later book, *The Arabs and Mediaeval Europe* (London, 1975), is structured chronologically, yet still offers a static picture, because it maintains the view that the attitude of Europeans towards the Arabs, as first developed in the eleventh and twelfth centuries, has remained fixed until modern times: see, for instance, p. 139 (on the First Crusade): 'The existing attitude of Europeans to the Arabic world was intensified and fixed. European persecutors and aggressors would always see the Arabs in the same capacity. It was as if future European aggression was endowed forever with a conviction of righteousness. In the long run the Crusades confirmed the European belief that it was not possible to share a culture with the Arabs; it was their own behaviour, as much as Arab behaviour, that taught them this. This experience strengthened the sense of difference which later ages would inherit', and p. 319: '... we can only say that Europeans have on the whole maintained towards the Arabs a constant reserve which seems to run consistently through the whole medieval period up to the present day'.
[34] Daniel, *Islam and the West*, pp. 27, 327 and n. 45.

much more than the poet of the *Song of Roland*.[35] Conversely William clearly implies that the commonest assumptions about Islam by Westerners of his own day were quite false. Although accurate knowledge of Islam spread more widely and quickly in the crusading era, distinctions clearly have to be drawn between the amount and quality of information possessed by the educated elite and the illiterate masses in medieval Europe at any one time, as well as between the 'average' levels of knowledge which existed at different periods. Any future study of this fascinating and important subject should be particularly sensitive to these problems.

[35] The image of the Saracen presented in vernacular, popular literature, however, remained stable for centuries, and may be more a matter of genre than of period; cf. above, n. 2.

10

WILLIAM AND THE *NOCTES ATTICAE*

UNTIL RECENTLY, WILLIAM'S florilegium of extracts from classical and patristic sources, the *Polyhistor*, attracted little attention. Now, however, that florilegia are seen to be illuminating cultural documents, not merely quarries for rare texts or useful readings, the *Polyhistor* has been edited, and some of the extracts in it discussed.[1] L. D. Reynolds, for instance, has shown that William was the first person after late antiquity to know the complete correspondence of Seneca, which circulated in two parts. William included excerpts from both parts in the *Polyhistor*, and his principle of selection was characteristically individual: he was more attracted by Seneca's wit than by his moralistic or edificatory utterances. This is no more than a reflection of the purpose of the *Polyhistor* as a whole. It is above all a collection of 'dicta et facta memorabilia', considerations of style and moral instruction being secondary though by no means absent.[2]

In this chapter I wish to draw attention to another set of extracts in the *Polyhistor*, this time from the *Noctes Atticae* of Aulus Gellius.[3] Gellius was not a common author in early Europe. In the ninth century his work was known, in part, to Lupus of Ferrières, but in the twelfth century a sizeable group of (mostly English) literati was familiar with it, and it passed into

---

[1] Stubbs was the first to tentatively identify the *Polyhistor* as a work of William's: GR I, pp. cxli–cxlii. The attribution was proved by James in *Two Ancient English Scholars*, pp. 18–19, 26–29. For the edition (PH) see the Abbreviations. Studies of extracts in it are James, op. cit.; Reynolds, *The Medieval Tradition of Seneca's Letters*, pp. 102–3; F. Granger (ed.), *Vitruvii De Architectura Libri Decem* (London, Loeb ed., 2 vols, 1931–4), II, p. xli.

[2] Reynolds, pp. 115, 117, 120, 122–3. William explains his principles of selection in the introduction (PH, p. 37), and in some of his authorial interventions.

[3] All references below to the text of Gellius are to the edition of P. K. Marshall (Oxford, 2 vols, 1968).

several well-known florilegia.[4] Surviving manuscripts of the *Noctes Atticae* confirm the impression that between these centuries Gellius seems to have suffered almost complete oblivion. Like Seneca's letters, the *Noctes* circulated in two sections after late antiquity: books 1–7, and 9–20, the contents of book 8 having been lost early on. Lupus knew only the later section; William, a generation earlier than John of Salisbury, knew both parts of the text, though whether complete or in the form of excerpts is less easy to determine. William is to our knowledge the first man since late antiquity to know the complete text of Seneca's letters; in the case of Gellius only the compiler of the TY florilegium may have known both parts of the textual tradition before William. William's extracts, moreover, are numerous, of reasonable length, normally verbatim and textually valuable.

The Gellius section in the *Polyhistor* opens with an introductory passage from Augustine:[5]

> Agellius Noctium defloraturus Atticarum, sentenciam beati Augustini quam in ix. libro De Ciuitate Dei honori eius dedit non pretermittam ... [Here follows an extract in Augustine from *N.A.* 19. 1] ... Hec Augustinus. Nunc audi Agellium.

This extract suggests that William did not know book 19 of the *Noctes* at first hand. In both manuscripts of the *Polyhistor* it is followed by two stories which do not come from Gellius. They read as follows:

> Inter mundi mirabilia est Neapoli olla uitrea ingens, digitalis grossitudinis os habens, in qua domus erea continetur, cuius ostiolum apertum est et nidus in medio domus ouumque anserino grossius in medio nidi. Quod si tangi posset per angustias ostioli ingredi non posset. Querat ergo qui potest quomodo intrauerit?
>
> In ultima Britannia quam Arthurus obtinuit precipua ferri materia est, sed aqua ferro uiolencior, quippe temperamento eius ferrum acrius redditur, nec ullum apud eos ferrum probatur, quod non fluuio Calibi tinguatur unde et finitum gladium eiusdem Arthurii Caliburh dicunt.[6]

---

[4] Apart from William, in the twelfth century he was known to John of Salisbury, Ralph of Diss (drawing partly on the *Polyhistor*), Walter Map and Gerald of Wales (both probably at second hand), and possibly to Peter Helias and Adam du Petit-Pont. He was included in the so-called TY anthology (of which the earliest manuscript is from Salisbury cathedral), the *Florilegium Angelicum* and *Florilegium Gallicum*. See Martin, 'John of Salisbury's Manuscripts of Frontinus and of Gellius', pp. 1–26. An outline of Gellius's *fortuna* is given by Marshall in *Texts and Transmission*, pp. 176–180. See also B. Smalley, *English Friars and Antiquity in the early Fourteenth Century* (Oxford, 1960), pp. 86, 92, 104n, 105, 117–8, 153, 232, 313, 349–50, for the use of Gellius in the later middle ages.

[5] PH, pp. 61–2.

[6] ibid., p. 62.

William's historical sense was too sharp for us to suppose that he really mistook these for the work of Gellius; nor is their homespun Latin at all in his vein. I think that they are interpolations, made between William's death and the date of the surviving manuscripts, both early fourteenth-century.[7] The closely related readings of the manuscripts suggest that they depend upon the same exemplar, and it is clear that this exemplar was imperfect in many ways.

After this follow 28 extracts from *Noctes Atticae* books 1–3, 5, 9–13, 15–16, in fairly random order. William also mentions but does not quote seven further passages from the same books.[8] In the light of this distribution, and of the prefatory passage from St Augustine, one imagines that William's exemplar was a copy of, or excerpts from the *Noctes* books 1–7, 9–16 at least, and perhaps 17–18.

William's extracts provide worthwhile testimony to the text of Aulus Gellius. For the second part of the *Noctes*, books 9–20, his exemplar seems to have belonged to the γ manuscripts O, X, π and N, with contaminations from the δ class, especially Q. His exemplar probably dated from no earlier than the eleventh century. It was not directly related to any of the extant manuscripts, although sharing a number of readings with π, written in France in 1170. For books 1–7, the earliest extant manuscripts of which are twelfth-century, he is a more important witness. His exemplar (or this part of it) was evidently closely related to P, a French manuscript from the second half of the century, but William's manuscript, which must have been earlier, was evidently better. It seems likely that P and William's exemplar derived from a common ancestor, probably continental.

Another apparently copious quoter of Gellius in the twelfth century was William's fellow-countryman and younger contemporary, John of Salis-

---

[7] The second of these stories is also repeated by Ralph of Diss in his *Abbreviationes Chronicorum: Radulfi de Diceto Opera Historica* I, p. 96. Ralph knew the *Polyhistor*; see above, n. 6.

[8] PH, pp. 64–5: 'Ista que posui Agellius se sumpsisse affirmat ex ignotis nobis auctoribus, Quadrigario, Higino, Catone, Herodoto. Hiis autem supersedeo que de recencioribus mutuatus est: de Valerio reconciliacionem Publii Scipionis cum Tiberio Gracco, Cresi filio muto uocem datam, iudicium a Dolabella dilatum de muliere que confiteretur occisos a se uirum et filium, Sicinium Romanum Achillem uocatum, de Plinio esse homines effascinantes et esse alios qui uidendo interimant Marsicorum scienciam; nam de taciturnitate Papirii pueri Macrobium Saturnaliorum narrasse quis nesciat? Proinde illa ponam qui alibi me legisse non recolo'. The references are to 12. 7, 12. 8, 2. 11, 5. 9. 1–3, 16. 11. 1, 9. 4. 7 and 1. 23.

bury. Apart from four alleged quotations in the *Metalogicon*, all of John's Gellius references are to be found in his *Policraticus*. Webb's *Index Auctorum* lists no fewer than 45 of them, but to take this figure at its face value creates an inflated impression of John's real acquaintance with Gellius. Nine of the alleged references are brief and vague, and Webb has cited Gellius in his notes only by way of comparison.[9] The supposed reference to *N.A.* 1. 9. 1–5 is a mere commonplace also cited in the *Metalogicon*, and, later in the century, by Richard of Devizes in his chronicle.[10] Another four brief references could come either from Gellius or, in each case more probably, from Macrobius, Valerius Maximus or Isidore.[11] Yet another three, as Webb points out, are really from Macrobius who in turn derived them from Gellius;[12] and another three supposedly direct references to *N.A.* 5. 5 and 15. 2 are really from Macrobius, *Sat.* 2. 2. 1 and 2. 8. 4.[13] Two more of Webb's references are ascribed by John himself to Gellius, but are not found there.[14] This leaves us with altogether eighteen genuine quotations.[15] Passing to Webb's notes to the *Metalogicon*, we find that the reference to *N.A.* 1. 10. 14 in *Met.* I. 15 is really from Macrobius, *Sat.*, 1. 5. 2, while that to 1. 9 in II. 6 is the same commonplace found in the *Policraticus* and Richard of Devizes.[16] The reference to 13. 25. 21 in the same chapter is vague and doubtful,[17] and that to 16. 2. 1 in III. 10, although John cites 'Agellius'

---

[9] *N.A.* 1. 2. 2 (not 1. 22. 2 as Webb in his *Index*), *Policr.* I, p. 120 line 27; 1. 5. 1, *Policr.* II, p. 330. 31; 3. 12. 2, *Policr.* II, p. 253. 7; 5. 17, *Policr.* I, p. 55. 15; 12. 2. 14, *Policr.* II, p. 318. 24; 15. 1. 4, *Policr.* II, p. 197. 1–2; 15. 24, *Policr.* I, p. 16. 20; 17. 12, *Policr.* I, p. 122. 17; 20. 5. 1–13, *Policr.* II, p. 112. 18.

[10] *Metal.*, p. 69; *The Chronicle of Richard of Devizes*, ed. and trans. J. Appleby (London, 1963), p. 2.

[11] 1. 9. 12, *Policr.* I, p. 249. 30; 3. 10, *Policr.* I, p. 68. 17; 14. 1. 1ff, *Policr.* I, p. 53. 9; 17. 14. 4, *Policr.* II, p. 299. 4.

[12] 1. 10. 4, *Policr.* II, p. 293. 22; 1. 15. 9, *Policr.* II, p. 310. 17; 13. 11. 2, *Policr.* II, p. 293. 22.

[13] *Policr.* II, p. 54. 23–4; II, p. 291. 15–16; II, p. 291. 21, 25–6.

[14] 18. 2. 13 (? – Webb's suggestion), *Policr.* I, p. 133. 2–3; 19. 1. 4–20 (?), *Policr.* II, p. 112. 18.

[15] 1. 8. 3–6, *Policr.* II, p. 65. 1; 1. 13. 10–13, *Policr.* II, p. 30. 30; 1. 14, *Policr.* I, p. 311. 1; 1. 17, *Policr.* I, p. 327. 16, II, p. 78. 38; 1. 26. 5–9, *Policr.* I, p. 265. 11; 2.2. 1–10, *Policr.* I, p. 261. 1; 3. 6, *Policr.* I, p. 303. 11; 3. 8, *Policr.* I, p. 311. 27; 5. 10, *Policr.* I, p. 337. 10; 5. 14. 5–28, *Policr.* I, p. 361. 21; 9. 3. 2–5, *Policr.* I, p. 255. 22; 9. 4. 7–8, *Policr.* I, p. 345. 10; 10. 8. 1–3, *Policr.* II, p. 30. 6; 10. 10, *Policr.* II, p. 30. 17; 11. 9. 2, *Policr.* I, p. 324. 30; 12. 7, *Policr.* I, p. 272. 20; 12. 12, *Policr.* I, p. 346. 25; 13. 8. 3–4, *Policr.* I, p. 257. 9.

[16] See above, n. 11.

[17] 'Procedo itaque, quoniam homo obtusioris ingenii sum, et cui fides est in auditu; cf. *N.A.* 13. 25. 21: 'Ceterum quis tam obtunso ingeniost ...' ('ingenio' some MSS): cf. the alternative possibilities listed by Martin, p. 25.

for it, is summary enough to suggest an intermediate source.[18] As mentioned, John quotes 'Agellius' wrongly on two occasions in the *Policraticus*, and he assigns one of his genuine quotations to Frontinus, another to Pliny.[19] Little reliance, it seems, can be placed on his naming of his sources. John's certainly direct, verbatim quotations from Gellius, then, are eighteen in number, all in the *Policraticus*. They are useful in establishing the text of the *Noctes Atticae*, and have been employed by its latest editors.

What is astonishing, however, is that all of these passages except one are found in William's *Polyhistor*. The exception is *N.A.* 12. 7, cited but not quoted by William. Two other passages quoted by both authors are extended by John; he gives 1. 17. 5–6 as well as 1. 17. 4 quoted by William, and adds a sentence not found in the *Polyhistor* to 10. 8. Nonetheless there is a remarkable correspondence between the series of passages quoted by the two writers, and this applies also to the readings shared by the sixteen passages which they have in common.[20] Many of the differences between their readings are not significant, given the fact that the two surviving manuscripts of the *Polyhistor* are late, corrupt, and dependent upon the same exemplar, also probably late and certainly corrupt. The *Policraticus*, on the other hand, is preserved in early and authoritative manuscripts. Examples of such insignificant variations are words omitted by William, inversions of Gellius's and John's word order in the *Polyhistor*, and differences such as 'at' or 'et' for 'atque', or 'nec' for 'neque'. Conversely, disagreements of John against both William and Gellius are not significant; they merely suggest that John was not quoting verbatim. Variants which *are* significant are: agreements between William and John against Gellius or a number of Gellius manuscripts, and agreements of either John or William with Gellius. Taking these considerations into account, of 155 readings which vary between Gellius, John and William, about 73 between John and William are not significant. Some 16 differences are important. Against these, there are 69 cases in which William and John agree, either against the text of Gellius, or against the readings of a number of other manuscripts. As with the passages themselves, these readings amount to a striking correspondence. How is it to be explained?

[18] *Metal.*, p. 158. 18: 'Vt enim est apud Agellium: Qui in talibus plus uel minus respondet quam quaeratur ab eo, lineam recte disputandi ignorat aut dissimulat'; cf. *N.A.* 16. 2. 1: 'Legem esse aiunt disciplinae dialecticae, si de quapiam re quaeratur disputeturque atque ibi quid rogere, ut respondeas, tum ne amplius quid dicas, quam id solum, quod es rogatus, aut aias aut neges; eamque legem qui non seruent et aut plus aut aliter, quam sunt rogati respondeant, existumantur indoctique esse disputandique morem atque rationem non tenere'. John's version cannot even be termed an accurate summary of Gellius.
[19] See above n. 15; *N.A.* 1. 13.10–13 is accredited to Frontinus in *Policr.* II, p. 30. 29–30, 10. 8. 1–3 to Pliny in *Policr.* II, p. 30. 6.
[20] See below, Appendix II.

Since William was dead by the time the *Policraticus* was written (c.1159) he could not have been dependent upon John. Neither was John directly dependent upon the *Polyhistor*, as indicated by his few additional passages, and those readings which he shares with Gellius against William. The most obvious explanation is that both authors were drawing upon the same pre-existing Gellius florilegium, and there is other evidence to prove that this was so.

Oxford, Bodleian Library MS Lat. class. d. 39 (formerly London, Sion College Arc. L. 40.2/L. 21), now given the siglum L, is an English *Sammelhandschrift*, its exact provenance uncertain.[21] I have shown above that it was copied from a single manuscript of the same contents, made by or for William, who annotated it, and who may have compiled some of the individual pieces in it.[22] The last seven folios (ff. 153–9) contain a set of 28 Gellius extracts.[23] No less than 21 of these are in William's *Polyhistor*, and a further five were known but not quoted by him. This, plus the fact that some of the other extracts in L are longer than their equivalents in the *Polyhistor*, shows that the *Polyhistor* was not the source for L's florilegium or its lost exemplar. Neither was William dependent upon this exemplar, for he gives seven quotations from Gellius not found in L. The extracts in L are nearly all whole chapters, whereas William often drops the sentences of comment with which Gellius usually rounds off each story or chapter. On the other hand, in no case is an extract in L briefer than its equivalent in the *Polyhistor*. The relationship between the L collection and John of Salisbury is similar. It has fourteen quotations not in the *Policraticus*, and John has four not in L. In three cases where John adds extra sentences to an extract also in William, L gives the same sentences. With these exceptions, passages common to L, John and/or William begin and end at similar points in the text, and have strikingly similar readings which sometimes set them apart from all other Gellius manuscripts. An example of extreme eccentricity shared by all three sources and not found elsewhere is at *N.A.* 13. 8. 3–4, where they all in identical fashion invert the word order and summarize slightly.[24] In passages common to William and L appear only twelve disagreements as against some 43 cases of significant identity, and the variants may all, I think, be explained in terms of scribal errors and contaminations in the transmission of the *Polyhistor* or the L extracts. L itself abounds in less important *lapsus calami*.

[21] Fully described in Ker, *Medieval Manuscripts in British Libraries*, I, pp. 278–9. He points out that it presumably has some relationship to a manuscript with the same main contents listed in the early fourteenth-century library catalogue from Christ Church Canterbury, although L does not have the usual Canterbury press-mark.

[22] See above, pp. 140–154.

[23] Listed and assigned alphabetical letters by Ker, op. cit., who however omits one passage and conflates two others. For a revised list see below, pp. 192–3.

[24] See below, Appendix II.

A comparison of passages common to William, John and L is also instructive. There are twelve such passages, and a collection of them yields the following results. L agrees ten times with William against John, in four of these cases agreeing also with the text of Gellius. L agrees 39 times with John against William, 34 times also with Gellius. L agrees in 27 cases with both John and William against Gellius, and nine times with Gellius against both of the others. These figures do not suggest that L is especially closely related to John, but rather that John is on the average closer to the text of Gellius than William, and L closer than either.[25]

There are some correspondences in the order of the passages as well as in readings. Thus John follows his quotation from *N.A.* 1. 14 with one from 3. 8 because they both refer to Fabricius.[26] William does the same, presumably for the same reason. Furthermore, William's first three quotations, all from *N.A.* 9, are the first two and fourth in L. Thereafter L goes on through books 9–16, then returns to eight extracts which proceed in order through books 1–2.[27] Here the collection ends, although there can be little doubt that its ultimate source continued on to book 7. I say 'ultimate source' and not 'exemplar' deliberately, for the collection does not break off abruptly, but is followed, in the same hand, by the poem *Cesar tantus eras*.[28] Presumably the scribe went no further with the Gellius florilegium because such was the condition of his exemplar. William's own order is fairly random after his first three passages, except for the occasional thematic connection, but again his extracts 17 and 18 correspond to L's extracts 6 and 7. It is also significant that both he, L and John quote from the same books, and none of the three go beyond book 16. We have already suggested that William's exemplar may not have gone further than this.

There is one further witness to the Gellius florilegium which lies behind the quotations in William, John and L. Oxford, Bodleian Library MS Rawl. G. 139 (K), was recently identified as having been written at Malmesbury under William's supervision.[29] Its main contents are Cicero, *Partitiones Oratoriae* and *De Officiis*, and pseudo-Quintilian, *Declamationes Maiores XIX*. On ff. 152v, 153v–154v, originally blank leaves, nine extracts from Gellius, books 3 and 5, were copied in an informal, continental hand not much later than those responsible for the main contents. Seven of these

---

[25] These readings are given in Table II of my earlier article, 'William of Malmesbury, John of Salisbury and the *Noctes Atticae*', *Hommages à André Boutemy*, ed. G. Cambier (*Collection Latomus* 145, Brussels, 1976), pp. 375–81.

[26] *Policr.* I, pp. 311–2.

[27] The position of 13. 8 after 16. 15 is the only anomaly; as there is no other quotation from books 13 or 14 between those from books 12 and 15, the probability is that the scribe made an omission which he then rectified.

[28] This version is not recorded in H. Walther, *Alphabetisches Verzeichnis des Versanfänge mittellateinischer Dichtungen* (Göttingen, 2nd edn, 1965), no. 2287. See above, p. 141.

[29] See above, p. 86.

extracts are also found in the *Polyhistor*, four in the *Policraticus*. Again the extracts in K are closer to the text of Gellius than either William's or John's. What is particularly interesting is that these extracts are obviously complementary to those in L; that is, they constitute the remainder of the Gellius florilegium available to William and John, which was omitted, for whatever reason, from L's exemplar. The fact that all Gellius passages quoted or mentioned by William and John are found in L and K, that all LK extracts are at least as long as their equivalents in the *Polyhistor* and *Policraticus*, and that two passages in L are not found elsewhere, indicates that LK is complete. This strengthens the other arguments which I have advanced for connecting L's contents with Malmesbury and William. The order of the Gellius extracts in L suggests that the original florilegium was taken either from a Gellius manuscript in which the two main parts of the text had been bound in reverse order, or from two separate manuscripts of each part which the excerptor used in reverse order, either because that was the sequence in which he obtained the exemplars, or because in them the books were not numbered. The combined testimony of William, John, K and L enables the contents of the original florilegium and their order to be reconstructed thus:

1.	*N.A.* 9. 3. 2–5	L Wm1 Joh
2.	*N.A.* 9. 4. 7–8	L Wm Joh
3.	*N.A.* 9. 11	L Wm2
4.	*N.A.* 9. 13. 7–20	L Wm3
5.	*N.A.* 9. 16. 5–7	L Wm9
6.	*N.A.* 10. 8	L Wm17 Joh
7.	*N.A.* 10. 10	L Wm18 Joh
8.	*N.A.* 10. 18. 3–7	L Wm25
9.	*N.A.* 10. 27	L Wm19
10.	*N.A.* 11. 9. 2	L Wm13 Joh
11.	*N.A.* 12. 7	L Wm Joh
12.	*N.A.* 12. 8	L Wm
13.	*N.A.* 12. 12	L Wm20 Joh
14.	*N.A.* 15. 6. 3	L
15.	*N.A.* 15. 16	L Wm22
16.	*N.A.* 15. 22. 1–2	L
17.	*N.A.* 15. 31	L Wm23
18.	*N.A.* 16. 11	L Wm7
19.	*N.A.* 16. 15	L Wm
20.	*N.A.* 13. 8. 3–4	L Wm14 Joh
21.	*N.A.* 1. 8. 3–6	L Wm12 Joh
22.	*N.A.* 1. 13. 10–13	L Wm21 Joh
23.	*N.A.* 1. 14	L Wm5 Joh
24.	*N.A.* 1. 17	L Wm10 Joh
25.	*N.A.* 1. 19	L Wm24
26.	*N.A.* 1. 23. 4–13	L Wm

27.	*N.A.* 1. 26. 5–9	L Wm15 Joh
28.	*N.A.* 2. 2. 1–10	L Wm16 Joh
29.	*N.A.* 2. 11	K Wm
30.	*N.A.* 3. 6	K Wm11 Joh
31.	*N.A.* 3. 7. 1–19	K Wm4
32.	*N.A.* 3. 8	K Wm6 Joh
33.	*N.A.* 3. 9	K Wm27
34.	*N.A.* 5. 2	K Wm26
35.	*N.A.* 5. 14. 5–28	K Wm28 Joh
36.	*N.A.* 5. 9. 1–3	K Wm
37.	*N.A.* 5. 10. 4–16	K Wm8 Joh

Before proceeding with the subject of William's relationship to the florilegium, we need to examine the possibility that John knew a complete text of Gellius. There are two cases which suggest that this might have been so. Firstly, in their rendition of *N.A.* 5. 10, both William and John have 'Pitagoras' for Gellius's 'Protagoras', John commenting 'Nec multum refert ad propositum Pitagoras an Protagoras, sicut Quintiliano placet et Agellio, litigauerit'.[30] The simplest translation of this, of course, is: 'Nor does it matter whether the litigant was Pythagoras, or Protagoras as Quintilian and Gellius have it'. But it is possible, on the reasonable presumption that John knew that the preceding passage was from Gellius, that his intended meaning is: 'Nor does it matter whether the litigant was Pythagoras, as Gellius has it, or Protagoras, as Quintilian'. Or could it be that John, name-dropping, has confused his authors, as he seems apt to do, except that this time he was coincidentally right? The other case consists of verbal correspondences between the prologues to the *Policraticus* and *Attic Nights*, first noticed by Hertz and discussed recently by Janet Martin.[31] Here there seems little doubt that John must have had Gellius's text in mind. It is possible that he had had access to a complete text when he was in France, and perhaps retained memories of it. What he had at hand in England, however, was the florilegium.

But to return to William. Given the strong connection of the original florilegium with Malmesbury and William, the question must arise: did he obtain it ready-made from elsewhere, or did he make it himself from a more complete text?

First it ought to be indicated that the florilegium can hardly have been made much before c.1100. The extract from *N.A.* 16. 11 in L ends with a postscript by the florilegium's compiler: '... magna hominum dementia inaudita et incomparabilis stulticia qui armorum uiolentia uento putabant resistere, quem Deus de thesauro suo disposuit producere'. The rhyming

---

[30] *Policr.* II, p. 338. 14–15.
[31] M. Hertz, *A. Gellii Noctes Atticae* (Berlin, 2 vols, 1883–5), II, p. xxviii; Martin, pp. 11–12.

prose in which this comment is written first came into vogue in the early twelfth century.[32] Now let us consider the case for William obtaining a pre-existing florilegium from elsewhere. The first point to make is that William gives no indication, in any of his works, that he knew any more Gellius than was contained in the florilegium.[33] In itself this is not a strong negative point, since William does not refer to Gellius at all other than in the *Polyhistor*. The same is true of several much commoner texts, such as Seneca, *De Beneficiis*.[34] There is, in fact, one piece of evidence which suggests that William might have known more of Gellius than was contained in the florilegium. In the excerpt from *N.A.* 3. 8 in the *Polyhistor* William refers to 'Quadrigarius in tercio *Annalium*'. Now the *Annales* are not named by Gellius at this point, but he does name them in 3. 7. 21, a passage not included in the florilegium. However they are also named by Frontinus in the *Stratagems*, of which William had a copy.[35] Secondly, P, a French mauscript of the later twelfth century containing books 1–7 of the *Noctes Atticae*, bears indications that its exemplar had been marked up for excerpting. In seven places the words 'hucusque' have been inserted in the text.[36] It will be remembered that an ancestor of this manuscript suppplied the excerpts from the early books of Gellius used in the florilegium known to William and John of Salisbury. In six of the seven cases 'hucusque' corresponds to the end of an extract in K; in the seventh, which comes at the end of 4. 5. 6, there is no corresponding extract. At the end of 2. 20 in P is 'hinc sursum', which may or may not represent marking-up for excerpting, but again there is no corresponding extract in K. Curiously enough, 4. 5. 6 is quoted by the St Albans chroniclers Roger of Wendover and Matthew Paris, writing in the first half of the next century.[37] However, since they do not quote any other passages from the florilegium, it is hard to know what to make of this. Nonetheless, there can be little doubt that P preserves the remnants of marking-up for the making of part of the florilegium used by William and John. Now since P is French (so the argument appears to run), so, probably, was its exemplar, and therefore the excerptor must have worked in that country. William, so far as we know, never left England, and therefore cannot have been the excerptor.[38] But this argument too is not

---

[32] R. W. Southern (ed. and trans.) *The Life of St Anselm by Eadmer* (London, 1962), pp. xxv–xxxiv.

[33] Marshall, Martin and Rouse, 'Clare College MS. 26 and the Circulation of Aulus Gellius 1–7 in Medieval England and France', pp. 372–3.

[34] PH, pp. 139–143.

[35] *Strat.* 4. 4. 2. See above, p. 87.

[36] Martin, pp. 8–9. They are sometimes noted in Marshall's edition: I, pp. 55. 22, 84. 12, 87. 2.

[37] Marshall, Martin and Rouse, 'Clare College MS. 26 and the Circulation of Aulus Gellius 1–7 in Medieval England and France', p. 383 and n. 74.

[38] Martin, p. 17.

strong. We have already seen that the second part of William's copy of John the Scot's *Periphyseon* shared an ancestor with a copy made at Mont St Michel later in the century,[39] and other extant manuscripts came to Malmesbury from the continent, probably acquired by William.[40] It appears, in fact, that his exemplars were more often continental than not, and that sometimes they were available on loan, to be returned after copying. The markings in P, therefore, are no bar to William's possible activity as excerptor, and neither is the apparent absence of early Gellius manuscripts from England.

At least two positive arguments can be mounted in favour of William as the florilegium's compiler. First of all, William preferred to have at his disposal complete texts, especially of classical works, actively seeking them out and in some cases putting them together from more than one incomplete manuscript. His use of the word 'defloraturus' at the head of the Gellius excerpts in the *Polyhistor* seems inappropriate if all he did was recopy into it most of a pre-existing florilegium made by someone else. Finally, we have the facts that the two manuscripts containing the florilegium are both connected with Malmesbury and William, and that the florilegium circulated in England but not, so far as we know, on the continent. Neither of these arguments is conclusive, and it is not clear whether in combination they outweigh those against William's role as compiler of the florilegium. But they are consistent with what we know of his scholarly habits of mind and modus operandi.

---

[39] See above, pp. 90–1.
[40] Ibid., pp. 79–80

APPENDIX I:

HANDLIST OF WORKS
KNOWN TO WILLIAM AT FIRST HAND

ABBO OF FLEURY, *Passio S. Edmundi*: GR I, p. 264ff; GP, pp. 144, 153ff, 249. 'Accipe astrolabii quartam'. This is one of a collection of astronomical works copied into Oxford, Bodl. Libr. MS Auct. F. 3. 14, ff. 153–164v, from a single source. The collection is headed 'Incipiunt regulae de astrolabio' and consists of: (i) Prol. and text of *De Utilitate Astrolabii*, variously ascribed to Gerbert, Hermann the Lame etc. (TKI 513, 1236), ending with the last chapter of Bk. I as PL 143. 389–404; (ii) *De Horologio secundum Alkoran* (TKI 654; N. Bubnov, *Gerberti Opera Mathematica* [Berlin, 1899], pp. xix, xli; Millas Vallicrosa, *Assaig*, pp. 288–90); (iii) 'Si fuerit nobis propositum inuenire' (TKI 1449; Millas Vallicrosa, pp. 324–7); (iv) 'Accipe astrolabii quartam et tertiam vi. hora' (TKI 16; Bubnov, *Gerberti Opera Mathematica*, p.lvi; Millas Vallicrosa, pp. 304–8); (v) *Compositio Astrolapsus* (TKI 801; Millas Vallicrosa, pp. 322–4). These works, in the same order, are known in only one other MS, Avranches, Bibl. Mun. 235, ff. 58–69v, late twelfth-century, from Mont St. Michel. Millas Vallicrosa printed them from this MS, and collation with his edition shows that William used the same exemplar as the scribe of the Avranches MS. It has recently been suggested that at least some of the items common to the two MSS came originally from Reims: Contreni, 'The Study and Practice of Medicine in northern France during the Reign of Charles the Bald', pp. 43–54, esp. p. 45.

ADALBOLD, *Ep. ad Gerbertum*: GR I, pp. 195–6; see below under GERBERT.

ADELARD, *Vita S. Dunstani*: VD.

ADO OF VIENNE, *Chronicon*. See above, p. 150.

AELFRIC, *Vita S. Ethelwoldi, Abbreviatio Passionis S. Edmundi*, unspecified translations. See above, p. 45.

AGROECIUS, *Ars Grammatica*. See above, p. 61.

ALCUIN, Letters: see above, ch. 8; *De Orthographia*: above, p. 61; *Comm. super Ecclesiasten*: above, pp. 42–3; *Dialectica, Rhetorica*: GR I, p. 68. Here William says of Alcuin 'dialectica et rhetorica et etiam astronomia probe composuit'. The third item presumably refers to one or more of Alcuin's lengthy letters on the subject (126, 149, or most probably 171 in MGH Epist. 4, p. 282). William could not have inferred the existence of Alcuin's works on dialectic and rhetoric from his collection of the latter's correspondence.

ALDHELM, *De Laudibus Virginitatis*, Letters, *Carmen de Virginitate*, *Enigmata*, ?Sermons. For all of these see above, pp. 44–5.

ALEXANDER OF CANTERBURY, *Dicta Anselmi*. See above, p. 47.

ALFRED, *Handboc*: GR I, p. 132; GP, pp. 333, 336; cf. R. M. Wilson, *The Lost Literature of Medieval England* (London, 2nd edn, 1970), pp. 62–3, 66–7. Translations of Gregory, *Reg. Past.*: GR I, pp. 132–3; Orosius and Bede, *Hist. Eccl.*: ibid. p. 132; Boethius, *De Consol.*: ibid.; GP, p. 177.

AMALARIUS, *De Ecclesiasticis Officiis*. See above, p. 43.

AMBROSE, *De Obitu Theodosii*, *De Officiis*, *Hexaemeron*, *De Virginitate*, *De Poenitentia*, Letters. For all these see above, p. 40.

AMPHILOCHIUS, *Vita S. Basilii*: Oxford, Bodl. Libr. MS Arch. Seld. B. 16, f. 175.

ANASTASIUS BIBLIOTHECARIUS, *Passio S. Demetrii*: See above, p. 150; and for others of his works see below under JOHN THE SCOT.

Anglo-Saxon Chronicle. See above, p. 70.

Annales Mettenses Priores. See above, pp. 146–7.

ANSELM, *Monologion*, *Proslogion*, (Gaunilo, *Pro Insipientem*), *Responsio*, *De Concordia Praescientiae*, *De Libero Arbitrio*, *De Incarnatione Verbi*, *De Conceptu Virginali*, *Unde Malum*, *De Veritate*, *De Grammatico*: all of these are in London, Lambeth Palace Library 224, for which see above, pp. 46, 87–9; *Cur Deus Homo*: ibid. and GP, pp. 77, 98; *De Processione Spiritus Sancti*: Lambeth MS 224 and GP, p. 100; *Orationes, Meditationes*: see above, pp. 46–7; Letters: Lambeth 224, GP, p. 260.

ANSELM the younger?, *Miracula B.V.M.*: *De Miraculis B.V.M.* (Carter, 'The Historical Content of William of Malmesbury's Miracles of the Virgin Mary', p. 137).

?APULEIUS, *De Platone, De Mundo, De Deo Socratis*. These works are found, in that order, in the fourteenth-century MS BL Harl. 3969, not used by the editors of Apuleius. They form part of a collection of works on natural and moral philosophy which occupies ff. 63–105v, following and written in the same hand as the copies of William's *Polyhistor* and Grammatical Collection at ff. 1–62v. The collection consists of (i) Censorinus, *De Die Natali*, beginning imperfectly at 'reperiri aues que ante oua generata sint' (1. 4; ed. Hultsch, p. 7 lines 9–10), due to the excision of a leaf, ending at Fragm. 14, 8, 9 on f. 74v, after which another leaf is lacking; (ii) Apuleius, *De Platone*, beginning on f. 75 at 1, 8, 5 (ed. Beaujeu, p. 67), and ending at f. 83 with 'Explicit liber primus de secte platonica. Incipit secundus secundum Theophrastum'. The author's name is not found in the running title or elsewhere. Bk. II opens with the rubric 'Superius de naturali philosophia locutus est, amodo de philosophia morali'; (iii) Apuleius, *De Mundo*, untitled except as in the *incipit*, finishing on f. 91 with 'Explicit liber secundus de secte platonica'. In the margin of f. 83v, in the scribe's hand, is 'Nota quod hec sunt uerba in quinto libro Tusculanarum Disputacionum: "O philosophia indagatrix uirtutum, expultrixque uiciorum", non "excultrix" ut quidam dicunt'. The text of Apuleius at this point has 'expultrix', the only MS with this reading, which has been adopted by modern editors from the *Tusculans*. (iv) Apuleius, *De Deo*, ff. 91–96v, ending imperfectly due to the excision of a leaf. It is preceded by a paragraph on Apuleius and the *De Deo* headed 'Ex libro vij Augustini de Ciuitate Dei'. (v) The anon. *Phisiognomia* (TKI 538) composed in the fourth century and common from the twelfth century on; beginning imperfectly at f. 97, concluding at f. 105v, the end of a quire. A new hand then begins another work on f. 106, although the original hand returns near the end of the MS, which includes, among many works, the first and third Apuleius items again. BL Harl. 3969 was clearly copied from several exemplars, and this collection seems to have come from a single one of them, since the Apuleius items are tied together by their textual ancestry and rubrics. All five items on ff. 63–105v are connected palaeographically. It is the marginal note at f. 83v and the paragraph from Augustine at f. 91 which tie the collection to William, for these are very much in his manner (cf. above, p. 34). The scribe of this part of Harl. 3969 often copied marginal notes, evidently from his exemplars; one of those to the Grammatical Collection is clearly by William, and William certainly knew the *Tusculans* (above, p. 50). Only two other English MSS of Apuleius are known: CUL Ff. 3. 2 (c.1150, from Bury abbey) has only the *De Deo*, while Cambridge, Corpus Christi Coll. 71 (later twelfth-century, from St Albans) has the same three works as Harl. 3969, in the same order. These two MSS derive (the second with contaminations) from the early eleventh-century Leiden Voss. lat. Q. 10, and this proves to be also true of Harl. 3969. The Leiden MS contains the same three works of Apuleius in the same order, the first two untitled. The ascription of the *De Mundo* to Theophrastus in Harl. 3969 is explained by its derivation from the Leiden MS. *De Mund.* 289 reads 'Quare nos Aristotelen prudentissimum et doctissimum philosophorum et Theophrastum auctorem secuti ...', but the Leiden MS and its descendents, including Harl. 3969, omit '-re nos ... philosophorum'. Someone, then, faced with an anonymous work, had the intelligence to lift the name of Theophrastus from its text, and that might have been William; it is certainly typical of his philological insight.

?ASSER, *Vita Alfredi*. See above, pp. 69–70.

AUGUSTINE, *De Doctrina Christiana*: AbAm, p. 129; *De Civitate Dei*: PH, pp. 37, 95–101, and see above, pp. 51–2; *Confessiones*: PH, pp. 90–92 and above, p. 52; *De Trinitate*: PH, p. 93; *Contra Quinque Hereseos*: ibid., p. 37; *Contra Mendacium*: ibid., p. 89; *Contra Iulianum*: ibid., p. 93; *De Cura pro Mortuis*: ibid., pp. 93–4; *De Vita Beata*: ibid., p. 118; *De Natura et Origine Animae*: ibid., p. 136; *Enchiridion*: ibid., p. 93; *De Sermone Domini in Monte*: ibid., pp. 89–90; *De Consensu Evangelistarum*: ibid., p. 102; *Enarrationes in Psalmos*: AbAm, p. 148 etc.; *De Genesi ad Litteram*: PH, pp. 94–5; *De Fide et Operibus*: AbAm, p. 136; *De Quantitate Animae*: Farmer, 'William of Malmesbury's Commentary on Lamentations', p. 309 *(Defloratio Gregorii); Tractatus in Ioannem*: Comm. Lam., f. 70, AbAm, p. 136 etc.; *Contra Achademicos*: Comm. Lam., f. 82; *De Diversis Quaestionibus*: AbAm, p. 135 (Pfaff, 'The "Abbreviatio Amalarii" of William of Malmesbury', p. 86 and n. 24); Sermons: PH, p. 137, VD, p. 322; Letters: PH, pp. 92–3.

(Pseudo-) AUGUSTINE, *De Assumptione B.V.M* (PL 40. 1141–8): *De Miraculis B.V.M*, p. 57 (Carter, 'The Historical Content of William of Malmesbury's Miracles of the Virgin Mary', p. 133).

AULUS GELLIUS, *Noctes Atticae*. See above, ch. 10.

BEDE, *Historia Ecclesiastica*: GR and GP, passim; *Historia Abbatum*: GP, p. 328, GR I, pp. 51, 54; *Vita S. Cuthberti*: GP, p. 267; *De Temporibus, Ep. ad Wicthredum, De Temporum Ratione, De Natura Rerum*: Oxford, Bodl. Libr. Auct. F. 3. 14; *De*

Orthographia: see above, p. 61; *De Locis Sanctis*: GR II, p. 422; *In Sam.*: GR I, p. 59; *In Proverb.*: Oxford, Merton Coll. MS 181; *In Cant.*: ibid. and PH, p. 87; *In Esdram.*: AbAm, p. 157, and cf. p. 171 'Si quid commode ... dixit, referes gratiam Patri luminum, a Quo est largitio omnium bonorum', and CCSL 119A, p. 392 '... memoriae se sui Creatoris ac Largitoris omnium bonorum commendat. Et tu, summe Pater luminum, a Quo omne datum optimum et omne donum perfectum descendit ...'. *Expositio Actuum* and *Nomina Regionum*: see above, p. 181 n. 27; *De Tabern.*: AbAm, p. 159.

BERNARD, *Itinerarium*. See above, p. 69.

BOETHIUS, *De Consol. Philosophiae*: GR II, p. 167, *De Miraculis B.V.M.*, p. 88; theological tractates: ibid.; *De Arithmetica*: VD, p. 251 and n. 2; *In Aristotelis Categ.*, *In Aristotelis De Interpr.*: see above, p. 62. See below under *Elogia Boethii*.

BONIFACE, two letters. See above, p. 44.

Breviarium Alaricum, *Epitome Gaii* and *Sententiae Pauli*. William's copy, Oxford, Bodl. Libr. Arch. Seld. B. 16 (O) is described in Mommsen, *Theodosiani Libri XVI*, I, pp. lxv–lxvii, cxxxii. According to the editor, 'Oxoniensis liber fortasse inter eos, quos habemus, primum locum obtinet'. William's text contains readings which place it close to the lost archetype of Mommsen's 'classis melior', despite omissions, summarizations, and William's usual intelligent but unauthoritative corrections. His exemplar included additional matter (as in other MSS) from the *Constitutiones Sirmondianae* and the complete *Cod. Theodos.* Bk. I is lacking but renumbering was carried out from Bk. II, presumably by William, as this is the only extant MS in which this was done (although other, related MSS also begin incompletely). One of William's notes indicates, however, that he knew the original number of 16 books. Probably his exemplar retained the remains of Bk. I, which he omitted for the sake of neatness; I think it unnecessary to posit a complete copy of *Cod. Theodos.* in his exemplar, as in the second edition of Mommsen (I, p. cccl). At the end of the *Breviarium*, as declared in William's prefatory note, are the *Epitome Gaii* and *Sententiae Pauli*. These are found similarly in other *Breviarium* MSS and were presumably in William's exemplar. It has been suggested that that exemplar was continental (ibid.). It must of course have been earlier than its earliest extant descendant, which is of the seventh century: Mommsen, I, pp. lxx–lxxi; CLA, XI, no. 1637 (before 669?); see above, pp. 62–4.

CAESAR, *De Bello Gallico*, ?*De Bello Ciuili*. See above, p. 57.

(Pseudo-) CAESAR, *De Bello Alexandrino*. See above, p. 57.

Caesar tantus eras. See above, p. 141.

CALCIDIUS. See under PLATO.

(Pseudo-) CAPER, *De Orthographia*. See above, p. 61.

CASSIAN, *Collationes*. PH, pp. 137–8.

CASSIODORUS, *Institutes*: PH, p. 137, and above, p. 59; *Historia Tripartita*: GR II, p. 411; Comm. Lam., f. 20v; *De Orthographia*: see above, p. 61; *In Psalmos*: PH. p. 137. William evidently had a MS containing the well-known corpus of bibliographical works on early Christian literature (R. A. B. Mynors, *Cassiodori Institutiones* [Oxford, 1937], pp. xxxix–xlii): Cassiodorus, *Institutes*, *Decretum Gelasianum de Libris Recipiendis et non Recipiendis*, Jerome-Gennadius-Isidore, *De Viris Illustribus*, and Isidore, *De Ecclesiasticis Officiis* he certainly knew, leaving another three or four usual items for which we have no evidence. These and three more Isidorean works are in CUL Kk. 4. 6, for which see above, ch. 6.

CATO MINOR, *Disticha*: Comm. Lam., f. 46; HN, p. 21.

?CENSORINUS, *De Die Natali*. For the manuscript see above under APULEIUS. This item was probably present in the manuscript from which the scribe of BL Harl. 3969 copied the works of Apuleius, but of course this does not constitute a firm connection with William. For the descent of Censorinus see *Texts and Transmission*, pp. 48–50. All medieval copies – rare before the fourteenth century – seem to be descended from Köln, Dombibl. 166 (D) of the eighth century and Rome, Vat. lat. 4929 (V), derived from a copy of D but corrected from its exemplar. This MS was at Orleans from the late ninth century, and in the twelfth century was recopied a number of times. The text in BL Harl. 3969 shares significant readings with V, although sometimes improving upon it, probably by conjecture. Several manuscripts of Censorinus dating from the ninth to the fourteenth century have not yet been examined, so that the place of BL Harl. 3969 in the stemma cannot yet be accurately determined. (Two of these, not mentioned in *Texts and Transmission* or the editions, are listed in B. Munk-Olsen, *L'Etude des Auteurs Classiques Latins aux XIe et XIIe Siècles* I [Paris, 1982], p. 97). Certainly Censorinus was available in England before the Renaissance; Roger Bacon quotes him in his *Moralis Philosophia* (ed. E. Massa [Zürich, n.d.], pp. 61–2) and he is quoted among the calendrical notes in London, BL Roy. 7 D. xxv, ff. 55–69 (s. xii ex). A copy is recorded in the early fourteenth century library-catalogue of Lanthony priory (*Texts and Transmission*, p. 49).

CICERO, *De Senectute, De Natura Deorum, De Divinatione, De Fato, De Legibus, Academica Priora, De Paradoxis, De Officiis, De Amicitia*, transl. of the *Timaeus, Tusculan Disputations, (De Re Publica), (Hortensius), De Inventione, Partitiones Oratoriae, Catilines, Philippics, Pro Marcello, Pro Ligario?, Pro Rege Deiotaro?, Pro Milone?, Pro Plancio?, Pro Caelio?, Pro Sulla?, Pro Pompeio?, Pro Caecina?, Pro Cluentio?* See above, pp. 50–6. The queried items are in CUL MS Dd. 13. 2.

(Pseudo-) CICERO, *Ad Herennium*: see above, p. 55; *Invectiva in Sallustium?* CUL MS Dd. 13. 2.

CLAUDIAN, *In Rufinum*: VW, p. 3, GR II, p. 296; *De Bello Getico?*: GR I, p. 41.

Pseudo-Clementine Recognitions: GR I, p. 202.

Collectio Quesnelliana. See above, pp. 64–6.

COLMAN, *Vita S. Wulfstani.* See above, p. 45.

Compositio Astrolapsus. See above under 'Accipe astrolabii quartam'.

Continuatio Adonis. See above, p. 149.

CUTHBERT, *Epistola de Obitu Bedae.* See above, p. 16.

CYPRIAN, *De Idola quod non sint Dii*: PH, p. 78; *De Mortalitate*: ibid., and Comm. Lam., f. 44; *De Oratione Domini*: AbAm, p. 161; Letters: 63. 13 is quoted in ibid., p. 159.

'Dardanus ex Ioue et Electra'. See above, p. 57.

DARES, *De Excidio Troiae.* See above, p. 66.

DAVID SCOTUS, *Historia Expeditionis Henrici V*: See above, p. 69.

De Horologio secundum Alkoran. See above under 'Accipe astrolabii quartam'.

De Septem Miraculis Mundi ab Hominibus Facta (ed. H. Omont in *Bibl. de l'Ecole des Chartes*, 43 [1882], 40–59; extra MSS listed by Jones, *Bedae Pseudepigrapha*, pp. 8–9): PH, pp. 70–71.

De Utilitate Astrolabii. See above under 'Accipe astrolabii quartam'.

Decretum (Pseudo-) Gelasianum. Oxford, Bodl. Libr. Arch. Seld. B. 16, f. 11. And see above under CASSIODORUS.

(Pseudo-) DIONYSIUS. See below under JOHN THE SCOT.

DIONYSIUS EXIGUUS, *De Ratione Paschae, De Ciclo Annorum*: Oxford, Bodl. Libr. Auct. F. 3. 14.

DIOSCORIDES, *Materia Medica*: (TKI 888) PH, p. 60 line 34.

DOMINIC OF EVESHAM, *Miracula B.V.M.: De Miraculis B.V.M.* (Carter, 'The Historical Content of William of Malmesbury's Miracles of the Virgin Mary', p. 137); *Vita Wistani* (Macray, *Chronicon Abbatiae de Evesham*, pp. 325–37): GR I, pp. 263–4, GP, p. 297; *Vita Ecgwini*: I. 9 is quoted in GP, p. 384, and the forged Evesham privilege in it (I. 11) is included in William's edition of the *Liber Pontificalis* (above, p. 135), sharing readings with Dominic against the four other known versions. Book I of Dominic is now ed. M. Lapidge in *Analecta Bollandiana*, 96 (1978), 65–104. In his account of the founding of Evesham (GP, pp. 296–7) William follows neither Dominic nor Dominic's main source Byrhtferth.

EADMER OF CANTERBURY, *Vita S. Anselmi, Historia Novorum, Miracula S. Dunstani, De Excellentia B. Mariae, Vita S. Oswaldi.* See above, p. 73.

EDDI STEPHANUS, *Vita S. Wilfridi.* See above, p. 69.

EINHARD, *Vita Karoli.* See above, pp. 144, 147.

?*Elogia Boethii: De Miraculis B.V.M.*, p. 88 (Carter, 'The Historical Content of William of Malmesbury's Miracles of the Virgin Mary', p. 159 and n. 3).

ETHELWEARD, *Chronicon.* See above, p. 69.

ETHELWOLD, translation of the Benedictine Rule. See above, p. 45.

?EUCHERIUS, *Passio Acaunensium Martyrum* (Clavis, no. 490): GR I, p. 150.

(Pseudo-) EUCHERIUS, *De Situ Ierosolim* (Clavis, no. 2326): GR II, p. 422.

EUSEBIUS-RUFINUS-JEROME, *Historia Ecclesiastica*: GR II, pp. 435–6; Comm. Lam., ff. 20, 87, 105, 107v, and see above, p. 93.

EUTROPIUS, *Breviarium.* See above, p. 66.

FARICIUS OF ABINGDON, *Vita S. Aldhelmi.* See above, p. 74.

FERRANDUS, *Vita Fulgentii: De Miraculis B.V.M.*, p. 87.

FLORUS OF LYONS, *Contra Ioannis Scoti Erroneas Definitiones Liber.* See above, p. 43.

FRECULF OF LISIEUX, *Chronicon.* See above, p. 68.

FRITHEGOD, *Breviloquium Vitae Wilfridi.* See above, p. 69.

FRONTINUS, *Strategematicon.* See above, p. 87.

FULBERT OF CHARTRES, Letters and *Opuscula.* See above, p. 45; *Responsoria: De Miraculis B.V.M.*, p. 82 and n.; Sermons *de Nat. B.V.M.*: IV and V quoted in ibid., pp. 82, 112.

FULBERT 'PECCATOR', *Vita S. Aychadri* (BHL 182): Oxford, Bodl. Libr. Bodl. 852.

FULCHER OF CHARTRES, *Gesta Peregrinorum.* See above, p. 69.

FULCO, *Epistola ad Alfredum*: GR I, p. 130.

FULGENTIUS OF RUSPE, *De Fide ad Petrum, Serm. III.* See above, p. 42.

FULGENTIUS MYTHOGRAPHUS, *Met.* See above, p. 61

GENNADIUS,   *De Viris Illustribus*: Oxford, Bodl. Libr. Arch. Seld. B. 16, f. 11; Oriel Coll. 42, f. 90. And see above under CASSIODORUS.

GERBERT,   *Regulae de Abaco*: GR I, p. 195. And see above under ADAL-BOLD.

GILBERT CRISPIN,   *Vita Herluini*: GP, pp. 37–9. Gibson, *Lanfranc of Bec*, p. 222.

GILDAS,   *De Excidio Britanniae*. See above, p. 69.

Glosae Cantabr. in Martianum.   See above, p. 82.

GODFREY OF WINCHESTER,   Epigrams and Verses. See above, p. 71.

GOSCELIN OF ST BERTIN,   *Vita et Translatio S. Augustini*: GR II, p. 389: *Vita S. Letardi*: GP, p. 7; *Vita S. Edithae*: VD, p. 310; *Vita S. Laurentii*: GP, p. 6; *Vita S. Adriani, Vita S. Mildredae*: GP, p. 8; *Vita S. Edwardi Regis et Martyris*: GR I, pp. 181–6.

GREGORY,   *Dialogi, Regula Pastoralis, Moralia in Iob, Homiliae in Evangelia, Homiliae in Ezechielem*: see above, p. 41; *Registrum: De Miraculis B.V.M.*, p. 73.

(Pseudo-) GREGORY,   *Hom. de Poenitentia: Defloratio Gregorii* (Farmer, 'William of Malmesbury's Commentary on Lamentations', p. 309).

GREGORY OF TOURS,   *De Gloria Martyrum: De Miraculis B.V.M.*, p. 74; *De Gloria Confessorum*: ibid., p. 76.

GUITMUND OF AVERSA,   *De Corpore et Sanguine Domini*. See above, p. 46.

HATTO OF REICHENAU,   *Visio Wettini: De Miraculis B.V.M.*, pp. 101–4.

HEGESIPPUS,   *Iosephus Latinus*: GR II, p. 415.

HELPERIC,   *De Compoto* (TKI 299): Oxford, Bodl. Libr. Auct. F. 3. 14.

HERMANN THE ARCHDEACON,   *De Miraculis S. Edmundi*: GP, p. 155ff.

HILDEBERT OF LE MANS,   *Carmina Minora* 1–43: see above, pp. 71–2. *De Mysterio Missae*: AbAm, p. 171.

HILDUIN,   *Vita S. Dionysii*. See above, p. 124.

HINCMAR OF REIMS,   *Vita S. Remigii*. See above, p. 124.

?*Historia Francorum Senonensis*.   See above, pp. 151–2.

HONORIUS AUGUSTUDUNENSIS,   *Sigillum B. Mariae*: Oxford, Merton Coll. MS 181; *Speculum Ecclesiae: De Miraculis B.V.M.*, pp. 137–8. Although William's main source at this point is Dominic of Evesham, Carter in his thesis noted striking verbal parallels between William's story and Honorius's work but, presuming that the *Speculum* was written c.1150 or later, concluded that both authors were using a common source. However Honorius's career is now dated to the first part of the century, and the *Speculum* was apparently composed for the community of Christ Church Canterbury (Southern, *St Anselm and his Biographer*, pp. 211–7).

HORACE,   *Carmina, Epistolae, Ars Poetica, Satires*. See above, p. 49.

HUGH OF FLEURY,   *Historia Francorum*. See above, p. 67.

(Pseudo-) HYGINUS,   *De Astronomia* (TKI 473): Oxford, Bodl. Libr. Auct. F. 3. 14.

ILDEFONSUS OF TOLEDO,   *De Virginitate Perpetua B.V.M.: De Miraculis B.V.M.*, p. 71.

ISIDORE, *Etymologiae*: PH, pp. 45, 102, GR II, p. 485; *De Natura Rerum*: Oxford, Bodl. Libr. Auct. F. 3. 14; ?*De Ecclesiasticis Officiis*: see above, p. 43; *De Viris Illustribus*: see above, p. 34; *Chronica Majora: De Miraculis B.V.M.*, p. 138 lines 328–30 (Carter, 'The Historical Content of William of Malmesbury's Miracles of the Virgin Mary', p. 146 and n. 3). See also above under CASSIODORUS.
(Pseudo-) ISIDORE, Decretals. See below under LANFRANC.
Itinerarium Urbis Romae. See above, pp. 68–9.
IVO OF CHARTRES, Sermons: AbAm, p. 144; *Decretum, Panormia*: see above, p. 43.
?(Pseudo-) IVO, *De Ecclesiasticis Officiis*. See above, p. 43.

JEROME, *In Isaiam*: GR I, pp. 230–1, PH, pp. 129–133; *In Ierem.*: ibid., pp. 135–6; *In Ecclesiasten*: Oxford, Merton Coll. MS 181; *In XII Prophetas Minores*: PH, pp. 122–7 (all except Malachi); *In Danielem*: ibid., pp. 127–9; *In Ezechielem*: ibid., pp. 133–5; *In Galat.*: ibid., pp. 118–120, CUL MS Dd. 13. 2; *In Ephes.*: PH, p. 138; *Liber Interpr. Nominum Hebraicorum*: Comm. Lam., f. 9, Oxford, Bodl. Libr. Marshall 19; *Contra Iovinianum*: PH, pp. 81–3; *Contra Rufinum*: ibid., pp. 120–1; *Contra Pelagianos*: PH, p. 121; *Adv. Vigilantium*: ibid., p. 86; *De Viris Illustribus*: Oxford, Balliol Coll. 79, f. 3 (and see above under CASSIODORUS); *Vita Hilarionis*: PH, p. 49, and above, p. 58; Letters: PH, pp. 84–9, a series found in many early MSS, e.g. Casin. 296 MM, BL Harl. 3044, Angers 154; Chronicle: see above under EUSEBIUS.
JOHN THE ARCHDEACON, *Translatio S. Nicholai*: William mentions a 'translatio S. Nicholai' (above, p. 64) containing the information that Nicholas of Myra was present at the Council of Nicaea. This identifies the work as that by John the Archdeacon, written after 1105; F. Nitti de Vito, 'La Traslazione delle Reliquie di San Nicola', *Iapigia*, new ser., 8 (1937), p. 359 lines 65–6.
JOHN CHRYSOSTOM, untraced: Comm. Lam., f. 119v 'omnis gloria Dei in hoc seculo et omnis salus hominum in Christi cruce consistit …'.
JOHN THE DEACON, *Vita Gregorii*: GR I, p. 46.
JOHN THE SCOT, *Periphyseon*: see above, pp. 43–4; translation of the works of pseudo-Dionysius, with the preface of ANASTASIUS BIBLIOTHECARIUS: In his letter to Peter (GR I, pp. cxliv–v) William quotes the letter of Anastasius to Charles the Bald concerning John the Scot (MGH Epist. 7, pp. 430–4), which travelled as a preface to a standard collection of John's Dionysian translations, and William's note that John 'se Heruligenam in titulo Ierarchiae inscribit' (GR I, p. cxliv) shows that he knew such a collection, introduced into England c.1100 (above, p. 104). The contents were: Anastasius's Letter, John's prose and verse prologues, the poem 'Lumine sidereo Dionisius', Dionysius, *De Hier. Celest.*, *De Hier. Eccl.*, *De Div Nom.*, *De Mystica Theol.*, *Epistulae X* (all glossed) *Epist. Polycratis Archiep. Ephes.*, *Serm. Clementis*, Philo, *De Vita Theorica*.
JORDANES, *Getica, Romana*. See above, pp. 66–7.
JOSEPHUS, *Antiquitates*: GR II, p. 422, Comm. Lam., ff. 41, 74v, 107v, 115.
JULIAN OF TOLEDO, *Prognosticon*: PH, pp. 101–2.
JULIUS FIRMICUS MATERNUS, *Mathesis.* PH, p. 104. See above, pp. 59–60.
JUSTIN, Epitome of Trogus Pompeius: Oxford, Bodl. Libr. Arch. Seld. B. 16.
JUSTINIAN, *Corpus Iuris Civilis.* See above, pp. 63–4.
JUVENAL. See above, p. 48.

LACTANTIUS, *Divinae Institutiones, De Opificio Dei, De Ira Dei.* See above, p. 42.
LANFRANC, *De Corpore et Sanguine Domini*, Letters, *Scriptum de Primatu, Collectio Lanfranci.* See above, pp. 46, 131–3.
LEO, Letters, Sermons. See above, pp. 97, 129, 132–3.
Liber Pontificalis, Class 2 type and Class E type. See above, pp. 119–20.
LUCAN. See above, p. 49.

MACROBIUS, *Saturnalia.* See above, p. 60.
MARIANUS SCOTUS, *Chronicon.* See above, p. 69.
MARTIAL. Ep. 1 praef. 9 is quoted in the Letter to Peter (ed. Jeauneau, p. 169). Possible echoes occur in GR.
MARTIANUS CAPELLA. See above, pp. 60, 81–2.
Mathematica Alhandrei (TKI 834). See above, p. 62.
MILRED OF WORCESTER, collection of epigrams and inscriptions. See above, pp. 126–30.
Miracula B.V.M (MB Series): De Miraculis B.V.M: Carter, 'The Historical Content of William of Malmesbury's Miracles of the Virgin Mary', p. 138 and n. 1; idem, 'Thesis', I, p. 45 n. 3, listing MSS.

'NENNIUS', *Historia Britonum.* See above, p. 69.

ODBERT, *Vita S. Frederici*: GP, pp. 11–15.
ODO OF CLUNY, *Narratio in Reversione S. Martini*: GR I, p. 127.
ORIGEN, *In Cant.*: Oxford, Merton Coll. 181.
OROSIUS: Oxford, Bodl. Libr. Arch. Seld. B. 16; HN, p. 34.
OSBERN, *Vita S. Dunstani*: GR I, p. 162ff, GP, p. 148ff; *Vita S. Elphegii*: GR I, p. 188, GP, p. 33.
OVID, *Tristia, Amores, Metamorphoses, De Remedio Amoris, Fasti.* See above, p. 50.

PALLADIUS, *De Agricultura.* See above, p. 59.
PASCHASINUS, *Epistola de Ratione Paschae.* Oxford, Bodl. Libr. Auct. F. 3. 14.
PASCHASIUS, *De Corpore et Sanguine Domini*: GR II, p. 341; *In Lamentationes*: Comm. Lam.; *Sermo in Nat. B.V.M.* ('Cogitis me'): *De Miraculis B.V.M.*, pp. 51, 53, 57, 85.
Passio S. Kenelmi (BHL 4642): GR I, pp. 95, 262, GP, p. 294; Levison, *England and the Continent in the Eighth Century*, p. 250 and nn.
PATRICK, *Confessio.* See above, p. 70.
PAUL THE DEACON, *Historia Langobardorum, Historia Romana*: Oxford, Bodl. Libr. Arch. Seld. B. 16; *Vita Gregorii I*: Oxford, Merton Coll. 181, *Defloratio Gregorii*; Homiliary. This was one of the sources used by William for his collection of Leo's sermons in Oxford, Oriel Coll. 42 (Chavasse in CCSL 188, pp. xxvii–xxxiv).
PAUL THE DEACON OF NAPLES, translation of *Vita S. Mariae Aegyptiacae* (BHL 5415). In *De Miraculis B.V.M.*, Mir. 41, for which his main source was Dominic of Evesham, William excuses himself for omitting the details of St Mary's physical privations thus: 'Rerum circuitum longo agmine uerborum uentilatum alio

insinuabunt litterae' (p. 150). Such details are one of the principal features of the *Vita* translated by Paul.

PAULINUS OF MILAN, *Vita S. Ambrosii.* See above, p. 16.

PERSIUS. See above, p. 48.

?*Phisiognomia.* See above under APULEIUS. But this work is only connected with William by the link, in palaeography and subject-matter, between this item and the preceding ones in the MS.

Physiologus: Comm. Lam., ff. 84–84v.

PLATO, *Timaeus,* transl. Calcidius. See above, p. 52.

PLINY, *Natural History.* See above, p. 59.

POSSIDIUS, *Vita S. Augustini.* PH, p. 101.

Praeceptum Canonis Ptolemaei (TKI 754): GR I, p. 194 ('Ptholomaeum in astrolabio'). It is in Avranches, Bibl. Mun. 235 (see above under 'Accipe astrolabii quartam').

PRUDENTIUS, *Peristephanon: De Miraculis B.V.M.,* p. 117.

(Pseudo-) QUINTILIAN, *Declamationes Maiores XIX.* Oxford, Bodl. Libr. Rawl. G. 139.

RABANUS, *De Officiis Ecclesiasticis, De Universo, De Computo, Enarrationes in Epistolas Pauli:* see above, p. 43. ?*De Laude S. Crucis.* William mentions a copy given to Glastonbury by Archbishop Aethelnoth (1012–38) (AG, p. 136). A copy was still there in Leland's time (*Collectanea,* III, p. 260), but no less than three in 1247 (Williams, *Somerset Mediaeval Libraries,* p. 66). Cf. H. Gneuss, 'Dunstan and Hrabanus Maurus', *Anglia,* 96 (1978), 136–148.

RADBOD OF DOL, Letter to Athelstan: GP, p. 399.

REMIGIUS, *Comm. super Martianum.* See above, p. 60.

ROBERT LOSINGA, Treatise on Chronology. See above, p. 69.

ROBERT OF TOMBELAINE, *Super Cantica.* See above, p. 46.

SALLUST, *Jugurthine War, Catiline.* See above, p. 58.

?(Pseudo-) SALLUST, *In Cic. Orat.:* CUL Dd. 13. 2.

SEDULIUS (CAELIUS), *Carm.* 1: GP, p. 31.

SENECA THE ELDER, *Controversiae.* See above, p. 56.

SENECA THE YOUNGER, *Apocolocyntosis, De Beneficiis,* ?*De Clementia,* Letters. See above, p. 56.

SERVIUS, *In Aeneidos.* See above, p. 48.

'Si fuerit nobis propositum inuenire'. See above under 'Accipe astrolabii quartam'.

SIDONIUS, *Carmina:* 2. 30ff in GR II, p. 411; Letters: IV. 18. 4–5 quoted in GR I, p. 127.

SIGIBERT OF GEMBLOUX, Chronicle. See above, p. 124.

SOLINUS: PH, pp. 38, 45, 47.

'Spiris locus est famosus' (miracle-story; A. Poncelet, 'Miraculorum B.V.Mariae quae saec. vi–xv latine conscripta sunt index', *Analecta Bollandiana,* 21 [1902], 241–360, no. 1671): *De Miraculis B.V.M.,* p. 138.

STATIUS, *Thebais.* See above, p. 50.

SUETONIUS. See above, p. 57.

Sylloge Inscriptionum. See above under MILRED OF WORCESTER.

TERENCE, *Andria, Eunuchus, Heauton Timorumenos*. See above, p. 49.
TERTULLIAN, *Apologeticum*. See above, p. 42.
THOMAS OF BAYEUX (archbishop of York 1070–1100), *Carmina*. William mentions 'multa ecclesiastica . . . carmina' which he wrote (GP, p. 258); they have not survived.

VALERIUS MAXIMUS: PH, pp. 38, 71.
VEGETIUS. See above, p. 87.
VENANTIUS FORTUNATUS, *Vita S. Paterni*: GP, p. 399.
VIRGIL, *Aeneid, Georgics, Eclogues*. See above, pp. 47–8.
Visio Eucherii: GR I, pp. 255–6. U. Nonn, 'Das Bild Karl Martells in den lateinischen Quellen vornehmlich des 8. und 9. Jahrhunderts', *Frümittelalterliche Studien*, 4 (1970), 111ff, and Brett, 'John of Worcester and his Contemporaries', p. 123 n. 2. Also in Cambridge, Corpus Christi Coll. 290, ff. 118–118v, early twelfth-century, from St Albans, and used in the *Annales S. Neoti*; Dumville and Lapidge, *The Anglo-Saxon Chronicle*, 17, pp. liv–lvi.
Visio Karoli Crassi. See above, p. 148.
Vita S. Aniani (BHL 473). See above, p. 124.
Vita Athelstani metrice. See above, p. 70.
Vitae S. Audoeni (unspecifiable): GP, p. 420.
Vita S. Birini (?BHL 1361): GP, p. 157ff.
Vita S. Bonitis metrice (BHL 1420): *De Miraculis B.V.M.*, pp. 76–8.
Vita S. Dunstani auctore B (BHL 2342). See above, p. 70.
Vita S. Edwardi Confessoris: GR I, p. 229ff. This was apparently an 'improved' form of the anon. Life ed. F. Barlow, *The Life of King Edward the Confessor* (London, 1962), pp. xxii and n. 5, xxx–xxxii, xli.
?*Vita S. Erkenwaldi* (BHL 2600): GP, pp. 142–4.
Vita S. Goaris (BHL 565): GR I, p. 84.
Vitae S. Patricii: Vita III, π-type, W type. See above, p. 70.
Vita S. Philiberti (BHL 6806 + 6805): Oxford, Bodl. Libr. Bodl. 852.
Vita S. Wulganii (BHL 8746): as above.
VITRUVIUS. PH, pp. 71–4, and see above, p. 59.

WILLIAM OF JUMIEGES, *Historia Normannorum*. See above, p. 69.
WILLIAM OF POITIERS, *Gesta Guillelmi*. See above, p. 69.
WULFSTAN CANTOR, *Vita S. Ethelwoldi*: GP, p. 181ff, VD, pp. 262, 299, GR I, p. 167; *De Tonorum Harmonia*: GR I, p. 167.

APPENDIX II:

CONTENTS AND SIGNIFICANT READINGS OF THE GELLIUS FLORILEGIUM

Gellius readings are taken from the Oxford edition of P. K. Marshall. The florilegium is represented by L (Oxford, Bodl. Libr. Lat. class. d. 39), K (Oxford, Bodl. Libr. Rawl. G. 139), William's *Polyhistor* (PH) and John of Salisbury's *Policraticus* (*Policr.*). The order of the extracts is as found in L and K. Readings recorded are: (i) Agreement between two or more representatives of the florilegium against those of the complete text; (ii) Agreements of the florilegium's extracts from bks 1–5 with MSS of the complete text other than P; (iii) Agreements of the florilegium's extracts from bks 9–16 with representatives of the complete text other than the γ family (OXπN); (iv) Interesting editorial modifications in the florilegium.

1. *9. 3. 2–5* (2–4 summarized *Policr.*) Philippus ... susceptione.
2 exercitusque: exercitatus L, PH
  quin: cum L, PH
  pleraque et: plura L, PH
4 liberorum: librorum L, PH
  hortamentum: ornamentum, L, PH
5 quod: quo
  eductus: educatus

2. *9. 4. 7–8* (not in PH) In libro quoque plinii ... binas habere.
8 laetiores infantes amoeniores: ameniores letiores infantes
  Illyriis: illiricis
  tam nocenti: nocentes

3. *9. 11* (not in *Policr.*) De maximo ualerio ... monumentum.
2 admiranda (FπN): ammiranda
3 L. Furio Claudio Appio: fuit furio apio claudio L; furio appio claudio PH; L. *om.* δ.
4 ingentes: gentes L; gentis PH
  Pomptinum: promptinum

5 armisque auro praefulgentibus grandia ingrediens et manu telum: auro gemmisque
   fulgentibus grandi auiditate gradiens manu L; armis auro gemmisque fulgentibus
   grandi auiditate gradiens manu PH
   perque: et per
7 in aduersari: inde aduersarii (aduersarii πN)
   os atque: *om.*
   pugnare: impugnare
   et ... arcebat: *om.* L; prospectum ... atque *om.* PH
10 Coruino isti: isti Coruino
   pugnaeque quam: pugne quam

4. *9. 13.* 7–20 (not in *Policr.*) Cum interim Gallus ... occiderat.
7 duos (F²πQB): duos
   atque: et
   antistabat: antestabat
8 utrisque quiescerent: ut utrique adquiescerent
11 inmanitatem facies: inhumanitatem faciei
12 linguam exertare: lingua execrare L; lingua execrari PH
13 perdolitum: delatum
   adcidere: accedere
   e tanto: et de tanto
14 Is ut dico: hoc dicto
   uirtutem romanam: romanam uirtutem
   Hispanico cinctus: concinctus L; cinctus PH
   constitit: consistit
16 cantabundus: cadabundus
   conturbauit: perturbauit (Xπ)
17 studet: studeret
   scuto scutum: scutum scuto
   usquam: *om.*
   icti: iterum
18 inponit: imposuit
20 inmitia: inimica

5. *9. 16.* 5–7 (not in *Policr.*) Hec refert plinius uir ... non reddo.
5 cuia: cuius
   fuit: fuerat
7 sententiolam: sententiam
   potest: potuit

6. *10. 8* Fuit hec ... qui delinquerent.
2 primitus: primis L: in primis PH: primo *Policr.*
   declinatis: declinantis (πQ)

7. *10. 10* Veteres grecos ... cordi uideretur.
1 in digito accipimus sinistrae manus qui minimo est proximus: in sinistra manu
   (sinistrae manus *Policr.*) digito qui minimo proximus est accepimus

2 humanis: *om.*
quas: quos
pergere: pertingere
propterea non inscitum: *om.*
cordis: cordi

8. *10. 18. 3–7* (not in *Policr.*) Mausolus ubi ... higinus refert.
3 pulueris: puluerem
multaque alia ... dicitur: *om.*
4 dignatumque: dignumque (Q)
spectacula: miracula
6 mandauerint: mandauerunt

9. *10. 27* (not in *Policr.*) In litteris ... fuerunt incisa.
1 fuit: *om.*
3 ad eos: eoⁱs L; eis PH
4 sese: se
posse: pro se
mallent relinquere: uellent eligerent
sibi pro electo: pro lecto sibi (lecto O²N)

10. *11. 9. 2* Demostenes cum ... ut tacerem.
actorem (FNδ): auctorem (LOXπ); auctori PH

11. *12. 7* (not in PH) D. G. N. Dolobella ... memorabilium nono.
No significant variants.

12. *12. 8* (in L only) Affricanus superior ... uixerunt.
1 P. Africanus ... pater: Affricanus superior et Tiberius Gracus et .C.
Gracchorum pater
inlustres: et illustres
siue qua alia: sine aliqua alia
2 epulum: *om.*
duo: *om.*
Tum: et
4 nam: namque
probauerat elegeratque exploratissimo: exprobrauerat oderatque exploratissime
4 inimicus est: inimicus erat
5 Aemilius ... conflictati sunt: *om.*

13. *12. 12* Si obiectum sit ... emptionis.
1 facias risu: *om.* L, PH; paraphr. *Policr.*
2 P.: *om.*
tum: tunc
mutua: mutuo
uiciens tacita: uicies tacite

3 tamen: *om.*
emeret: emeretur
4 Tum: tunc
quoque se empturum negauit: quoque empturum se negauit L, PH; accepisse se
negauit *Policr.*

14. *15. 6. 3* (in L only) Aiax cum hectore ... gloria uiuet.
agit: ait
forte: morte
post: *om.*

15. *15. 16* (not in *Policr.*) Milo crothomensis ... feris prebuit.
1 e uita: uite
et mirandum: admirandum
2 athleticam desisset: dialecticam (dialeticam) didicisset
proxime uiam: proximam uie
3 Tum experiri credo: Experiri L; experirique PH
cauernas: cauernis (QZB)
4 partis: partes

16. *15. 22. 1–2* (in L only) [S]ertonus uir acer ... adiuuabant.
1 et utendi: utendi
2 Is: his
prodesset: profuisset
religiones: regiones
si quid: si quidem
adiutabant: adiuuabant

17. *15. 31* (not in *Policr.*) [R]odum insulam ... ciuitati peperit.
1 inclutus: inclitus
peritia disciplinaque: pueritia disciplina
2 Tum ibi: *om.*
publice: *om.*
4 malum inquiunt ratiost: inquiunt Rhodii causas L; ratio est PH
nos omnes: omnes
5 Hoc: hec

18. *16. 11* (not in *Policr.*; PH beg. in *3*) Gens in italia ... occupatos (+
add.).
1 esse fertur (FONZ): esse fertur
filio: filia solis L
3 quarto: quinto
5 eo flatu aquam: eoque flatu
7 eosque (X²Q): eosque (eoque FOπNZ)
copiis: corpusculis L; corporibus PH
8 L *adds* magna hominum dementia inaudita et incomparabilis stulticia, qui

armorum uiolentia uento putabant resistere, quem Deus de thesauro suo disposuit producere; PH *adds* Ingens hominum stultitia qui putabant armis posse resisti uento.

19. *16. 15* (in L only)
Refert Theophratus philosophus de perdicibus omnes in Perphagonia perdices bina corda habere in Bisaltia uero bina iecora

20. *13. 8. 3–4*
Philosophi ueteres imaginem sapientie pro foribus omnium templorum pingi et hec uerba scribi (*om.* L) debere censebant: Vsus me genuit, peperit Memoria; Sophiam me uocant (uocant me L) Grai, uos Sapientiam. Item: Ego odi homines stultos et (*om.* PH) ignaua opera et philosophicas sententias

21. *1. 8. 3–6* Tais corinthia ... non emo.
3 ditiorum: diuorum L *Policr.; om.* PH
   quod: que (quae)
4 apud Graecos adagium: prouerbium apud Grecos
   Gr. *om.*
5 ut sibi: ut L *Policr.; om.* PH

22. *1. 13. 10–13* Crassus a sempnio ... responderit.
10 Asellione (asellone VPR): Assellone L; Asello *Policr.*; et Asellione PH
11 oppugnareque: atque obpugnare (oppugnare PH)
   magistratum Mylattensium: magnum .G. more atthenensium L; magistratum Atheniensium PH (mag. G. more atheniensium P); Magnum Gaium maiorem Atheniensium *Policr.*
12 Tum: tunc
   desideraret: desiderasset
   esse magis: magis esse
13 dictitabat: dictabat R
   imperauit: iussit
   respondeat: responderit

23. *1. 14* Iulius yginus ... non accipere.
1 dixisse: dicebant L, PH; paraphr. *Policr.*
2 inde: deinde

24. *1. 17* [X]antippe socratis ... sunt.
1 perque: et L, PH; paraphr. *Policr.*
3 domi: *om.* L, PH
4 aut ferendum est: est aut ferendum

25. *1. 19* (not in *Policr.*) In annalibus antiquis ... sunt.
2 quos esse (TY): quos
   uelle (P): dixit uelle (uelle dixit VR)
3 percontatus est: percunctatus L; percunctatur PH

5 coram cum igni: coram rege
5 ecquid: *om.*
9 constitit: constat
10 appellati: appellati sunt
11 eos: eos quippe

26. *1. 23. 4–13* (in L only) Mos antea ... pretexte prudentiam.
5 Tum cum: cum
   in diem: in
   placuitque: placuit
   super qua: super quam
   enuntiaret: enuntiarent
7 audiendi cupidior: cupidior audiendi
   animum: animumque
   compressius uiolentiusque: uiolentius compressiusque
8 Tum: tunc
11 Senatores: senatores uero

27. *1. 26. 5–9* [P]ultarcus ... tu hoc age.
7 facere: iacere L, PH: iaculabatur *Policr.*
8 inquit: *om.* (ait *over line* L)
   ruboremue: ruboremque L *Policr.*; ruborem PH
9 Haec enim omnia: hec (haec) omnia quippe

28. *2. 2. 1–10* Ad philosophum ... priorem decet.
2 cubiculi: cubilis L, PH; paraphr. *Policr.*
5 Allata mox una sella est: allata est mox una sella
   uti: ut
6 Atque: at L, PH; atque *Policr.* VR (ad que P)
7 inspicimus: conspicimus
8 quoque: quodcumque L, PH; paraphr. *Policr.*
9 actionibus: dictionibus L, PH; *om. Policr.*
   familiari (familiaris VPR): familiari
10 colloquimur: loquimur
   disceptamus: detrectamur L; dissertamus PH *Policr.*

29. *2. 11* (K only) [L]ucium sicinum ... triumphos nouem.
1 L.: Lucium
   plebi: plebis
   Sp.: Spurio
   A.: Aulo
   Aternio: Artenio
   strenuum: strenunum
   ei: *om.*
   ob: *om.*
2 donatus esse aureis centum sexaginta: donata est lx. centum

3 uiciesque spolia: uicies quae populi post
habuit: habuerit
4 prouocatoria: prouocaria

30. *3. 6* [P]er herculem ... non cedat.
2 tam: tantum
intra (in terra TY): in terram PH, *Policr.*: iter K

31. *3. 7. 1–19* (K, PH) [P]ulcrum dii boni ... ceterum seruauit.
3 in terra Sicilia: intra Siciliam
Carthaginiensi: Carthaginensi
6 illam: *om.*
id: *om.*
unoque: uno atque
11 tribunus (tribunum VPR): tribunus
quadringenti: quadringenti uiri
12 demirantur: admirantur (amm- PH)
13 ad eam: ad eandem P²
aduersum: aduersus
equitatumque: equitumque
19 tribuno (P²; tribunus P): tribuno
ita euenit (euenit ita VPR): ita euenit ita K; ita euenit quod PH
sanguen eius: sanguis
Eum: eum atque K: atque PH

32. *3. 8* (*1–7* heavily summarized in PH and *Policr.*) [C]um pirrus ... ia-
cebis.
1 filii sui: filius suus PK
8 tenus: *om.*
negauimus: negamus VPRK, PH: negauimus *Policr.*

33. *3. 9* (K, PH, which omits *7–9*) [G]aius bassus ... puniceum diximus.
2 quos (quod VPRT): quos Y
3 flora (florea Y) et comanti: florea et iubanti
sed: sed et
familia: et familia
4 M.: Mar. K
Deinde ... interisse: *om.*
de hominibus: de *om.*

34. *5. 2* (K, PH) [E]quus alex ... appellauit.
1 Alexandri: Alexandri magni
Bucephalas: Bucefal
Chares (cares VR; ikares P): kares K; cares PH
2 talentis tredecim: .c. talentis .xiii. K: centum talentis PH
nostri summa: summa nostra (summa ... nostra PH)

3 erat: fuit
  inscendi: ascendi
  ab rege: a rege
4 de isto: deuicto K: de dicto PH
  cuneum (cum eum P): cuneum
  esset (est VPR): est K, esset PH
  eum extra: eum *om.*
  extulerat: retulerat
5 Tum: tunc
  Bucephalon: Bucifallonia K: Bucefalonio PH

35 *5. 14. 5–28* (*5–8, 29–30* summarized only in *Policr.*; *17–30* summarized only in
PH) [In] icirio maximo ... medicus leonis.
5 inquit: *om.* P
6 rei: re causa K; rei causa PH *Policr.*
7 inuisitata aut: inusitata
8 praeter alia: praeter
9 toris: thoro K *Policr.; om.* PH
  sese: se
10 13 Androclus: Androcus K; Andronicus PH *Policr.*
  compluris: complures
11 repente inquit: repente
  ac: ac K; et PH *Policr.*
  noscitabundus: iocabundus PH *Policr.*: uocitabundum K
  leniter (leuiter VPR): leniter K *Policr.*; leni PH
12 exanimati metu: exanimati metu K; metu exanimati PH *Policr.*
14 Tum: tunc K *Policr.; om.* PH
  et gratulabundos uideres hominem et leonem: uideres et gratulabundos leonem et
  hominem K *Policr.*; uideres leonem et hominem PH
15 Androclum: androcum K; Andronicum PH
  illi (ille VPR): ille K, PH; illi *Policr.*
18 Tum PH: cum K *Policr.*
  inquit PH: *om.* K *Policr.*
  specum K: caueam PH *Policr.*
19 me: *om.*
20 commiserantia: cum miserantia K *Policr.*
21 re: res K *Policr.*
  inquit: *om.* K *Policr.*
  mansues: mansuetus K *Policr.*; mansuete PH
  porrigere (pergere P): porrigere
22 stirpem: stipem K; stipitem PH *Policr.*
  medicinae: medele (-lle)
23 Illa: ille K *Policr.*; Leo PH
25 eodemque et uictu (VP): eodem uictu K, PH; eodemque uictu R *Policr.*
26 leone in: leone
28 curauit: procurauit K *Policr.*
  autem inquit: autem
  mihi: *om.* K *Policr.*

29 Androclum (*bis*): andromacum (–chum) K, PH; andronicum *Policr.*

36. *5. 9. 1–3* (K only) [F]ilius cresis ... loqui incepit.

37. *5. 10. 4–16* [E]uathlus adolescens ... distulerunt.
5 causarumque: causarumque K: causasque PH *Policr.*
6 disciplinam: disciplina K, PH: disciplinam *Policr.*
   Protagorae (*etc. semper*): Pitagore (Pytagore K; *etc. semper*)
   sese: se
   petiuerat: petierat
7 adsectatorque: assertorque K *Policr.*: assessorque PH
   iam: *om.*
   transcurreret: transcurrisset K PH
9 consistendaeque: consistendeque KP; coniciende PH;
   constituendaeque *Policr.*
   tum: *om.*
11 respondit Euathlus potui (opto P): placide (placidit K) Euathlus (Euatlus PH)
opto
12 mihi: *om.*
   prolubium: prolubium K; proludium PH *Policr.*
14 pronuntiauerint: pronuntiatum (pronunatum K) fuerit
   debebo: debeo
15 and 16 transposed
15 utramcumque: utramque K *Policr.*; utram PH
   esset: *om.*
   longissimam: longissimum
16 suo sibi: suo
   uersute: uersute et P

INDEX OF MANUSCRIPTS

GENERAL INDEX